DATE DUE

JUN 0 5 2008			
NOV 1 8 2010			

Demco

The Language of the Heart

By the Same Author

The Broken Heart (1977)

The Language of the Heart

The Body's Response to
Human Dialogue

JAMES J. LYNCH

Basic Books, Inc., Publishers   New York

Figure 3.2, p. 68, from "Effects of Human Contact on the Heart Activity of Curarized Patients in a Shock-Trauma Unit," by J. J. Lynch et al., reprinted by permission from August 1974 issue of *American Heart Journal*.

Figures 4.1, 4.2, and 4.3, pp. 79–81, from "Patients' Cardiac Responses to Nursing Interviews in a CCU," by S. A. Thomas et al., reprinted by permission from July–August 1982 issue of *Dimensions of Critical Care Nursing*.

Table 6.1, p. 124, from "Human Speech and Blood Pressure," by J. J. Lynch et al., from *Journal of Nervous and Mental Disease* 168:9, © 1980, The Williams and Wilkins Co., Baltimore.

Reprinted by permission of the Elsevier Science Publishing Co., Inc.: Table 6.4, p. 130, from "The Effects of Talking on the Blood Pressure of Hypertensive and Normotensive Individuals," by J. J. Lynch et al., *Psychosomatic Medicine* 43:1, pp. 25–33, © 1981; and figures 6.5 and 6.6, pp. 143–44, from "The Effects of Normal and Rapid Speech on Blood Pressure," by E. Friedmann, et al., *Psychosomatic Medicine* 44:6, pp. 545–53, © 1982 The American Psychosomatic Society, Inc.

Table 6.5, p. 132, from "Automated Blood Pressure Recording: The Phenomenon of Blood Pressure Elevations During Speech," by K. L. Malinow et al., reprinted by permission from *Angiology-Journal of Vascular Diseases* 33:7, 1982.

Figure 6.8, p. 154, from "Social Interaction and Blood Pressure: Influence of Animal Companions," by E. Friedmann et al., from *Journal of Nervous and Mental Disease* 171:8, © 1983 The Williams and Wilkins Co., Baltimore.

Library of Congress Cataloging in Publication Data

Lynch, James J., 1938–
  The language of the heart.

  References: p. 322
  Includes index.
    1. Hypertension—Psychosomatic aspects.
  2. Migraine—Psychosomatic aspects.   3.   Transactional
  analysis.   4.   Biofeedback training.   5.   Relaxation.
  6. Cardiovascular system—Diseases—Psychosomatic
  aspects.   7. Mind and body.   I. Title.   [DNLM:
  1. Heart Diseases—psychology.   2.   Hypertension—
  therapy.   3.   Interpersonal Relations.   4.   Migraine—
  therapy.   WG 100 L987L]
  RC682.L86   1985   616.1′3208   83–46082
  ISBN 0-465-03795-X

This book is dedicated to

the memory of my teacher

W. Horsley Gantt, M.D.,

who gave this book his "Effect of Person,"

and

to my colleague

Sue Ann Thomas, R.N., PH.D.,

who gave this book its life

CONTENTS

CHAPTER 5

No Language But a Cry   104

CHAPTER 6

Examining the Cardiovascular–Communication Links   118

CHAPTER 7

The Social Membrane   174

CHAPTER 8

The Hidden Dialogue   202

CHAPTER 9

Decoding the Heart's Language   241

ACKNOWLEDGMENTS

This book describes a journey of discovery that began over twenty years ago, one that has involved the loving support and intellectual brilliance of dozens of colleagues, the pain and suffering of hundreds of patients, and the willing participation in our research studies of thousands of individuals. Their collective support has made the writing of this book a joyous yet humbling endeavor. While no statement of acknowledgment or expression of gratitude could ever sufficiently convey the debt I owe to others, nevertheless it is important to emphasize that this book could never have been completed by one person alone.

To the patients and staff of the coronary-care unit of the University of Maryland Hospital, who first led us to see the links between human loneliness and heart disease, a special debt of gratitude is owed. In addition, many patients at the University of Maryland's Psychophysiological Center shared the most precious and pained aspects of their lives so that we could hear and understand the language of the human heart. I pray that this book fulfills their deepest hope that others may be helped by the sharing of their personal struggles. A very special debt is owed as well to the administrative staffs of the University of Maryland Medical and Nursing Schools, and in particular those in the Department of Psychiatry who have generously supported my research for the past fifteen years. To Eugene B. Brody, M.D., and Russell R. Monroe, M.D., I owe a special note of thanks.

In this book are the results of the work of a group of dedicated research colleagues who have brought a special quality of warmth and excellence to the Psychophysiological Center of the University of Maryland Medical School. Though a simple listing of their names does not convey the crucial role they played in the development of our understanding, nevertheless this book could not have been written without their inspired commitment, as well as their care and concern for the well-being of their fellow men and women. I thank all of them for the way they have enriched my life, and hope they are pleased with the fruits of their labor.

Ruth Brownell, R.N., M.S.

Grace Chicadonz, R.N., PH.D.

William Convey, M.D.

Ann Creamer, B.A.

Jay Perry Foreman, B.S.

Carolyn Freed, R.N., M.S.

Erika Friedmann, PH.D.

Sally Gresty, R.N., M.S.

Pamela Sue Hall, R.N., M.S.

Gayle Holcomb, R.N., M.S.

John Hsiao, M.D.

Katie Jones, R.N., M.S.

Aaron H. Katcher, M.D.

Denise Kulick-Ciuffo, R.N., M.S.

Debbie Lewandowski

Pat Liehr, R.N., M.S.N.

Jack Long, D.S.W.

Linda Sue Lottes, R.N., M.S.

Kenneth L. Malinow, M.D.

Paula Mason, R.N., M.S.

Cindy Miller, R.N., M.S.

Mary Etta Mills, R.N., SCD.

Katie Mosley, R.N., M.S.

Margaret Noctor, R.N., M.S.

Lourdes F. Orta, B.S., PH.D.

David A. Paskewitz, PH.D.

Christine Peterson, B.S., M.S.

Maureen Richey, R.N., M.S.

Marycarol Rossignol, R.N., M.S.

Ellen Sappington, R.N., M.S.

Eliot Siegel, M.D.

Sue Snedker, R.N., B.S.N., M.A.

Fran Wimbush, R.N., M.S.

Raymond Rochkind of the Illustrative Services Department of the University of Maryland Baltimore Campus drew most of the figures and graphs included in this text. His uniquely accurate portrayal of Stephen Hales's first measurement of blood pressure is but one of the many fine contributions he made to our efforts.

Two physicians—Dr. Paul Rosch, president of the American Institute of Stress in New York, and Dr. Kenneth Gimbel, a cardiologist in Atlanta—at great personal expense, generously gave their time, expertise, and unsparing criticism to earlier drafts of this book. I smile even now as I recall the many ingenious ways they tried to rescue me—and spare my readers—from as much ambiguity as possible. I hope these lovable critics are at least mildly pleased with this final draft, one that escaped their reading and

thus did not receive their final scientific *nihil obstat.* Likewise, I
owe a special debt to Dr. Richard B. Carter, who insisted that I
not avoid certain broader philosophical issues raised by our experiments. His insights into the philosophical writings of René Descartes
and the contributions of Adolf Portmann proved to be of particular
value. In like manner, Elinore Detiger of the Netherlands was
particularly helpful in leading me to understand the broader
philosophical implications of our work. I hope this book does her
gentle teaching justice. Finally, I would like to thank Dr. Herbert
S. Gross, co-director of the Psychophysiological Clinic: his psychodynamic insights, encouragement, and support helped to crystallize
many of the clinical issues raised by our new techniques.

For two years, Mary Horka typed and retyped numerous drafts
of this manuscript. For her patience, perseverance, and kindness, I
am particularly grateful.

It has been my particular good fortune to have worked with
Martin Kessler, president of Basic Books, and Phoebe Hoss, my
editor, both of whom worked long and hard to make this book as
good as the limitations of its author would allow. To them both, I
and this book owe a great deal.

To my wife Eileen, and my sons, Joe and Jim, and my daughter,
Kathleen, I owe more than gratitude. They are the language of my
heart, the reason this book exists, and the source of any inspiration
in these pages. They are indeed what is infinitely beautiful about
the *dia-Logos*—in which heart truly speaks to heart.

The Language of the Heart

INTRODUCTION

The Language of the Heart

> Unlearn'd, he knew no schoolman's subtle art,
> No language but the language of the heart.
> —Alexander Pope

> Out of the abundance of the heart the mouth
> speaketh. —Matthew 12:34

> Cor ad cor Loquitur ("Heart speaks to heart")
> —Motto of John Henry Newman

> But still the heart doth need a language.
> —Samuel T. Coleridge

> Oh Lord, who shall abide in thy tabernacle, who
> shall dwell in thy holy hill?

> He that walketh uprightly, and worketh righteous-
> ness, and speaketh the truth in his heart.
> —Psalms 15:1–2

It is obvious that we human beings are distinguished from all other living creatures by the fact that we speak. Whether man or woman or child, we can share our desires, thoughts, plans, and—above all—feelings with each other through dialogue. Coupled to this is another simple yet sublime truth: that while we speak with words, we speak also with our flesh and blood. As we shall see, study after study reveals that human dialogue not only affects our hearts significantly but can even alter the biochemistry of individual tissues at the furthest extremities of the body. Since blood flows through every human tissue, the entire body is influenced by human dialogue. Thus, it is true that when we speak we do so with every fiber of our being.

This "language of the heart" is integral to the health and

emotional life of every one of us. Yet this vital truth has been largely obscured by a scientific-philosophical perspective we all share and that leads us to think about the human body solely in terms of its mechanical functions. In an age dominated by dramatic images of heart transplants, artificial heart machines, and even the implantation of a baboon's heart into a human baby, it is all too easy to look on the human body solely as a machine incapable of either listening or speaking to others. Nonetheless, the essence of the human being is the body's involvement in dialogue—a process in which no machine can ever engage. For the human heart speaks a language that not only is vital to our well-being but makes possible human feelings and binds human beings together.

In this book I will delineate that language in the light of new scientific data about the links between the spoken word and the human heart and show how that relationship influences two major cardiovascular disorders, hypertension and migraine headaches.* Human dialogue is involved significantly in the development as well as the treatment of these diseases. While I hope that the information in this book will help to alleviate some of the suffering and pain caused by these diseases, I hasten to add that my overall purpose goes far beyond describing a new way to look at their causes and treatment or, by extension, one that implicates other diseases as being symptomatic of dysfunctional human dialogue. Rather, it is to show through these two diseases what it means for a person to live in a body that speaks.

To appreciate why we tend to think about the body as a machine, we need only recall an outstanding event of late 1982 and early 1983. For the first time ever, at the University of Utah's Medical Center in Salt Lake City, the life of a human being was sustained by an artificial heart machine. The public's response to this endeavor was electric, perhaps equaled only by the excitement over the first heart transplant operation performed by Christiaan Barnard in Capetown, South Africa, in 1969. And, as in that earlier operation, hourly news bulletins told the world of Dr. Clark's progress, as relentlessly and efficiently pulsating with the timed sighs of its own air compressors, a machine outside of his body

---

* Since a host of excellent texts are already available which describe the technical aspects of these diseases, every effort has been made in this book to keep technical terminology to a minimum.

kept the life-sustaining fluid—blood—flowing through it. For 112 days, the machine kept beating, pumping blood through his body, until with the failure of other organs, his circulatory system collapsed, and he died. Thirteen hundred mourners, including a personal representative of the President of the United States, attended his funeral in the town of Federal Way in the state of Washington.

Clearly, not only Dr. Clark but the medical profession had attempted, and accomplished, a heroic and extraordinary feat. Moreover, this feat, heralded all over the world, was the culmination of a belief on which medical scientists have acted for over three centuries: that is, that the human body is made up of a group of essentially mechanical organs that, when not running properly, can be tinkered with, like any mechanism, in the hope of setting it right again.

At about the same time, my colleagues and I at the Psychophysiological Clinic at the University of Maryland Medical School, were seeing, also for the first time, quite a different aspect of the human cardiovascular system that would lead us to develop an entirely new type of clinic, one based on an understanding of the connection between human communication and the cardiovascular system. For computer technology allowed us to see that as soon as one begins to speak, one's blood pressure increases significantly, one's heart beats faster and harder, and microscopic blood vessels in distant parts of the body change as well. Conversely, when one listens to others speak or truly attends to the external environment in a relaxed manner, then blood pressure usually falls and heart rate slows, frequently below its normal resting levels.

Initially, this discovery seemed more a curiosity than a conceptual breakthrough, especially when contrasted with the human and technical drama in Utah. Yet the data were so clear and so predictably consistent that we could not ignore them. They showed us that centuries of religious, philosophical, literary, and poetic wisdom that had suggested links between words and the human heart contained the core of an astonishingly fertile truth, and one central to medicine. Once aware of this truth, we tested for it in a variety of cases and research studies. We examined thousands of individuals, from newborn babies crying in their cribs; to preschool children reciting their ABCs; to grade-school children reading aloud from textbooks; to nursing and medical students describing their daily work routine; to hypertensive patients in our clinic, and those waiting anxiously for cardiac by-pass surgery; to schizophrenics in psychiatric wards; to elderly patients in nursing homes describing their loneliness, and in patients close to death. In each and every one, the link between language and the heart was clear and undeniable.

Yet, as I shall discuss, there was a powerful force that made it initially difficult for us to appreciate fully that we were indeed creating a new type of clinic. That force had to do, as I have said, with an unexamined philosophical perspective we brought to our own research. It included a vision of the human body shared by virtually everyone in our society, and first formulated by the French philosopher René Descartes in the seventeenth century. Living in an era that witnessed the beginnings of modern science, Descartes harnessed the discoveries of scientists like Galileo, Copernicus, Kepler, Harvey, and Pascal and cast their findings into a new and comprehensive philosophical system. As Descartes himself stated, he intended to create a totally new medicine, one based on the idea that the human body is a machine. He accomplished his goal so brilliantly that his influence, though pervasive, is scarcely understood today. Rather, like the air we breathe, his perspective is simply taken for granted.

Descartes promulgated and defended the idea that the human body functions like all other bodies in nature, according to mechanical principles. He separated mental functioning from bodily mechanics, arguing that the capacity to think has to be the result of the existence of the human soul. While ostensibly innocent, it was an extraordinary vision, one that permeates the way we in the Western world came to understand the nature of human beings, the human body, human health, and the links between our individual bodies and our social existence. After Descartes, issues of health and illness were relegated strictly to medical science; while spiritual and social concerns came to be seen as having little in common with physical health.* Physicians would come to be trained much

* Descartes's influence was every bit as pronounced in religious circles as in medicine. Thus, today no theological school—be it Catholic, Protestant, or Rabbinical—deems it necessary to teach its students elementary anatomy and physiology. The body is considered utterly irrelevant to religious questions, even though the Bible was rooted in such concerns (for example, Talmudic

as were the highly skilled technicians who maintained the French water gardens where statues were cleverly designed to move by means of water pressure, and that helped to inspire Descartes's concept. Three centuries after him, it would make "perfect sense" to think about a heart transplant in a human being much as a mechanic thinks about replacing a faulty water pump in an automobile: heart disease had become a mechanical problem in a faulty hydraulic system. Indeed, as the doctor treating the baby girl with the transplanted baboon heart, said, "The heart ... 'is a muscular pump and is not the seat of the soul.' "[1]

The stage, thus, was set with Descartes. From then on, thinker after thinker, scientist after scientist—including, as we shall see, those seminal masters of modern times, Marx, Darwin, Freud, and Pavlov—thought about the human body in mechanical terms. Whether in social evolution or in social revolution, the body was uncritically accepted to be an isolated, self-contained group of organs functioning strictly according to mechanical principles. In the process, the emotional life of human beings came to be seen as a reflection of mechanical functions inside a well-regulated machine. Unique aspects of human emotional life and the unique nature of human speech were obscured by a scientific perspective that accepted the human body as mechanically similar to other animal bodies, and human emotional life as comparable to the emotional life of animals.*

My plan in this book reflects the development in our thinking about these issues over two decades of research. When we originally began our journey, we sought to understand how human relationships and human loneliness affect cardiovascular health. In 1977, I summarized our findings in *The Broken Heart*.[2] That book was based on the fact that human loneliness is among the most important causes of premature death in modern America. In our

---

dietary regulations, or Christian and Judaic notions about blood and the heart). Hospital chaplains are today trained so as to feel no need to understand even the most rudimentary aspects of physical disease; instead, they see their job as caring for the soul. Likewise, psychologists can go through college and graduate school without any training in anatomy and physiology. And even the most elementary introductory courses in psychology or philosophy are not required to gain entrance to medical schools, though such schools do require advanced training in calculus, physics, and chemistry.

* As I shall describe in chapters 4 and 9, it was this idea that prompted scientists to use animal models to study stress-induced physical diseases in human beings.

studies, for virtually every cause of death—whether suicide, cancer, cirrhosis of the liver, automobile accident, or heart disease—the incidence of premature death was far higher among people who lived alone than among those who were married. While in certain cases—such as suicide, cirrhosis of the liver, or lung cancer—we could easily detect the factors that caused premature death, in others the mechanisms were far less clearcut, especially for heart disease, the leading cause of death in the United States. It was far from obvious why the single, the widowed, and the divorced were two to four times more likely than married people to die prematurely from hypertension, stroke, and coronary heart disease.

While human loneliness appeared to be the single most important and compelling emotional factor in these premature deaths, we were at a loss to explain how this feeling state influenced the heart. Though the statistics were unambiguous, we did not understand how a human experience such as loss or bereavement could lead to premature death from hypertension, stroke, or heart attack any more than we understood how loneliness caused elevations in blood pressure. While pondering this question, we were equally troubled about how to counteract this problem effectively, since many of the patients who appeared in the coronary-care unit recapitulated the very statistics we had uncovered linking loneliness to increased risk of heart disease.

These questions led us to explore loneliness in hypertensive patients. Since hypertension was, and still is, the single most important medical problem in modern America (it has been estimated that anywhere between forty million to sixty million Americans are hypertensive), we assumed that loneliness played an important role in the problem in at least a significant percentage of these cases.

Yet our efforts to examine the interlocking problem of human loneliness and hypertension quickly confronted us with a whole series of paradoxes. While it seemed intuitively obvious that human dialogue ought to be the best antidote to human loneliness, a large and well-documented literature had amply warned that certain types of social interaction can cause marked increases in the blood pressure of hypertensive patients. Even more to the point, the type of psychotherapeutic dialogue that seemed best suited to delve into issues surrounding the loneliness of hypertensive patients had already been shown to be precisely the type of encounter that would cause their blood pressure to rise to dangerous levels. This problem was compounded further when we discovered a striking relationship between speaking and blood pressure. While the blood pressure of almost everyone we tested rose during speech, that of hypertensive patients increased far more than that of any other group. Sometimes a hypertensive person's blood pressure would surge 50 percent above the resting baseline level as soon as he or she began to speak. Thus, we were forced to recognize that our psychotherapeutic "cure" could make hypertension worse. We began to wonder whether hypertensive patients were trapped inside their own bodies, damned if they withdrew from their fellow human beings and damned if they tried to relate to them.

Through our efforts to reconcile this dilemma, we uncovered a new dimension of the cardiovascular system which allowed us to develop an entirely new way to approach the treatment of vascular disorders, such as hypertension and migraine headaches. And we came finally to recognize that the human cardiovascular system does far more than change in response to internal and external demands: it also communicates. Since our hearts can speak a language that no one hears or sees and therefore cannot understand, we can get sick at heart.

I shall, in the following chapters, describe clinical cases treated by me and other staff members at the Psychophysiological Laboratories and Clinic of the University of Maryland School of Medicine. These patients are people who, literally and all unwittingly, talked their way into such cardiovascular disease, and whom we taught to talk their way back to health.*

In machines created by humans, it is perfectly clear who and what controls the internal mechanisms and why a particular machine, such as the pump that replaced Barney Clark's heart, was created. That pump was designed to fill a particular purpose, and it was absolutely regulated by its creators. Yet who is in charge of,

---

* In order to ensure the patients' rights to privacy, I have altered certain of their characteristics, such as name, occupation, family characteristics, and home town. In addition, the dialogues described in the text are not verbatim transcripts but are instead intended to capture the overall flavor of the communications between therapist and patient. In most cases the dialogue was reconstructed from brief clinical notes taken during therapeutic encounters. Neither the changes in patient characteristics nor the nature of the "recorded" dialogue should significantly alter the reader's ability to understand these cases, the course of therapy, or their outcome.

and what controls, the machinery of the human heart is another matter. Control is exercised from both inside and outside. This idea, though simple when it first occurred to us, gradually led us to understand that internal bodily mechanisms, such as blood pressure, long thought to be primarily regulated by the internal machinery of the human body, are also powerfully influenced by a force is human dialogue. Once this force was recognized, we came to understand that dialogue gives the body its very humanity.

Since human dialogue, and its relationship to our hearts and feelings, is the central issue of this book, let me define it as I did in *The Broken Heart:*

In its most general meaning, dialogue consists of reciprocal communication between two or more living creatures. It involves the sharing of thoughts, physical sensations, ideas, ideals, hopes, and feelings. In sum, dialogue involves the reciprocal sharing of any and all life experiences. . . .

Other characteristics of the process of dialogue are that it is reciprocal, spontaneous, often nonverbal, *and* alive.[3]

At the core of this book is the idea that we human beings are biologically interrelated—and that any attempt to maintain or restore health must be based on that reality. Scientific attempts to understand the human body apart from the most basic of all human traits—the fact that we speak—is all too likely to produce a medicine that brilliantly treats isolated parts of the human body, while it seriously neglects the individual as a whole and as a part of nature. We can understand and cope with illness only when we are able to view ourselves as part of a complex world beyond the confines of our own individual skin. The response of our hearts, blood vessels, and muscles when we communicate with spouse, children, friends, colleagues, and the larger community has as much to do with our cardiovascular health as do factors such as exercise or diet.

So vital to human health is the language of our hearts that—if ignored, unheard, or misunderstood—it can produce terrible physical suffering, even premature death. For the language of our hearts cries out to be heard. It demands to be understood. And it must not be denied. Our hearts speak with an eloquence that poets have always, and truly, sensed. It is for us to learn to listen and to understand.

CHAPTER 1

Bodies in Revolt

> It is in moments of illness that we are compelled
> to recognize that we live not alone but chained to
> a creature of a different kingdom, whole worlds
> apart, who has no knowledge of us and by whom
> it is impossible to make ourselves understood:
> our body.
> —Marcel Proust, *The Guermantes Way*

PSYCHOSOMATIC ILLNESS

As Proust suggests, we tend to take our bodies for granted until we fall ill. Even though citizens in our society are becoming ever more aware of the importance of taking care of their bodies, with ever more people actively exercising and dieting, nevertheless we seldom wonder what our relationship is to our own bodies. Instead, such a question is usually reserved for periods of illness or for when one is confronted by life-threatening disease. Only then—and in a truly profound, albeit inadvertent way—does one come face to face with the notion that perhaps oneself and one's body are two separate entities.

During illness, one instinctively searches for its causes in what is perceived to be a highly sophisticated biological machine. And if the mechanical cause is found—whether infection, germ, parasite, or contagious disease—one tends to heave a sigh of relief in the expectation that the problem can be fixed by medicine. For medical science and technology have so thoroughly and triumphantly probed the intricacies of bodily mechanics that many of the diseases that once plagued mankind have been conquered. This triumph, in turn, has led to a better understanding of certain more complex sources of disease and death. As scientists have probed ever deeper, a new dimension of the human body has been identified, one involving the influence a person has on his or her own physical health; and it has become clear that bodily mechanisms can be influenced for better or worse not only by external forces but by forces inside the body as well. This dimension, variously called "psychophysiological" or "psychosomatic," has gradually come to be understood as being every bit as important to human health as the traditional causes of illness.

Human beings have always recognized their own penchant for self-destruction. Overt suicide or covert forms of self-destruction, such as cigarette smoking or alcoholism, have long been seen as a real part of the human condition. Coupled with this recognition has come the gradual realization that psychosomatic processes also can cause human pain, disease, and even premature death. This source of self-destruction is even more unsettling than overt acts of self-destruction precisely because it can occur outside a person's conscious awareness; or even if one is aware of the problem, one still may be unable to control it.

Indicative of the growing awareness of this problem is the increasing acceptance of the idea that psychological stress can have dire effects on the body or make one ill. The concept of stress-induced illness is now frequently mentioned in the news and entertainment media and is readily accepted by the public at large. Virtually everyone accepts the idea that stress can cause someone else's illness and can exact a brutal price on the human body. While the notion of stress is readily accepted on an abstract level, at a personal level its acceptance is somewhat equivocal, especially when the problem occurs outside of a person's awareness.

Yet, even at a personal level, "stress" is readily accepted as a major cause of bodily illness, as long as that stress is seen as external to the person and as something that victimizes him or her. Exemplifying such acceptance is the 1982 air-traffic controllers' strike. Thousands walked off their jobs and defied a presidential order to return to work because they had been led to believe that their occupation was causing extreme psychological stress, including dangerous elevations in blood pressure. While it is most likely that their jobs were no more stressful than a wide variety of others, and were indeed far less stressful than unemployment itself, nevertheless the idea that external psychological stress can cause serious cardio-vascular illness was readily accepted by the air-traffic controllers.*

Yet while people grow ever more comfortable with the idea that external stressors can influence the body, one perception has not changed. The body is still thought about the same way it has been viewed for nearly four hundred years: as a self-regulating, self-adjusting machine. Psychological stress has merely been added to a list of other factors that can attack the body and, thus, is merely an extension of the infectious disease model. Now, as in 1600, the human body is treated as a highly sophisticated biochemical machine which breaks down only gradually—unless, that is, it is victimized by forces it cannot control, irrespective of whether those forces are mental or physical.

The separation of the mind from the body, embodied in such terms as *psychosomatic,* has made it particularly difficult for patients to come to grips with quite a different source of stress in their lives. For, as we shall see, not all stress-induced bodily problems are a reflection of a struggle between one's mind and body. Quite the contrary. The belief that mind and body live together in some sort of self-contained dual existence, apart from everything and everyone else, has obscured the fact that human beings also live in and are biologically linked to their natural environment as well as to other human beings. Thus, a major source of stress arises from a breakdown in dialogue and a blindness to the links between human communication and bodily function: that is, when one is emotionally isolated.†

In order to help clarify this source of stress and its effects on the human body, I will begin by describing three health professionals

---

* Their belief was based on medical studies that had found blood pressure to be higher than normal when air-traffic controllers were working in the flight towers.[1] The medical investigators who conducted these studies were unaware of the links between speaking and blood pressure, and in all likelihood, had recorded blood pressure elevations that were due not to the stress of the job but to the fact that blood pressure was recorded in a task requiring the controllers to talk. Many air-traffic controllers were so thoroughly convinced that their jobs imperiled their health that they went out on strike and even defied a presidential order. They probably lost their jobs because of an unfortunate misinterpretation of blood-pressure readings in the flight towers in a job that may have been only modestly stressful.

† As I shall later explain, especially in chapters 8 and 9, this emotional isolation is complex: One can be cut off from one's own emotions and, thus, literally cannot relate to oneself. Unable to relate even to oneself, then one is unable truly to relate to others. Even if one attempts to break that emotional barrier and communicate to others, they themselves may be unwilling to respond.

who struggled against recognizing that their physical problems—migraine headaches and hypertension—reflected a profound disturbance in their communication and relationships to other people. Each of these professionals knew a great deal about human physiology and human psychology; and indeed, all were well versed in the most up-to-date theories about psychosomatic disease. Nevertheless, this knowledge did not help them conquer their own bodily distress, nor did it help alleviate the suffering that came from misunderstanding the language of their own hearts.

WHEN ALL THE TESTS ARE NEGATIVE

Patty nervously flicked the ashes from her cigarette into an ashtray on my desk, settled back into a black sofa chair, and slowly exhaled smoke from her lungs. She pensively watched the thin grayish white cloud from her half-spent cigarette waft slowly toward the ceiling of my office. Staring at the smoke, as if hypnotized by its slow upward journey, she commented in a subdued voice, "All the tests were negative—not even a little tumor or blood clot—not even the hint of any problem. So, I guess the migraines must be psychosomatic after all." She paused for a moment, then turned and looked at me with a quizzical, somewhat strained smile, and added wistfully, "Hard, though, to really admit that you're some kind of a nut. Better to have cancer or some kind of brain tumor, you know what I mean?"

Outwardly she seemed completely calm, but the physiological monitors beside her chair reflected another, internal reality (see figure 1.1). Her hands were a freezing 76 degrees Fahrenheit, almost twenty degrees colder than normal; her heart was pounding along at 125 beats per minute, twice as fast as normal; and her blood pressure registered a surprisingly low 98/50 millimeters of mercury.* When I asked her how she felt, however, she said fine. She seemed completely oblivious to the excessive pounding of her heart as well as to the other major changes occurring in her body.

I was surprised the first few times I heard patients express anxiety at the suggestion that their migraines, hypertension, muscle spasms,

---

* In the measurement of blood pressure, the top number, here 98, refers to the systolic, or peak, blood pressure; while the bottom number, here 50, is the diastolic, or lowest, pressure measured in the pressure wave. Normal pressure in a patient of Patty's age would be around 120/60, and normal resting heart rate would be between 60 to 70 beats per minute. The measurement of blood pressure and its implications will be further explained in chapter 2.

Figure 1.1.   Therapeutic setting with patient and therapist watching digital and computer graphic displays of various physiological responses.

spastic colons, or facial pain might not stem from exclusively mechanical causes. Yet even though such anxieties are common in patients, I could not help feeling that Patty ought to have known better and to have felt differently. A bright and attractive nurse, thirty-three years of age, divorced and forced to support a six-year-old son by herself, she hardly seemed like the type of person who would be depressed to discover that her migraines were not the result of a brain tumor.

She had just returned from seeing a neurologist who had conducted an exhaustive series of medical tests to rule out the possibility that some previously undetected neurological problem might have caused her headaches. In recent months, they had grown so severe that she could no longer effectively function at work; blinding pain and visual disturbances were at times making it difficult for her to see the intravenous drips she was supposed to regulate in very sick hospital patients. Intramuscular injections of Gynergin no longer seemed to quash her headaches, nor did an entire battery of painkillers help. She had even been thinking about stealing codeine from a hospital supply cabinet in order to escape her misery.

And yet, in spite of her misery, Patty had agreed to come to our clinic only because her neurologist strongly insisted that she do so. She stated that she had originally perceived our clinic to be "some kind of biofeedback place where I could come and learn to control the headaches with the help of computers." Her attitude shifted when she learned that our therapy involved far more than learning how to control her body, and that, indeed, we believed that she could never really "control" her body but could only listen to it when it reacted during human dialogue. She appeared to be uneasy about the prospect of having her body monitored while she talked to us about various topics. She responded to that approach by noting that a clinic labeled "psychophysiological" had to be the end of the line—a place you went only after all other treatment possibilities had been exhausted.

Her strong ambivalence prompted me to reflect on the irony inherent in her desire to find a physical explanation for her problems: "You know, Patty, if your problem with migraines stems from interpersonal sources, then there may be a great deal you can do to help. But what would your options be if cancer or a brain tumor had been discovered?"

"I know! I know!" she shot back impatiently, as she leaned forward to extinguish her cigarette in the ashtray. Then quickly glancing at the computer screen that, minute by minute, was silently graphing the marked changes in her heart rate and blood pressure, she smiled wanly and commented, "That machine kind of undresses you, doesn't it?" Without allowing me time to respond, she continued, "So let's get on with whatever it is you do in this place." (I shall continue with Patty's treatment later in chapter 8, where I deal specifically with migraines.)

THE UNHEARD MESSAGE

At forty-nine years of age, Michael was a physician who had spent over twenty years in a family medical practice, routinely measuring the blood pressure of thousands of patients. Friendly and outgoing, and a dedicated physician, he did not appear to be in danger of dying from what the American Heart Association has labeled America's number one "silent killer"—hypertension. Like many other hypertensive patients seen in our clinic, he seemed to be doing all the "right things." He exercised regularly, did not smoke, watched his diet carefully, and in general seemed to be in excellent physical shape. Yet his blood pressure was elevated up to levels that had to be considered alarming.

Unlike other hypertensive patients treated in our university clinic, however, Michael was well informed about the cardiovascular system. He clearly understood that emotional arousal, tension, and stress can produce high readings, and that if patients are relaxed their blood pressure can fall. As is true of virtually all physicians, he recognized the importance of taking blood pressure several times in order to get an accurate reading. He also readily accepted the idea that emotional stress can be linked to the development or exacerbation of hypertension. Even more personally troubling, he clearly understood the serious medical risks associated with sustained high blood pressure. He knew all about the sharply increased risks of having a heart attack or a stroke that had been linked to hypertension. He had seen more than enough pathology and sudden death in his clinical practice to question the seriousness of his own high blood pressure. His understanding of the cardiovascular system, and his clinical sophistication, had only made his struggle with hypertension all the more frustrating—or as he initially said to me, "embarrassing."

Michael first recognized the sudden and alarming rise of his own blood pressure into dangerous hypertensive ranges five years before we met when he felt dizzy upon standing. He also began to experience transient blurring of vision. His internist quickly prescribed a variety of conventional antihypertensive medicines, which did lower his blood pressure. Unfortunately the drugs caused a variety of side effects which he felt were even more problematic than his hypertension. He was depressed and alarmed because his medicines were significantly contributing to his struggle with sexual impotency and to his overall feeling of loss of energy.

He had recently remarried after a painful and emotionally distressing divorce from a marriage of almost twenty years. Shortly after his second marriage—two years before our meeting—Michael decided to cease taking his medicines and run the risks associated with hypertension. He felt trapped between the dangers inherent in his elevated blood pressure and the potential dissolution of his second marriage because of the drug-related impotence and his general sense of lethargy and depression. He had come to our clinic at the recommendation of his internist who felt that our treatment techniques might be helpful.

During our initial meeting, his blood pressure was quite high, averaging around 170/110,* well into hypertensive ranges. His heart rate averaged about 90 beats per minute, some twenty to twenty-five beats per minute faster than normal. In spite of these high readings, Michael initially stared in a rather detached way at the computer screen that was automatically recording his heart rate and blood pressure while we talked. He seemed as calmly objective as a television newsman reporting "live" from the scene of catastrophe. Each minute the cuff on Michael's arm was automatically inflated to measure his pressure, and each time the results on the computer screen were consistent. His blood pressure was elevated into levels that were alarming. Although halfway through our first meeting, he gradually began to express some surprise at the way his blood pressure changed when he spoke, he nevertheless appeared absolutely relaxed, smiling pleasantly as he chatted about "his concern" with "that blood pressure showing up each minute on the screen." He spoke with only the slightest hint of forced articulation, and most noticeably, when he spoke, he breathed in a remarkably shallow fashion. He seemed to speak without commas in his sentences—commas, that is, at the points where one ordinarily stops to breathe. He talked softly, yet with breathless intensity, virtually never pausing until he had completed what he wanted to say.

Externally his demeanor appeared typical of many hypertensive patients. I said that I would hate to play poker with him, in light of the fact that he showed no emotion on the surface—except for his pleasant smile. It was impossible to tell what he was feeling by looking at his poker face, as I commented to him, remarking on the paradox of his appearing so calm while his pressure was out of control.

"Spent all of my life perfecting this smile," he countered, smiling.

---

* Normal pressure in a patient forty-nine years old ranges between 120–140/60–80, with a normal resting heart rate of 60 to 75 beats per minute. Hypertension is usually diagnosed for pressures that average above 155/95 on two or more successive readings. The measurements are in millimeters of mercury—for example, 155/95 mm Hg. Measuring blood pressure will be further explained in chapter 2.

"It's worth a million dollars, you know. Patients love it. After all, you can't have your friendly family doctor looking unhappy and sick, now can you?" Glancing at the computer screen, which was tracing out the rise in his pressure, he continued, "Strange how I spent all my life controlling things. Do you know how hard it is to look at that? Just when I finally got everything under control, that thing goes out of control."

"That thing!" The phrase struck me as symptomatic of his problems with hypertension, and I repeated it for emphasis.

"That thing is part of you!" I then pointed out that his language was typical of the way virtually everyone disconnects medical symptoms from their personal selves. "Why do you think 'that thing' has gone out of control?" I asked.

He paused to reflect on the question and, while continuing to smile, quipped, somewhat sarcastically, "Maybe it's my arterioles? Or kidneys? Or the extracellular fluid system? Who knows, maybe my whole body has turned against me!" His voice then became more intense, his speech more rapid, and he stopped smiling. He alluded briefly to his divorce from his wife five years earlier, and the trauma it had caused. His adolescent children had great difficulty coming to terms with his leaving their mother, and their distress had been especially painful for him. Within sixty seconds his blood pressure rocketed up to 210/125, and his heart rate began to pound over 110 beats per minute. Concerned about the rapid rise in his pressure, I asked him to be quiet and breathe deeply. Within one minute, his pressure fell back to 175/108, and his heart rate to 85 beats per minute.

"That's amazing!" He seemed genuinely stunned by the abrupt rise in his pressure when he spoke, and equally surprised by the precipitate drop when he breathed quietly. And yet in spite of what he had seen, he could not remain silent for long, nor did he continue to breathe deeply. He seemed driven to talk, even while commenting on the relationship between his speech and his pressure. "It seems that every time I talk about the past, that thing shoots up."

Three times during the session, Michael returned to the topic of his divorce, and three times his pressure rose as high as 216/139; and each time I interrupted him to request that he be quiet and breathe deeply.

Toward the end of our first hour-long session, he finally stopped talking and silently watched the computer tracings of his blood pressure and heart rate. His systolic blood pressure had gone as high as 216 and as low as 159—57 millimeters of pressure change in an hour in which he had hardly moved in his chair. His diastolic pressure had likewise changed dramatically, rising as high as 139 and falling as low as 103. Still appearing absolutely calm on the surface and still smiling, he quietly reflected, "Kind of makes you wonder about measurements of blood pressure using a stethoscope, doesn't it? Wonder how many patients have come into my office with pressure changing as wildly as this? That pressure's just amazing." Pausing just momentarily and still neglecting to breathe in spite of numerous reminders during the session, he continued, "Thought I had gotten the past out of my system—but it appears what I did was push it out of my head and into the cardiovascular system. How do you control your own body when it revolts on you?"

Therapy had begun. Within eight months Michael had learned to regulate his blood pressure back down to more normal levels without having to depend on drugs.

During his treatment, Michael saw how his blood pressure and heart rate changed when he talked to us at the clinic. The dangerously high rises in his blood pressure had been spurred by his talking. As I shall later describe, what he talked about, the way he spoke, the way he breathed and failed to breathe, and, above all else, the way in which he had managed to hide from himself and others major increases in blood pressure when he spoke—all had contributed to the dangerous rise in his blood pressure. Seeing it all graphically plotted by a computer while he chatted with us led him to realize how totally disconnected he had been from his own body. He was, in turn, led to realize how completely unaware he had been of the feelings that went along with such major bodily changes. Simple conversations, and everyday social interactions that he had previously thought irrelevant to his problems with hypertension, were now seen as central to his disease. During the treatment, Michael learned that he had been disconnected from far more than an awareness of his blood pressure and his own feelings: he had been disconnected from his fellow men and women.

CARING IN ISOLATION

Several years ago a seasoned psychiatrist gave me a glimpse of the difficulty even the most sophisticated clinicians can have when it comes to thinking about bodily functions and bodily communications in an interpersonal context, or when they try to grasp the idea that bodies can destroy themselves when dialogue breaks down. This physician had a great deal of training and knowledge about psychological conflicts and psychological stress. Like Michael and Patty, Henry understood the links between psychological problems and physical difficulties; but even though he knew all about their theoretical connections and interplay, this knowledge did not seem to apply to his own medical problems with hypertension.

I first met this fifty-three-year-old psychiatrist at a medical conference on the interpersonal factors that influence human blood pressure. He was in an audience of about eight hundred health professionals as I demonstrated a phenomenon we had discovered several years earlier. My lecture was on human blood pressure and the way it rapidly and dramatically increases when people talk. Henry watched silently for over an hour as one health professional after another volunteered to have his or her blood pressure recorded by a computer. Each volunteer was asked to sit quietly for four minutes, then to talk to the audience for two minutes on any topic, and then to sit quietly again for an additional two minutes. The computer automatically recorded each person's blood pressure and heart rate every minute and displayed these functions on a large screen. In every case, blood pressure and heart rate soared dramatically when the volunteers began to speak. One nurse increased her heart rate from 70 beats a minute while quiet, up to 155 beats per minute as she talked about her work with coronary-care patients, and then watched her heart rate plummet back down to 70 when she was quiet once again. A young physician proudly announced that he jogged five miles a day and was certain his blood pressure was well regulated and would not rise when he talked. He confidently asserted that he "would beat the machine!" His certainty turned to disbelief as the audience began to laugh nervously after his blood pressure quickly increased from 115/60 while quiet up to 170/95 when he spoke. Almost every volunteer's blood pressure rose from normal levels while quiet to hypertensive levels when he or she began to speak.

The audience was clearly startled by vascular responses that I had grown used to. After observing them on thousands of occasions, I understood these rises in blood pressure to be a routine response within the body when one is speaking. Henry, too, was astonished. He, like most health professionals there, had not been educated to think about the links between language and the cardiovascular system. And though he and they were well aware that psychological stress could elevate blood pressure, they were not prepared to see how dramatically and rapidly it was altered by the mere act of speaking. Indeed, since the traditional way of taking blood pressure required the use of a stethoscope, silence was built into the measurement procedure. Thus the very technique of measurement kept clinicians from recognizing the links between human communication and the cardiovascular system.

Toward the end of the demonstration, Henry decided to test this phenomenon for himself. He felt that he had detected a possible explanation for the large changes in blood pressure in the volunteers. He repeated the younger physician's assertion that his blood pressure could "beat the machine." I did not know at the time that Henry was a psychiatrist suffering from hypertension, nor did I know he was taking large dosages of antihypertensive medicines that he believed would keep his pressure from rising. His blood pressure while he was resting quietly was a bit high, around 155/90. Then he spoke, telling the audience that he was a psychiatrist, and that he suspected "the response of the other volunteers may have been due to anxiety and stage fright, and that with insight and training in dealing with these aspects of human communication, the blood pressure responses could be reduced." He was convinced that his blood pressure would not change during the two minutes he spoke—and he watched in shocked disbelief as his blood pressure boiled up to 225/130 in spite of his medicines. He seemed forlorn and alone as he sat quietly for the final two minutes of the demonstration in front of that large audience, even though his blood pressure fell back down to 155/90 when he was quiet once again.

Several weeks later, he telephoned me and asked if he could fly to Baltimore and spend a couple of days studying our techniques in the clinic. He wanted to see if he could learn to use our methods to help reduce his blood pressure and apply it to other patients. I told him that he could come, but that our methods did not work quickly; also, that it usually took us five to six months—and, in some cases, even longer—to lower a patient's blood pressure to a point where it would remain down without the use of drugs. And our results depended on whether there were other physical or psychological complications.

On the telephone Henry was insistent: "The damn medicines aren't working, you know—and besides, they're making me feel awful. After six years with my internist trying every medicine in the books, the blood pressure is still out of control."

He listened patiently as I repeated that he could come for a diagnostic work-up, but that we could not perform miracles by conducting a brief crash course, or intensive two-day workshop, on blood-pressure control. He said that he understood all that. He was, he reminded me again, a trained psychiatrist who knew that there was no quick cure for his problems. "What have I got to lose," he continued in a subdued tone, "if all I've got to look forward to is more of what I've been going through for the last six years?" He paused and then said, "I'd appreciate it if I could come anyhow."

I asked him if he would consider coming with his wife, in spite of the expense of two air fares. I said that it would help to see both of them together, since such disorders often involve a person's mate, one way or another. "Living with a hypertensive individual sometimes involves communication problems, you know." I felt his own clinical expertise allowed me to be a bit more blunt than I might ordinarily have been. He said he would check with her and get back to me.

Several weeks later, after receiving and reviewing his medical records with an internist, and having both him and his wife, Louise, take a series of routine health and psychological inventories, they arrived to begin working on their problems. Although Henry had spent years treating neurotic and emotionally disturbed people, he had obviously missed several important points in terms of his own struggles with hypertension. In common with Patty and Michael, he was astonishingly insensitive to changes in his own body, especially those that occurred when he was speaking to others. The fact that communicating with other human beings was his life's work did not seem to make the large changes in his blood pressure any easier to appreciate. Like Patty and Michael, his feelings seemed to be disconnected from an awareness of changes in his body. Like them, he had difficulty understanding how his hypertension was linked to any emotional problems he might be having, even though he readily acknowledged that stress can alter one's blood pressure. Ironically, it seemed as if his extensive medical knowledge about the physiological mechanisms that influence blood pressure and his in-depth understanding of psychology made it all the more difficult for him to grasp how these two factors were simultaneously operating to make him hypertensive. It was almost as if he believed his acknowledgment of the problem ought to have afforded him immunity.

During the first hour we met together, his blood pressure and heart rate were monitored every minute. As was true in our first encounter at the medical meeting, his blood pressure fluctuated significantly as we spoke even though he was on high dosages of antihypertensive medicines. Within an hour, however, his pressure gradually settled down just on the borderline of hypertensive ranges. When he seemed a bit more relaxed, I asked him whether his parents were still alive. The question seemed to startle him. He shook his head to indicate that they were dead, held his body more rigidly, and began to breathe more irregularly. Yet he continued to speak softly and without much emotion.

In a flat, controlled, monotone, he began to describe his earlier life as if he were a television commentator passively describing a news event of only marginal significance. "My dad died a few years ago, my mother when I was twelve." He paused for a moment, sighed softly, and continued, "I still remember the last time I saw her. It was snowing, one of these wild mountain blizzards, and the police car could hardly make it up the hill. She'd had a stroke earlier that autumn, and Dad just couldn't handle it any more. He'd been drinking heavily and steadily for almost two months. Drank himself into a stupor that Christmas. Thank God for my grandparents. I think the whole thing must have gotten to him. I—I guess that's what it was. Funny, but I don't even remember crying at that time—I can still remember my mother groaning softly though, like she didn't want to be taken away to the State Hospital.

It was snowing so hard that the blanket she was wrapped in was all covered in white even before they could get her into the police car. She looked far away, like she was in some other place—and that's the last time I ever saw her, all covered in white and looking far away. She died the next day."

Although he showed virtually no emotion while telling his story, his blood pressure rose to 230/125. I asked him to stop talking for a couple of minutes and begin breathing deeply in order to lower his pressure. In order to allow him time to breathe, I directed the conversation to Louise and asked if she was aware of the story he had just told. Appearing every bit as calm as her husband, she nodded affirmatively and then added with a warm smile, "He's got a great deal more than that to tell—but I think it would take days." Neither of them seemed to notice his abnormally high blood pressure.

I asked her if she would object to our monitoring her blood pressure along with her husband's. First joking that she was not the patient, she nevertheless seemed willing to have her cardiovascular reactions monitored. Both she and her physician husband were surprised to discover that her heart rate was around 120 beats a minute, and her blood pressure was also elevated into hypertensive levels, around 165/100. Like her husband, her blood pressure gradually fell over the next hour to more normal levels, although her heart rate remained high. Both of them were expending an amount of cardiovascular energy more appropriate for runners in a marathon than for people chatting quietly in an office. Even more surprising was the fact that, while chatting quietly—and unrecognized by either husband or wife—their cardiovascular systems were seesawing wildly in response to one another. When Henry spoke, his blood pressure and heart rate rapidly increased, and Louise's changed just as rapidly when she spoke. It was a revelation to both of them to discover that her body was as hyperreactive as his and, especially, almost as hypertensive.

Later in the day, after exploring a wide range of topics with both of them, and correlating these topics to changes in their cardiac systems, I asked Louise whether she could summarize her feeling about our hours together. Suddenly her eyes filled with tears. She glanced at the computer monitoring her own body and then stared intensely at the day-long tracing of her husband's blood pressure, saying, "I don't like to see that." And as if she felt we had not heard her the first time, she repeated again, "I don't like to see that. We've got every reason to have a good life together now. The kids are grown up and out on their own and doing quite well. That pleases us both, you know. Now when everything should be going all right, he seems to be drinking too much, fighting depression, worried about hypertension, struggling in our sex life. Why now? Why has everything come undone now?"

Shaking her head in bewilderment, and for the first time in over five hours dropping the appearance of absolute external calm, she began to sob. With an air of quiet desperation, she added softly, "I don't want him to die. I don't want him to die." Her heart rate began to pound at a high rate of 165 beats per minute, and her blood pressure rose to marked hypertensive ranges.

Reaching over to pat her on the shoulder, her husband exclaimed, with a sad smile, "Good God! Your body reacts even more than mine." And, having learned at least one lesson from our session together, he added, "Why don't you breathe deeply a few times?"

By the end of our second day together, Henry and Louise began to reflect on how they had been speaking softly to each other with words that said nothing about how their bodies were crying inside. Indeed, their bodies were involved in a dialogue that had led him inevitably to develop hypertension, while she lived with the overwhelming fear that a hidden disease was threatening her husband's life. Yet once they could look beyond each other's tranquil exterior, and come to understand just how deeply their bodies cared about each other, they began to listen to each other, to the intense bodily dialogue—the dialogue within each of them, and the one between the two of them—which neither had heard in all their married life. They began to accept that there was a variety of things they could do, such as breathing properly and pacing their dialogue, that would ameliorate the marked swings in their heart rate and blood pressure. Each also saw the links between his or her blood pressure and the painful memories of love lost in childhood. But, most of all, each began to look beyond the surface calm of the other's body, and to pay attention to the meaning of its pained and caring internal dialogue. Henry and Louise's bodies had revolted because neither was listening to or understanding the other's hidden communications, in part because neither could tolerate the other's suffering. In a strange paradox, which I shall discuss later, this couple *cared too much.*

BODIES IN REVOLT

Migraine headache and hypertension are but two of the problems that can involve significant interpersonal factors. While certain of these disorders may more frequently afflict one sex or one specific race, in general a broad range of people, from a wide variety of backgrounds and life experiences, are vulnerable to them.

Blood pressure can be elevated, as it was in the case of a fifty-one-year-old woman, because she had carefully concealed from her thirty-two-year-old daughter the fact that she had been an illegitimate child. The woman said that her life with her daughter had always been a lie, and she lived in fear that some day her daughter would find out. She felt that she resented her daughter because "she makes me feel my struggles—even though that's not her fault." Only after a number of sessions, and her confession to her daughter that her father was not some heroic figure who had died in the Korean War, only then did her blood pressure drop precipitately from its hypertensive levels. This mother's body had refused to cooperate with her deception.

Blood pressure can also rise dramatically, as it did in the case of one hypertensive, hard-driving lawyer, who told me, with a burst of excited enthusiasm and forceful, rapid speech, that he could make a million bucks selling our treatment approach—assuming, that is, "you can cure me so that I can slow down long enough to live." He never heard me counter with the idea that he would have to participate in the cure, and that our clinic was no "fix-it," overnight, auto-body shop. He did smile, though, when I suggested that he first slow his speech down a bit so that I could absorb everything he was trying to say to me.

Surface blood flow in the arm can totally shut down, as it did in one woman biochemist afflicted with a vascular disorder (Raynaud's disease) when she began to talk about how she hated her mother.

And the patient's blood just as suddenly began to flow again when she began to think about pleasant things in her life: "You mean that arm turns on and off like some fire hydrant that periodically gains and loses water pressure? Amazing!" She could not describe exactly what "amazing" meant to her, nor could she immediately grasp the utility of expressing love rather than hatred toward her mother.

"You came right out of her belly, you know," I said, in an effort to remind her of the implication of the fact that genetically her body was half her mother's, "so how can you love yourself if you hate her?"

"You don't know my mother!" the chemist countered, adding that she'd rather die than forgive her mother.

"Maybe your immune system is trying to oblige you?" I suggested, and emphasized that the therapy would take some time.

"Amazing!" she replied again, looking at the computer record of the blood flow in her arm. "That arm is just amazing."

These are only a few of the many people in our society whose bodies, unheard by them and unseen by others, react drastically when they attempt to communicate, endangering themselves and hurting those others whom they most love. Such people are often educated, successful, sophisticated, bright, and sensitive. They are usually wonderfully pleasant and seem to care about their fellow human beings. And yet, for all that, their deafness to the internal message of their own bodies causes suffering, emotional isolation, and interpersonal pain.

Why do bodies revolt? Why and how do sensitive, well-informed, and intelligent people literally allow their own bodies to push them around? The reason is, I believe, that they do not—indeed, have never been allowed to—understand the language of their own hearts—a language expressed in ways both obvious and subtle, through variations in the cardiovascular system. Before delving further into this language and its meaning, let us look at one aspect of the cardiovascular system—blood pressure—to see how it is measured, and at the cardiovascular system as a whole.

CHAPTER 2

The Vital Sign

> The heart has its reasons that reason knows not of. . . . Do you love by reason?
> —Blaise Pascal, *Pensées*

The television screen crackles with drama. Amid the wreckage of half a dozen automobiles, a critically injured woman lies motionless on the soft shoulder of an interstate highway, while a team of paramedics hovers over her. In the background an oil truck explodes in flames. Then the scene shifts to a hospital emergency room where a doctor, surrounded by nurses, holds a dataphone.

"Vital signs!" he commands and then listens as two of the paramedics, with split-second precision, provide him with the critical figures:

"Female, approximately thirty-five years old."

"Pulse, fifty-eight and weak."

"Heartbeat, irregular."

"Respiration, eight per minute and labored."

"Blood pressure, 105 over 50."

"Pupils, dilated but responsive."

"Victim, pale and clammy."

The physician momentarily strokes his chin, obviously concentrating on the crucial information he has just received and the vital decisions he must make in a matter of seconds. His commands flash over the dataphone: "Start I.V., Ringers Lactate, two liters oxygen, nasal cannula. Send rhythm strip and transport immediately."

Days pass. Then, from her hospital bed, a cheery, attractive blonde greets the paramedics and her physician and nurses with all the intense gratitude and awe due those who have brought her back from the brink of death.

An eight-year-old munches on his Sunday evening snack, transfixed by the drama unfolding on the television screen. In addition to the excitement generated by the billowing flames and the heroism of the paramedics, when he trundles off to bed the child has absorbed an invaluable lesson. Via the wizardry of modern electronics, he has been taught something that our ancestors first learned in caves thousands of years ago—the importance of what the doctor called "vital signs." Heartbeat, pulse, respiration, pupillary reflexes (that is, central nervous system responsiveness), body temperature, and blood pressure—these were the crucial functions the paramedic team barked over the roar of exploding gasoline tanks.

In spite of the drama, the television program contains an important lesson, which is difficult to witness anywhere but on television. The lesson concerns death itself and the importance of what the doctor called "vital signs."* For in our modern world, the drama of life and death has been removed from the personal experience of most people, and is witnessed instead as high-action, tension-filled soap opera. Unlike earlier generations, most people today would have to make a real effort to witness the demise of a fellow human being. Few of us are able to watch the change in bodily functions—the vital signs—that mark the transition from life to death. Once a routine part of everyone's consciousness, that drama is now played out in hospital intensive-care units and old-age facilities and is usually hidden from public view, except when television brings it into our homes.

It is not at all clear who coined the term *vital signs,* but I suppose that even a man or a woman living in a cave ten thousand years ago knew what to look for to determine whether someone was dead or alive. The physical drama has remained unchanged even if our philosophical understanding of the source of the "vitality" has shifted. The lifeless lungs no longer inhaling the vital air; the coldness of a body no longer warmed by circulating blood; the

---

* Another, far less helpful notion has also been subtly suggested: that is, no matter what happens or how one behaves, concerned medical personnel, standing vigilant beside emergency-room dataphones, and a highway paramedic team will always be ready to rescue one from disaster.

absence of heartbeat or pulse: These are fundamental differences between life and death that have been observed and monitored since the dawn of mankind. It is indeed humbling to realize how little we have added to our understanding since our ancestors living in caves struggled with the drama. For in spite of our leaps in knowledge, over the millenniums only one qualitatively new vital sign—blood pressure—has been added to the roster of physical signs of life. Of course, we have new drugs, and our understanding of cardiac function and of the danger of cardiac arrhythmias has vastly improved; but nevertheless, as vital signs they are not new. Only blood pressure is "new." It is the only vital sign that could not have been measured or, for that matter, even conceived of by our ancestors in their caves. It is the only new vital sign that has managed to get itself prominent billing in the flaming wreckage of the highway medical dataphone. Make no mistake about it, the blood-pressure numbers flashed across telephone lines to emergency centers are big-league information: they are numbers that separate life from death.

In spite of the recent discovery of this vital sign, people have come to attach meaning to blood-pressure numbers in a way that has made it the pre-eminent indicator of health and illness. One goes to one's doctor and "gets" a number—say, 140/90—and somehow just knows that this rating is not as good as their next-door neighbor's. When they come to our clinic, patients seldom talk about or even think about their respiration or pulse rate, temperature or pupillary reflexes, but they do "know" their blood pressure is 140/90 and view "it"—that number—with awe. More than one patient has pulled out a card or note from a wallet, pointed to it with smug satisfaction, and said, "My blood pressure was 136 over 72 the last time I visited my physician." It is the only vital sign that has managed to get itself emblazoned in red-banner print on highway billboards and announced solemnly on television commercials: "If you have high blood pressure, see your doctor."

This "Johnny-come-lately" vital sign is now routinely measured in almost every medical examination and is undoubtedly the most common medical measurement. The National Center for Health Statistics estimates that, in 1975 and 1976, there were over one hundred million office visits to physicians in the United States for treatment of diseases of the circulatory system—a statistic that provides an absolute minimum of the frequency with which blood pressure is measured annually by physicians and nurses in the Western world. It has been estimated that blood pressure is measured at least one billion times annually in the United States alone.[1]

WHAT IS BLOOD PRESSURE?

Blood pressure is a measure of the force liquid blood exerts against the walls of blood vessels throughout the body during the cardiac cycle. With each heartbeat, two or three ounces of blood is pumped under pressure into the major artery exiting the heart, the aorta. The aorta subdivides into smaller branches throughout the body. The smaller arteries lead into a system of microscopic vessels, the arterioles, which have the capacity to dilate and constrict.

The relationship between arteries and arterioles can be understood through the analogy of an ordinary garden hose. When a water spigot is turned on, water enters the hose. If the nozzle at the far end of the hose is closed, the pressure behind the nozzle in the hose is very high, and no water flows through the nozzle. (You can sense this pressure by squeezing the hose.) As you open the nozzle, water flows out, the pressure falls, and the hose feels softer. When the nozzle is entirely open, the amount of flow is at a maximum, and the pressure is at its lowest. Within the body, the small arterioles function like millions of nozzles: that is, they can open (dilate) and close (constrict). When they constrict, the pressure behind them (in the arteries) increases.

Blood pressure is determined by the volume of blood pumped from the heart during each heartbeat (this is called "stroke volume") and by the resistance the blood encounters in its passage throughout the peripheral circulation: that is, blood pressure varies directly with stroke volume and peripheral resistance. Cardiac output is described as the volume of blood pumped by the heart per minute, and therefore simply represents the product of stroke volume and heart rate. In this book I shall focus on dynamic variables affecting the flow of blood throughout the circulatory system, including heart rate, blood pressure and peripheral resistance, and the relationship between these variables, when people communicate.

WHAT ARE NORMAL AND ABNORMAL BLOOD PRESSURES?

If one measured blood pressure in a large group of people at any specific age, one would quickly discover a range of values, with a high and a low end. It has been noted that those people whose pressures are in the high end of the spectrum are at greater risk for a variety of cardiovascular diseases. Normal blood pressure, then, is a statistical notion, which indicates that there is no absolute value or cut-off point separating normal from abnormal. Rather, there is a range of pressures; and the higher the pressure, the greater the probability of cardiovascular dysfunction. Sustained blood-pressure elevations at the upper end of the curve are considered to indicate a disease called "hypertension."

THE DANGER OF HIGH BLOOD PRESSURE

For the past three to four decades, cardiovascular disease has led the list of killers in virtually every industrialized society. Heart diseases now account for slightly more than 50 percent of all deaths reported in the United States.[2] In 1980, almost one million Americans died from either atherosclerosis or hypertension, while an additional forty million Americans were identified as suffering from diseases of the heart and blood vessels.[3] In 1980, the National Institutes of Health estimated that the economic costs of cardiovascular disorders, including loss of productivity and health expenditures, exceeded eighty billion dollars annually in the United States alone.[4] Hypertension or sustained elevated blood pressure has long been recognized as a leading contributor to a variety of cardiovascular diseases, including stroke and heart attacks. It has been estimated, for example, that hypertensive individuals are two to three times more likely to develop coronary artery disease than those with normal blood pressure, and are four times more likely to suffer from a stroke. It is also widely suspected that sustained elevations in blood pressure or rapid changes in pressure may be an important cause of atherosclerosis, a process that leads to the gradual hardening of the arteries.[5]

It has been estimated that approximately sixty million Americans are hypertensive. Only 24 percent of these sixty million are effectively treated with drugs; while twenty-six million (44 percent of those with hypertension) are aware of their elevated blood pressures, but their condition remains untreated or inadequately controlled.[6] This lack of effective treatment is particularly worrisome because high blood pressure may damage the lining of blood vessels. It is the damage to those blood vessels supplying vital organs such as brain, heart, kidneys, and eyes that results in the clinical manifestations of hypertension, such as stroke, heart attack, and heart and kidney failure. Since hypertension usually presents no detectable symptoms until secondary-organ damage occurs, medical scientists have labeled this disease "America's number-one silent killer." All of these facts have long convinced physicians of the necessity of routinely recording blood pressure in all patients.

High blood pressure acts in four especially destructive ways:

1. Sustained high blood pressure forces the heart to work harder when it ejects blood in order to overcome the resistance. The increased pressure in the arteries can cause enlargement of the heart muscle, especially of the left ventricle, the chamber that ejects blood out into the entire body. This condition, called "left ventricular hypertrophy," places the heart muscle, the myocardium, under ever-increasing risk of a heart attack, or what is called a "myocardial infarction."

2. A second important problem caused by sustained high blood pressure occurs in the brain. The constant strain of hypertension in the blood vessels in the brain may cause certain of these smaller vessels to burst, leading to a stroke, which will deprive certain vital nerve centers of oxygen. Such brain hemorrhages are four times more common in people with hypertension than in those with normal pressure. In addition, blockages in the larger central vessels commonly result in strokes.

3. Other major organs that can suffer damage from sustained high blood pressure include the eyes and the kidneys. Kidney damage brought on by hypertension can create a vicious circle in which the damage may cause the kidney to secrete renin, a substance that will drive the pressure even higher.

4. Finally, it is suspected that high blood pressure accelerates the process of atherosclerosis (hardening of the arteries). Atherosclerosis—especially in the coronary arteries, the arterial vessels that supply blood to the

heart muscle itself—is the underlying pathology responsible for heart attacks—that is, myocardial infarctions.

Recognition of the relationship between high blood pressure and these major medical problems led the American Heart Association, about ten years ago, to launch a concerted national public education program on hypertension. Its message was twofold: first, hypertension has to be considered a serious medical disorder; and secondly, if treated by a physician, high blood pressure can be managed effectively. Hypertension was defined as a systolic pressure greater than 155 and a diastolic pressure greater than 95 (usually determined after several measurements of blood pressure). Initially, diastolic pressure was considered more important than systolic, insofar as it tended to reflect overall baseline levels of pressure; but systolic pressure came to be seen as equally important. If one accepts repeated readings of blood pressure of 155/95 or higher as indicating hypertension, then approximately thirty-five million Americans now suffer from this disease. A second group of five million to ten million people, with diastolic blood pressure readings between 90 and 94, are classified as borderline hypertensive. The campaign to get more of these people treated clearly has had its intended effects. Within the past few years, the number of people seeking treatment for hypertension doubled, and an increasing variety of drugs was developed to help treat the problem.

Along with these efforts to educate the public about the dangers of high blood pressure, medical scientists redoubled their efforts to identify the cause or causes of high blood pressure. Before turning to this issue, however, I shall sketch a brief history of the technique of measuring blood pressure. For, embedded in this history are certain crucial ideas that lead us to understand why certain interpersonal aspects of blood pressure regulation had been vastly underrated, and why such phenomena have to be considered in the development of more effective treatment approaches for hypertension.

THE TECHNIQUE OF MEASURING BLOOD PRESSURE

THE CIRCULATORY SYSTEM: WILLIAM HARVEY

Most medical historians credit the beginnings of modern under-standing of the heart and circulation with the scientific studies of William Harvey (1578–1657). In his classic text *Anatomica de Motu Cordis,** published in 1628, Harvey wrote, "I was almost tempted to think with Fracastorius† that the motion of the heart was only to be comprehended by God."[7] Thus he began a text that is now widely acknowledged to be a milestone in the history of medicine, the first complete explanation of the anatomy and physiology of the heart and its circulation. This work did much to enlighten humanity about the true nature of the cardiovascular system and set aside many of the myths that surrounded this central organ of the body.

Harvey's studies were the first to reveal how the heart functions and how the vast array of arteries and veins in the body are all connected in one, unified, extraordinary complex network that he called the "circulatory system." He showed that the vascular system is circular in nature, and that the blood pumped out of the heart travels in a circle—circulation—to return to the heart once again. Even more remarkable, in that the microscope was not yet widely available, he predicted the necessary existence of capillary circulation which he called "pores": that is, the way in which blood in the arteries is able to pass over to the veins.

In 1616, Harvey described the outlines of his theory as follows:

It is plain from the structure of the heart that the blood is passed continuously through the lungs to the aorta as by the two clacks of a water bellows to raise water.

It is shown by the application of a ligature that the passage of the blood is from the arteries into the veins.

Whence it follows that the movement of the blood is constantly in a circle, and is brought about by the beat of the heart.[8]

It is clear from these quotations that Harvey's ideas about the heart and circulation were rooted in a mechanical model. When

---

* The full title of Harvey's book is *On the Movement of the Heart and Blood in Animals,* or, in the original Latin, *Exercitatio Anatomica de Motu Cordis et Sanguinis in Animalibus.*

† Girolamo Fracastoro (1483–1553), Italian physician and poet; a long poem of his gave the disease of syphilis its name.

he speaks of "two clacks of a water bellows," the analogy to hydraulics is obvious. I emphasize this point in order to indicate that scientists were already thinking about the human body in terms of physics and hydraulics decades before Descartes's major philosophical treatise, *Discourse on Method,* appeared in 1637.*[9] The same system of thought that allowed scientists to study heavenly "bodies" (the stars and planets) and physical "bodies" (chemical structures) was applied by Harvey and other scientists to the human body as well. It was, after all, a "body" that occupied space: it had a certain mass and moved in space. Therefore the human body appeared to be amenable to the same type of scientific scrutiny that was being successfully applied to the study of other bodies by Renaissance scientists. As I shall discuss in chapter 10, Descartes's proposition that the human body obeys machinelike laws was by no means new. Rather, he added a perspective that was qualitatively different from Harvey's. Descartes extended the mechanical view of the human body to include the emotional life of human beings and, in the process, rendered this fundamental aspect of human life irrelevant to anything that could be seen as unique to the human body. Emotions were included as a problem to be addressed in terms of physics and hydraulics.

The immediate question that greeted Harvey's description of the heart and circulation, however, was far more technical than philosophical. His descriptions led many people to question how the heart can beat so as to enable blood to travel all around the body and to the extremities and still return to the heart at the same rate and flow as it is being pumped out.

HYDRAULICS IN LIVING ANIMALS:
THE DISCOVERY OF BLOOD PRESSURE

In 1733, about one hundred years after Harvey's discoveries, an English clergyman, the Reverend Stephen Hales (1677–1761), demonstrated the existence of a physical force that explained how Harvey's model of circulation worked. Hales called the force "blood pressure" and described his findings in a text entitled *An Account of Some Hydraulic and Hydrostatical Experiments Made on the*

---

* As one can discover from the *Discourse,* Descartes and Harvey had somewhat different notions about the mechanics of the heart; they corresponded and debated their respective ideas. While history was to vindicate Harvey's technical descriptions, it was the larger philosophical context in which Descartes cast these findings that deeply influenced science and medicine.

Blood and Blood Vessels of Animals.[10] As is clear from the title of his book, Hales's frame of reference about blood pressure was rooted in the emerging scientific fields of mechanics and physics. He sought to demonstrate that human blood obeys the same laws of hydraulics and hydrostatics that other liquids in nature obey.

Hales's ability to conceive of blood as having a "pressure" that could be defined in terms of hydraulics and hydrostatics was itself dependent on the scientific formulations of another extraordinary individual, Monsieur Blaise Pascal (1623–62). In 1663, almost forty years after the appearance of Harvey's book, Pascal's brother-in-law (Perier) posthumously published his discoveries in *Traité de l'equilibre des liqueurs* and *Traité de la pesanteur de la masse de l'air* ("Dissertation on the Equilibrium of Liquids" and "Dissertation on the Weight of Air").[11] In this text Pascal clearly and concisely established two facts that had long eluded scientific understanding: namely, that air has weight; and that, therefore, liquids must have a pressure that can be measured.

Pascal began his quest attempting to answer a problem raised by Galileo in 1638. Galileo reported in his *Discorsi* that a suction pump could raise water to a fixed height of only about 10 meters, a finding he believed contradicted Aristotle's theory that nature abhors a vacuum. Three years later, Evangelista Torricelli (1608–48) modified Galileo's experiment, substituting mercury for water. He observed that the height of the column of mercury reached only 76 centimeters, instead of the 10 meters that water attained. Torricelli correctly deduced that the different heights attained by these two liquids had to do with the weight of the external column of air. More important, he also reaffirmed Galileo's observation that a vacuum can exist in nature.

Torricelli's experiment initially could not be confirmed and was ignored until Pascal successfully achieved the same result in 1646. In a series of brilliant experiments, Pascal focused on the crucial idea that air had weight and, in so doing, created an entirely new understanding of the physics of liquids. He described a phenomenon he called "hydrostatic pressure," a marvelously simple and clear demonstration that water, as well as all other liquids, has a certain pressure that depends on various physical forces. The most important of these forces is air itself. Pascal proved that air can exert a counter pressure on the pressure of liquids, that air itself has weight. He went on to show that the weight of air interacts with water in a way that can be mathematically measured. With elegant simplicity he proceeded to work out the mathematics of barometric pressure and the fundamental physics of fluids, while confirming Galileo's suspicions that nature does not abhor a vacuum.[12]

On two occasions, 23 and 24 September 1647, Pascal discussed his findings about the existence of vacuums and the concept of fluid pressure with an older contemporary, René Descartes. Since Descartes had recently published his major philosophical treatises, including *Discourse on Method* (1637) and *Passions of the Soul* (1645–46), Pascal was well acquainted with the central thrust of his philosophy. Like Harvey, both Descartes and Pascal shared a keen interest in the nature of the human heart and its circulation— but from a philosophical perspective beyond Harvey's clinical one. Descartes and Pascal recognized that the body was a physical object which had much in common with other physical objects in nature. The question was whether there was anything about the body that made it uniquely human.

It is also clear that Pascal differed sharply with Descartes's fundamental notion that bodily systems such as the heart and circulation are solely mechanical parts of a sophisticated bodily machine.* Pascal understood that his proof that air has weight, and that liquids can be measured in terms of pressure, was of profound consequence to Descartes's entire philosophical system. Since the latter had already stated that the heart and circulation function strictly according to mechanical principles, and that these functions are identical in humans and animals, Pascal would have recognized that his own notion of the "pressure of liquids" would make Descartes's concept of a mechanical heart work. After all, blood being a liquid could, like other liquids, be measured in terms of its pressure.

Yet at the same time Pascal was deeply troubled by the essential core of Cartesian philosophy, even though he sensed it would sweep the Western world. He differed sharply with Descartes about the nature of human emotions and about their links to the human

---

* While space precludes any detailed account of the overlapping interests of Pascal and Descartes, both made major contributions to mathematics and physics. Both shared as well a keen interest in the scientific method and its potential application to solving certain fundamental questions about man's essential relationship to the rest of nature and, by extension, to God.

body. His reflection that "the heart has its reasons that reason knows not of. . . . Do you love by reason?"[13] was no romantic metaphor but a penetrating assault on the essential core of Cartesian philosophy. He believed that Descartes's mechanical model of the body trivialized the nature of human feeling: if the human body was to be considered solely a machine, Pascal recognized that emotions, which arise in the body, would have to be considered as no more than imprecise thoughts. Thus the heart (and, by extension, the entire body) could no longer be the source of any emotion that could be considered uniquely human, since the bodily mechanics of emotions were obviously quite similar in humans and in animals.* The controversy between these two men about the nature of human emotion and its links to the body forms the core issue to be addressed in the latter part of this book with the discovery (or rediscovery) of the language of the heart.

Pascal's demonstrations of air and hydraulic pressure made it possible for the Reverend Hales to deduce that another liquid—blood—must also have a pressure that can be mathematically defined. In a broad range of experiments, he followed the experimental designs originally outlined by Pascal. He measured blood pressure in horses, (and later in sheep and dogs) by tying these animals down and then inserting a brass pipe, $\frac{1}{6}$ inch in diameter, into an artery 3 inches from the horse's belly. To the small brass pipe Hales then attached another larger brass pipe and a glass tube nearly 9 feet long. By this method he was able to watch the blood

---

* Pascal's concerns about the human heart had a greal deal to do with religious issues and his conviction that faith is based on emotions, not on reason. In this same passage in the *Pensées,* Pascal also noted: "It is the heart that experiences God, and not reason. That is what faith is: God felt by the heart, not by reason."[14]

To appreciate fully the context of the debate between Descartes and Pascal, however, recall that, at that time, not only was Galileo's life threatened by orthodox theological interests, but a series of dreadful religious persecutions had erupted throughout Europe. In a deeply ironic sense, Pascal lent support to a movement opposed to the primacy of rational explanations for all natural phenomena. I say "ironic" because he also was a firm believer in the utility of the scientific method and he quarreled with Descartes only about its limits. For Pascal established the guiding principle of modern science when he noted in his book *Traité de la pesanteur de la masse de l'air:* "Experiments are the true teachers which one must follow in physics."[15] This statement embodied his belief that man must be submissive to nature, and was intended to oppose Descartes's central belief that human reason can dictate laws to nature and, in doing so, is not altered by the objects it considers. Pascal believed that the human heart is involved, and therefore altered, whenever two human beings interact. Yet given the emotional tenor of the time, few intellectuals were in a mood to listen to any philosophical position that questioned the limits of reason or espoused the importance of human emotions. For in those dark times (and many dark times since) it appeared as if in objective reason lay the best hope for human beings to survive the dangers of human irrationality.

Figure 2.1. The first experiment Reverend Stephen Hales conducted to measure blood pressure in a horse. His assistant is shown marking the level (8 feet 3 inches) to which the blood rose in the glass tube at its full height.

in a horse's artery rise and fall with each heartbeat (see figure 2.1). Hales describes what he observed with his method as follows:

When I untied the ligature in the artery, the blood rose in the tube 8 feet 3 inches perpendicular above the level of the left ventricle of the heart, but it did not attain to its full height at once; it rushed half way in an instant, and afterwards gradually at each pulse 12, 8, 6, 4, 2 and sometimes 1 inch: when it was at its full height, it would rise and fall at and after each pulse 2, 3, 4 inches; and sometimes it would fall 12 or 14 inches, and have there for a time the same vibrations up and down, at and after each pulse, as it had, when it was at its full height; to which it would rise again after forty or fifty pulses.[16]*

* About ten years ago, research questions about the effects of human contact led our clinic to examine cardiac changes in the horse. Hales reported the average pulse of a horse to be 36 beats per minute, and stated that it could rise as high as 100 beats per minute when excited. With sophisticated telemetering devices almost 250 years later, we found exactly the same cardiac reactions.[17]

Hales deduced that the height of the blood in the glass cylinder, and the changes in this height, were a result of pressure from the horse's bloodstream interacting with the pressure of the air. It was a brilliant extension into the realm of physiology of Pascal's demonstrations of hydrostatic pressure. Hales observed that the horse's blood pressure changed with each heartbeat in wavelike fashion, rising and falling in the glass cylinder. It was also clear that the magnitude of changes in pressure varied from one heartbeat to the next. Sometimes the blood would rise 10 inches and fall 4 inches; sometimes, rise 4 inches and fall 10; and so on.

Thus, Hales simultaneously demonstrated three ideas:

1. the existence of blood pressure;
2. that blood travels through the arteries in wavelike fashion, with a peak wave and a trough or low point; and
3. that blood pressure varies, sometimes quite markedly, with each beat of the heart.

Hales worked out the mechanics of the vascular response by demonstrating that the blood pressure in the artery was determined by the size of the horse and the heart rate of the animal. In what are remarkable experiments even in the light of modern standards, Hales went on to prove that the peak increases and decreases in the blood volume in the glass cylinder were directly related to the filling (diastole) and emptying (systole) of the left ventricle of the horse's heart. He noted that when blood was filling the left ventricle, in the so-called diastole, then blood pressure in the artery (that is, the volume of blood in the glass cylinder) would fall to its lowest point. When the ventricle emptied with the contraction of the heart, in the so-called systole, pressure in the artery rose to its highest level. These two pressure points were therefore called "systolic" and "diastolic" blood pressure because they were linked to the emptying and the filling of the ventricles in the heart.* Systolic was the peak, and diastolic the lowest, pressure in the artery. While Hales's techniques and conceptual thinking were brilliant, the price the horse had to pay—namely, the sacrifice of its life—clearly precluded the use of any similar experiment on human beings. It is ironic that what Hales observed by means of a glass cylinder was remarkably similar to the blood-pressure changes

---

* The terms *systolic* and *diastolic* owe their origins to the Greek terms *systole,* which means "contraction," and *diastole,* which means "to expand" or "to inflate."

now seen with the aid of modern mini-computer technology—blood pressure that can fluctuate markedly with each beat of the heart.

HYDRAULICS IN HUMAN BEINGS: N. S. KOROTKOV

For the next 150 years scientists tried a variety of alternative techniques (other than inserting brass pipes) to measure blood pressure in humans without placing the person at risk, but none was satisfactory until 1904 when N. S. Korotkov (1874–1920) devised an elegant technical solution to the problem. The Russian physician based his technique on an ostensibly simple development that had occurred only six years before. In 1898, an Italian scientist, Scipione Riva-Rocci (1863–1937), developed a pneumatic cuff that could be wrapped around the arm and inflated gradually so as to squeeze the arm tight enough to obliterate the pulse normally felt in the radial (wrist) artery.[18] The cuff was linked to a sphygmomanometer (*sphygmus* = "pulse"), which made possible an accurate gauge of the amount of pressure required to obliterate the pulse at the wrist. With this technique, one could measure systolic blood pressure (see figure 2.2).

In 1904, Korotkov reasoned that he could use a modified version of Riva-Rocci's device while simultaneously using a stethoscope to listen to the pulsations of the brachial artery just below the point of cuff placement, near the elbow (see figure 2.3). By first feeling the pulse manually (that is, palpating the pulse) and then listening to the pulsations of the artery with a stethoscope, Korotkov worked out how to measure human blood pressure:

This reporter has arrived at the conclusion that a completely compressed artery in a normal condition does not produce any sound. Taking advantage of this situation the reporter proposes the sound method for determining the blood pressure in humans. The sleeve [cuff] of Riva-Rocci is placed on the middle ½ of the arm toward the shoulder. The pressure in the sleeve is raised quickly until it stops the circulation of the blood beyond the sleeve. Thereupon, permitting the mercury manometer to drop, a child's stethoscope is used to listen to the artery directly beyond the sleeve. At first no audible sound is heard at all. As the mercury manometer falls to a certain height the first short tones appear; the appearance of which indicates the passage of part of the pulse wave under the sleeve. Consequently, the manometer reading at which the first tones appear corresponds to the maximum pressure. With a further fall of the mercury in the manometer, systolic pressure murmurs are heard which change again to a

Figure 2.2.   Dr. Riva-Rocci feeling the cessation of the pulse in the radial
artery as he gradually tightened the cuff on his patient's arm, while the
mercury manometer simultaneously gauged the pressure in the cuff.

sound (secondary). Finally, all sounds disappear. The time at which the
sounds disappear indicates a free passage of the pulse wave; in other words
at the moment the sounds disappear, the minimum blood pressure in the
artery exceeds the pressure in the sleeve. Consequently the reading of the
manometer at this time corresponds to the minimum blood pressure.[19]

By listening with a stethoscope for two distinctive arterial sounds—
today called the "Korotkov sounds"—he was able to determine the
two extremes of blood pressure:

1. *Systolic pressure,* the point, on the sphygmomanometer, to which the
   mercury has dropped when the pulse begins to beat again, after
   having been totally cut off or obliterated by inflation of the cuff.
2. *Diastolic pressure,* the point, on the sphygmomanometer, to which

Figure 2.3. Dr. Korotkoff in Leningrad adding a stethoscope to Riva-Rocci's technique in order to hear the pulsations of blood in the brachial artery. For the first time both systolic and diastolic blood pressure could be gauged.

the mercury has dropped when the secondary tones stop, indicating that the cuff pressure is so reduced that the pulse pressure in the artery has returned to its normal flow.

While the eighteenth-century philosophical context that determined modern views about blood pressure has remained largely unchanged, there were crucial differences in Korotkov and Hales's methods. Since Korotkov's technique requires a stethoscope in order to hear the pulsations of the artery, silence was explicitly required from both physician and patient while pressure was being measured. In addition, unlike Hales's observations of the changes in blood pressure with each heartbeat of a horse, Korotkov could measure systolic and diastolic pressure in a human being only once each time the cuff was inflated.

Of these two major differences in technique, silence was the crucial variable that no one saw as problematical. For what Hales's horse and a silent human being have in common is that neither could speak during the measurement period. Surely Hales had seen that when an animal was aroused, its heartbeat and blood pressure were altered. From the very beginning, scientists were well aware of the importance of arousal and stress on the circulation. When it was finally possible to measure blood pressure in humans, scientists quickly seized upon the idea that emotional arousal could influence blood pressure. *The emotional content of conversations* was readily seen as influencing blood pressure, while at the same time physicians were blinded to the idea that the *act of talking*—quite independent of emotional content—can also influence blood pressure.

The discrete, single measurement of blood pressure was quickly recognized by physicians to be a limitation of Korotkov's technique, but a limitation that, it was generally assumed, could be circumvented by measuring blood pressure several times to get an accurate reading.

In spite of these two limitations, Korotkov's technique was a major technical breakthrough, all the more remarkable because of its simplicity and cost-effectiveness. It was quickly accepted all over the world, and one simply cannot overestimate its impact on twentieth-century medicine. For the first time, physicians had a way to monitor not only the heartbeat but also the systolic and the diastolic blood pressures of individual patients. The method allowed a far more comprehensive and accurate idea of the overall state of the heart and its circulation than had up to then been possible; and within a few years, an impressive amount of data made it possible to establish norms for healthy levels of blood pressure.

GETTING MY BLOOD PRESSURE TAKEN

Owing to the importance of blood pressure, the rituals and the instruments involved in its measurement have profoundly shaped our modern views about the human body and reinforced our attitudes about the causes of health and illness.* The inflatable cuff wrapped around the patient's arm, the column of mercury rising in the sphygmomanometer (the gauge that moves up—to 180, say—as the physician or the nurse pumps up the cuff) and—most important—the stethoscope, an instrument that allows the clinician to listen to the pulsating blood in the brachial artery: these are the tools that most of us have grown up with, and we all recognize them as essential symbols of modern medicine. I dare say no modern physician or nurse would really feel fully dressed who was not wearing a stethoscope or carrying one in a black bag or in the pocket of a clinical jacket.†

While many aspects of the ritual of blood-pressure assessment deserve closer scrutiny, none is more important than the notion that one has a fixed blood pressure, a number gauged by an instrument which can be "taken" from your body by someone else. Virtually everyone has experienced the ritual at least once; most of us have participated in it a dozen times or more. I vividly remember my own rite of passage. At about seven or eight years of age, struggling with a fever and cold that refused to disappear with the standard remedies of bed rest, avoidance of school, chicken soup, and that most important of health tonics, ginger ale, I waited for hours with my mother, and twenty to twenty-five other people, in the subdued waiting room of our family doctor's office. When the long winter afternoon was beginning to fade into evening, the nurse finally called my name and silently ushered by mother and me into one of the doctor's examining rooms. She took my temperature while solemnly discussing my cough and fever with my mother and scribbling on a medical sheet attached to her clipboard. The physician arrived shortly thereafter—a friendly and kind man who, I knew, had been entrusted with the well-being of my family for almost two decades, although I had never seen him before.

After a minute of quiet conversation with my mother and a few benevolent comments, he asked me to take off my sweater and T-shirt. Naked, I shivered in embarrassment as the room grew absolutely silent. He attached a stethoscope to his ears and slowly

---

* Space precludes a detailed discussion of the crucial power that symbols and rituals have in organizing societal values and influencing thinking. For readers who may be interested, I recommend Mary Douglas's *Natural Symbols: Explorations in Cosmology* (1972).[20]

† The stethoscope has many functions in addition to its use in assessing blood pressure.

moved the cold metal microphone across my back and chest: "Breathe in. That's right. Now breathe out.... Good.... Now cough a few times.... Wonderful! Now breathe in again.... Breathe out.... That's great!"

Then he reached for an oblong case beside the examining table, wrapped a black strap, or cuff, around my arm, securing it with a longer rubber belt, and began to inflate the cuff by squeezing a black bulb held in his hand. The cuff tightened on my arm while a silver column of mercury inside a thin glass tube shot rapidly upward in the sphygmomanometer. Placing the stethoscope's microphone on my arm, he slowly released a soft stream of air through a valve on the rubber ball. He leaned forward and listened intently, while the column of mercury slowly fell in the glass tube. He repeated the procedure, and this time, in the absolute silence, I could feel my pulse beating forcefully against the ever-tightening cuff. Then he released it, and the air hissing softly from the valve broke the silence.

"Excellent, James, excellent." He scribbled the crucial numbers on his clipboard and, turning to my mother, said with assurance, "He'll feel fine in a few days. There's no sign of pneumonia."

His words rang with authority and infallibility; and as he looped the stethoscope around his neck and removed the cuff from my arm, I knew with the same certainty that I knew there was a heaven that these were extraordinary tools, and that only the most gifted and talented of human beings could have access to such mystical devices.

At that time indeed, in the middle of the Second World War, only doctors usually measured blood pressure. Because of the recent appearance of a technique that yielded such vital information, even nurses were not generally permitted to take blood pressure before the Second World War.

Today the ritual is rapidly disappearing. A high school student can be taught to use a stethoscope and cuff to measure blood pressure. A development even more shocking in comparison with the old ritual of doctor and stethoscope is that, by 1980, anyone could put one's arm in a computerized machine in virtually any shopping mall or drugstore in the United States and have one's blood pressure recorded automatically. Today one no longer needs another human being to measure this vital sign. The mystique of the ritual has been ruptured forever.

THE IMPLICATIONS

In addition to its symbolic importance, however, the use of the stethoscope and the sphygmomanometer in blood-pressure assessment profoundly influenced our understanding of the overall regulation of the cardiovascular system. It reinforced the eighteenth-century idea that hydraulic principles underlie the human circulatory system, and that such principles could be used to explain all circulatory phenomena in human beings.* In addition, this mechanical view of the cardiovascular system directed attention away from other factors that could influence blood pressure, such as communication and human relationships, and emphasized instead the mechanics involved.

Mechanistic thinking about blood pressure was further reinforced by the fact that the stethoscope requires that *both physician and patient remain quiet during the measurement. Silence is structurally built into the procedure.* This procedural necessity blinded clinicians to the fact that blood pressure is significantly influenced by one of the most elementary aspects of human relationships—our capacity to communicate with one another. Little wonder, therefore, that when computers first showed my colleagues and me that human speech has a major influence on blood pressure, we completely ignored the implications of our own discovery. No other hydraulic or hydrostatic system in physics was known to be influenced by simple conversations. It therefore initially struck us as a curious finding, but not one that had a great deal to do with the *real—that is, mechanical—factors that influence blood pressure.* After all, several billion measurements of blood pressure taken in silence annually in the world cannot be misleading? Or can they?

---

* Recent discoveries by investigators like Cornell Medical School's John Laragh, M.D., of peptides in the right atrium—which have a potent influence on lowering blood pressure—lead one to a new perspective about the human heart (*Wall Street Journal,* 7 December 1984). These hormones are produced by the right atrium and released into the blood stream when the heart senses that blood pressure is too high. This occurs when the walls of the right atrium are stretched. Though cast within the framework of mechanistic thinking, these findings certainly put blood pressure changes when humans speak into a new perspective. Commenting on these implications in a personal communication, Paul Rosch, M.D., president of the American Institute of Stress, remarked, "It creates a new way to think about the heart: one that indicates it is far more than a pumping machine. It does indeed suggest that there is a language of the human heart."

CHAPTER 3

The Human Machine

> She seemed cut off from everyone and everything
> by walls of agony, and the sense of the solitude of
> each human soul suddenly overwhelmed me. Ever
> since my marriage my emotional life had been
> calm and superficial. I had forgotten all the deeper
> issues, and had been content with flippant clev-
> erness. Suddenly the ground seemed to give way
> beneath me, and I found myself in quite another
> region. Within five minutes I went through some
> reflections as the following: the loneliness of the
> human soul is unendurable; nothing can penetrate
> it except the highest intensity of the sort of love
> that religious teachers have preached; whatever
> does not spring from this motive is harmful, or at
> best useless; it follows that war is wrong; that a
> public school education is abominable, that the
> use of force is to be deprecated, and that in human
> relations one should penetrate to the core of
> loneliness in each person and speak to that.
> —Bertrand Russell, *Autobiography*

A telephone call I received in the spring of 1983 led me to reflect
once again on my own blindness about the links between communication and blood pressure.

"Valerie and I have decided to get married, and we thought—
ah, excuse me—to use your vernacular, we *felt* that you and Sue*
should be among the first to know. So that's the occasion for this
call. We divided up the joy of transmitting the news, so Valerie is
calling Sue, and that leaves me calling you."

As Ed bubbled over about his wedding plans, it was not difficult

---

* Dr. Sue Ann Thomas, co-therapist in the treatment of this patient.

for me to sense some of his feelings: joy, triumph over loneliness, love. Yet there was more. In a deeply personal way I, too, shared in the joy of his accomplishment and the complex feelings that were an inextricable part of our relationship. For Ed was not just any patient calling to inform me about a happy event in his life. He was also a true pioneer, the very first person who participated in an endeavor that helped my colleagues and me to conceive of the human body and human feelings in an entirely new way. His contribution was truly unique. It was through our treatment of Ed that we came to understand how human hearts and blood vessels speak a language that is often more articulate than human speech itself. Ed was the first patient in whom we understood the deeper meaning of the phrase "the language of the heart," and the tragic consequences of the inability to hear, see, attend to, or understand it. In treating Ed, we at the clinic discovered how to decode that language in a way that could be used to guide people back to health.

As Ed continued to talk about his engagement, I reflected on how much had changed since we first met almost seven years earlier. Ed's cardiovascular system literally cried out for attention for over a year before we were able to listen. It was disconcerting to recall once again how long we had resisted seeing the very phenomenon we had set out to discover. Yet in some ways that was the most fascinating aspect of our entire struggle. We had set out to convince Ed that his interpersonal life was linked to his hypertension, but we had completely ignored the crucial evidence that explained the linkage. Perhaps the only redeeming feature of our blindness in this regard was the realization that we were not alone: a legion of medical investigators and physicians had been equally blind in the past.

When I met Ed in the autumn of 1977, however, there was no hint of the role he would play in our research or in the development of our conceptual thinking. Quite the contrary. He was initially particularly embarrassed by his neurologist's suggestion that he consult us. Ed did not like the idea of being sent to a "psycho-physiological" clinic nor did he accept the possibility that hidden emotional struggles might be contributing to his hypertension. If anything, Ed viewed himself as a bedrock of emotional stability. While he acknowledged that certain job-related stresses might occasionally drive up his blood pressure, he nevertheless smiled as he wondered about whether he might have to endure, as he phrased it, "a clinical treatment that appeared to be a form of psychotherapy." While he appeared friendly enough on the surface, he was not enthusiastic about our approach, one that initially involved a mixture of the most general supportive psychotherapeutic dialogue, interspersed with frequent instructions to breathe properly and relax.

Even the most gentle, general probing of his personal life seemed to make him uncomfortable. He appeared to have spent a lifetime nurturing the self-image of a person free from psychological conflict, a kind of Kellogg's cornflakes, friendly all-American tower of emotional strength. Any hint that his hypertension might be linked to some ill-defined emotional or interpersonal struggle had to be rejected out of hand, as implying some moral weakness. Ed was not a man who easily tolerated moral weakness in himself or the thought of unknown psychological conflicts that might expose him to such weakness.

Although he was friendly, talkative, outgoing, and almost always smiling, he nevertheless used logic and questions in a way that kept us from getting too close. He had to challenge and scrutinize every procedure, maneuver, and concept. He spoke rapidly, his words bursting out in phrases that had a controlled, breathless intensity.

And yet viewed in the larger context of the health crisis engulfing his life in the autumn of 1977, Ed's doubts were easy to appreciate. Fifty years old, unmarried, and a stockbroker with a distinguished record in a leading corporate firm in Washington, D.C., he had finally confronted the frightening realization that not only his career but his very life was in mortal peril. He was deeply troubled by the fact that the first-step antihypertensive medicines* had not

---

* The goal of the "stepped care" approach to the treatment of hypertension is to use the least toxic agents first and to combine drugs logically for the most effective usage. The first-step drugs—the thiazide diuretics—are the most widely used and well known and have been thought to have few side effects. Step-2 drugs are given in combination with the diuretic and in some manner interfere with sympathetic nervous system functioning either through central nervous system action or through an effect on peripheral sympathetic activity. Step-2 agents are added only if control of blood pressure is not maintained on step-1 drugs. Beta blockers were originally designated step-2 drugs; however, with the recent data implicating diuretic agents as potentially more toxic, beta blockers have become the first-step agents for many practitioners. If blood pressure is not controlled with step-1 and step-2 drugs, the next drug added would be another complementary step-2 agent. The step-3 drug, hydralazine, is a potent direct-acting vasodilator. With each increasing step in this approach, the risk of drug side effects also increases. The step-

controlled his blood pressure, and that he might have to take even more powerful drugs for the rest of his life.

"Why," he wondered aloud, "should a treatment so manifestly less precise than the antihypertensive medicines prescribed by my doctors offer any hope? Then again, I must admit that your therapy can't be considered any great danger either. It can't have the side effects of my drugs."

The anxiety and repressed anger behind his statement were difficult to discern beneath his pleasant demeanor. At that time we did not share with him our overriding concern that perhaps our approach might have side effects even worse than drugs. As I subsequently describe in more detail, our treatment approach was based on the assumption that human interactions are an integral aspect of the cardiovascular system, and that loneliness is a major factor that needs to be considered in various cardiovascular diseases. Yet research studies had shown that psychotherapeutic or interactive treatment approaches for hypertension can lead to marked elevations in blood pressure.[2] While various studies might have lent credence to Ed's doubt about the effectiveness of psychotherapy in other situations, there was little question about its potential impact on hypertension. Most of the available data suggested that the type of therapy we were considering, one that was inherently socially interactive, should be avoided with hypertensive patients, as either it would not help or, more likely, would drive a patient's blood pressure higher. Yet these data actually helped reinforce our central thesis that human relationships have an important influence on the heart. The only problem was that most of these studies had focused on the negative, even disastrous, consequences of unpleasant human interactions for the heart. It was not at all clear how much more cardiovascular stress Ed could tolerate, and we knew we had to tread with great care.

He had just been released from a hospital after an extensive

---

4 drug is guanethedine, which acts to decrease the response of the sympathetic nerve terminals and depletes norepinephrine storage. Again, this is an increasingly difficult drug to tolerate, with potential serious side effects. Other agents recently introduced for the treatment of hypertension are calcium channel blockers and Captopril, for example. These new drugs are useful and popular but have not been incorporated into the stepped-care approach. New recommendations for adjustments on the stepped-care regimen continue to evolve as data on drug usage becomes available. For more details, see the recent review by Dr. David Roffman and Dr. Sue Ann Thomas.[1]

diagnostic work-up for a transient ischemic attack.* He had collapsed in a boardroom meeting while discussing a client's portfolio. For the past two years his blood pressure had risen into hypertensive ranges that ultimately culminated in his ischemic attack. Ed felt that his own career was haunted by the specter of a possible crippling stroke or sudden death.

For five years he had reluctantly followed the prescriptive medicines recommended by his physicians. Unfortunately he was less successful in following what he readily acknowledged to be their common-sense medical advice. In spite of repeated warnings to slow down his pace of work, alter his dietary habits, and lose thirty to forty pounds of the excess weight he carried on his six-foot frame, he was unable to change. He was a classic example of the Type A personality described by Dr. Meyer Friedman and Dr. Ray Rosenman.[3] Restlessly ambitious, fast-talking, and hard-driving, Ed seemed unable to slow the pace of his relentless march toward the grave. He had tried in vain to change, only to find himself trapped by his own personality. "It appears as if my doctors believe my salvation rests in adopting the life style of a scholastic monk," he remarked with grudging laughter. He shrugged off further questions about his personality, as if he had decided in advance that certain topics were off limits or useless to discuss. Generally he spoke in the past tense, and the passive voice, almost as if he had resigned himself to the inevitability of his own premature death. His sense of foreboding was not that far removed from clinical reality. His blood pressure averaged around 185/110 during our first meeting, in spite of the fact that he was on first-step antihypertension medication.

Available medical statistics unfortunately underscored the reality of Ed's sense of foreboding.[4] Table 3.1 shows the relative increase or decrease in overall death rates from standard life-insurance risk tables for different levels of blood pressure. In this table, 100 percent equals the average death rate for any given age. Percentages below 100 represent a life expectancy longer than normal, while those higher than 100 reflect a mortality rate higher than normal. As shown in this table, Ed's reading of 185/110 was in excess of

* A transient ischemic attack is a short-term decrease in blood flow and oxygen to a small region of the brain. It frequently causes weakness in extremities, dizziness, and a short loss of memory and is considered a warning sign of a possible impending stroke.

TABLE 3.1

Relative Mortality of Insured Lives 1954–72
According to Blood Pressure Levels

Systolic Pressure	Mortality Ratio		Diastolic Pressure	Mortality Ratio	
	Men	*Women*		*Men*	*Women*
Under 108	71%	83%	Under 73	85%	87%
108–17	77	90	73–77	92	96
118–27	89	93	78–82	99	103
128–37	111	107	83–87	118	114
138–47	135	121	88–92	136	132
148–57	166	135	93–97	169	167
158–67	206	169	98–102	200	181
168–77	218	178	103–07	258	208
178–87	232	200	108–12	244	195

Source: Blood Pressure Study, 1979, Society of Actuaries and Association of Life Insurance Medical Directors of America (November 1980).

the average by 132 percent for systolic blood pressure and by 158 percent for diastolic blood pressure: that is, his chances of dying were more than double that of men his age whose blood pressures averaged around 125/80.

Another way of assessing the seriousness of Ed's health problem was to look at the effects of his blood pressure in terms of the years it could take away from his normal life expectancy. The data made it clear that the higher one's blood pressure, the shorter one's life expectancy (see table 3.2).

Based on these statistics, even the most optimistic forecast of Ed's chances for long-term survival indicated that he would likely die at least five to eight years earlier than men his age with lower blood pressure. Coupled with the fact that he was exhibiting signs of cerebrovascular problems, it seemed possible that he might not live long enough to enjoy his retirement.

Seven years later, however, in the early winter of 1984, Ed's blood pressure averaged around 130/75, both at home and on follow-up visits in our clinic. He had managed to lower his blood pressure significantly and, in the process, to change dramatically the odds for his long-term survival. More surprisingly, he no longer

TABLE 3.2

Years of Life Lost Due to Hypertension

	Men		Women	
Blood Pressure Level	Age 35	Age 65	Age 35	Age 65
140/90	3 years	2 years	2 years	1.5 years
160/95	6 years	4 years	4 years	3 years
180/100	8 years	5 years	5.5 years	4 years

Source: Blood Pressure Study, 1979, Society of Actuaries and Association of Life Insurance Medical Directors of America (November 1980).

needed medicines to control his pressure, although in the intervening years he had not lost any weight.

What brought about the change? How did he rid himself of a cardiovascular problem that had posed a serious threat to his life? What was it about his life style, or his personality, or, indeed, his body that had caused his blood pressure to rise to dangerous levels in the first place? Did he have a disease that was somehow miraculously turned around at the eleventh hour, or was it really a symptomatic reflection of some other problem? And why had it been hard for Ed to modify his hard-driving personality, when he himself acknowledged that it might contribute to his cardiovascular problems? What were we blind to—like many investigators before us—that held the key to his recovery?

THE TRADITIONAL PARADIGM OF THE BODY

In order to clarify the changes in Ed, I shall first outline the point of view about cardiovascular disease we at the clinic held when we began to work with him. For only in retrospect did it become clear that the very questions we were asking about his blood pressure could not be answered until we changed certain fundamental assumptions we held about the human body.

In his seminal *Structure of Scientific Revolutions* (1970), Thomas

Kuhn describes a phenomenon he calls the "scientific paradigm."[5] Kuhn defines the term *paradigm,* in its most general meaning, as a construct embracing the entire constellation of beliefs, values, techniques, and attitudes that are shared by members of a given scientific community. As he outlines it, the paradigm determines how scientists approach the study of phenomena in their specific area of interest and how they understand and interpret the data they observe. The paradigm is a way of looking at scientific data, and one remains in force until enough conflicting data accumulate to cause it to be seriously questioned. A shift in paradigms occurs when an alternative way of looking at data is developed and found to deal more effectively with the conflicting data.

Our struggle with Ed involved precisely one such paradigm and our shift toward a new one. As I said in chapter 2, when we began our treatment of Ed's hypertension, we uncritically accepted the idea of the human body as a machine—a belief we held in common with virtually all medical scientists and physicians. Thus, we viewed the human heart and its blood vessels as part of an incredibly sophisticated bodily machine, a marvelously sensitive hydraulic system which keeps blood flowing to all the tissues of the body. We knew that the cardiovascular system is highly adaptive and can quickly adjust to the internal demands of the body and to the external demands of a constantly changing world. Any of a whole host of internal and external factors can cause a person's heart rate to increase and blood pressure to rise. Conversely, we knew that certain homeostatic mechanisms can be called into action to slow the system down. In like manner, we recognized that mechanical problems can cause the entire system to break down.

Our own particular interest centered on understanding one particular external stimulus that seemed to have a major impact on the heart. While many scientists had already focused on the ways a host of internal and external factors can influence the cardiovascular system, it struck us that one obvious stimulus had been overlooked: relatively little attention had been paid to the influence of other people. Little effort had been made to study how friends, children, one's mate, the gentle touch of another human being, or, indeed, even one's enemies might influence the human heart. This area became the focus of our interest.

Yet when we began our studies, the overall paradigm we accepted was no different from that held by other scientists. We examined the effects of people the same way other scientists studied such factors as diet, exercise, or smoking. Our methods were essentially no different from those of a scientist studying how a golf club drives a golf ball down a fairway. Just as various physical factors, such as the intensity of a person's swing and the angle of the club, would determine the flight path and distance of a golf drive, so we viewed other people as a class of "social stimuli" that impinges on a person's heart. We viewed human relationships as merely a neglected class of environmental stimuli, qualitatively no different really than any other stimuli. The paradigm we had uncritically accepted offered no alternative. If the human body is a finely tuned biological machine, then human relationships can influence heart and blood vessels only by impinging on bodily mechanisms that cause this system to respond.

Our attempts to treat Ed's hypertension first led us to recognize the serious limitations of that perspective. In attempting to lower his blood pressure, we were confronted with certain questions that had been present in our earlier work but were obscured by the cardiovascular paradigm. After treating Ed, however, we began to understand that beyond the concept of people as "social stimuli" impinging on the cardiovascular mechanics of other human beings, there is another dimension to human relationships: one involving the essential interrelatedness of human beings and the "humanness" of the human body. We began to understand that human relationships, far from being just another stimulus affecting the heart, have an impact that is qualitatively different. Not only do one's heart and blood vessels respond to human "stimuli," but these responses can be seen, heard, and felt by others as communications. As we shall see, this dimension of human relationships casts bodily mechanisms into a realm far different from any we had previously considered.

In order to help differentiate these paradigms, and their effect on our understanding of the human cardiovascular system and on our treatment approach to problems such as hypertension and migraines, I shall briefly trace certain crucial background experiences that led us to shift from one paradigm to the other.

THE EFFECT OF PERSON

I began my research training in the quiet atmosphere of an animal laboratory far removed from the issues raised by Ed's hypertension. Indeed, nothing was further from my mind than questions about human relationships and cardiovascular health when I began my graduate school training. I had come to the Pavlovian Laboratory at Perry Point, Maryland, in 1962 for an entirely different purpose. Under the tutelage of one of the world's foremost authorities on Pavlovian conditioning, I intended to study how the brain processes information and how learning occurs. It was not long, however, before my career plans and goals were changed. I soon found myself listening to the rhythm of a recording pen as it scratched out the electrical waveform of a dog's heartbeat on polygraphic paper. In the quiet darkness of a laboratory observation room, seated beside my teacher, Dr. W. Horsley Gantt (1893–1979), I peered through a one-way mirror in fascination, as I was introduced to a scientific phenomenon he called the "effect of person."

On a table stood a mongrel dog, quietly relaxed and restrained ever so gently by a leash. The animal was all alone, isolated from contact with the outside world, as surface electrodes recorded each heartbeat and respiration (see figure 3.1).

"You are monitoring just a tiny portion of what Claude Bernard* called the milieu interior," commented the director of the Pavlovian Laboratory at Johns Hopkins Medical School,† as he began to demonstrate his remarkable discovery to me for the first time. Already a retired professor emeritus, Dr. Gantt was the only living American scientist who had studied with the great Russian physiologist Ivan Pavlov (1849–1936).‡ Gantt's advanced age and

* Claude Bernard (1813–78), French physiologist who investigated, among other things, the sympathetic nervous system.

† The Pavlovian Laboratory at Johns Hopkins was linked to the Pavlovian Laboratory at the Veterans Administration Hospital at Perry Point, Maryland. Both laboratories had the same director, Dr. W. Horsley Gantt, and both conducted interdisciplinary research. My initial research was supported by the Veterans Administration for a three-year period at the Perry Point V.A. Hospital, and I am deeply grateful for that support.

‡ Dr. Gantt had originally gone to Russia in 1922 as a medical officer serving in the Russian Famine Relief efforts organized by President Herbert Hoover. While serving in Leningrad he met Pavlov and was electrified by his bold new concepts. Pavlov's theories seemed to offer great hope for the development of a new type of psychiatry, one that would be based on objective scientific principles, freed up from the quagmire of ill-defined terms and uncertain clinical treatments that had left psychiatric patients languishing without hope in psychiatric hospitals. Gantt stayed in Russia for seven years, and helped bring Pavlov's research to the attention of

Pavlovian Chamber

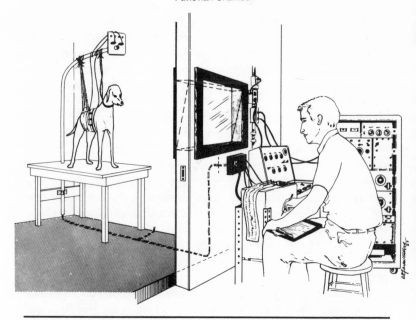

Figure 3.1. An example of a typical experimental chamber originally devised by Pavlov to isolate an animal from all extraneous environmental stimuli while simultaneously measuring changes, such as heart rate and respiration, in the animal's physiology.

breadth of experience enhanced the importance I attached to his insights. After fifty years in scientific research, Dr. Gantt was a storehouse of information. If he insisted that an experiment was worth watching, then clearly it was, and I watched and listened intently.*

the English-speaking world. When he returned to America, he dedicated his own research career to expanding the work of his famous Russian teacher. So faithfully had he duplicated his teacher's methods that his laboratories at Hopkins and Perry Point looked exactly like the pictures I had seen in introductory psychology textbooks of Pavlov's dogs salivating to conditional signals in their isolation chambers.

    * The quotes in this section are recollections of a variety of conversations I had with Dr. Gantt during our ten years of association. They are not literal quotes in the sense that they were tape recorded or written down by me, but are rather a summary of his overall views. Each of these ideas was repeated frequently by him and has also been described in a series of articles Dr. Gantt published on these topics.[6] I have chosen to place his ideas in a conversational context in

He continued: "The heart is the most important part of our internal life. The circulatory system interacts with every organ and cell in the body, and so you must understand it and the factors that influence it. Changes in the heart and circulation can lead to changes anywhere in the body. This system is the great unifier of the living organism, the system that integrates our body into one whole.

"As you can see on the polygraph, there is one world on the surface, and quite another dynamic, constantly changing life inside the living body. If you truly want to understand what you're seeing, then you must observe patiently for many hours. Pavlov's motto was observation and more observation." He chuckled, and his strong, gravelly voice firmly conveyed the importance he attached to Pavlov's methods and the deep admiration he held for his Russian teacher.

Sixty to eighty times each minute, the pen recorded the traces of the dog's heartbeat, the rhythm shifting faster and slower with each inspiration and expiration. For over thirty minutes Dr. Gantt sat beside the polygraph, squinting slightly to observe the dog, while he continued to talk quietly about the way biologists and psychologists study animals in isolation. "The links between our social existence and the functioning of our bodies has been totally ignored by science. They [the scientists and biologists] focus, instead, on understanding the homeostatic mechanisms of the body. The dilemma is inherent in the very methods scientists use to study physiology."

He paused momentarily to scribble several notes about the dog's behavior in a laboratory notebook and then continued to speak in the rhythmic accent of Southwestern Virginia which had been tempered by years of study in England and Russia: "In order to be objective, the scientist is forced to maintain a distance between himself and the object of his study. Yet, clearly, we also interact with the objects of our study when we investigate living organisms.

---

an attempt to convey the intellectual vigor and vitality with which he pursued his investigations and the way in which he interacted with colleagues and students. Dr. Gantt spent a great deal of time with younger students, out of his conviction that the young student is most impressionable, not yet encumbered with beliefs and attitudes that might freeze one's capacity to see things in a novel way. I was by no means the first or the last student he tutored in this unselfish and truly caring way.

Heisenberg discovered this phenomenon in physics in 1929."*

He seemed both amused by the paradox and excited about the phenomenon he was about to show me: "As you will see, looking at a dog's physiology is quite different from being with that same animal. The entire cardiovascular system changes when a person is present."

When he then opened the steel door to the dog's isolation chamber, the polygraphic pen began to scratch frantically as the animal's heart pounded with excitement: 120, 130, 140, 150, 160, 170 beats per minute. The dog's heart rate almost tripled the moment Dr. Gantt entered the room. Suddenly the pen virtually stopped, and the room grew strangely quiet, as the dog's heart rate abruptly slowed to 30 beats per minute. It had plummeted almost instantaneously in response to Dr. Gantt's gentle stroking. Petting had had an astounding infuence. On the surface I could see little change in the dog's behavior. The entire response had occurred in a hidden bodily universe whose operation I glimpsed for the first time.

"It is a part of the effect of person!" Dr. Gantt said enthusiastically. "We have seen such responses for many years now. Indeed far greater changes can be seen in other animals. I believe it is one of the most important of all biological phenomena.

"The effect of person is one of the most ignored phenomena in all of modern medicine. Even though every doctor pays lip service to the importance of bedside manner, young physicians are hypnotized by scientific technology. They have forgotten their most important therapeutic tool. Perhaps it is ignored because its influence is so pervasive. It is much like the air we breathe, taken for granted unless it is poisoned or polluted. Maybe in your lifetime——" He smiled wistfully, implying that at his advanced age of seventy-two

* Werner Heisenberg (1901–76), German physicist; this phenomenon was his uncertainty principle. In his marvelous essays *What Is Life?* and *Mind and Matter,* Erwin Schrodinger (1887–1961) describes this revolutionary aspect of Heisenberg's discovery: "We cannot make any factual statement about a given natural object (or physical system) without 'getting in touch' with it. This 'touch' is a real physical interaction. Even if it consists only in our 'looking at the object' the latter must be hit by light-rays and reflect them into the eye, or into some instrument of observation. This means that the object is affected by our observation. You cannot obtain any knowledge about an object while leaving it strictly isolated. The theory goes on to assert that this disturbance is neither irrelevant nor completely surveyable. Thus after any number of painstaking observations the object is left in a state of which some features (the last observed) are not known, or not accurately known. This state of affairs is offered as an explanation why no complete, gapless description of any physical object is ever possible."[7]

he would never see the discovery gain the scientific recognition he felt it deserved: "Maybe in your lifetime——" He repeated the phrase almost absent-mindedly, as if he himself did not really understand why the importance of the effect of person was not more clearly recognized within modern medicine.

He then continued: "Osler* knew all about the effect of person and the power of bedside manner. He was truly the greatest medical teacher Hopkins ever had. He once remarked that just one visit from an optimistic and cheerful physician had led a patient dying of terminal cancer to suddenly gain three to four pounds. You should read his descriptions of the effects of bedside manner on cardiac patients."

Then, as if to emphasize the unique scientific nature of his observations—one in contrast to the traditional clinical descriptions of bedside manner—he added, "We would not have discovered this response had we not used Pavlov's methods of isolating the dog from all external stimuli. Pavlov knew how important human contact was for the dog. That is why he took such care to isolate it from all external stimuli. It was the only way he could study the conditional reflex."

From the very beginning of my research training at the Pavlovian Laboratory, it struck me as utterly incongruous that Dr. Gantt could be totally dedicated to extending the research methods of his beloved teacher and yet, at the same time, use the isolation chamber—the Pavlovian chamber—to study the effect of person. On the one hand, his teacher, Ivan P. Pavlov was an outspoken proponent of a strict mechanistic point-of-view about physiology. He believed the body to be regulated by automatic reflexes—his so-called unconditional reflexes. Pavlov thought about physiology in terms of its reflex wiring. Animals do not learn to speed up their heart rate when they exercise, nor do they learn to salivate when food is in their mouth: this is the way they are wired. (I discuss Pavlov's influence at greater length in chapter 10.)

It was in the context of the Pavlovian paradigm and its tradition of isolating animals from all extraneous stimuli that, in 1938, Dr.

* Sir William Osler (1849–1919) was one of the founding pioneers of the Johns Hopkins Medical School and a leading figure in early twentieth century medicine. He was a pre-eminent medical spokesman who spent his life emphasizing the importance of bedside manner to a generation of medical students.

Gantt first observed the effect of person. Using one of the first electrocardiographic recording devices ever developed, he noticed the remarkable way a dog's heart responded to human contact. There was one type of physiology when the dog was alone, and quite a different physiology when a human being was present.

For decades Gantt and his research colleagues mapped out various dimensions of this previously hidden cardiovascular world.[8] In one of the more intriguing of these experiments, two of his colleagues, Dr. Joseph Newton and Dr. Walter Ehrlich, observed that the presence of a human being significantly influenced the flow of blood through a dog's coronary arteries. (These vessels are of special importance since they carry blood directly to the heart muscles themselves and are vital for the healthy functioning of the heart.) In the course of their physiological experiments, these investigators commented that "during experiments on the effects of eating and exercise on coronary blood flow, we were surprised to find such large coronary flow increases due to a person entering the room. Indeed in some dogs the person was almost as potent a stimulus to coronary flow as violent exercise on a treadmill, despite the small increase in motor activity caused by the person."[9] As we were subsequently to understand from patients like Ed, such hidden cardiovascular responses are a routine aspect of many human interactions and are sometimes far more dramatic than in dogs.

For seven years I absorbed Dr. Gantt's unique, and paradoxical perspective, while participating in a variety of laboratory studies of his effect of person. Deeper questions about the effect of person, ones involving human relationships which went beyond the reflex wiring of homeostatically regulated machines, would occasionally come up in conversations. Yet in the laboratory itself the phenomenon was studied within the context of Pavlov's paradigm. But even within this mechanistic, stimulus-response paradigm the cardiovascular changes were truly remarkable. There was one heart rate and blood pressure when those animals were alone and quite a different rate and pressure when a person was present. It became the focus of my own research: to me, there seemed to be no biological phenomenon more important or more deserving of study.

THE EDGE OF LIFE

When, in 1969, I accepted a faculty position at the University of Maryland Medical School, I had hoped to extend the laboratory observations of the effect of person to the human level. I was initially struck by the similarities between patients lying all alone in hospital coronary-care units and dogs resting quietly, all alone, in Pavlovian isolation chambers. It seemed reasonable to assume that if human touch affects the hearts of animals, then coronary-care patients might be similarly affected. Advancing medical technology made it possible continuously to monitor the heartbeats of these patients in much the same way that the physiology of animals had been monitored in the laboratory. As had been done earlier, we could watch the heart rate and heart rhythm of the patients when they were alone, and then compare what happened when nurse, doctor, or loved one came to their bedside.

There were differences from earlier laboratory studies, of course. Since in the coronary-care unit, patients were struggling for their lives, the type of controlled experiments conducted in the laboratory were simply out of the question. All that could be done was to monitor the patients' heartbeats, and note when they were alone, and when someone came to their bedside. In order to study and evaluate even the simplest human interaction, such as a pulse taking, patients had to be monitored continuously for twenty-four hours and their electrocardiograms coded whenever someone came to their bedside. Yet, in spite of all the factors that could obscure the effects of routine pulse palpation, it soon became apparent that even this elementary human interaction affected a patient's heart rate and heart rhythm.[10]

The gentle touch of a nurse palpating a pulse, a brief visit from wife or loved one, all of these human interactions were found to influence coronary-care patients' hearts compared with baseline readings when these patients were alone.[11] Yet all of these observations raised certain fundamental questions about mechanisms. Were these cardiac changes due specifically to human contact, or were they really the result of changes in muscle movement or breathing patterns when a person came to a patient's bedside? The shock-trauma patients permitted us to study the effects of human contact in patients from whom all normal physiological mediating variables had been eliminated. If their cardiovascular system responded to human touch, then the responses had to be directly regulated by the central nervous system.

Thus, one evening in 1972, I sat alone in the hushed silence of the central monitoring station of the University of Maryland's shock trauma unit. Computers were silently recording the figures for the vital signs of the patients in the eight beds surrounding the central monitoring station console. Blood pressure, heart rate, core temperature, respiration, blood gases: each number flashed with unfeeling objective precision, continuously delineating the border between life and death. If the numbers fell below certain critical levels, then alarms would sound, and a trauma team of nurses and physicians would rush to a patient's bedside. It had been a day of repeated emergencies, and I had found it a strain, over the past eight hours, quietly to observe acute human suffering. For the first time in over eight hours, the unit had grown quiet, almost eerily so.

For those hours I had been watching the motionless body of a thirteen-year-old girl who had been fighting for her life since she had been injured by an automobile on the highway the previous week. She had taken a turn for the worse the day before, and a team of doctors and nurses were struggling to save her. The central console was continuously recording her heartbeat, while the soft beep of her bedside heart monitor confirmed the fact that she was still alive. A trachial airway pumped oxygen into her lungs, while an artificial respirator sighed predictably every six seconds, helping to sustain her life.

In an effort to stabilize her, she had been administered the drug d-tubocurarine which, even had she not been in a deep coma, would have made her unable to move, breathe on her own, speak, or even open her eyes. She could, however, hear sounds and feel the touch of a person, since the drug paralyzed only her muscles but left intact her sensory system.

Throughout the day I had watched and waited. The trauma team had been at her bedside almost constantly. Now for the first time in eight hours, she had been left alone for fifteen minutes. Her heartbeat was steady (averaging between 105 and 125 beats per minute), rising and falling in rhythm with the paced inspiration and expiration of the respirator. At my request, a nurse colleague approached the bed and held the young girl's hand and, for three minutes, gently stroked her head, softly murmuring to her. The nurse told her that she was in a hospital and assured her that a nurse or a doctor would always be near, that she was cared for and loved very much, and that everything would be fine.

As can be seen in figure 3.2, while the nurse was at her bedside, the girl's heart rate did not change. She did not appear to hear or to feel. Yet as soon as the nurse put her hand down and left the bedside, the girl's heart rate rose higher than it had been in over eighteen minutes, up to 135 beats per minute; then it fell below resting levels, down to 95 beats per minute, before cycling back into rhythm with the respirator once again. The effects of this simple human interaction appeared to be reflected in changes in her heart rate. It was the first of many such heart responses we would see in a variety of patients in this unit.[12] They were part of a constellation of studies that helped persuade us that human contact does have a measurable influence on the heart.

FROM HUMAN CONTACT TO HUMAN LONELINESS

For several years we continued to focus almost exclusively on brief, nonverbal interactions for two reasons. First, such periods could be easily differentiated from periods when a patient rested alone in bed. In a sense, it best approximated the animal studies we had conducted earlier: both involved touch and could be differentiated from periods of quiet isolation. Also, both adhered to the Pavlovian paradigm that had first revealed the influence of the effect of person. The second reason was the realization that more complex forms of human interaction, such as those involving verbal communications, posed serious methodological problems. The emotional content of conversations can vary enormously, and its effects on a patient's heart are far more difficult to evaluate than are brief, nonverbal interactions.

Yet at the same time we recognized that human relationships are characterized not by the brief interactions we were studying, but by longer-lasting ones which, we assumed, have far more powerful consequences. One did not have to watch many wives visiting their critically ill husbands to realize that life-long relationships are far more important than a one-minute pulse palpation. This realization prompted other questions. If enduring human

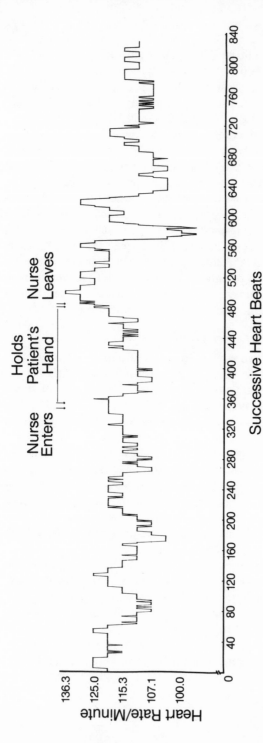

Figure 3.2. Beat-to-beat changes in the heart rate of a thirteen-year-old girl in a shock trauma unit before, during, and after a nurse held her hand. At this time the girl was in a coma, her muscles were paralyzed by *d*-tubocurarine, and she was artificially respirated. Note the sudden increase and then sudden decrease in this girl's heart rate after the nurse left her bedside.

relationships are so powerful and central to our lives, then how does lack of such potent relationships affect the heart? Does such lack lead to a lesser risk of heart disease or make matters worse?

Medical statistics on the loss of human companionship, the lack of love, and human loneliness quickly revealed that the expression *broken heart* is not just a poetic image for loneliness and despair but is an overwhelming medical reality. All the available data pointed to the lack of human companionship, chronic loneliness, social isolation, and the sudden loss of a loved one as being among the leading causes of premature death in the United States. And while we found that the effects of human loneliness were related to virtually every major disease—whether cancer, pneumonia, or mental disease—they were particularly apparent in heart disease, the leading cause of death in the United States. Evidently millions of people were dying, quite literally, of broken or lonely hearts.[13]

One example of this remarkable influence could be seen in the overall death rates for men between the ages of fifteen and sixty-four in the United States. Almost without exception those who were single, widowed, or divorced had significantly higher death rates than married individuals from virtually every cause of death (see table 3.3).* By no means is the influence of marital status on health idiosyncratic to white males. At virtually every age, for both sexes and all races, death rates for the single, the widowed, and the divorced range anywhere from two to ten times higher than for married individuals, depending on the cause of death.

The implications of the mortality statistics, however, quickly led us to confront another troubling reality. Statistical probabilities, even those that unambiguously point to the destructive effects of human loneliness, are small comfort to individual patients all alone in hospital beds, trying to put their lives back together again after a heart attack. And equally important, the question had to be raised, what could be done to prevent problems from reaching such a painful and destructive endpoint?

In addition, in spite of all the statistics we had gathered, it was not at all clear how loneliness contributes to the development of heart disease or to elevations in blood pressure. While certain fatal consequences of human loneliness—such as suicide, lung cancer,

---

* See Lynch, *The Broken Heart*, for further elaboration and detailed discussion of these statistics.[14]

TABLE 3.3

Marital Status and Mortality: Death Rates per 100,000 Population in the United States (Ages 15–64)

| | Death Rates for White Men | | | |
Cause of Death	Married	Single	Widowed	Divorced
Coronary disease and other myocardial (heart) degeneration	176	237	275	362
Motor vehicle accidents	35	54	142	128
Cancer of respiratory system	28	32	43	65
Cancer of digestive organs	27	38	39	48
Vascular lesions (stroke)	24	42	46	58
Suicide	17	32	92	73
Cancer of lymph glands and of blood-making tissues	12	13	11	16
Cirrhosis of liver	11	31	48	79
Rheumatic fever (heart)	10	14	21	19
Hypertensive heart disease	8	16	16	20
Pneumonia	6	31	25	44
Diabetes mellitus	6	13	12	17
Homicide	4	7	16	30
Chronic nephritis (kidney)	4	7	7	7
Accidental falls	4	12	11	23
Tuberculosis, all forms	3	17	18	30
Cancer of prostate gland	3	3	3	4
Accidental fire or explosion	2	6	18	16
Syphilis	1	2	2	4

cirrhosis of the liver, and automobile accidents—are unambiguously linked to human behavior, it was far less certain how human loneliness influences the heart. Our ignorance in this regard was partly the result of the focus of our own research, and partly the result of the orientation of virtually all other research studies.

By 1977 the need for change was obvious. It no longer seemed useful merely to continue gathering additional evidence to prove that human relationships influence cardiovascular health. Rather the weight of existing evidence made it imperative to try to extend this knowledge to the treatment process. Our sense of urgency about translating our research findings into an effective treatment program was reinforced by Dr. Sue Ann Thomas, a nurse who, from the very beginning of our coronary-care research, had organized and directed the nursing and research team that helped us carry out our investigations. Dr. Thomas was also responsible for educating coronary-care patients about their heart disease before they were released from the hospital. In this capacity she routinely confronted a whole dimension of cardiac rehabilitation that was usually glossed over in the critical environment of the coronary-care unit itself. Significant numbers of her patients seemed to be suffering from loneliness and to be living proof of the very statistics we had uncovered. These patients were single, widowed, divorced, or unhappily married. Many had seen their children move far away; while still others had, upon retirement, lost the social network their jobs provided. Yet, at the same time, many of these heart patients seemed strangely oblivious to their own loneliness, disconnected from any real awareness of their emotional pain. That pain seemed to have been translated directly into cardiovascular disease, almost as if they had used their hearts and blood vessels to short-circuit and deaden their pain. Many patients were like Ed, still relatively young and well educated, with a great deal to live for, yet utterly unaware of their loneliness or of any link between their interpersonal emotional life and their heart disease. For years they had suffered from symptoms such as hypertension which should have warned them that something was wrong in their lives, that some corrective action ought to be taken. Yet the warnings went unheeded.

Prevention would clearly be far more efficacious than efforts aimed at restoring a patient to health after serious damage had been done to the heart itself. At the same time, both our research experiences and the statistical data made it clear that such a prevention program had to deal squarely with an issue that had been ignored for decades—the interplay between human relationships and the healthy functioning of the heart.

THE TREATMENT OF HYPERTENSION

The disease that was most obvious to address in terms of a meaningful preventive health-care program was hypertension. Not only was it the single most pervasive medical problem in the United States, but any effort that could help patients lower their blood pressure would have major health benefits in terms of preventing the development of more serious cardiovascular problems. Upward of sixty million adult Americans are suspected of having this disease. Yet in spite of its pervasiveness, in 90 percent of all cases, the fundamental cause of the hypertension is not known. In only 5 percent to 10 percent of all cases has it been possible to identify clearly the cause of this disease.

While medical experts debated the relative importance of various factors that potentially contribute to hypertension, there was virtually unanimous agreement that no single factor was likely to be identified as the sole cause of all instances of it—in contrast to nineteenth-century infectious disease models, where a single germ caused a specific problem.[15] Existing evidence overwhelmingly supported the idea that the disease could be caused by a combination of factors, including physical, biochemical, central nervous system, social, psychological, and personality variables.[16] Not only had different bodily mechanisms been identified that could lead to elevations in blood pressure; but, more important, the mechanisms that led to sustained elevations apparently could be quite different from those that transiently elevated blood pressure.[17] The doubling of hypertensive death rates for the single, the widowed, and the divorced strongly implied that human relationships have an important influence on this disease. Yet, in spite of the statistics, conventional medical treatment of hypertension adhered to the fundamental notion of hypertension as a hydraulic problem that could be effectively regulated with drugs. Beyond this conceptual point of view, however, another compelling factor determined the treatment prescribed by physicians. The United States government itself recommended drug treatment as the approach to be used. Drug treatment for hypertension was established as part of national public health policy, because scientific data had made clear the risks involved in not treating extremes in blood-pressure elevation (a diastolic pressure of 110 or higher), and available studies showed that drugs were the most effective treatment method.

While the roots of this public health policy could be traced back to the very earliest notions about the hydraulic nature of blood pressure, the specific treatment recommendations were based on a variety of scientific evidence. In 1967, and again in 1970, the Veterans Administration published the first results of a major health survey they had conducted on hypertensive patients. These studies presented convincing evidence that drug treatment of male patients with moderate hypertension (a diastolic blood pressure of at least 105) was helpful in preventing stroke, heart attacks, and heart failure.[18] In 1979, the National Heart, Lung and Blood Institute released the findings of another major study—the Hypertension Detection and Follow-Up Program.[19] As was true of the earlier V.A. studies, this large-scale study also supported the vigorous drug treatment of hypertension.

Yet while these studies found that drugs can lower the overall mortality of patients with dangerously high blood pressure, questions began to arise about the risk-benefit ratio of treating borderline hypertensives with powerful drugs. In 1983 the National Heart, Lung and Blood Institute reported the findings of a major long-term screening study—the Multiple Risk Factor Intervention Trail, or MRFIT survey—of the effects of factors in addition to drugs, including diet and exercise. This study revealed a *comparatively higher mortality* among those mild hypertensives who had electrical abnormalities in their resting electrocardiograms and who were given drug therapy than among those who were not treated with drugs. This unexpected finding created uncertainty and some confusion about what treatment a physician ought to recommend for mild hypertension.[20]

In addition to the recent scientific controversies over the effectiveness of various drug therapies, however, other problems with pharmacological treatment approaches to hypertension were recognized long before the 1983 MRFIT report. First of all, large numbers of patients simply refused to comply with their physicians' prescriptive advice because of the occasional side effects—lethargy, impotency, and depression—of these antihypertensive medications. And while the problem was not widely recognized by patients, the fact is that sudden withdrawal from certain antihypertensive agents can cause a variety of side effects that place one at risk for having cardiac problems, including a sudden heart attack. The problem of drug compliance is further complicated by the fact that since hypertension usually has no detectable symptoms, many patients are simply not prepared to take drugs year after year for a disorder whose symptoms are not obvious. Adherence to prescriptive regimens is no better among people with dangerously elevated blood pressure and actually diminishes for those taking medicines for five or more years.[21]

By the early 1970s, it had become obvious that the problems inherent in hypertensive drug therapy demanded the development both of alternatives to drugs and of safer drugs. In 1983, the assistant secretary for health for the Department of Health and Human Services issued to physicians new treatment guidelines that included, for the first time, a recommendation that did not rely only on drugs: "Initiate treatment of mild high blood pressure, particularly in the range of 90/94 mm Hg diastolic pressure, with nonpharmacologic measures as long as this treatment is effective in maintaining normal blood pressure."[22]

These recommendations also reflected a change in attitudes concerning the effects of long-term medication usage in a group of patients with mild elevation in blood pressure. That is, the question was raised whether, in the long run, the negative side effects of various drugs outweigh potential benefits accrued from the control of mild hypertension?

In response to the growing demand for viable alternatives to drugs, investigators began seriously to examine a variety of approaches, such as yoga, biofeedback, meditation, and exercise regimens. Each alternative appeared at least partially effective in helping some hypertensive patients regulate their pressure without drugs. Yet at the same time each alternative to drugs seemed to provide only marginal relief or was restricted to a relatively small subgroup capable of utilizing the technique. In addition to questions about their efficacy, however, all of these alternatives ironically share a common feature with drugs: they are all fundamentally solitary, using techniques that do not focus on issues of human relationships.

While each of these non-drug techniques may involve social interactions, the essence of these techniques is solitary. Each of these therapeutic maneuvers is aimed at altering different bodily mechanisms, and they differ only in the techniques used to influence blood pressure mechanically. Neither weight loss, nor exercise, nor yoga, nor relaxation, nor biofeedback, nor transcendental meditation requires other people as an essential part of the regimen. These are all techniques that can be carried out alone. Yet, on the other hand, one can also engage in them in the company of others.* Elsewhere my colleagues and I have shown that the greater the degree of interpersonal involvement in these techniques, the greater their effectiveness in lowering blood pressure.[23]

In 1977 we decided to experiment with an innovative treatment, focusing on the link between a patient's interpersonal life and his or her struggles with hypertension, while simultaneously utilizing some of the non-drug techniques others had shown to be potentially effective in lowering blood pressure. Ed was the first case in which we attempted to translate what we felt to be an intuitively and empirically obvious life force into a treatment that would involve the links between human relationships and the human cardiovascular system.

Yet as Dr. Thomas and I reviewed Ed's medical records before accepting him for treatment, we were concerned. We were considering an interactive treatment whose outcome was far from predictable, and that, according to existing data, as I shall describe in the next chapter, could markedly increase the blood pressure of a man whose chances of having a heart attack or a stroke not only were more than double that of men with normal blood pressure but also were statistically compounded by his solitary life. Our choice of what was at that point an unconventional therapy was a compromise that emerged from Ed's misgivings about the effects of long-term drug therapy, from his scepticism about the utility of psychotherapy, and from our conviction that human relationships are an important aspect of cardiovascular health.

---

* While many of these activities are frequently carried out in the company of other people— and, indeed, often appear to be more effective when others are engaged in the process—their effectiveness in terms of bodily health is usually thought of in terms of the mechanics of physiology.

CHAPTER 4

Lethal Dialogue

> My life is in the hands of any rascal who chooses
> to annoy or tease me."
> —John Hunter, M.D., *c.* 1790

The fate of John Hunter did little to assuage our anxiety when Dr. Thomas and I first began outlining a treatment plan to help Ed. A legend in the history of medicine, Hunter was an English physician, renowned in surgical societies for his discovery of the connection between the placenta and the uterus, and for his superb surgical skill which led him to develop the first successful operation for aneurysms. He was also highly regarded for his brilliant work in comparative anatomy, which today is immortalized in the Hunterian Museum of the Royal College of Surgeons in London. Ironically, though, John Hunter was destined to be remembered not just for these accomplishments but even more for his eerie prediction of the circumstances of his own death. Apparently rather irritable and spirited by nature, he often engaged in vitriolic arguments, including a bitter dispute with his older physician brother William, who had started John on his illustrious career. For twenty-five years they argued over the priority of the discovery about the placenta and the uterus, William apparently feeling that John had taken his ideas without properly acknowledging the debt.

One can only speculate whether his irritable temperament led to the development of severe angina pectoris;* but in 1785 at the age

* Angina pectoris, commonly perceived as chest pain (although not necessarily limited to the chest), reflects imbalance between the metabolic demands of the heart and the adequacy of one's coronary circulation, and is caused by a lack of oxygen brought on by a sudden decrease in the blood supply. The pain is usually intermittent and is triggered by exercise, cold weather, eating, and frequently by emotional stress. The pain occurs because the heart muscle continues to work in spite of the decrease in oxygen, and is akin to cutting off the blood supply to your finger with a tight rubber band; if you exercise your finger under such circumstances, it will become increasingly painful.

of sixty-five, John Hunter began to suffer from recurrent chest pain. An astute observer of his own medical condition and of the factors contributing to his anginal attacks, he stated publicly, "My life is in the hands of any rascal who chooses to annoy or tease me." On 16 October 1793, after a colleague teased him at a medical staff meeting, Hunter got into an argument with the board of governors of St. George's Hospital. He stormed out of the meeting room in anger and immediately fell dead. He was the same age, sixty-five, as his equally irascible older brother William had been when he died.

The ghost of John Hunter haunted the subsequent history of medicine as an outstanding example of one way that human interaction can profoundly influence the cardiovascular system. After his death nobody seriously questioned whether human interaction influences the heart, or the potency of that influence, or that it did not seem wholly beneficial. This attitude was reinforced by the infectious and communicable disease models of the nineteenth and twentieth centuries. Again, human relationships were seen as crucial to health, but in a largely negative way. Other human beings were viewed as carriers of contagious germs and deadly infections, as a threat to one's very existence, not as a source of health. In this century, furthermore, a wide range of scientific studies more than amply attested to Hunter's prophetic wisdom. Clearly, human interaction, especially emotionally upsetting conversation, can undermine cardiovascular health. And, as I shall outline shortly, a large body of scientific data indicates that hypertensive individuals are particularly vulnerable in this regard.[1]

CONVERSATION WITH CORONARY PATIENTS

Certain of our own experiences with coronary patients sensitized us to the dangers long before we thought about treating patients like Ed. In one study we observed that ordinary conversations with these patients could elicit changes in heart rate and heart rhythm that were, to say the very least, worrisome. While most of our research focused on the generally calming effects of nonverbal interaction, we were also interested in more complex interaction, especially human dialogue. Our interest was initially stimulated by Dr. Thomas who, as coronary care clinical specialist taught cardiac patients about proper diet, exercise regimens, and work programs after they were released from the hospital. While her patients usually showed great interest in her educational program, many also used these sessions to begin talking about far more pressing concerns, which had been difficult to express while they were in the coronary-care unit itself. Some patients expressed anxiety about leaving the hospital or described their struggles at home, their fear of dying, their terror of becoming a cardiac cripple, their poverty and economic misery, and their sense of isolation and loneliness. The regularity of these outpourings, as well as their apparent intensity, gradually led us to question how such unburdening would affect their hearts. Was it therapeutic for patients to discuss their fears and anxieties and unburden themselves of problems they had bottled up inside? Or did such discussions make matters worse? This question was especially worrisome in the context of their cardiovascular vulnerability. If a person's heart and blood vessels were quite healthy, then it seemed likely that transient emotional disturbances triggered during discussions, even if they produced major changes in heart rate and blood pressure, would not be a serious threat to life. On the other hand, it was clear that if one already had a myocardial infarction or any of a variety of other heart diseases, then any sudden surge in blood pressure or a marked increase in heart rate could pose a variety of health risks.

In order objectively to assess the seriousness of this problem, we began to monitor the effects of conversations on the heart rate and heart rhythm of patients while they were still in the coronary-care unit. Rather than deliberately search for hidden emotional concerns, however, we engaged patients in an open-ended dialogue in which they were free to chat about anything they wished. They were interviewed several days after the immediate medical crisis that brought them to the coronary unit had passed and their medical condition had been stabilized. Each patient was then asked to describe the symptoms and events that had brought him or her to the unit. The question was designed as a starting point, and from there each patient was encouraged to talk about anything that might be of concern or interest. Each interview lasted approximately thirty minutes and was preceded and followed by thirty-minute

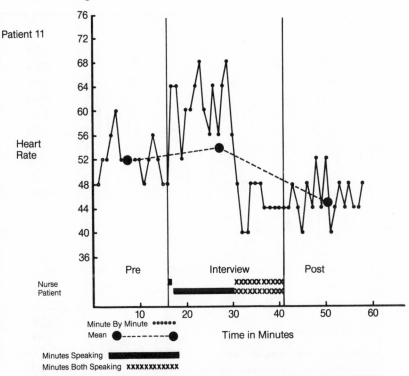

Figure 4.1. Minute-to-minute changes in the heart rate of a coronary patient before, during, and after an interview with a nurse. Note that, during this interview, the patient's heart increased significantly and then fell to a lower resting level than before the interview.

periods when a patient rested alone while his or her electrocardiogram was continuously recorded. The interview itself was tape-recorded for later independent analysis of its emotional content.

Twelve of the nineteen patients exhibited significant increases in heart rate during the interview, but the pattern of changes varied widely. Some patients increased their heart rate almost as soon as the conversations began, while others exhibited the greatest changes halfway through their conversations. As shown in figures 4.1 and 4.2, some patients significantly lowered their resting heart rates after the conversations, while others exhibited just the opposite pattern.

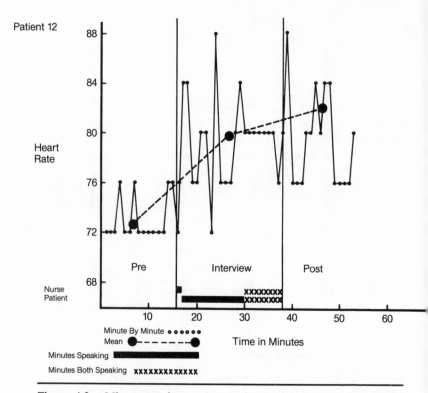

Figure 4.2.   Minute-to-minute changes in the heart rate of a second coronary patient before, during, and after an interview with a nurse. Again, the patient's heart rate rose during the interview but did not return to the resting levels seen before the interview.

In addition to the heart-rate changes, eight of the nineteen patients also exhibited intermittent arrhythmia during the resting period before their conversations. Predisposition to such abnormal heartbeats frequently increases after a heart attack and has been strongly linked to an increased risk of sudden death: the greater the frequency of such abnormal beats, the greater the risk.* Four patients showed significant increases in the incidence of ventricular

* Often after a heart attack, cardiac rhythm may be quite unstable. It is not unusual to observe an increased incidence of abnormal heartbeats. One of the reasons specialized coronary-care units were developed was to monitor carefully these rhythm irregularities and, when necessary, to suppress their occurrence with drugs.

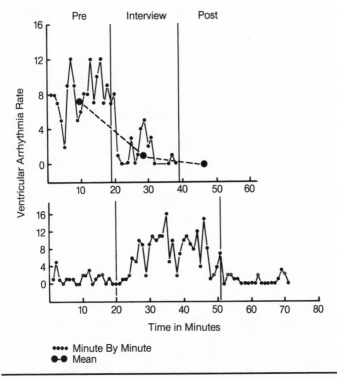

Figure 4.3. Changes in the frequency of ventricular arrhythmia in two coronary patients before, during, and after an interview with a nurse. The patients exhibited opposite patterns of these potentially life-threatening abnormal heart beats. The first patient exhibited a marked reduction in the frequency of these beats during the interview and a total cessation of such heart-rhythm disturbances after the interview. The second patient exhibited a significant rise in the incidence of these abnormal beats during the interview but a similar pattern both before and after the interview.

arrhythmia during conversation with Dr. Thomas. Figure 4.3 illustrates the changes in two such patients. As can be seen in the graph, one particular patient had an average of one to two abnormal heartbeats per minute both before and after the conversation. Yet during the interview itself, the frequency of these abnormal heartbeats increased significantly, rising as high as sixteen per minute. Surprisingly, this patient showed very little change in heart rate during the same interview.[2] By contrast, the other patient exhibited a marked reduction in these abnormal heartbeats during and after the conversation.

As we expected, the emotional content of the conversations varied enormously. Some patients talked about what appeared to be mundane, emotionally neutral topics, while others openly expressed terror at the thought of dying or being incapacitated. The impact of the conversations on the patients' hearts also varied: heart rate and heart rhythm changed in ways that were both helpful and, as shown in figure 4.3, sometimes dangerous. To our surprise, the changes did not always correlate highly with the emotional content of the conversation. On the basis of earlier research studies, we had assumed that emotionally provocative material would cause more significant cardiac changes; but in some patients, neutral topics appeared to be linked to the significant effects. We assumed that certain of the changes, such as the increase in the incidence of ventricular arrhythmia, had to result from interaction between the cardiovascular status of the patient and the conversations themselves. Yet even if this assumption were accurate, it did not really help clarify why such changes occurred during neutral conversations.

Almost three decades before our study, Dr. Ian Stevenson, Dr. Charles Duncan, Dr. Stewart Wolf, Dr. Herbert Ripley, and Dr. Harold Wolff, part of a medical research group at Cornell University Medical School, had similarly monitored patients who had come to the hospital complaining of heart palpitations or chest pain.[3] As in our study, they observed that eight of the first twelve patients they monitored exhibited significant elevations in heart rate during their interviews. Several patients also exhibited a significantly increased incidence of cardiac arrhythmia. Unlike our study, however, the cardiac changes in their study appeared to be most prominent when patients discussed emotionally stressful topics, an impression that led these investigators to conclude that the emotional content of conversations posed the health hazard.* These findings were subsequently confirmed by other investigators.[4] It appeared that Hunter was right: that the lives of individuals already suffering

---

* As I shall discuss later, in this study and in many subsequent studies, little attention was paid to the act of communicating or to who was speaking; rather, the focus was on the emotional content of a communication.

from cardiovascular disease were in the "hands of any rascal who chooses to annoy or tease" them. While it was puzzling that the cardiac changes we observed in our coronary-care patients were not always linked to the degree of emotional arousal in the conversations, nevertheless in general our findings did confirm the overall phenomenon that human dialogue can significantly influence the heart.*

THE DILEMMA OF HYPERTENSIVE DIALOGUE

Yet it was not just the changes in heart rate and heart rhythm we had observed in coronary patients that made us uncertain about how to treat Ed. Far more unsettling were data from an extensive series of studies on blood-pressure changes of hypertensive patients. In the 1940s and 1950s, thirty years before we met Ed, investigators had already found that hypertensive patients frequently exhibited major elevations in blood pressure during stressful interviews.[5] These findings were important in guiding our initial approach. Because the data from previous studies appeared consistent, we were determined to avoid provocative emotional topics with Ed, choosing instead to be supportive and reassuring. The strategy that seemed best was one in which we would interact in a therapeutically supportive and emotionally unprovocative manner for an hour's session each week, while at the same time teaching Ed basic relaxation techniques which might help him to lower his blood pressure. Thus, Dr. Thomas and I began to chat with Ed, much as we had done with coronary patients, while measuring his blood pressure with a stethoscope four or five times during the hour. Ed was informed that our approach was experimental, and that, indeed, the entire endeavor might prove fruitless.

Yet in spite of our intention to avoid emotional confrontations,

---

* One of the main differences between our coronary-care observations and other studies is that our determination of emotional arousal was established by objective rating scales and independent psychiatric judgments. Other studies relied on the clinical ratings of the experimenters themselves to judge emotional arousal. There was one other variable that struck us as important only in retrospect: that is, we not only coded the content of the conversation but also recorded who was speaking. Later we were to understand that who was speaking was far more important than the emotional content of the words spoken.

TABLE 4.1

Death Rates per 100,000 Population in the United States
for White Males between the Ages of 45 and 54 for
Various Cardiovascular Diseases

	Coronary Heart Disease	Hypertensive Disease	Cerebrovascular Disease
Married	330	16	35
Single	458	35	70
Widowed	548	36	78
Divorced	713	48	96

Source: James J. Lynch, *The Broken Heart: The Medical Consequences of Loneliness* (New York: Basic Books, 1977).

Ed insisted on quickly challenging the theoretical basis of our approach. Like a moth drawn toward the very flame that sears it, Ed seemed inexorably drawn toward topics that were by their nature emotionally provocative. Even though we tried to focus his attention on general relaxation techniques which had been shown to be useful in transiently lowering blood pressure—such as muscle relaxation, deep breathing, and modified forms of biofeedback—it seemed as if our mere presence in the room precipitated emotional arousal.

In our second session, Ed questioned the overall philosophy of our clinic and the basic assumptions behind our approach. While he agreed that various relaxation techniques might help lower his pressure, he asserted that he believed the main source of his hypertension to be overweight and his excessive salt intake, which causes fluid retention. While he readily admitted that losing weight was hard to do, he nevertheless attributed his hypertension to his excess weight rather than to any hidden emotional or interpersonal struggle. By no means did we think Ed's ideas about the importance of weight and salt intake were unimportant in blood-pressure regulation. To the contrary, we knew them to be very important. We simply believed there were other crucial factors Ed was unaware of. Unable to convince him in any other way, we reluctantly showed him some of the statistics on heart disease and marital status for men his age (table 4.1).* Indeed, Ed insisted on seeing "hard data to evaluate the *raison d'être*" of our approach. He was

* See Lynch, *The Broken Heart,* for elaboration and detailed discussion of these statistics.[6]

in a "hurry to get better," he said, "and was willing to try anything that seemed even remotely sensible" if we could show him evidence to substantiate our thesis. Though we feared these data would be emotionally provocative, Ed appeared quite amused. "They are just correlations!" he remarked laughing, in regard to the doubling of hypertensive and stroke death rates for single men his age. Scanning the table casually, almost as if he were trying to emphasize his lack of concern, he added with a kind of stockbroker's objectivity, "Correlations prove nothing about cause. You could just as easily have correlated the incidence of insanity with various phases of the moon, and derived an argument about lunacy comparable to your theories about loneliness."

Though he continued to smile, he went on to speak with increased emphasis, without pausing to breathe. He also failed to look at us while speaking. At first he flatly denied that he was lonely or that he might have difficulty with human relationships. He insisted the contrary, that his life was full of business acquaintances and a constant whirl of social activities that led him to treasure the time he spent by himself. Though he did live alone, and though he also readily acknowledged that he lacked a close friend or confidant with whom he could share his experiences, he found it difficult to conceive how we could possibly link these situations to hypertension. Almost as an afterthought, he added that several years earlier his closest friend, a professional colleague, had died unexpectedly from a heart attack. Since that time he had been unable to establish a comparable friendship. Ed also alluded to the fact that he was "struggling a bit to establish a closer relationship with a woman he had admired for several years"—yet categorized this struggle as "one that any middle-aged man would find a bit difficult to negotiate."

In spite of what appeared to us to be a significant list of interpersonal struggles, he denied feeling any discomfort in connection with other people and was emphatic about not being lonely or in need of the intimate companionship of others. He appeared to become increasingly uneasy the longer he spoke. When we asked whether he was irritated, however, he professed bewilderment, laughing as he countered, "Irritated? No, not at all! I find your attempts to link hypertension to loneliness amusing. Although I know it's a pet theory of yours, I'm sorry to say that it simply doesn't ring true in my case. I've already got more than my quota of problems without your adding to the list."

At that point, mindful of the link between emotional arousal and blood pressure, Dr. Thomas interrupted the discussion and instructed Ed, "Take a few deep breaths and relax while I take your blood pressure." She then teased him about his failure to breathe properly when he spoke. As she picked up the stethoscope, she asked, "Do all stockbrokers talk the way you do? It's hard to argue with someone who never stops to take a breath. I think it's a way you have of winning arguments. You just keep talking without breathing so that others can't argue with you." Then pointing to her stethoscope, she added, "But we have a secret weapon. We have a way of seizing the floor by taking your blood pressure."

The room grew quiet as she pumped the bulb to inflate the cuff. As she listened intensely for the Korotkov sounds in his brachial artery, I reflected on Ed's comments. In one sense he was absolutely correct. Without doubt we were foisting a "pet theory" on him, and there seemed to be no way, beyond statistical data and research studies, to persuade him of the influence of human relationships on vascular problems. The lack of explicit proof was especially frustrating because not only was loneliness unacceptable to Ed as a cause of hypertension but—even more to the point—he did not believe it was a real problem in his life.

As Dr. Thomas slowly released the air from the cuff, I reflected on Ed's rejoinder that correlations prove nothing about cause. He was absolutely right. Not only had he quickly made mincemeat of the medical statistics we showed him, he also underscored our ignorance. We simply did not understand the how or the why of the increased cardiovascular mortality in lonely people. We did not understand how divorce or living alone increases the risk of cardiovascular death. Granted there was a sudden surge in cardiovascular mortality for bereaved widowers, or a doubling of hypertensive death rates for single people, Ed's central question remained unanswered. How do bereavement, loss, or loneliness contribute to hypertension, heart disease, and sudden death? And why hypertension in Ed's case? Why not ulcers, cancer, migraine headaches, or a spastic colon? What are the mechanisms?

Dr. Thomas removed the stethoscope from her ears and recorded her findings. Ed's pressure had risen to 192/128, and his pulse was pounding at 96 beats per minute! Earlier in the session, his pressure had been 160/101, and his pulse 71. Alarmed at the rise in his pressure, she instructed him to relax.

"Your pressure is up a bit right now, so why don't you just remain quiet for a few minutes and relax by breathing deeply." Although Ed did not appear particularly upset, his blood pressure clearly revealed another reality. Even more surprising, he seemed utterly unconcerned about the rapid rise in his pressure. After three to four minutes of quiet deep breathing, Dr. Thomas again took his blood pressure, and this time it had fallen back to 170/105, while his heart rate had settled to 68 beats per minute.

After remarking to Ed that his pressure had dropped, Dr. Thomas said, "Maybe you're not lonely and maybe you're not struggling with relationships, but that discussion sure elevated your blood pressure quickly." She then added, "But look at how quickly you were able to lower it when you relaxed!"

"How about that?" Ed responded, appearing a bit more involved after hearing that his blood pressure had fallen once again.

Dr. Thomas then instructed him to take his blood pressure at home each day, both before and after five minutes of relaxed deep breathing. A number of studies, including recently published work from Dr. Herbert Benson's laboratory at Harvard University's Medical School, had indicated that quiet meditation and relaxation could help transiently lower blood pressure.[7] She hoped to reassure Ed that there were ways beside losing weight, that he could use to help improve his health. Furthermore, since it appeared that Ed was unaware of his feelings, I asked him to write down how he felt each time before he took his pressure at home. I thought that this device might help him attend to the potential links between his feelings and his blood pressure.

Yet after several additional treatment sessions with Ed, we were discouraged. For one thing, our initial misgivings had changed from simple theoretical concerns about blood pressure to a very real concern about Ed's cardiovascular health. His blood pressure followed a truly disconcerting pattern. Any time he discussed emotionally provocative topics, his blood pressure went up. Similarly, whenever he relaxed and breathed deeply, his blood pressure came down. It seemed to be a therapeutic catch-22. On the one hand, we assumed that certain psychological conflicts surrounding interpersonal relationships contributed to his hypertension. Yet, at the same time, it had become obvious that any discussion of these conflicts precipitated marked increases in his blood pressure.

In spite of this dilemma and our own misgivings, we decided to continue. This decision was based on two inescapable facts. First, it was obvious that our clinic was not the only place where Ed was likely to engage in emotionally provocative topics or encounter stressful interaction. Any number of social and business situations were likely to elicit similar marked increases in blood pressure. Yet unlike our clinic where we could at least record his pressure five or six times during each session, there was no way he could similarly monitor his pressure in his everyday life. Though he could measure his pressure in the privacy of his home, he could not similarly measure it while dealing with a cantankerous client. Since Ed appeared to be completely unaware of major increases in his blood pressure, he had no way to recognize or differentiate interpersonal situations that elevated pressure from those that lowered it. Furthermore, his inability to detect major blood pressure shifts in his body appeared to be linked to his inability to sense or discriminate his own feelings. Unlike Dr. Hunter who could at least feel his own chest pain and thus link it to the misfortune of meeting a "rascal," Ed apparently had no way to differentiate potentially lethal encounters from those that might be comforting. He had no way to recognize what was stressful and what was not stressful, or to sort rascals from friends. We thought this might be something we could teach him.

Recognition of these issues led us to alter our initial therapeutic strategy. Perhaps Ed would first have to be made aware of his emotional struggles and his feelings before he could deal with his blood pressure. Yet this possibility quickly raised a host of other questions. Could Ed be alerted to the fact that he had problems hidden in his blood pressure when that system could be monitored only indirectly and infrequently? Even more perplexing, how could he alter blood-pressure increases when he discussed emotional topics? Should he avoid all business interactions involving emotional stress and similarly avoid all meaningful emotional encounters in his life? Should he withdraw from a professional life that he professed to enjoy, even though it required him to constantly deal with other people?

We also began to wonder about another more subtle question. Could the marked transient surges in Ed's blood pressure help explain why he had insulated himself from intimate relationships? Was he unconsciously trying to protect himself from emotional interactions that could be lethal? Did his pressure rise to such dangerous levels, when he was emotionally aroused, that he was forced to withdraw from people and unconsciously protect himself from more drastic consequences? Were loneliness and hypertension part of a vicious circle?

Forty years before we began to ask these questions, investigators, using psychotherapeutic models that had successfully treated other types of psychological conflict, had explored whether insight-oriented psychotherapy could be helpful for treating hypertension.[8] A considerable body of evidence supported the idea that certain personality characteristics, psychological conflicts, and emotional problems contributed substantially to this disease; but, as I have said, insight-oriented psychotherapy did not appear to be an effective way to treat it.

When we first reviewed these studies, we thought that perhaps some crucial interpersonal factor had been overlooked that might explain their lack of clinical success. After all, our earlier research had thoroughly convinced us that human relationships are therapeutically beneficial for the heart, while loneliness and social isolation are major causes of cardiovascular disease. Yet after a few therapeutic encounters with Ed, we formulated a totally different hypothesis. We began to believe that he was psychologically trapped by his own body. His blood pressure apparently surged during conversations the way a fuse box responds to a sudden surge in electric power. The analogy led us to a new insight, as we began to suspect that topics in psychotherapy that markedly increase blood pressure can have only one of two outcomes: either one short-circuits the conversation by turning it off or withdrawing from it; or a fuse inside one's body may threaten to blow. Hence, to avoid the latter in the form of heart attack or stroke, hypertensive patients like Ed could either control the emotion—that is, the power surge of human interaction—by keeping a comfortable distance from other people, or they could flee from situations that threaten to overload the vascular system.

This hypothesis made plain the dilemma of hypertensive dialogue. If we interacted with Ed solely by being reassuring and emotionally supportive, and kept at a safe distance, his pressure would remain relatively lower. On the other hand, if we began to discuss emotionally provocative issues in an effort to get at the underlying source of his emotional pain, his blood pressure would quickly rise to dangerous levels. It was a dilemma that at least helped us understand one facet of Ed's life: that is, why he was lonely.

THE FOUNDATIONS OF LETHAL DIALOGUE

Our observations of the rapid rise in Ed's blood pressure and heart rate whenever he discussed emotionally provocative subjects appeared to duplicate findings made by Dr. Franz Alexander four decades earlier. In 1939, this pioneering psychoanalyst reported on the first of what was to prove to be a series of studies that attempted to use insight-oriented psychotherapy to treat hypertension.[9] Alexander's studies were conducted in an era in which no effective drug treatments for hypertension existed, and some effective way to manage the problem was urgently needed. Alexander hypothesized that deeply hidden emotional conflicts are the principle cause of hypertension, and he assumed that a psychoanalytically based psychotherapy would be the best way to uncover the conflicts and thus help patients lower blood pressure.

Alexander's hypothesis was based on the psychoanalytic studies of Sigmund Freud[10] and on the classic physiological studies of Walter Cannon,[11] and he hoped to bridge the findings of those two investigators. In order to provide the context for Alexander's studies, however, let me first review Cannon's central findings.

In his *Bodily Changes in Pain, Hunger, Fear and Rage* (1929), Cannon described the way the autonomic nervous and the neuroendocrine systems influence the cardiovascular system. His book was a milestone in the history of medicine because it was among the very first to emphasize the crucial role that emotional stress plays in the development of disease. Before Cannon's studies, medical scientists had a very different perspective on emotions. It was not that physicians did not recognize the influence of emotions on the heart. To the contrary, as already noted in the case of Dr. Hunter, medical history was filled with evidence about the influence of emotions on the heart. What Cannon added to this anecdotal history, however, was a scientific way of understanding the phenomenon. By the sheer force and clarity of his experimental demonstrations, his text left no doubt about the importance of emotions to bodily functions. He almost casually notes how emotions rapidly alter blood pressure.

Great excitement is accompanied by sympathetic innervations [that is, firing of the sympathetic nerves of the autonomic nervous system] which contract the small blood vessels, accelerate the heart rate and thus increase arterial pressure. In 100 cases studied by Gallavardin and Haour the blood pressure at first when the subjects were excited, was 25 to 35 millimeters of mercury higher than it was later when they became accustomed to the procedure. In a patient observed by Schrumpf fear of serious diagnosis was attended by a pressure 33 percent higher than it was after the patient was reassured. In extreme pleasure, anger or fright a rise of 90 millimeters may occur.[12]

Cannon outlined a bold new thesis about the utility of bodily changes accompanying emotional arousal as being part of a primitive "fight or flight" response. He noted that the physiological organs of both humans and animals are constructed to allow them to mobilize for emergencies. He reasoned that, in times of stress or emotional upheaval, the body has to have the adaptive capacity either to fight for survival or to flee. Cannon's thesis became the core theoretical idea that framed the way subsequent investigators would think about emotions. He noted:

Our inquiry thus far has revealed that the adrenin [adrenalin] secreted in times of stress has all the effects in the body that are produced by injected adrenin. It cooperates with sympathetic nerve impulses thus flooding the blood with sugar; it helps in distributing the blood to the heart, lungs, central nervous system and limbs, while taking it away from the inhibited organs of the abdomen; it quickly abolishes the effects of muscular fatigue; and it renders the blood more rapidly coagulable. These remarkable facts are, furthermore, associated with some of the most primitive experiences in the life of higher organisms, experiences common to all, both man and beast, *the elementary experiences of pain and fear and rage that come suddenly in critical emergencies*. What is the significance of these profound bodily alterations? What are the emergency functions of the sympathico-adrenal system? (Italics added)[13]

This was the basis of Cannon's now thoroughly accepted theory of the "fight or flight" response. The body's automatic chain of events in this response are those already quoted—the pouring out of adrenalin, markedly increased heart rate and blood pressure, the constriction and dilatation of blood flow in the various parts of the body. These were the changes Cannon brilliantly charted as major bodily mechanisms that prepare humans to fight or to flee. He also recognized that this "primitive" alarm system, while adaptive in certain conditions, can also be a significant cause of subsequent maladaptation and disease: that is, the same fight or flight reactions that prepare the body for action may also occur in situations where a person no longer can fight or flee, and hence, the body would begin to prepare itself for action—fire its own boilers, if you will—without being able to follow through. Cannon thus added a new dimension, one that charted the hidden bodily responses that are mobilized, along with the more overt expression of emotions. He postulated that animals have to be able to respond to life-threatening danger not only by expressing their emotions but also by mobilizing their bodies to fight or to flee. He suggested that when an animal perceives danger, it mobilizes its entire body to optimize its capacity to respond appropriately. As Cannon pointed out, not only were there *visible manifestations* of the *expression of emotions,* there were also *internal correlates* that cannot be seen and, indeed, are often not even felt. Heart-rate increases, blood-pressure elevations, blood-flow shifts stimulated by the secretion of adrenalin and the activation of the autonomic nervous system—all are part of an elaborate bodily system that prepares animals to either fight or flee. This general framework about the physiology of emotions profoundly shaped subsequent approaches to the study of such diseases as hypertension. After Cannon's work it was widely accepted that emotional arousal can trigger "fight or flight" reactions which include significant increases in blood pressure and heart rate.

PSYCHOLOGICAL INSIGHT: FRANZ ALEXANDER

Deeply influenced by this scientific background, Alexander assumed hypertension to be in all likelihood the end result of unconscious conflicts that place a person in a state of hypervigilance or a chronic condition of fight or flight. For two decades Alexander studied the personality of hypertensive individuals in order to understand the nature of their emotional conflicts as well as to evaluate whether psychotherapy could be used to help alleviate their struggles and thus lower blood pressure.

In the mid 1930s, he began treating a hypertensive man five days each week in classic hour-long psychoanalytic psychotherapy. For two years he systematically measured the patient's blood pressure with a stethoscope, both before and after each therapy session. In what was one of the most exhaustive series of measurements of the day-to-day fluctuations in a hypertensive's blood pressure ever conducted up to that time, Alexander observed that in sessions when the patient was relatively calm, blood pressure was almost always lower. By contrast, in sessions when the patient discussed emotionally provocative topics, blood pressure was consistently higher. Alexander was convinced that the emotional state of this man and the topics discussed in the therapeutic hour were the single most important factor influencing his overall blood-pressure levels.

Alexander traced the patient's problems with hypertension back to psychological conflicts of early childhood. The emotional struggles had to do with dysfunctional parent-child communications. Since the patient's infantile needs to be taken care of and understood were not adequately met, he grew up driven to seek support and affection. He was led to form dependent relationships, thus becoming trapped in a vicious circle, especially in regard to the open expression of anger. The patient was torn apart by a chronic struggle against overtly expressing hostile impulses, always trying to appear outwardly friendly, in order to be liked by others. His personality was dominated by excessive but inhibited hostility, which stemmed from conflicts early in his life.

After two years of intensive psychoanalysis the patient had gained certain psychological insights but was still hypertensive. Although Alexander did allude to modest decreases in blood pressure as the patient became emotionally calmer, it was clear that this therapeutic approach was neither an inexpensive nor a particularly useful way to lower blood pressure. Unlike other types of neurotic patient he had seen, Alexander's hypertensive patient appeared to respond to psychotherapy almost as if the therapy itself confronted the patient with a fight or flight situation in an environment in which he could neither fight nor run away.

PSYCHOLOGICAL INSIGHT: OTHER STUDIES

Subsequent efforts by other investigators to use various forms of psychotherapy to treat hypertensive patients supported the original conclusions made by Dr. Alexander.[14] A consensus emerged that there was a "hypertensive personality" characterized by lifelong unconscious conflicts involving the expression of hostility, aggression, dependency, and ambition. Confronted by these conflicts when interacting with other people, the hypertensive individual is forced to confront his or her own rage. This in turn triggers marked fight or flight responses lest the other person see one's anger and either attack—or even more disabling—be rejecting.

In 1951, Morton Reiser, M. Rosenbaum, and E. B. Ferris described twelve patients with malignant hypertension* who had been studied at the University of Cincinnati College of Medicine.[15] As was true in Alexander's studies, their overall impression was that the precursors of hypertension were rooted in early childhood and conflicts over dependency with parents. The onset of the disease itself usually occurred in early adult life (between the ages of twenty and thirty), during an intense emotional crisis, and then proceeded to the malignant stage between the ages of forty and fifty, concomitant with the recurrence of some major life crisis (such as death of a spouse or divorce). In virtually every case, the major stress was linked to a disruption of core relationships on which the patient depended for emotional support. It left the patient in a social vacuum, unable to express anger, while cut off from meaningful human relationships.

It was particularly striking in the Reiser study, however, that some of their patients were able to lower their pressure to achieve a more benign phase of the disease with a moderate amount of what the authors described as supportive therapy, although, as in Alexander's studies, these psychotherapeutic effects had not eliminated the hypertension. These investigators had in essence confirmed

---

* Malignant hypertension is the condition where a prolonged state of elevated blood pressure has caused end-organ damage—for example, kidney problems, cerebral edema, and/or changes in the retina.

Alexander's overall findings in a more severe form of the disease.

Elaborating on their findings, Reiser and his colleagues investigated the use of reassurance and emotional support, rather than insight-oriented psychotherapy, to lower blood pressure in hypertensive patients. In 1953, these investigators reported the results of ninety-eight hypertensive patients who were given three different levels of what was called "therapeutic support."[16] They observed that, at the end of therapy, anywhere from 22 percent to 58 percent of the patients had lower blood pressure, while 20 percent had higher pressure. Reiser and his colleagues described the most intensive of their therapeutic interactions as "superficial insight therapy," thus differentiating it from the in-depth approach used by earlier investigators. In their study, almost 50 percent of the population derived some benefit from "therapeutic support," with success apparently linked to a patient's ability to maintain his or her unconscious defense mechanisms, and to social distance in the therapeutic relationship.

One other study of interest conducted during the same era was reported by a psychoanalyst, Dr. Leon Moses.[17] Like Alexander, he engaged ten patients in psychoanalytically oriented, intensive psychotherapy. Four of the patients, whom he labeled as "transiently hypertensive," were found to be normotensive after six months of therapy. By contrast, the two patients with the highest pressures—or what Moses labeled "accelerated hypertension" (200–230/110–130)—quickly dropped out of therapy. Those with blood pressures in the intermediate ranges were still hypertensive at the end of therapy. The severest hypertensives could not tolerate insight-oriented psychotherapy and thus withdrew from treatment.

These studies were important for another reason that went unrecognized for some time. They were to be the last of their kind for over twenty-five years. In the early 1950s, the first of a variety of drugs became available which appeared to lower blood pressure effectively. The availability of these drug treatments, in turn, led to a decline in interest in nonpharmacological approaches. Interest in psychotherapeutic treatments that were time consuming, expensive, and marginally productive rapidly waned as hope rose that a more effective and efficient treatment of hypertension had at long last been found.

Although the transition in treatment approaches was dramatic, its full impact was not recognized at that time. A few years ago, Dr. Alvin Shapiro commented on the change in conceptual thinking brought about by the introduction of antihypertensive drugs. He wrote of Reiser's pioneering efforts:

It is unfortunate that in the explosion of information about physiologic mechanisms and pharmacologic influence in hypertension which has accumulated in the past twenty years, this small paper [Reiser's study] remains a gem only appreciated by those internists who have sought for confirmation of their own clinical experiences in handling malignant hypertensives with a "listening ear." Those who have "listened" have repeatedly confirmed Reiser's observation that one can almost always find emotional conflict of considerable meaning to the patient when hypertension accelerates to the malignant phase, but because of the other more easily communicated facts about this disease, the importance of the emotional factors is not transmitted sufficiently well in current teaching.[18]

Although treatment of hypertension shifted almost exclusively to drugs in the 1950s, nevertheless the personality of hypertensive patients continued to be investigated.[19] In study after study, a consistent pattern began to emerge. It became clear that many hypertensive patients were burdened by lifelong unconscious struggles over the expression of rage, hostility, resentment, rebellion, ambition, and aggression. The original source of the rage was almost always traced back to unfulfilled or unmet childhood needs for dependency. As adults these patients unconsciously demanded to be taken care of. Yet trapped by the possibility that their rage and resentment might be seen or detected by those on whom they depended, hypertensive patients employed a variety of defense mechanisms to hide their negative feelings. Typically their anger and aggression were covered over by emotional expressions that were exactly opposite to what they felt inside. They appeared to be friendly, lacking in assertiveness, even submissive. In general, since these problems were rooted in childhood conflicts over dependency, typically the hypertensive individual would experience the most serious conflicts with authority figures who were symbolic representations of his or her parents. While various aspects of the psychodynamic roots of the conflicts were debated, there was general agreement about the overall personality. Repressed anger in interpersonal encounters appeared to be a dominant feature. Alexander and his colleagues summarized the findings of many investigators as follows:

The patients were afraid to lose the affection of others and had to control the expression of their hostility. In childhood the patients were prone to outbursts of rage and aggression. As they matured and developed the angry attacks came under control. Consequently they became overtly compliant and unassertive. As adults they persevered doggedly, often against insuperable obstacles. When promoted to executive positions they encountered difficulties because they could not assert themselves or make others follow their orders. They were overconscientious and too responsible. Their conscientiousness only increased their feelings of resentment at self-imposed tasks.[20]

LIFE STRESS AND ESSENTIAL HYPERTENSION

Of all the research findings that influenced our initial approach to Ed, none was more central than the studies by Dr. Stewart Wolf and Dr. Harold Wolff at Cornell Medical School. In their pioneering book *Life Stress and Essential Hypertension* (1951)[21] these physicians, along with several co-workers, described in great detail the truly profound elevations in blood pressure that hypertensive patients could exhibit during stressful interviews. These studies were of central importance not only because they greatly expanded the observations of clinicians such as Dr. Alexander, but even more because they monitored a host of cardiovascular and neurochemical changes that occurred during stressful interviews. Their central thesis was that emotional stress is a major cause of hypertension. These investigators, like many others, did not see talking or conversation as a major stress, but rather they used stress interviews as a means of eliciting emotional arousal. They assumed that talking about unpleasant life experiences or discussing earlier emotional upheavals would cause emotional reactions similar to those once produced by the event itself.

In their studies Wolf and Wolff instructed hypertensive patients to rest for thirty to forty minutes while their blood pressure was periodically taken (along with many other physical measures).* Following a period of rest, these patients were then interviewed for thirty minutes about topics the investigators already knew were

* These studies were conducted in the 1940s, when no effective drug remedies for hypertension existed. Many of these patients were subsequently treated by various surgical procedures that included cutting their sympathetic nervous systems.

upsetting; each patient's blood pressure was measured periodically during the interview.

What these investigators observed was remarkably consistent across a wide range of patients. Blood pressure frequently surged extraordinarily high during the stress interviews. Extraordinary changes were seen not only in blood pressure but also in the relative clotting time of the blood, in the thickness (or viscosity) of the blood, in the hematocrit (or number of red blood cells), and in the erythrocyte sedimentation rate. Figure 4.4 shows an example of the types of pressure increases and changes in blood flow which patients exhibited during stress interviews. In addition to blood pressure and heart rate, also measured were stroke volume (the amount of blood pumped out of the heart with each beat), renal blood flow variation (the change in the percentage of blood passing through the kidneys both before and during the interview), as well as the filtration fraction (the amount of blood that passes through the glomeruli in the kidney—the filtering system of the kidneys). The stress interview had a major impact on every cardiovascular parameter measured. By contrast, when patients were reassured, asked to discuss emotionally neutral topics, and instructed to "ventilate," there was little change in these cardiovascular measures.

Typical of these patients and their blood-pressure changes is the case described in the following clinical vignette:

A 45 year-old Swedish housewife was referred to the clinic because of dizziness and headaches related to hypertension, which had been first noted 16 years earlier during her first pregnancy. Episodes of dizziness were closely correlated with stressful incidents in her life, chiefly concerning her alcoholic husband. At her first visit to the clinic her blood pressure was 236/148. The physical examination showed her heart to be moderately enlarged and there was a faint basal systolic murmur. The radiological examination of her chest also showed enlargement of the left heart; electrocardiogram showed left axis deviation. The results of observations on this patient during an interview are shown in [figure 4.5]. After a preliminary period of rest and relaxation in which there was no conversation, the patient was engaged in the discussion of marital life by one of the physicians. She described the alcoholism of her husband and its effects upon her son and herself. During the discussion she appeared anxious and resentful. Her blood pressure rose from 186/128 to 242/168 and there were concomitant elevations in the heart rate, "stroke volume," and "cardiac output." During this period the "peripheral resistance," which is not shown in the figure, fell from 89 to 43. There was a decrease in renal

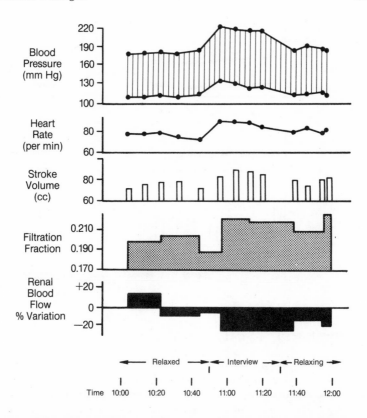

Figure 4.4.   Changes in blood pressure, heart rate, stroke volume, and renal blood flow of a hypertensive patient before, during, and after a stress interview. This figure is redrawn from data first reported by Dr. Stewart Wolf and his colleagues in 1951 in *Life, Stress and Essential Hypertension* (Baltimore: Williams & Wilkins, 1955).

flow and an increase in the filtration fraction. At the end of the interview the patient became quiet and apparently calm. The stroke volume and pulse fell but there was a persistent elevation of the blood pressure associated with a sharp rise in peripheral resistance of 98 units. During this period the renal flow remained decreased. Finally, the blood pressure, peripheral resistance, and renal blood flow all returned to essentially their original values.[22]

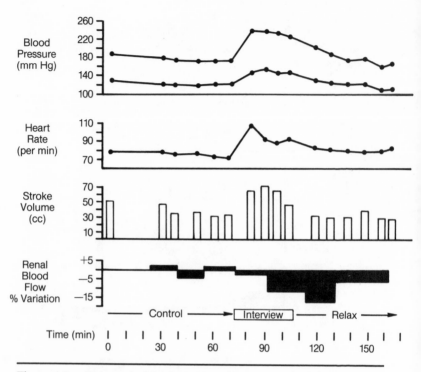

Figure 4.5. Changes in blood pressure, heart rate, stroke volume, and renal blood flow of a forty-five-year-old hypertensive woman before, during, and after a thirty-minute stress interview. This figure is redrawn from data first reported by Dr. Stewart Wolf and his colleagues in 1951 in *Life, Stress and Essential Hypertension* (Baltimore: Williams & Wilkins, 1955).

While general practitioners, and even experts in hypertension, tended to ignore these data (partly, I suspect, because of the extraordinary difficulty of monitoring all these cardiovascular measures), they nevertheless deeply influenced our initial approach to Ed.

The conclusion of these pioneering studies, aspects of which were subsequently confirmed by dozens of similar studies,[23] were unequivocal. The data from the studies of Alexander, Reiser, Wolf and Wolff, and dozens of other investigators, as well as our own initial observations of the reactivity of Ed's blood pressure, made it clear that emotionally provocative topics had to be avoided with hypertensive patients. Virtually every study reached similar conclusions:

1. Emotional arousal stirred up in psychotherapeutic dialogue can lead to major transient elevations in blood pressure.
2. By contrast, supportive therapy that involves a great deal of reassurance and instructions to relax can bring blood pressure down from dangerously high levels but cannot by itself eliminate hypertension.
3. In virtually every study, the central interpersonal conflicts could be traced back to emotional struggles in childhood.
4. Certain adult life crises can trigger major increases in blood pressure which, if combined with certain unknown physiological and/or genetic predisposing factors, can lead to essential hypertension and then to end-organ damage.
5. In many hypertensive patients, repressed rage or inhibited hostility, combined with a surface appearance of submissive friendliness, seemed to be a dominant personality trait.
6. In a number of studies, investigators alluded to the fact that it was possible to have conversations with hypertensive patients, as long as the encounters avoided emotionally provocative topics and the patient was reassured and instructed to "ventilate."

AN ANTIDOTE TO LETHAL DIALOGUE

The question was, how could we help Ed establish supportive relationships and at the same time identify sources of emotional stress in his life? How could we help shift him from a life of lethal dialogue to a world of human relationships in which he could communicate in a way that would not drive his body to ruin?

One clue resided in the way hypertensive patients themselves attempt to solve this problem. After all, most hypertensive patients do not drop dead in the middle of emotional social encounters, nor do they retreat to desert islands to avoid contact with their fellow man. Somehow the majority of hypertensive individuals manage to adapt and cope, at least most of the time.

Based on the supposition that repressed hostility is a major personality trait of hypertensive patients, a number of investigators had studied the interpersonal coping styles of these patients. Two research teams in particular, one directed by Dr. Margaret Thaler-Singer and the other by Dr. Herbert Weiner, investigated how hypertensive patients perceive other people, and how that perception leads them to relate to others.[24] These studies noted that hypertensive patients perceive others as threatening, derisive, and untrustworthy. Because of these negative perceptions, these patients made great efforts to maintain distant relationships while simultaneously attempting to appear friendly and submissive. As Dr. Weiner pointed out, the ambivalence of hypertensive patients paradoxically provokes anger in those with whom they are trying to relate—the very reaction the hypertensive fears most. In essence the hypertensive has to relate to others with all the finesse required of a circus performer attempting to traverse a high wire. It is the threat of falling, not the walking itself, that produces the anxiety! As Weiner noted: "When hypertensive patients successively maintained their distance and avoided relationships, the blood pressure levels remained unchanged, but when this habitual defensive style fails, critical elevations of blood pressure occur."[25]

The hypertensive patients in these studies had continually to readjust the closeness and the distance of their relationships according to what they could tolerate. Dr. W. J. Grace and Dr. David Graham at the University of Wisconsin alluded to this problem when they observed that hypertensive patients were always caught by an "awareness of threat of bodily harm, without any possibility of running away or fighting back."[26] Too many relationships, or too invasive ones, produce marked increases in pressure; too few produce loneliness and a sense of abandonment.

These data led us to several conclusions. We decided continually to readjust the emotional distance we maintained in our dialogue—just as, in medical parlance, one titrates dosages of medication. While we would try to reassure and comfort Ed, we would also do our best to keep at a distance by avoiding emotional discussions that would elevate his blood pressure. In addition, we decided to emphasize a variety of mechanical steps by which he could alter his breathing patterns, as well as to have him practice standard relaxation exercises. In an effort to control the emotional level of the conversations and keep them as emotionally unprovocative as possible, we began to talk as much and sometimes even more than

Ed did during our sessions. The focus was to be on blood pressure rather than on interpersonal issues.

Very much in the style of an intricate dance, we tried to maintain an emotional rhythm to the dialogue, in order to allow Ed to establish a comfortable social distance, and we approached emotional topics as one would train an inexperienced fighter for a boxing match. We sparred and maneuvered to regulate the intensity of dialogue and not overburden his cardiovascular system. We interrupted conversations to measure his blood pressure every ten minutes; and whenever he was emotionally aroused, we would stop the conversation and instruct him to relax and breathe deeply. We felt that this was the best way to teach Ed about his feelings and to train him to deal with them. We followed this program every week for several months on the assumption that it was a first step in counteracting the impact of lethal dialogue.

CHAPTER 5

No Language But a Cry

So runs my dream: but what am I?
An infant crying in the night:
An infant crying for the light:
And with no language but a cry.
   —Alfred Lord Tennyson, "In Memoriam"

TITRATING THE DIALOGUE

For several months we continued to see Ed on a weekly basis, and his blood pressure began to fall. Both in our clinic and at home, his blood pressure readings were slowly but surely approaching normal levels. While it was hard to determine precisely why his blood pressure was dropping, several factors appeared to be significant. Most notable was deep breathing. Whenever Ed got intensely involved in any dialogue, he began to speak more rapidly and frequently failed to breathe. We repeatedly pointed this pattern out to him, and instructed him to measure his pressure twice daily at home, once in the morning and once in the evening. He was instructed to record the pressure once while he was quiet, then to practice relaxed deep breathing for five minutes, and take his pressure again. Soon Ed came to recognize a highly consistent trend: his blood pressure was almost always lower after deep breathing exercises.

Beyond the mechanics of breathing, however, Ed made another major adjustment in his personal life. While it took several weeks for him to mention it, the major source of interpersonal stress in Ed's life was a woman called Valerie. Although he proudly touted the advantages of remaining a confirmed bachelor, it turned out that he "deeply admired a woman, approximately the same age as me, who recently divorced her husband." Yet it was clearly hard for Ed to begin dating Valerie after decades of confirmed bachelor-hood.

Rather than force the interpersonal issues involved in his anxieties about Valerie, Dr. Thomas and I identified with his struggles and made every effort to reassure him. "Of course it would be difficult to begin dating," Dr. Thomas answered him. "It was bad enough going through all those emotional struggles as an adolescent, at a point when you don't really have the sense to recognize all that's involved in a relationship. Of course it's a major problem to date when you're older and wiser."

Again and again we assured Ed that his struggles were not foolish, that his concerns were understandable. Dr. Thomas also emphasized that she suspected that Valerie would have an equally difficult time—a notion that seemed genuinely to astonish Ed so involved was he in his own struggles. He perceived Valerie to be a "divorced woman who knew all about men and dating," and felt he was the one who had problems with their relationship. Ed's first dinner engagement with Valerie was a major interpersonal victory for both of them—and for Dr. Thomas and me as well.

While supporting Ed in his efforts to broaden his social life, we continued to search for an alternative way to measure his blood pressure continuously. As he grew to trust us, Ed appeared to be more at ease about raising interpersonal issues that he earlier would have felt to be emotionally provocative. I say "appeared" because we had no real way of knowing which of our discussions elevated his blood pressure.

The difficulty of keeping a therapeutically appropriate emotional distance from Ed was compounded by a problem that had plagued virtually every other investigator who had attempted to treat hypertensive patients in the past. We simply had no continuous or direct way to measure his blood pressure. Like everyone else who had previously treated hypertensive patients, we were severely limited by the blood-pressure-measuring techniques available to us. Unless we put a catheter directly into his artery (a procedure that was clearly out of the question), the only way we could measure Ed's blood pressure was with stethoscope and cuff. This limitation required us to stop all conversation every five or ten minutes and be quiet while Dr. Thomas listened to his arterial pulsations with a stethoscope.

It was, in one sense, a major step backward from the blood-pressure studies I had conducted with animals fifteen years earlier when, by inserting catheters directly in a dog's arteries, I could measure blood pressure with every beat of its heart. Those studies revealed not only the potent influence of human contact on blood pressure but also the extraordinary changes in blood-pressure levels within a few heartbeats. It seemed likely that a similar reactivity existed in human blood pressure, and that we were missing a great deal by measuring Ed's blood pressure only every ten minutes or so. It was clear we needed a device that would allow us to measure blood pressure on a continuous basis, one that would allow us to titrate our dialogue more precisely. We needed a way to persuade Ed that interpersonal struggles significantly affected his blood pressure, in spite of his claiming to feel no discomfort dealing with other people.

After several months of searching, we came across a scientific report describing the measurement of something called "pulse-transit time." It was an experimental tool that several recent studies had suggested might provide an indirect way to calculate blood pressure with every beat of the heart. This device proved to be a major turning point in our treatment of Ed.[1]

PULSE-TRANSIT TIME: THE BEGINNING OF VASCULAR DIALOGUE

"When do we take off?" Ed asked in good humor as he listened to the aging teletype machine noisily printing numbers on the paper. Like a carpenter's hammer driving a nail into solid oak, the printer vibrated and shuddered as it banged out the number of milliseconds between each beat of his heart and the subsequent pulse waves at his wrist. "I rather imagine Dick Van Dyke in his chitty-chitty bang-bang motor car would feel right at home in this clinic. How are we supposed to carry on a conversation with that thing clacking in the background?"

Ed chuckled at his own image as the teletype pounded louder and more rapidly, almost as if it were demanding the last word.

"Don't worry about it," I countered in a voice decidedly louder than it had been in previous conversations. "Sue and I will do most of the talking. We can always resort to arguing the way we did in our first few meetings."

Ed grinned at the allusion to those strained earlier sessions. He was able to smile, I thought, at least in part because his blood pressure had dropped so markedly. "What's all the rigmarole for, Sue?" he asked, while brushing aside the electrode wires that were monitoring his heartbeat and wrist pulse.

"It's a way of measuring pulse-transit time," she replied, "which means that it records the amount of time it takes your pulse to reach your wrist after each heartbeat. We think it may give us an indirect way of measuring your blood pressure without having to stop our conversations every ten minutes to measure it with a stethoscope. Several investigators have recently suggested that the time it takes the pulse wave to travel from your heart to your wrist is influenced by blood pressure. So we thought we'd give it a try. It sure beats inserting a catheter into your artery to measure your pressure directly, don't you think?"

Without waiting for Ed's response, she added, "Look at all the trouble we've gone to in order to talk to you without interruptions! Those electrode wires on your chest and wrist send your heartbeat signal to a polygraph, which then transmits it to the computer. A clock in the computer starts whirring after each heartbeat, recording the time it takes the pulse to arrive at your wrist. And bang! That's the chitty-chitty-bang-bang you hear."

"Great, that's just great!" Ed exclaimed in feigned annoyance. "Now we won't be interrupted every ten minutes! We can just stop talking all together!" The teletype began to pound more rapidly as he continued to speak. "That noise would drive up anyone's blood pressure. Is this some perverse experiment you've devised to stop the progress I'm making?"

His question was, I thought, his way of reminding us of the progress he had made, for by now we were focusing not just on lowering his pressure but on reducing the dosage of his hypertensive medications. Originally we had not really considered this latter possibility, but had initiated therapy to persuade him to take his medicines regularly. Noncompliance with his drug regimens had been one of Ed's major problems, and our original goal had been to help him lower his pressure with medication in order to minimize his chances of having a stroke. Yet now after four months of therapy, his pressure had dropped so dramatically that his referring neurologist thought it worthwhile to experiment with lowering Ed's medication. The risks seemed minimal. If his pressure rose again, he could quickly increase his drug dosage. Furthermore, any sudden rise in pressure might convince Ed once and for all of the necessity of complying with his physician's prescriptions.

I quietly reviewed the chart of his home recordings of blood pressure, while Dr. Thomas measured his pressure with her stethoscope. The teletype continued to pound with every heartbeat. The drop in pressure at home correlated exactly with the lowering of pressure in the clinic.

"Beautiful!" Dr. Thomas commented, as she removed the stethoscope from her ears. "It's 130 over 75! Couldn't be better."

"It must be your breathing exercises," I said, adding, as the teletype printer slowed, "That combined with dealing with your loneliness."

"Good heavens! You never give up on that theory, do you?" Ed parried. He had learned to counter notions about human relationships and blood pressure almost as quickly as we suggested them. It was like a chess game in which our every move was quickly countered by a countermove of his. In all of Ed's sparring, however, one fact was glaringly obvious. While, as I have said, he was unusually sophisticated, highly educated, and sensitive, Ed seemed oblivious to his own emotional sensitivity, frequently denying that specific topics bothered him even though his blood pressure revealed a different reality. He appeared to be totally disconnected from his body and thus from the feelings that accompanied major changes in his cardiovascular system.

Ed continued, "I wish I could go along with you on your loneliness theory, but I really think you're barking up the wrong tree." He then leaned forward in his chair as the printer began to pound more rapidly.

"How's your relationship with Valerie coming along?" Dr. Thomas interjected.

Ed became animated and began to speak more rapidly and to

breathe more irregularly as well. He explained that he and Valerie had decided to see each other on a regular basis, and that they had just spent a very pleasant weekend together. The printer began to pound noticeably faster as he described his weekend, and Dr. Thomas stopped the conversation. Ed had grown accustomed to such interruptions during our therapy, knowing in advance precisely what she would say. They smiled broadly at each other as she quietly instructed him, "Breathe!"—the now-familiar command in our strategy of titrating the conversation to lower his blood pressure.

The pulse-transit device had been introduced at this session in the hope that it would make our strategy more precise. If the device worked, it would significantly improve our ability both to detect changes in blood pressure and, as a result, to gauge emotionally stressful topics more accurately.

Pausing in response to Dr. Thomas's instructions, Ed took several deep breaths. As he began to breathe deeply, he was able to hear the printer's pounding slow down. He pointed his thumb toward the teletype without saying a word. Then, pausing a bit longer to breathe deeply, he looked at us with a surprised smile and murmured, "You know, it's hard to remember to breathe when you're talking about something of interest."

Toward the end of the session, at a point when we were all tired of the hammering of the teletype machine, I asked half in jest, "Well, did you learn anything today?" It was an indirect way of apologizing for the inconvenience Ed had endured in the experiment. It hardly seemed worth all the effort. The maze of wires and the pounding teletype did not seem useful. There had to be another way to measure blood pressure.

"You bet!" Ed exclaimed loudly, as Dr. Thomas lifted up his shirt to remove the electrodes from his chest. "You had that thing rigged against me. Every time I went to talk, it pounded louder and faster. It's a great way to keep me quiet in these sessions, if that's what you wanted to do!"

Dr. Thomas laughed. Perhaps it was our collective imagination, but it did seem that Ed was right. Every time he spoke, the teletype seemed to pound faster and louder.

"It would be nice," I responded, "if we could monitor your blood pressure with a catheter—but if you don't mind, we'll stick with this monitoring system for a few more sessions."

Ed's pressure rose about 10 percent the first week after he reduced his blood pressure medicines, and then began its slow course downward once again. There was only one problem. We still had no idea what was succeeding in lowering his blood pressure.

For six sessions we continued to use the pulse-transit-timer but moved the printer into an adjacent room, so that its noise was barely audible. Yet, on the whole, the experiment was disappointing. Instead of providing us with data about blood pressure once every ten minutes, the device buried us under an avalanche of numbers that gave us the milliseconds of pulse-transit time for every beat of Ed's heart. There had to be some manageable middle ground. Several months after initiating this experiment, we inadvertently found it.

THE HUMAN MACHINE AND
THE BLOOD-PRESSURE MACHINE

At about the same time we became aware of a new device—a computer—that permitted the automatic and repetitive determination of blood pressure and heart rate. The cuff on the arm periodically inflated and the device displayed a person's blood pressure and heart rate digitally from minute to minute.* This device was exciting not only because it permitted the relatively unobtrusive determination of these measurements, but did so in a way that permitted dialogue to continue uninterrupted. It also permitted far more frequent determinations of blood pressure than were possible using the traditional stethoscope. Prior to this device, the only reliable way to obtain similar information required invasive procedures, the placement of indwelling arterial catheters.

"Aha! I see you have a new toy!" Ed greeted the appearance of the computerized blood-pressure machine with every bit as much curiosity and enthusiasm as we had. "Just when I'm about to finish

* The Dinamap automated blood-pressure machine is manufactured by the Critikon Corporation and was donated to our clinic by Dr. Maynard Ramsey and Dr. Bernard Krause of the Critikon Corporation. In addition to providing us with several of these computer devices, they also provided us with technical information. We are deeply grateful for their generosity, without which we would have been unable to carry out our research studies.

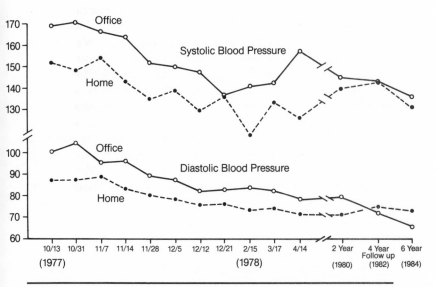

Figure 5.1. Blood-pressure changes at home and during therapy for a hypertensive patient, and measures of pressure during six years of follow-up recording. Each point on the chart represents the average of repeated measurements of blood pressure. Note that the changes in home pressure corresponded closely to changes occurring in the clinic; though, in general, home pressures were usually lower. (Home pressures were always taken when the patient was quiet, while laboratory pressures usually occurred during conversations.

treatment, you bring in the fancy stuff. Ah, well, perhaps the next patient won't have to be wired up like our astronauts in space."

I smiled at Ed's reference to the fact that our therapy was nearing an end. His blood pressure had come down to normal levels, and he had successfully withdrawn from all his medicines. As shown in figure 5.1, in seven months of therapy he had come a long way.*

"Still gaining weight?" Dr. Thomas asked, smiling, as Ed stepped off the scale. "What's the matter? Are you afraid Valerie might find you irresistible if you began to lose weight?"

* Figure 5.1 also includes follow-up blood-pressure readings from 1977 to 1984 to show that Ed has continued to control his blood pressure successfully.

During our therapy, though his blood pressure had fallen steadily, Ed had gained eight pounds.

"I swear," Ed protested, as I wrapped the blood-pressure cuff around his arm, "I gain weight by just thinking about food."

"Maybe it's your diuretic," she interjected. "Now that you're off your medicines, you may retain fluid for a while. We'll just have to monitor you closely. Watch your sodium intake, and after a while your body should adjust."

Ed smiled in surprise as the computer automatically began to inflate the pressure cuff on his arm. I waited eagerly for it to register the first blood pressure, feeling as I do when someone is opening a gift from me. Ed sat quietly smiling as the cuff loosened its grip on his arm. The red lights on the front panel of the computer flashed their first recordings:

Systolic 148
Diastolic 78
Heart Rate 82
Mean Arterial Pressure 98*

"I'll be darned!" Ed exploded in excitement. "That's quite a toy. The readings seem a bit high compared to those I've taken at home, but it sure beats all the wires and the clacking of the teletype machine we had a few months ago."

Then, shifting the topic abruptly back, he continued light-heartedly as the cuff reinflated, "Valerie says she doesn't object to my being heavy, but she agrees with you that if I lost twenty pounds it would probably increase her competition. If I took off twenty pounds, quite a few ladies might take a second look. So it's a bit of a quandary for me, you see."

The numbers flashed again and this time were all startlingly higher:

Systolic 162
Diastolic 91
Heart Rate 85
Mean Arterial Pressure 115

Ed caught the puzzled look on my face and glanced at the numbers. He then smiled and commented: "That was the fastest

---

* *Mean arterial pressure* equals diastolic pressure plus two thirds of the difference between systolic and diastolic pressure.

cure that wasn't. According to the computer, we'll have to postpone the end of therapy a bit longer."

Observing that Ed had begun to speak more rapidly, and that his blood pressure had risen up to hypertensive levels, Dr. Thomas interrupted the conversation and instructed him, "Breathe!"

Ed remained quiet and breathed deeply as the cuff again inflated. This time the numbers dropped dramatically:

Systolic 138
Diastolic 72
Heart Rate 76
Mean Arterial Pressure 93

"You see," she said, "if you just breath properly you can keep your blood pressure down."

Ed countered, "That's quite a demonstration! But are you sure that thing's working? Blood pressure can't jump around like that. I mean, when I've taken it at home after deep breathing, the numbers drop a few millimeters but nothing like that."

Again the computer registered its findings:

Systolic 152
Diastolic 86
Heart Rate 83
Mean Arterial Pressure 106

Ed's blood pressure had risen once again!

The computer had arrived only the previous afternoon; and as I watched the rapid changes in his blood pressure, I knew we would have to correlate the machine against pressure measured with a catheter.* Nonetheless, Ed's failure to breathe when he spoke was noticeable, and I asked, "After all this time in therapy don't you think emotions can drive up your blood pressure?"

"Sure," Ed answered quickly, as the cuff began to inflate once again. "There's no doubt emotions and stress can drive up anyone's blood pressure, but for the life of me, I don't feel emotionally aroused. If it was an earlier session, then sure, I'd grant you at times my pressure would have gone sky-high. But I feel quite relaxed today, and my blood pressure was 128 over 68 at home early this morning." Then laughing briefly, he added an afterthought,

---

* Subsequent experiments with catheterized patients did convince us that the machine was highly accurate and reliable.

"Well, maybe there're a few stressors I'm still unaware of."

The numbers flashed again:

Systolic 170
Diastolic 98
Heart Rate 85
Mean Arterial Pressure 118

Again, his pressure had risen markedly, and again Dr. Thomas almost shouted to Ed, "Breathe!" As he obeyed, I tried to counter his logical argument. Then the numbers appeared again:

Systolic 132
Diastolic 72
Heart Rate 76
Mean Arterial Pressure 92

His mean pressure had fallen more than 25 percent after one minute of deep breathing. Ed's blood pressure was bouncing around like a yo-yo. I, too, began to question the accuracy of the computer.

For the remainder of the session, we chatted back and forth, with similar results. Ed's blood pressure continued to fluctuate dramatically. Late in the session our scepticism about the computer's accuracy had grown so strong that Dr. Thomas began to measure his pressure with a stethoscope while the computer simultaneously gave its own readings. Her readings closely paralleled those recorded on the machine.

The next day we began systematically to check its accuracy. It turned out to be highly reliable, leaving us with only one conclusion. Ed's blood pressure was fluctuating far more rapidly and drastically than we had ever believed possible when he was talking to us. The next question concerned the nature of his blood-pressure reactivity. Were such changes peculiar to him or to hypertensive patients in general, or do other people respond in the same way?

To answer this question, we quickly measured the blood pressure of twenty laboratory staff members and found that everyone's blood pressure shifted substantially when engaged in conversation. When people were quiet, their blood pressure appeared to be almost always lower than it was when they were speaking.

At the time we viewed these findings as confirming, by way of sophisticated technology, those of earlier investigators: that is, that emotions can quickly drive up blood pressure; although the rapidity of the rises was surprising. Since Alexander, Weiner, Reiser, Wolf, Wolff, and other investigators had shown that interviews with hypertensive patients could lead to marked elevations and wide fluctuations in blood pressure, and theorized that the emotional arousal inherent in their clinical interviews was the major factor altering blood pressure, we assumed that the computer had simply shown the phenomenon to be pervasive: not only hypertensives', but literally everyone's blood pressure goes up when one is interviewed. We were still not able to see the full implication of our obervations.

All of these considerations led us to feel more at ease about Ed's blood-pressure fluctuations. After all, his basal or resting pressure measured at home and in the laboratory had fallen steadily and dramatically in the past seven months. And he no longer needed antihypertensive medicines to control his pressure. The following week I showed him how my own blood pressure fluctuated while we chatted together, and assured him that his fluctuations were normal. I told him that Dr. Thomas would continue to see him for routine check-ups every two months, since I was about to leave for a six months' sabbatical in Ireland. And it was there—across the Atlantic—that quite unexpectedly I found the key to the language of the heart.

AN INFANT'S CRY

I had planned to explore a variety of aspects of psychosomatic disease in Ireland. Circumstances, however, drastically altered my plans, and I found myself spending all of my time in a most unlikely laboratory—the newborn nursery of the National Maternity Hospital in Dublin.

For several months I had the opportunity to monitor the blood pressure of a group of newborns. Before the advent of computer-assisted devices, it had been virtually impossible to measure diastolic blood pressure in infants. One simply could not hear the muffled sounds of blood pulsating through their tiny arteries, and little was known about the dynamics of neonatal blood pressure. Now I was spending my sabbatical watching Irish babies sleeping soundly in their basinettes while the computer measured their heart rate and blood pressure. Hour after hour in this fabled land of gregarious people, I sat alone, talking to no one but fat, red-cheeked Irish babies who ever so often would open their eyes and stare at me for a few minutes in bewilderment before falling back to sleep. There were a few moments of diversion when they screamed hungrily for their fair share of milk. Then their blood pressure would rise markedly; and their systolic and diastolic pressures would frequently double from their somnolent levels and then drop back to baseline when they fell asleep again. And the longer the babies cried, the longer their blood pressure remained elevated.

Even though I understood that no one had ever measured blood pressure in newborns in this manner before, at first the broader implications of my observations eluded me. It was only after several months of repeated observations and further reflection that I was struck finally by the consistent association between crying and blood pressure. My attention had been focused on fluctuations in blood pressure itself, rather than on those factors that might be influencing it. At first the consistent rise in blood pressure during periods of crying seemed perfectly logical, simply a consequence of increased emotional arousal and increased physical activity.

Suddenly, though, it occurred to me that the blood-pressure elevations when the babies cried were similar to the changes in Ed when he spoke. Were the babies attempting to speak? Or was Ed crying? Did the simple act of human communication have a fundamental influence on blood pressure, the heart, and the human circulatory system?

The more I reflected on these questions, the broader the implications of the links between human communication and blood pressure began to appear. It is not just hypertensive adults like Ed who increase their blood pressure when they speak; babies do it, too, when they cry! It is vocalizing that is crucial! It is communicating that is important! Like a puzzle suddenly fitting together for the first time, it occurred to me that the computer was showing us something different from what Alexander, Wolf and Wolff, and many other doctors thought they had seen. Even in our coronary-care research, we had ignored the fundamental fact that *who* was speaking—nurse or patient—might be far more important in terms of a patient's cardiac changes than *what* they were talking about! I recalled once again the pulse-transit teletype machine pounding out the digital data whenever Ed spoke, and, for the first time, understood its message. Ed was quite right! It had been rigged to keep him quiet because it was directly linked to his speaking. The computer machine had also been giving us the exact same message. Blood pressure was not just fluctuating with the waxing and waning of human emotions. The pressure increases were directly linked to speaking. Whenever Ed spoke his pressure rose. And so did everyone else's in the laboratory. It was not just the emotional content of one's conversation that was elevating blood pressure when people communicated with one another. It was talking itself. The response we had been staring at so blandly for years was far more basic than we had realized. It was not just the emotional content of conversations that was important to the heart; talking itself was vital.

I began to think about Ed, the precision of his language, his loneliness, and his hypertension in an entirely new way. Maybe there was a baby inside Ed crying to be heard? As the infants screamed their hungry protest in the Irish National Hospital, I began to wonder whether Ed's words were really the coded cries of an infant. Was human dialogue a replacement for the umbilical cord that is cut at birth? Were we connected—biologically—to one another by our words and cries in a way that influenced our very survival? Perhaps Ed's hypertension was not just the result of emotional struggles he had in his adult life? Maybe he used words— even precise words—in a way that could not be understood, in a way that concealed rather than revealed what he needed to communicate? Did he lower his blood pressure because we heard his cry and decoded its meaning without being aware we had done so? Had we somehow managed to hear the language of his heart without being aware of it?

CHAPTER 6

Examining the Cardiovascular–
Communication Links

> The contributions of chronic arousal to mortality
> cannot be mitigated solely within a medical frame-
> work because the forces that generate arousal are
> powerful and deeply ingrained in our social struc-
> ture and culture. Nor could we, even if it were
> desirable, return to a primitive life style. We can
> and must, however, move toward a more reason-
> able balance between work and play, striving and
> living, individuality and interdependency. At least
> this is what the radio-immune assays and chro-
> matograms seem to be telling us!
> —Peter Sterling and Joe Eyer,
> "Biological Basis of Stress-Related Mortality"

The capacity to speak is the chief distinguishing characteristic of
the species *Homo sapiens* and the most common feature of our
everyday lives. Except for breathing, there is nothing we human
beings do more routinely and repetitively than communicate to
one another. If, as the computers in the clinic indicated, speech
itself is powerfully linked to the cardiovascular system, then speech
itself has to have a major influence on cardiovascular health.

Once we recognized the relationship between talking and blood
pressure, we began to wonder how we had ignored the phenomenon
for so long, even though we had often observed it in our twenty
years of research on human relationships and cardiovascular health.
Nor were we peculiar in this oversight. For all of the billions of
dollars spent in this country to isolate various factors influencing

cardiovascular health, researchers had failed to notice the vital role of common everyday human speech.

At first we speculated that the enforced silence of the blood-pressure monitoring procedure might have blinded investigators to the links between communication and the cardiovascular system. This interpretation was tempered by our realization that the blood pressure of tens of thousands of hospitalized patients had been continuously monitored with catheters: surely the phenomenon would have been noticed there. Of course, most of these patients were very sick or comatose, and thus unlikely to have engaged in conversation. Not only had the blood-pressure response to talking been missed, so also had its component, heart rate, which does not require silence to be measured. Literally billions of polygraphic measurements of heart rate had been taken in hospital units and university laboratories, yet links to talking were similarly overlooked. Indeed, the sheer mass of such measurements made us hesitant about our own observations on the computer long after we were thoroughly convinced of their reliability. Clearly something other than technical limitations had obscured the relationship between blood pressure and talking.

Certainly aspects of the relationship had been noted previously. Scientists had long since refined polygraphic techniques to gauge phenomena such as "lie detection." The diagnostic power of these techniques lies in the reactivity of the human body to verbal answers. Whether a person is "speaking" the truth or lying can be differentiated by the pattern of changes in his or her autonomic nervous system. Yet these changes were considered in a framework in which human speech was seen as one of many components of the global phenomenon of emotional arousal. With a similar point of view, as I have said, investigators like Alexander and Wolf likewise attended to the emotional content of patient conversations rather than to talking itself. Scientific understanding of the autonomic nervous system had combined with theories about emotional arousal to dominate the way in which investigators and clinicians alike thought about human communication. Thus, human speech was seen more as an epiphenomenon—as one of many factors subsumed under the central phenomenon of emotional arousal—than as a process crucial in its own right.

And this perspective did far more than blind investigators to the special nature of human speech. It also encouraged scientists to develop models of the physiology of emotions based on animal research, guided by the assumption that such models could be applied to human beings as well. Darwin's notions of evolution, and the belief that the difference between humans and higher animals was quantitative rather than qualitative, also reinforced these fundamental attitudes. Since animals cannot speak, and yet an elaborate physiology of emotions had nevertheless been worked out on them, there appeared little reason to assume that talking itself would be important in the physiology of human emotions.

It was this general framework, and the deeply rooted philosophical ideas supporting it, that guided investigators who observed phenomena similar to our own. Dr. Stanley Kaplan and his associates, for example, noticed in 1960 that, after hypertensive subjects had finished speaking, their blood pressure remained elevated for an extended period and that there was a significant correlation between the hostile content of their speech and elevations in their diastolic blood pressure.[1] In similar fashion, Dr. George Innes and his colleagues observed that, after clinical interviews, hypertensives were different from people with normal blood pressure. Even when they talked at the same speed as normotensive individuals, the blood pressure of hypertensive patients remained elevated longer when they were silent once again.[2] In a study in which blood pressure was measured directly with an indwelling catheter, Dr. Rolf Adler and his colleagues reported in 1976 that blood pressure of hypertensives rose in response not just to the emotional content of conversations but to the rate of speech and the number of words spoken by a patient. These investigators deduced, however, that this phenomenon was peculiar to hypertensive individuals.[3] Following up on the studies in the mid-1950s by Meyer Friedman and Ray Rosenman on the links between the Type A personality and coronary heart disease (see pages 140–45),[4] Dr. Ted Dembrowski again commented on the strong relationship between the verbal behavior of Type A personalities and their overall elevations in blood pressure.[5] Indeed, in many studies that had explored the link between psychological stress and cardiovascular changes, subtracting backward or doing other forms of mathematics aloud was used as the stressor. Yet in all these studies the stress of the task rather than vocalization was seen as the crucial factor. In these and similar studies, talking was viewed in the context of emotional arousal, rather than as a process directly linked to the human cardiovascular system.

A similar perspective dominated our own studies. We had spent several years directly studying the effects of conversations on the heart rate and the heart rhythm of coronary patients and yet missed the most crucial aspect of the response.[6] To be sure, we observed significant increases in heart rate in patients when they talked to us. Each and every facet of our conversations was scrutinized in terms of its emotional content; each and every minute of conversation and each minute of heart rate were painstakingly examined in an effort to isolate various physiological, psychological, emotional, and interactional factors that might potentially influence a patient's heart rate and rhythm. Yet not once had we attended to the most elementary aspect of our dialogue: that is, to *who* was speaking. To us, *what* was discussed, the emotional content of the conversations, appeared much more important. Even when the pulse-transit time hammered at us when Ed spoke, we had looked elsewhere. More remarkably, we had paid no attention when the blood-pressure computer itself unequivocally showed the marked elevations in pressure when Ed spoke, and revealed that the pressure of everyone else in our laboratory similarly rose. Ed's heart was literally crying out for our attention for over a year before we were able to listen. Yet perhaps that was the most fascinating aspect of the entire struggle. Having set out to prove to Ed that his interpersonal life was crucially linked to his hypertension, for well over a year we had completely ignored the phenomenon that explained the linkage.

THE MODEL FOR THE BLOOD PRESSURE-COMMUNICATION RESPONSE

One of the reasons the link between blood pressure and talking finally emerged with compelling clarity was the decision we made about the empirical model designed to study the phenomenon in a systematic and consistent fashion. The model emerged from two basic considerations. First and foremost, computer technology gave us a way of measuring blood pressure while simultaneously permitting people to talk. Second, it seemed that blood pressure ought to be examined in a way that simulated the clarity of the newborn communications I had heard in the Dublin nursery. The context of that neonatal environment, the long periods of quiet slumber that were suddenly disrupted by the piercing cries of an infant, made the concomitant surges in blood pressure impossible to ignore. We felt that an analogous context ought to be used with adults, one where a period of quiet would be followed by talking, to be following by a quiet period once again. Since infants usually do not engage in the "stop and go" or "switching" back-and-forth dialogue that is typical of adult conversations, we decided to isolate *who* was speaking as well as *what* was being discussed. In a sense, this model implied that adult language could be examined both as a cry and as a highly evolved and sophisticated message.

Thus, we began systematically to monitor blood pressure and heart rate when subjects were quiet, when they spoke to us, and when they were quiet once again. It was a simple model we eventually used to measure blood pressure and heart rate in thousands of people, and its very simplicity ultimately led us to think about the human heart in a new way.

Experiment 1. Once a model had been worked out, it was simply a matter of beginning our research on the populations most immediately accessible to us in our clinic—our own graduate nursing and medical students. In the first experiment, six healthy female graduate nursing students, between the ages of twenty-five and thirty-eight, were asked to volunteer to have their blood pressure taken in their seminar class when they were quiet as well as when they talked to their fellow students about anything of interest to them. They were told that the purpose of the demonstration was to monitor blood pressure and heart rate with an automated computer device.[7]

As illustrated in figure 6.1, the blood pressure of all six nurses rapidly and significantly rose when they spoke and just as quickly lowered to baseline levels when they were quiet once again. The blood pressure of three of the six nurses increased to ranges considered borderline hypertensive as soon as they began to speak, while the heart rate of five of the six increased to over one hundred

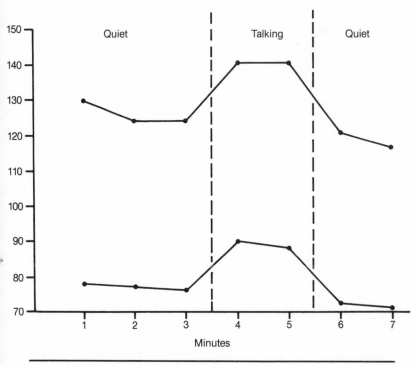

Figure 6.1.   The effects of talking on the systolic and the diastolic blood pressure of six nurses.

beats per minute—rates far in excess both of their resting levels and of the physical demands of speaking.

Though these students knew each other well, had often spoken in class in the past, and did not appear to be stressed, all six exhibited significant elevations in blood pressure and heart rate as soon as they spoke to their classmates. Curiously, the nurse with the largest heart-rate increases had the lowest blood-pressure increases, while the nurse with the least increase in heart rate exhibited the greatest proportional increases in blood pressure.

No demands were made about the specific content of their communications. Each woman talked calmly about some of the problems she was confronting with patients in her daily hospital

TABLE 6.1

*Comparison of Average Blood Pressure and Heart Rate of
10 Nursing and Medical Students for Experimental Phases*

Minutes of Study	Quiet Baseline (minute 3)	First Talking (minute 4)	Second Talking (minute 5)	Return to Quiet (minute 6)
Average mean arterial pressure	92	100	97	92
Systolic pressure	121	127	130	121
Diastolic pressure	75	82	79	71
Heart rate	82	94	86	78

All figures have been rounded off to the nearest decimal point. All increases in blood pressure and heart rate while speaking are statistically significant.

duties. Though these topics did not appear to be personally stressful, and all six nurses smiled as they talked, their heart rate and blood pressure suggested that the topics they were discussing were stressful. Because of the magnitude of the changes, we hypothesized that they might be explained by the stress of speaking before a small group of peers or before their teacher.

Experiment 2. In order to assess this possibility, a second similar experiment was designed in which only experimenter and individual student were in the room together. In order to help make the experimental situation even more comfortable, a fellow graduate student was chosen as the experimenter. Ten additional medical and graduate nursing students volunteered to have their blood pressure and heart rate recorded while they rested quietly and when they spoke. The format duplicated the first experimental protocol. During the speaking phase, they were asked to talk about themselves or describe how their day was going for a couple of minutes.

Again, as in the first study, all the students exhibited significant rises in blood pressure and heart rate as soon as they began to talk; and these readings just as quickly dropped when the students were quiet once again (see table 6.1).

Although the students chose to talk about a wide variety of topics, the pattern of increases while speaking was consistent across the entire group. Again, as in the first experiment, the magnitude of the changes was surprising. Unlike the first experiment when they spoke in front of a small group, this time they were speaking alone to one of their peers, a classmate, who was simply acting as an assistant helping to conduct the experiment. Nor did they appear to be psychologically or emotionally stressed in the slightest by the task. And even if the experimental situation itself were stressful, it seemed as if such stress would have increased resting blood pressure levels far more than levels while they were talking. In addition, since all students appeared to be in excellent physical shape, and most reported that they exercised regularly, we assumed their blood pressure would be less reactive to something as ostensibly innocuous as talking about their daily routine to a fellow student.

In light of both the consistency and the magnitude of these changes, we began to wonder whether they were caused by the act of communicating to another person or simply by vocalizing itself.

Experiment 3. To answer this question, as well as to evaluate other potential hidden factors such as the sex of experimenter and volunteers, twenty additional student volunteers (medical and nursing students) were recruited for a third experiment. Ten male and ten female students were randomly assigned to either a male or a female experimenter. Again, as in the previous study, the experimenters were fellow students of equal status. Each person was told that his or her blood pressure and heart rate were going to be automatically recorded both when the experimenter was in the room and when each was alone. In addition, these volunteers were told that, under each of these conditions, they would be asked to remain silent at certain times and then would be asked to read a book aloud.[8]

As shown in table 6.2, blood pressure and heart rate were recorded at one-minute intervals for thirty-five consecutive minutes under a variety of conditions. Each person was left alone for fifteen of these recording minutes and then with the experimenter for the next twenty measurements.

In the reading phase, the students were asked to read aloud from a bland school text, both when they were alone and when an experimenter was present in the room. During the talking phase, the experimenter asked each student to tell a little about himself or herself. During the listening phase, the experimenter gave a

TABLE 6.2

Sequence of Experimental Procedure

Subject Alone (taps signal change of condition)							Subject with Experimenter Present						
Time (minutes)													
1 2 3 4 5	6 7 8	9 10	11 12 13	14 15	16 17	18 19 20	21 22	23 24 25	26 27 28	29 30	31 32	33	34 35
Quiet	Reading	Quiet	Reading	Quiet	Quiet	Reading	Quiet	Talking	Listening	Responding to Inquiry	Sharing Feelings	Pulse	Quiet

three-minute summary of the experiment. Then each person was asked whether he or she understood the experiment or what each perceived the experiment to be about. Finally in the "sharing feelings" stage, each person was asked to relate his or her feelings about the experiment in general. There followed a minute of pulse palpation to evaluate the effects of silent tactile interaction on their cardiovascular system.

As shown in table 6.3, blood pressure and heart rate rose rapidly every time these students vocalized. Whether they read a book aloud all alone in a room or when the experimenter was present, the effects were similar. When the experimenter entered the room while the person remained quiet, or talked to the student or took his or her pulse, there were no significant differences from the blood-pressure readings when a student was quiet all alone in the room. As soon as a student spoke or read a book aloud to the experimenter, however, there was an immediate and significant rise in blood pressure and heart rate. Surprisingly, talking about feelings did not increase a student's pressure more than simply reading a book aloud: that is, all verbal activities elicited statistically equal rises in blood pressure and heart rate, while all quiet periods were accompanied by significantly lower blood-pressure readings. There were no differences in the magnitude of the cardiovascular changes due to the sex either of the experimenter or of the students.

In each of these first three studies, vocalization was clearly linked to rapid increases in blood pressure and heart rate. In all three experiments, every effort was made to minimize the stress of the situation, and the experimental atmosphere was kept as casual as possible. In addition, all of the volunteers were, as I have said, healthy normotensive graduate students in medicine and nursing, and most of them reported taking regular exercise.

The fact that healthy young students exhibited such marked increases in blood pressure when speaking naturally led to the question whether hypertensive patients would exhibit similar changes. This question was of particular interest not only because of the potential link between talking and high blood pressure, but also because physicians were unaware of this relationship. It was obvious that many patients talk to their physicians out of either friendliness or nervousness just before their blood pressure is measured. In light of our findings, it appeared that such verbal

TABLE 6.3

Comparison of Average Blood Pressure and Heart Rate of 20 Subjects for Experimental Phases*

Average Minutes of Study	Baseline (5)	First Minute Reading (6)	Average Reading with Experimenter (18, 19, 20)	First Minute Reading with Experimenter (18)	First Minute Talking (23)	Average Talking (23, 24, 25)	Average Responding to Inquiry (29, 30)	Sharing Feeling (31, 32)	Pulse Taking (33)
Average mean arterial pressure	87†	94	92	94	91	93	94	93	88†
Systolic pressure	116†	127	127	121	122	121	123	125	118†
Diastolic pressure	68†	75	73	74	73	74	74	74	70†
Heart rate	73†	80	78	79	80	78	78	75	68

* All figures have been rounded off to the nearest decimal point.
† Except for these figures, all others are statistically significant.

behavior would significantly influence one's blood pressure as it was being measured by a physician, and that ignorance of this influence could lead to highly misleading information about blood pressure. ("Impossible!" a senior cardiologist recently exclaimed, in the presence of several colleagues, when this problem was explained to him: "You mean that for the past thirty years I've been listening to patients' blood pressure, something as simple as talking could have been altering the pressure readings I was getting? That's impossible! Surely I would have noticed it.")

Over and above a general lack of awareness about the link between talking and blood pressure, another aspect of doctor-patient interaction was even more troubling. It was part of entrenched medical folklore that emotions and anxiety can cause a patient's blood pressure to be higher than normal. Virtually every physician and nurse understood that, whenever they obtained high blood-pressure readings from a patient, they ought routinely to take a second reading after calming the patient down for five to ten minutes. Clinicians who followed conventional psychiatric wisdom might very well assume that the best way to get a patient to relax would be to prompt him or her to talk about any troubling problems. This idea, conventionally known as "emotional catharsis," was commonly understood to be a useful way to alleviate anxiety. Our observations, however, made it clear that if a physician chose this strategy and prompted a patient to talk, then the next blood-pressure reading would be considerably higher than the first. On the other hand, if the doctor talked or left the patient quietly alone for five minutes, and then measured the pressure again, the second reading was likely to be lower. Thus, one simple strategic decision about whether an emotionally upset patient should talk or be quiet could influence a physician's judgment about a patient's hypertension. Such clinical implications led to a fourth study.

Experiment 4. In order to evaluate the effects of talking on blood pressure in a medical setting, thirty hypertensive and fifteen normotensive adults were studied in a physician's office. The patients were chosen as they appeared one after another in a doctor's office for what usually were routine medical visits. As shown in table 6.4, the patients who volunteered to participate in the study varied in age, race, and sex. All of the hypertensive patients were in the

TABLE 6.4

Mean Arterial Pressures for 30 Hypertensive Subjects during Quiet and Talking Periods

| | | | | Experimental Minutes | | | | | |
| | | | | Quiet† | | Talking | | Quiet | |
Subject	Age	Sex/Race	Medications*	3	4	1	2	5	6
1	56	M B	D, M, I	109	104	110	118	113	113
2	60	M W	None	101	99	143	139	105	101
3	61	F W	D, T	109	110	154	137	107	113
4	32	F W	None	107	106	122	117	122	109
5	59	F W	D	85	99	105	105	95	90
6	42	F W	I	123	112	133	160	118	109
7	43	F W	D	85	87	91	92	87	81
8	48	M W	D, I	123	125	179	132	125	117
9	54	M B	D, M, A	82	84	104	93	104	87
10	46	F W	None	102	110	102	103	93	86
11	52	M B	D, M	130	119	180	197	116	118
12	35	M W	I	111	115	126	118	112	100
13	50	M W	D	102	90	115	104	101	100
14	63	M W	M	105	105	100	101	92	90
15	53	F W	B	100	102	117	120	107	97
16	62	F W	D	97	88	96	96	93	101
17	27	M W	D	85	80	89	89	87	82
18	77	M W	D, T, A	89	87	112	96	90	95
19	65	M W	M, T	88	83	88	90	85	85
20	76	F W	D	88	96	105	102	86	93
21	69	F W	D	102	93	107	112	88	95
22	66	M B	D, I	87	90	100	105	97	92
23	76	M W	D	104	105	109	110	106	112
24	65	F W	D	108	109	124	122	118	112
25	60	F B	D	102	98	98	111	96	84
26	65	M B	D, I	123	114	106	146	105	104
27	55	M W	L	116	109	122	116	117	111
28	56	M W	D	118	113	128	134	118	127
29	47	M B	None	107	102	111	161	118	114
30	27	F W	None	88	98	101	117	110	93
			M T A D						
Means	54.9		5 6 2 19	102.4	101.1	115.9	118.2	103.7	100.4

* Codes for drug type: D = diuretic; M = Minipress; T = tranquilizer; A = Aldomet; B = Butazalodine; I = Inderal, Lopressor; L = Lanoxin.
† Quiet 3, 4 are the last two blood-pressure quiet periods before the talking measurements.

clinic for a routine medical check-up, and twenty-five of them were already taking a variety of antihypertensive medicines. The normotensive individuals either had come for a routine medical check-up or had accompanied someone else who was using the medical facility. None of the normotensive subjects were taking any medicines, and none had ever been told he or she had a problem with blood pressure.[9] During the talking phase of the experiment, each person was asked by a graduate student experimenter to "tell me about your work or tell me how your day is going." As in the previous experiments, every effort was made to keep the atmosphere casual and relaxed.

As happened among nursing and medical students, the blood pressure and the heart rate of both hypertensive and normotensive individuals significanty rose as soon as they began to speak. Furthermore, none of the antihypertensive medicines the patients were taking appeared to effectively block the pressure from rising. Even more revealing was the magnitude of the increases in the hypertensive patients. Some of these increases were truly extraordinary. In subject 11, for example, a mean arterial pressure of 180 equals a blood pressure of approximately 200/148. One minute before this patient spoke, his mean arterial pressure was 119. It rose to 180 and then to 197 as he continued to speak, before plummeting down to 116 when he was quiet. His responses after being asked how his day was going had caused an alarming rise in his blood pressure and an equally rapid fall when he was quiet again. Even more surprising was the fact that none of the patients seemed to have the slightest awareness of these pressure changes. These people appeared not only calm—most smiled and expressed interest in the computer we were using to take their pressures—but also completely oblivious to the vascular changes occurring inside their bodies.

Sixteen of the patients elevated their pressures into hypertensive ranges (150/95) while speaking; even though in most cases, their blood pressure was fairly well controlled with drugs when they were quiet. Patient 2, for example, had a resting quiet blood pressure of 157/86, which rapidly rose to 200/120 within a minute after he began to describe his job.

Yet of all the findings that emerged from this study, the most intriguing was the very strong correlation observed among the

TABLE 6.5

*Blood Pressures and Heart Rates of Four Experimental
Subjects in Each Period**

Cardiac Measure	Group	Quiet	Talking	Quiet
Mean arterial pressure	normotensive	88	97	90
	hypertensive	109	122	105
Systolic blood pressure	normotensive	125	133	128
	hypertensive	151	165	152
Diastolic blood pressure	normotensive	71	81	71
	hypertensive	87	102	86
Heart rate	normotensive	76	81	74
	hypertensive	81	86	78

* Each period contains two measures at 1-minute intervals; all measures have been
rounded off to the nearest decimal point.

hypertensive patients between the magnitude of the rise and their
resting blood-pressure levels: the higher a patient's resting blood
pressure, the more it tended to increase when he or she spoke.

There was an amazingly consistent and striking increase in blood
pressure when people spoke. The pressure rises in some hypertensive
patients after two minutes of relaxed conversation were of the same
magnitude that Dr. Stewart Wolf and others had described in
thirty-minute stress interviews.[10] The difference between these stress
interviews, however, and our casual conversations appeared enor-
mous. We had made every effort to keep the conversations brief
and emotionally neutral and unstressful, and we wondered just
how high a patient's blood pressure would have risen if we had
discussed emotionally provocative topics or deliberately stressed
them.

In light of both the medical importance of these findings and
their implications for the diagnosis and treatment of high blood
pressure, we repeated this study with twenty additional hypertensive
patients and twenty more normotensive individuals.[11] Again, as
can be seen in table 6.5, the same findings emerged. Blood pressure
and heart rate increased in all forty subjects when they talked about
their daily lives, and quickly lowered when they were quiet once
again. And, as in our previous study, the blood pressure of
hypertensive patients rose higher than did that of normotensive

individuals in spite of the fact that many of the former were taking a variety of antihypertensive medications. The mean average talking blood pressure of 165/102 of these hypertensive patients was well into ranges considered clinically problematic.

THE PERVASIVENESS OF THE RESPONSE

Beyond problems dealing specifically with adult hypertension and the interpersonal context in which blood pressure was measured, questions arose about the pervasiveness of the link between blood pressure and talking.* Was the link idiosyncratic to certain populations or to the settings in which we had measured blood pressure? Or was this relationship far more fundamental, an essential part of the human condition?

In order to begin evaluating these questions, we examined the blood pressure–talking response across a broad spectrum of the population and in a variety of settings. Everywhere we looked, the findings appeared to be the same. Blood pressure rose rapidly whenever human beings began to communicate. Whether it was newborn babies crying in their cribs, pre-school children reciting their ABCs, grammar-school children reading a textbook aloud, university and graduate students telling us about their day, physicians and nurses reading books aloud or talking about their work, the elderly talking about their lives and their loneliness, or patients in coronary units and cardiac catheterization laboratories telling us about their fears and anxieties—virtually everyone's blood pressure

* Even as our first studies began to confirm the ubiquity of the link between talking and blood pressure, automated blood-pressure machines began to appear in drug stores and shopping malls across the United States. Just as physicians are informed about the implications of particular levels of blood pressure, these machines had clearly posted guidelines denoting normal blood pressure, borderline levels of danger, and levels (usually 155/95 and above) that ought to send a person straight to a physician. The absolute definitiveness of these guidelines now appeared potentially misleading, as they had been established through a method that precluded talking during the measurement period, and none instructed people to remain quiet while pressure was being measured. One was now free to speak to one's friends or mate as a computer automatically measured one's pressure. Furthermore, the precise numbers for the various levels of blood pressure showed how entrenched was the belief in the relative stability of blood pressure and in the unlikeliness of its being significantly influenced by common talk.

While these computer devices were being made available to the public, equally important technical breakthroughs were allowing physicians to monitor patients' blood pressure for twenty-four hours outside medical offices. These computer devices were capable of recording a person's blood pressure every five to ten minutes for an entire day.[12] When pressure was found to be higher on the job, or when one was talking on the telephone compared with watching television, physicians tended to infer that certain activities might be inherently more stressful than others. An equally valid interpretation, however, was that certain of these activities involved human speech, while in others patients were quiet.

rose when they spoke. No matter whether the blood pressure was measured at home or in laboratory, medical clinic, classroom, or diagnostic facility; or whether one spoke aloud by oneself, to one other individual, or in front of small or large groups—a person's blood pressure rose with remarkable consistency whenever he or she began to talk.[13]

The consistency of the response was truly remarkable. For example, in one study of 178 individuals who ranged in age from nine to eighty-three years, mean arterial blood pressure rose in 98 percent. Again, as in the initial studies with hypertensive patients, there was a strong relationship between the resting baseline blood pressure and the magnitude of the rise: the higher the resting blood pressure, the more it tended to go up when a person spoke.[14]

While in certain settings, such as coronary units and cardiac catheterization laboratories, one might intuitively suspect that stress and anxiety contributed to the rise in pressure, in other settings they seemed unlike to do so. In one pre-school setting, for example, my wife, Eileen, and her colleague, Christine Peterson,[15] monitored the blood pressure of twenty-five kindergarten children (average age, six years) whom the two women had been teaching for almost a year.* While in many of our studies the experimenter was a relative stranger to the person whose blood pressure was being measured, in this case the children were familiar with their teachers. And rather than engage in highly complex, emotionally charged dialogue, these children were simply asked to recite their ABCs or count numbers aloud—tasks they had often performed during the year. The children appeared to be delighted to participate in what seemed to be a game. None of the children had any difficulty reciting the alphabet or counting; yet without exception they all showed an increase in blood pressure and heart rate when they spoke. The vascular responses of two six-year-old boys are shown in tables 6.6 and 6.7. Figure 6.2 shows the average heart-rate and blood-pressure increases for all twenty-five children. While not shown in this figure, the blood pressure and heart rate of all twenty-five increased when they began to speak.

As our population sample grew ever larger, several patterns began to emerge. One was the striking contrast between the external calm

---

* We are grateful to the Good Shepherd School in Ruxton, Maryland, for helping us to carry out this study.

TABLE 6.6

*Blood Pressure and Heart Rate of Six-Year-Old Kindergarten
Child Before, During, and After Reciting His ABCs
and Counting for Two Minutes*

	Mean Arterial Pressure	Systolic Blood Pressure	Diastolic Blood Pressure	Heart Rate
Resting 1	81	117	77	87
2	91	123	77	90
3	78	104	65	79
Talking 1	102	131	81	92
2	109	133	92	100
Resting 1	89	118	76	85
2	84	121	61	80

Note dramatic increase in diastolic, systolic, and mean arterial pressures while the child was speaking.

of many of the people we monitored and the magnitude of their cardiovascular reactions when they spoke. Even while their blood pressure surged into hypertensive ranges, and their hearts began to pound rapidly, many of these individuals appeared absolutely calm,

TABLE 6.7

*Blood Pressure and Heart Rate of Six-Year-Old Boy
in Kindergarten While Reciting ABCs and Counting*

	Mean Arterial Pressure	Systolic Blood Pressure	Diastolic Blood Pressure	Heart Rate
Resting 1	84	115	55	72
2	75	110	58	71
3	78	107	55	68
Talking 1	82	108	70	91
2	91	122	60	83
Resting 1	73	108	55	72
2	69	104	50	75

Note the rapid increase in systolic blood pressure and the significant increase in heart rate while speaking.

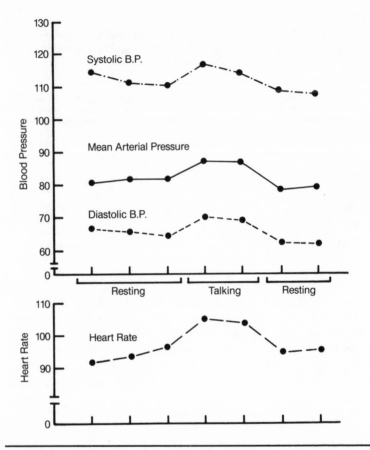

Figure 6.2. Increases in blood pressure and heart rate in a group of twenty-five kindergarten children while reciting their ABCs.

typically smiling as they spoke. A corollary of this clinical observation was even more suggestive. It appeared that the greater the cardio-vascular change when one spoke, the less likely was one to report being aware of any internal changes whatsoever. As we reconfirmed the correlation between baseline blood pressure and the magnitude of increase when a person speaks, we began to notice that there was something truly dysfunctional about the communicative style of many hypertensive patients. Part of the dysfunction involved the contrast between their pleasant external demeanor and the cardiovascular storm raging inside. Other people could no more see or sense these changes in hypertensive people than could the latter in themselves. Oblivious to their own internal cardiovascular message, they would continue talking, apparently innocuously, even though their blood pressure was rising dangerously high.

CLINICAL STUDIES

Even as we expanded the experimental model to ever more people in order to answer questions our data had generated, we simultaneously began to use the computer system as part of our treatment to help hypertensive patients lower their blood pressure. Unlike the experimental model in which eight to ten minutes of blood pressure and heart rate were measured once by a volunteer, the clinical sessions involved hour-long periods in which blood pressure and heart rate were measured each minute. And these hourly sessions were held weekly for a period that usually lasted for six months or more.

The extension of the experimental model into the treatment setting required modifications in the way information about blood pressure was communicated to the patients. Irrespective of who was speaking—therapist or patient—blood pressure and heart rate were measured and plotted on a video monitor, and the content of the conversations was coded on the bottom of the screen. There were four numbers—systolic, diastolic, and mean arterial pressure, as well as heart rate, which flashed each minute on the front panel of the monitor. It was clear that it would be virtually impossible for patients to remember all these varying numbers for an hour's session, especially when the sessions were repeated over six months. Without the aid of computer graphics it would have been difficult for patients to recall what their heart rate or diastolic pressure was ten minutes earlier, let alone ten weeks earlier, or to fully appreciate the dynamic way their pressure changed when they discussed certain topics. Thus it was necessary to store this information and display the data in a manner that allowed each patient to appreciate fully the dynamic nature of his or her internal vascular universe.*

* A special debt of gratitude is owed to Dr. David Paskewitz of Digital Psychophysiological Systems for developing the necessary hardware and software that allowed us to add this new dimension to our treatment regimen.

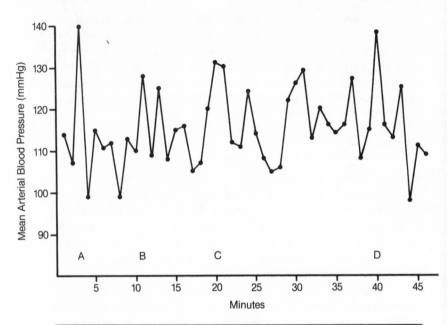

Figure 6.3. Minute-to-minute changes in mean arterial blood pressure in a male hypertensive patient during a typical therapeutic session. Points A, B, C, and D identify specific areas of discussion considered of particular significance. Note the marked fluctuation in blood pressure, averaging close to 50 percent, even though the patient was seated in a comfortable chair and exhibited little unusual muscle movement.

Similar to the patterns seen in the experimental model, patients' cardiovascular systems changed significantly during speech. The chief difference between patients and normotensive individuals was that the former's blood pressure and heart-rate increases frequently were far more exaggerated. At the end of an hour-long session, the computer tracings of a patient's blood pressure and heart rate frequently looked like waves in a storm-tossed ocean. It was not at all uncommon to see blood pressure repeatedly surging up and down more than 50 percent in a typical hour. Though little physical exercise or violent movement was involved, and though the conversations often appeared light-hearted and unstressed, these patients' cardiovascular systems revealed a different reality.

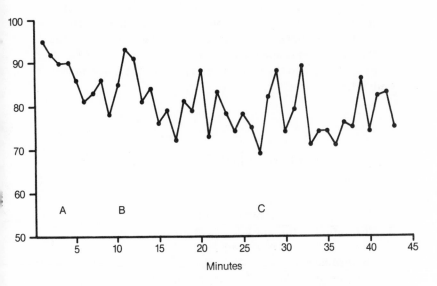

Figure 6.4. Minute-to-minute changes in mean arterial pressure in a female migraine patient during a typical therapeutic session. Points A, B, and C identify discussion topics considered to be particularly significant by the therapist. Though the mean pressure is far lower than in a hypertensive patient, the minute-to-minute variability is nevertheless significant.

The graphs in figures 6.3 and 6.4 show pressure changes that were typical of the hundreds upon hundreds of hour-long therapy sessions we began to accumulate with patients. Figure 6.3 shows a typical tracing of the mean arterial blood pressure seen in one hypertensive patient during a therapeutic hour, while figure 6.4 shows comparable tracings recorded in a migraine patient. Though the average resting blood pressure is far lower in the migraine patient, nevertheless the variability of this patient's cardiovascular system was just as pronounced as that seen in the hypertensive patient.

Blood pressure and heart rate frequently changed from minute to minute in these patients. The magnitude of the changes was influenced by other factors than the fact of their speaking. The emotional content of the discussions, what they talked about, and the way they spoke compounded or amplified the responses. Furthermore, it was apparent that the mechanics of speech, respiratory patterns, and the emotional content of the communications were interconnected.

TALKING BLOOD PRESSURE UP:
THE TYPE A PERSONALITY

Of the various mechanisms that appeared to play a role in the blood pressure–communication response, none seemed more immediately obvious than the way hypertensive patients spoke with a certain breathless intensity, often increasing the rate of their speech when trying to make a point or discuss an emotionally charged topic. And when they increased the cadence or the intensity of their speech, their blood pressure usually rose far higher than normal and fell back more slowly to its resting level when they were quiet once again.

The importance of speech patterns was reinforced by a thoroughly documented research literature that had linked a cluster of personality traits—called the "Type A personality"—to the premature development of coronary heart disease. In the mid-1950s, two California investigators, Dr. Meyer Friedman and Dr. Ray Rosenman, initiated what turned out to be a wide-ranging series of studies of thousands of individuals, aimed at exploring various physiological, psychological, and personality factors that might contribute to the development of coronary heart disease.[16] What emerged from this Western Collaborative Group Study was surprising. While these investigators had expected various well-known factors, such as weight and poor diet, and physiological factors, such as elevated serum cholesterol, to be the strongest predictors of who would get sick and die, the strongest predictor turned out to be an individual's personality. They found that a certain cluster of personality traits, which they labeled "Type A," is strongly linked to a predisposition to develop coronary atherosclerosis, as well as to an enhanced risk of heart attack and sudden death. The Type A personality is characterized by an aggressive, "workaholic," restlessly impulsive, hard-driving approach to life. But, of all the personality characteristics, the most dominant is speech pattern and the manner in which one communicates to others. Type A individuals speak faster and louder, have a tendency to interrupt and speak over others, and use more emphatic gestures when they talk.

When Friedman and Rosenman first identified the Type A personality, they did not observe this trait to be linked to changes in blood pressure or to hypertension. Rather, they specifically linked this personality type to the development of coronary atherosclerosis. In light of our observations of marked rises in blood pressure when people spoke, as well as some of our clinical observations on the peculiar speech patterns of hypertensive patients, it seemed reasonable to re-examine Type A speech patterns. We suspected that perhaps Friedman and Rosenman might have been unable to link Type A speech patterns to blood pressure because of the limitations of the technology available to them. When they developed the concept of Type A, they did not assume that speech patterns are directly linked to the cardiovascular system, or that the communicative style of Type A individuals directly causes cardiovascular disease. Rather, they assumed that speech is one of a constellation of traits that combine to make up the Type A personality, and that the emotional overdrive of these individuals leads them to develop coronary heart disease. Since Friedman and Rosenman found the Type A personality specifically linked to the premature development of atherosclerosis, but not particularly related to chronic elevations of blood pressure, another theoretical possibility began to occur to us: perhaps Type A speech patterns cause unusually large, sudden surges in blood pressure, which might lead to the development of tiny bruises in the inner walls of the coronary arteries and to the subsequent development of atherotomous plaques. Such bruising and the development of such plaques had been postulated to be a significant contributor to the development of atherosclerosis. And as we shall see in chapter 9, hypertensive patients occasionally exhibited truly remarkable sudden surges in blood pressure when discussing certain topics.

The possibility that certain predominant speech characteristics of Type A personalities might have a direct influence on the heart led us to study thirty white normotensive adults. Fifteen men and fifteen women were recruited from a medical residents housing unit. The volunteers ranged in age from twenty-one to thirty-three. Twenty of the thirty volunteers jogged at least five miles, three times a week. The nurse experimenter (Denise Kulick-Ciuffo), also a resident in the same housing unit, was well known to the volunteers. Of the thirty volunteers, twenty-five had completed college, and twelve had completed medical school.[17] Thus, the population was not only unusually well educated but also in unusually good physical shape. They were among the brightest and healthiest young adults we could find.

Each subject was asked to read a book under two conditions: one that involved reading a book at their own personal tempo, and one that involved reading aloud at maximal tempo. Under each condition, they were further asked to read both aloud and silently. They were then assigned randomly to read either fast or at normal tempo first. (Reading was chosen to minimize any emotional differences that might arise in talking to the experimenter.) They were asked to read the Articles of Constitution of the United States, which was judged to be more or less emotionally neutral. The reading was tape-recorded so that the number of words spoken could be gauged accurately.

As shown in figures 6.5 and 6.6, reading aloud led to significant elevations in blood pressure and heart rate in all thirty participants; blood pressure and heart rate also quickly returned to baseline when they were quiet once again. By contrast, reading silently had little effect on the cardiovascular system. More importantly in terms of Type A personality theory, reading faster led to significantly greater blood-pressure increases than did reading at normal tempo. In like manner, the number of words read per minute also correlated significantly with the magnitude of the blood-pressure elevations.

It is important to emphasize that all of the subjects in this study were in excellent physical health and highly educated, and their resting heart rates and blood-pressure levels were normal. Thus, it is all the more surprising that a task as simple as reading aloud would cause significant increases in their blood pressure. Since it was already known that the higher the blood pressure the greater the increase, it seemed obvious that if we had used hypertensive

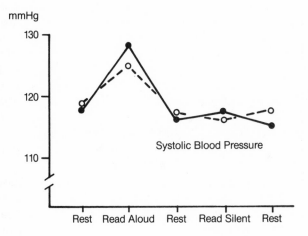

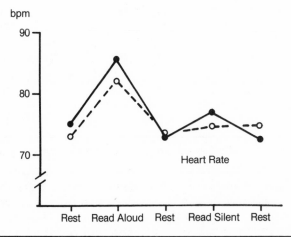

Figure 6.5. Systolic blood-pressure and heart-rate changes while resting and reading aloud and silently both at maximal tempo (●) and at personal tempo (O). Note that only reading aloud had an effect on blood pressure.

patients in this experiment, they would have exhibited far greater increases in comparable circumstances.

These data helped to confirm our initial clinical impressions that the speed of a patient's speech can significantly influence the

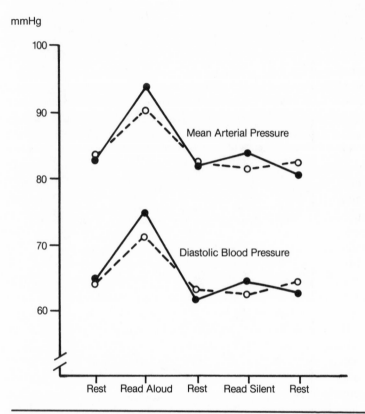

Figure 6.6. Mean arterial and diastolic blood pressure changes while resting and reading aloud both at maximal tempo (●) and at personal tempo (O). Note that only reading aloud had an effect on blood pressure.

magnitude of blood pressure elevations during therapy. In terms of treating hypertensive patients, the data also suggested that instructions to speak more slowly, less emphatically, as well as to breathe properly, can directly effect their blood pressure and heart rate when talking.

These findings also led us to consider a theoretical possibility quite different from the original assumptions of investigators like Wolf and Alexander. We began to suspect that it is not the emotional quality of a specific conversation that drives blood pressure up to hypertensive levels, but rather the way a person talks when communicating emotionally meaningful material. It seemed possible to teach hypertensive patients to talk about emotionally provocative or personally upsetting material without their blood pressure rising dangerously high. One would have to discuss such topics slowly, less emphatically, while breathing properly. In a sense, when "ventilating" feelings, one would have to "ventilate" properly: that is, to breathe and pace oneself.

While the volunteers in this study were not classified according to personality, the findings indicated that two of the key personality traits of Type A—rapid and loud talking—have a direct and immediate effect on blood pressure and heart rate. Thus these speech characteristics appeared not only to be part of the Type A personality but, far more importantly, to have a direct physiological influence on a Type A person's cardiovascular system. The study also suggested that if Type A, coronary-prone individuals were able through computer technology to see the direct vascular consequences of their rapid, loud speaking style, they might find it easier to modify this maladaptive behavior.

The crucial importance of developing methods to help alter Type A behavior has been demonstrated in a most persuasive way by recent reports which have indicated that changes in such behavioral patterns can reduce the risk of recurrent heart attacks by up to 50 percent in people who have already had at least one myocardial infarction.[18] Commenting on the obvious significance of these findings Dr. Paul Rosch, president of the American Institute of Stress, recently noted:

Attempts to reduce the rate of recurrent heart attacks by lowering such standard risk factors as blood pressure, cholesterol, and cigarette smoking have generally proved unsuccessful. A prime example is afforded by the seven year multiple risk factors intervention trial, in which hypertensives treated with diuretics actually had a higher mortality rate than controls. On the other hand, two other studies conducted during the same period proved so successful that they were halted prematurely so that controls would not be denied the benefits of intervention. One was designed to reduce Type A coronary prone behavior and the other was treatment with propranolol. The protective effect in both instances is most probably related to lowering the effects of stress related catecholamine secretion known to produce cardiac damage and sudden death.[19]

THE ELDERLY

The fact that altering certain speech characteristics of the Type A personality could have a direct influence on blood pressure increases while a person communicates led us to consider another population at risk for cardiovascular dysfunction—the elderly. The gradual advancement of atherosclerosis is widely recognized to be part of the aging process. Because of this problem, blood pressure tends to rise with age; and, indeed, hypertension is far more prevalent in people over sixty-five than it is in those who are younger.[20] Owing to the strong correlation, revealed in our studies, between resting blood pressure and its elevation during speech, verbal communications seemed to pose special problems for the elderly, in many of whom we observed striking increases in blood pressure when they talked. As was true of hypertensive patients in general, elderly individuals, when speaking, increased their blood pressure proportionately more than younger people. These increases were at times so great that we wondered whether some elderly persons might find it particularly difficult to communicate, or become emotionally agitated and quick-tempered with others, or even be susceptible to mental confusion when they talked. Could such high surges of blood pressure tax one's entire system? Could anything be done to ameliorate what appears to be inherent to the aging process? Are human beings really "wired" in such a way as to make verbal communications increasingly difficult and taxing in terms of the cardiovascular system as one grows older? Are children more capable of "fighting and making up" because of the elasticity of their cardiovascular system? Does the lack of vascular elasticity in the aged contribute to their loneliness, trapped as many appear to be by the stress of interacting with others? Does the stress of communication force an old person to withdraw into social isolation?

While answers to these questions await additional research, it is clear that elderly individuals, and particularly those who are hypertensive, can take several steps to modulate the rise in blood pressure when they talk. As is the case with Type A individuals, they can slow down the rate of their speech as well as breathe deeply and regularly when they talk. In addition, they can utilize the specific techniques taught to our hypertensive patients, which I shall describe in the appendix.

THE EFFECTS OF STATUS

While certain aspects of speech clearly influenced the blood-pressure response, interviews with patients suggested that the interview situation itself also distinctly affects the magnitude of cardiovascular changes. Aspects of the issue were first brought to our attention by patients' descriptions of visits to their regular physicians. Having grown accustomed to hundreds, even thousands, of measurements of their blood pressure, several of the hypertensive patients we were treating began to express surprise at the elevations in their blood pressure when they went for routine medical checkups during our therapy. The patients themselves began to speculate about undetected anxiety they must have felt during such visits. Such experiences were by no means peculiar to these patients. A number of studies had revealed that blood-pressure recordings taken in a physician's office are almost always higher than those recorded at home.[21] The potential for misdiagnosis or misinterpretation of blood-pressure levels was clear. If a patient's resting blood pressure is elevated in a physician's office and then rises proportionately higher while he or she talks to the doctor, misinterpretation can be seriously compounded. Without home readings (which, historically, have always had the potential for error since one has to learn how to use a stethoscope and to listen for the Korotkov sounds), the physician traditionally had no way of knowing whether a patient's blood pressure is elevated simply because of the office setting.

While numerous factors had been cited as potentially contributing to these elevations (such as anxiety about the diagnosis, the stress of waiting a long time to see the doctor, or the cost of the visit), a variable of particular interest to us was any status difference between doctor and patient. Might the higher status of the physician make one's pressure rise? If a person speaks to someone whose status is perceived to be higher, does that person's blood pressure tend to rise correspondingly? Hypertensive patients frequently alluded to status problems in their job, to conflict with people in positions of authority, and to their low self-esteem; and it began to appear as if such embedded variables could crucially affect overall cardiovascular health.

To evaluate the importance of this issue on the blood pressure—

communication response, we randomly distributed forty normotensive college students into two groups and asked them to participate
in an experiment.[22] As in previous studies, they were asked to be
quiet, then to talk to an experimenter, to be quiet once again, then
to read a book aloud. In this experiment, however, the experimenter
had a dual role. For twenty of the students, he (Jack Long) dressed
in a casual manner (blue jeans, sport shirt, tennis shoes) and
described himself as a graduate student working as a research
assistant in our laboratory. For the other twenty students, he dressed
neatly (white shirt and tie) in a white laboratory jacket which
identified him as a resident in internal medicine. He also told this
group of students that he was an internist conducting a research
project in blood pressure. Other than this alteration of identity, the
experimental protocol was identical.

The dual status of the experimenter made a significant difference.
As in all previous studies, the blood pressure of all forty students
significantly rose when they spoke. As shown in figure 6.7, both
the magnitude of the rise as well as the baseline pressures were
altered significantly by the students' perception of the experimenter.
Blood-pressure elevations were significantly higher when the students
spoke to Dr. Jack Long the internist than when they spoke to Jack
Long fellow graduate student. It is important to emphasize that
not only was the magnitude of their speaking blood pressure greater,
but even their resting blood pressure was significantly higher when
the students perceived themselves to be in the presence of a person
of higher status.

While the design of this study was simple and straightforward,
the implications were far-reaching. If something as basic as "social
status" can have a significant impact on the blood pressure of
healthy college students, then how do comparable social, economic,
and psychological status differences affect people's blood pressure
in everyday life? Are the significantly higher death rates from
hypertension among black Americans and the economically disad-
vantaged due, at least in part, to their low status in society? Are
they frequently thrust into situations where they are "talking up":
that is, forced to communicate in a world where virtually everyone
else is of higher status?

Similar questions can be raised about the significantly higher
incidence of hypertension and cardiovascular death rates of school

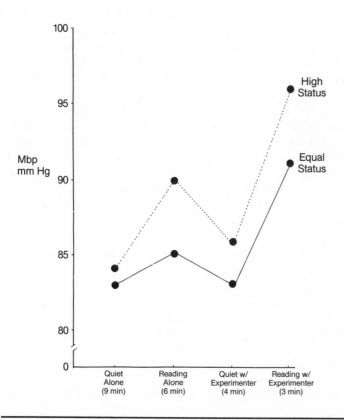

Figure 6.7.   Mean arterial blood-pressure changes while reading alone and reading with an experimenter of different status. Note that the high-status experimenter led to elevations in mean arterial pressure and to significantly greater changes while reading aloud.

dropouts. In an earlier report we questioned whether this increased mortality also was linked to their psychological identity and sense of self-worth.[23] Even when all other factors, such as economics and living standards, are factored out of the equations—that is, even where school dropouts have succeeded in life—nevertheless they appeared to be particularly vulnerable to hypertension.[24] Using data obtained from a major governmental study called the Hypertension Detection and Follow-up Program, Dr. H. A. Tyroler at the University of North Carolina recently examined the five-year mortality patterns of 2,094 male subjects between the ages of thirty and sixty-nine.[25] These men were gathered from fourteen study centers across the United States in 1973 and 1974. What they all had in common at the beginning of the study was mild hypertension (diastolic pressures between 90 and 105). At the beginning of the study, they all had equivalent blood-pressure readings. During the next five years, 182 of these men died. Two variables made a difference: race and education. With other factors held constant, the death rate for blacks was twice as high as for whites—13 percent for blacks versus 7 percent for whites. Educational levels had an even more pronounced effect. The risk of dying was significantly higher among the whites with less education than among those with more. For blacks the differences were even more startling: there was a sevenfold increase in death rates among the blacks with the least education.

All of these data raise the tantalizing question whether there is a fundamental relationship between psychosocial aspects of human interaction and cardiovascular health.

TALKING BLOOD PRESSURE DOWN

The fact that a pet animal, or "man's best friend," can help lower blood pressure was a phenomenon that seemed at first glance to be more a joke than a problem deserving of scientific scrutiny. After all, highly sophisticated pharmaceutical companies had spent billions of dollars researching and promoting various drugs to lower blood pressure, and it hardly seemed possible that a lowly dog wagging its tail could have anything remotely resembling such potency. Yet a variety of studies we conducted indicated that the effect has to be taken seriously.

Interest in questions about the influence of pets on human blood pressure was itself an ironic reversal from the point, two decades earlier, when my research studies had originated with questions about the profound effects of human petting on a dog's cardiovascular system. Now the research had come full circle; and instead of studying the effects that humans can have on dogs, we began to study the influence that pet dogs can have on the cardiovascular health of human beings.

Curiosity about this problem arose from a surprising finding during our coronary-care research. In a study conducted with several colleagues—including Dr. Erika Friedmann and Aaron Katcher, at the University of Pennsylvania, and Dr. Sue Ann Thomas at the University of Maryland—we were assessing the relative importance of social, psychological, economic, and physical factors on patients' survival after being released from a coronary-care unit. Our involvement in this problem had been stimulated by statistical data suggesting that human relationships and human loneliness play an important role in cardiovascular health. While the statistics implied that various aspects of a patient's social life might significantly affect recovery from a serious illness, there had been no systematic investigation of the problem.

In our effort to explore this question, ninety-six patients—twenty-nine women and sixty-seven men—in the University of Maryland Hospital's coronary-care unit were interviewed just before they were discharged from the hospital. Only patients who had had a myocardial infarction or angina pectoris were included in the study. Included in the survey data were well-known physiological predictors of survival longer than four months after a heart attack, as well as a general physical assessment of the patients' overall health. In addition, each patient was given a comprehensive checklist of social and psychological data, which included many questions about their socioeconomic status, social network, geographic mobility, and general living conditions. Among the hundreds of questions asked was one about pet ownership.

All patients were followed on a monthly basis for a full year in an effort to gauge what factors influenced both their overall health and their survival. Within one year, fourteen of the ninety-six patients had died. Not surprisingly, their general physical health and extent of cardiovascular disease upon release from the hospital proved to be the most potent predictor of who would die. Those who had suffered the most serious physical problems, and the greatest extent of heart damage, clearly ran the greatest risk of dying. A major surprise, however, was that pets also had an

TABLE 6.8

*The Effects of Pet Ownership on
One-Year Survival after Release
from a Coronary-Care Unit*

Patient Status on One-Year Follow-up	Number of Patients with:		
	No Pet	*Pets*	*Total*
Alive	28	50	78
Dead	11	3	14
Total	39	53	92*

* The discrepancy in the original total of 96 is due to
the fact that four people dropped out of the study.

independent predictive effect over and above the predictive power
of well-known physiological indicators of survival.[26]

Of the total population studied, 58 percent reported having a pet
living with them. As shown in table 6.8, there proved to be a
relationship between pet ownership and one-year survival. Of the
39 patients who did not own pets, 11 (or 28 percent) died, whereas
only 3 (6 percent) of the 53 pet owners died—a difference that was
highly significant both clinically and statistically. While this finding
had many implications, it certainly forced us to wonder how a
person is benefited by pets in ways that actually affect survival. Is
a dog really that much of a friend to man?

We had completed a series of studies on blood-pressure elevations
in children and adults when reading aloud, and felt it might be
possible to use the same experimental model to help examine this
phenomenon. Much as status differences had been part of the
context of our experimental model, we aimed to study the effects
of a dog on the blood pressure of children when reading a book
aloud.

To conduct this study, my three children—Joe, Jim, and Kathleen—recruited thirty-six neighborhood children between the ages
of nine and sixteen and asked them to participate in a blood-
pressure study. The experiment was conducted in the recreation
room of my home. Each child was monitored individually by a

researcher (Erika Friedman), and the blood pressure of each was measured both while quiet and while reading aloud. These two conditions were studied both when a friendly dog was in the room and when the dog was not present. When the dog was in the room, it was held next to the experimenter. The children did not know the animal nor did they talk to or touch it during the experiment. Three different dogs were used in the experiment, and all were pets belonging to various research colleagues.[27]

As in all previous experiments, the children's blood pressure and heart rate rose significantly when they were reading aloud, both when the dog was present and when they were alone with the experimenter. When the dog was present, however, the children's blood pressure was significantly lower, both at rest and while reading (see figure 6.8). There were no differences in the children's vascular responses to the three dogs, but the effect of a dog was greater if it was introduced at the beginning of an experiment, rather than later. In a sense, the dog seemed to speed up the process of relaxation that naturally occurred after the children had grown accustomed to the experiment.

How did the presence of a friendly animal produce such changes in children's blood pressure? And how did the effects occur? Did the presence of a dog make the entire experiment less threatening? Or did the animals distract the children so as to make the reading task less emotionally charged?

Questions of this sort led Dr. Aaron Katcher and his associate, Dr. Alan Beck, to begin examining the nature of human–pet interaction.[28] Availing themselves of a perfect ethological setting, Dr. Katcher began to watch people and their pets in the waiting room of the University of Pennsylvania Veterinary Clinic. There he noted that people interacted with their dogs in a manner quite different from the hurly-burly, gruff, suspicious, superficial, or distant ways that human beings frequently talk to each other. Dr. Katcher noted that, when speaking to their pets, these people tended to speak far more softly, gently, and slowly. Not only did they appear to communicate differently but, they also petted and stroked their animals while talking to them.

Taking a cue from this observation, we decided to ascertain whether blood-pressure changes are the same when human beings talk to their pet animals as when humans speak to each other.

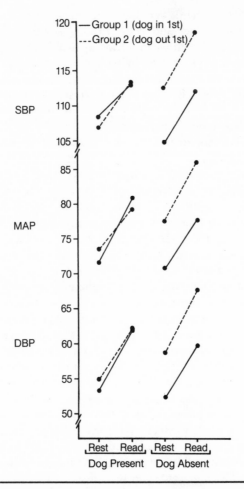

Figure 6.8. Average mean arterial systolic and diastolic blood pressure while reading with and without the presence of a dog. Note higher reading pressures when the dog was not in the room.

Unlike previous experiments, however, in which only talking was studied, people were allowed to stroke their animals while speaking to them. It would have been difficult to do otherwise, as people seemed naturally to touch their animals when speaking to them.

The overall results were revealing. While blood pressure rose significantly when these pet owners talked to an experimenter, it either did not change or actually decreased when they talked to their pets.

Again the question why had to be asked. What is it about the way a person interacts with a pet that produces different vascular effects from those seen when human beings interact with one another? Is it the lower status of the animal? Were these people in a sense talking down to a creature lower than they? Or was it that pets are nonjudgmental? Or was the effect due to the different ways people spoke to their pets?

THE CARDIAC ORIENTING RESPONSE

All of these questions brought into sharper focus the contrast between the way people talked to their pets and the way hypertensive patients talked to us in the clinic. It often seemed as if the hypertensive patients were using words as a smokescreen or a weapon to fend us off, keep us at a distance, while they prepared to fight or to run away. It was clear that when their blood pressure surged unusually high, we had to be a threat of some kind. Equally clear was the defensive, rather than relaxed, nature of their listening: they appeared to decode our messages as a radar operator interprets the sudden blips from the direction of an enemy's territory.

When, during therapy, the computer indicated that our dialogue was apparently deteriorating into something more akin to a state of war than any peaceful discourse, I would try to shift the focus of conversation. Occasionally at such times, in order to help a patient be less defensive by showing myself as vulnerable as him or her, I would reveal something of a personal nature, some incident that had caused me certain discomfort or embarrassment in my own life. Or I would read something that had personal meaning to me, some passage from a medical text or even poetry that I felt might help give a patient a clearer perspective of his or her struggles. At these moments—unlike the ongoing dialogue, which was dominated by fight or flight vigilance and defensive listening—the patients seemed truly to be able to listen. They could momentarily forget themselves and attend to what I was saying. And on such occasions their blood pressure invariably fell to the lowest levels in the session and sometimes to levels far below those usually seen in therapy, occasionally even below levels patients themselves had not observed in years.

The plummeting of pressure during these periods suggested a link between attentional mechanisms and the cardiovascular system. It appeared that if hypertensive people could momentarily forget themselves, drop their defensive listening, and truly attend to others outside of themselves, then blood pressure would fall correspondingly. While such moments were all too infrequent in the clinic, it was this type of outer-focused attention that appeared to characterize the human–pet interactions in the Veterinary Clinic. The reason blood pressure fell when these people were stroking their dogs appeared to be linked to the fact that they were able to forget themselves, step outside of their normal defensive armor, and wholly attend to their pet animals.

An ingenious way to test this idea was devised by Dr. Katcher. He asked fifteen hypertensive patients and twenty normotensive individuals to participate in our research model of reading a book aloud as well as being quiet. As in all earlier studies, blood pressure rose significantly when they read aloud. And also as in previous studies, blood pressure rose porportionately more in hypertensive patients than it did in normotensive individuals. After participating in this protocol, each person was asked to stare in a relaxed manner at a blank wall for twenty minutes while the computer continued to record his or her blood pressure each minute. Finally each person was asked to watch a school of tropical fish swimming in a twenty-five-gallon tank for an additional twenty minutes. Blood pressure was highest when people spoke, and lowest when they attended to the fish swimming in the tank. More important, blood pressure was lower when the people attended to the fish then when they rested quietly in a comfortable chair staring at a blank wall. There was a difference between passive relaxation and actively attending to the external environment in a relaxed state.

The links between attending to one's environment, and nondefensive listening in terms of blood pressure was in a sense a rediscovery and a reaffirmation of a large scientific literature that previously had described a phenomenon called the "cardiac orienting reflex." Yet, as was the case in our original resistance to seeing the links between talking and blood pressure, it was the context of these fish-tank observations that gave these earlier studies new meaning. Again, there was deep irony in this rediscovery, for one of the very first scientific papers I had ever published centered on the way heart rate in a dog slows when it attends to its external environment.[29]

Pavlov had first observed what he called the "orienting reflex" in dogs at the turn of the century. His description of the orienting reflex involves a behavioral pattern probably every reader of this book has observed: if a dog is presented with a soft noise or sound, or a sudden movement in its environment, it will stop all activity and attend to that stimulus. The dog will stand motionless, prick its ears, and cock its head back and forth as it orients to the stimulus. It is, as Pavlov noted, a fundamental reflex without which an animal would be unable to adapt to, or survive in, a constantly changing world. The reflex permits animals to differentiate changes in their environment and to decode the novel from other stimuli that pose a threat. Pavlov noted that the orienting reflex involves a constellation of behavior that is seen only when the dog attends to its environment. What gave the reflex its special meaning was that it could be easily distinguished from other behavior, such as fight or flight or defensive reactions. Thus the same stimulus—say, a tone—can elicit either an orienting or a defensive reaction from a dog. What makes the difference is the stimulus qualities of the sound: if a sound is soft, then a dog will orient to it; but if it is too loud, then a dog will recoil and respond defensively.

The importance of this reflex in terms of the cardiovascular system was studied subsequently in great detail by the Russian scientist Professor E. N. Sokolov as well as by a group of American scientists.[30] They observed that during the orienting reflex, when animals and human beings attend to their environment, idiosyncratic cardiovascular changes also occur. Among the prominent, characteristic changes, Sokolov observed that the heart rate slows precipitately. In human beings, distinctive changes in blood flow also occur that clearly indicate that one is orienting to one's environment. Sokolov noted that when human beings orient or pay attention to their environment, their heart rate slows while blood flow increases into the brain and decreases in the surface regions of the fingers. Even more noteworthy was his additional observation that the vascular changes in human beings, when they pay attention or orient, are different from the changes that occur when they defend against or are frightened by stimuli in the environment. Sokolov's studies beautifully demonstrated that the monitoring of blood flow and heart rate makes it possible to distinguish whether a person is attending to the environment or defending against it.

Sokolov's book[31] was published at virtually the same time I began my research with dogs. In an effort to verify his findings, we studied the cardiac orienting reflex in twenty-four dogs.[32] As he predicted, there was indeed a marked reduction in heart rate when the dogs oriented to soft tones. Typical of the cardiac orienting response we observed is the electrocardiographic tracing in figure 6.9. As can be seen in this figure, just as soon as the tone was introduced there was a marked slowing in the animal's heart rate.*

Equally fascinating was the way the cardiac orienting response disappeared or was extinguished once a dog habituated to the novelty of the stimulus. If the tone was sounded repetitively, the dog would eventually stop attending to it: that is, the animal would stop orienting. Along with the cessation of orienting, the dog's heart rate also would no longer fall when the tone was sounded. In a sense, the novelty had worn off. It is a fundamental part of the learning process. The capacity to habituate to novelty means that the animal learned to respond to the tone as part of its natural environment. If animals responded to every stimulus as if it were continually novel, then they would have no capacity to learn or adapt to their environment.

Extending these findings to human dialogue, we began to wonder whether hypertensive patients minimize the amount of time they spend orienting or listening to others, and thus are unable to avail themselves of a natural way to lower heart rate and blood pressures? As I have suggested, hypertensive patients frequently appear to defend against a message instead of listening. Words that ought to lead them to pay attention or to orient are responded to as a threat. In addition, we began to wonder whether these patients also cannot listen because the novelty of the incoming message has been lost? This possibility struck us as especially important in relationships that are central to a patient's life. If, for example, a hypertensive person can no longer react to the novelty of verbal communications

---

* Space precludes a more detailed discussion of this fascinating topic, but to interested readers I highly recommend either Sokolov's book or a review published by Frances K. Graham and R. K. Clifton.[33]

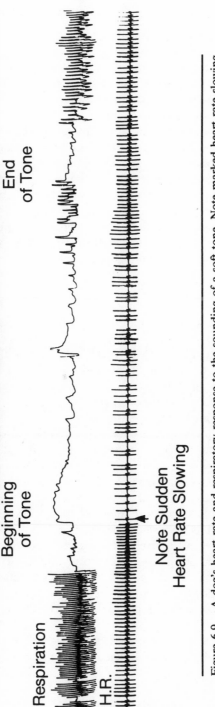

Figure 6.9. A dog's heart rate and respiratory response to the sounding of a soft tone. Note marked heart rate slowing when the dog attended to the tone.

from his or her spouse; if orienting no longer occurs in dialogue; if one no longer can attend to one's mate and the novelty of one's relationship, have they inadvertently lost a natural way to lower blood pressure? Even more important, if the "incoming" messages elicit defensive listening rather than orienting, will the entire dialogue prime blood pressure rise?

These observations and questions also provided a new perspective on the various alternative nonpharmacological treatments used to lower blood pressure. Whether the approaches involved transcendental meditation, the relaxation response, or biofeedback, each appeared to involve alterations in attentional mechanisms. In addition to their emphasis on deep breathing and relaxation of various muscle groups, each of these techniques emphasized in one way or another that a person ought to focus attention on some object or stimulus outside of his or her own body.

TALKING AND LISTENING

The fundamental idea that emerged from these animal studies underscored the second component of the dialogic equation. Human communication clearly involves two intertwined components— talking *and* listening—each of which has a powerful influence on the regulation of human blood pressure. Human dialogue is a seesaw, whose rhythm is sensitively registered by the vascular system. Dysfunctional speaking patterns appear to be accompanied by equally dysfunctional listening skills.

As the computer systems traced the blood-pressure responses during therapeutic dialogue, it became apparent that there are two aspects of the vascular response to human communication: that is, in addition to the elevation in blood pressure when a person speaks, there is a *decrease* in blood pressure when one *listens.* At first we thought that blood pressure more or less reflexively returns to baseline after a person stops speaking; and thus, for a time, the difference between passively relaxing and actively listening or attending to another person escaped our notice. Yet gradually we began to see that when one listens to someone else, one's blood pressure goes down, sometimes even below its baseline level. We began to visualize blood pressure as part of a communicative seesaw.

In normal dialogue, there appears to be sufficient switching back and forth between speakers so that a person's blood pressure usually can settle back to resting baseline. Hypertensive dialogue, however, seems to be characterized not just by marked elevations in blood pressure when one speaks, but by an equally marked inability to listen when spoken to. Rather than listening, our hypertensive patients appeared to be preoccupied, thinking about what they wanted to say next, almost as if they were continuously engaged in a contest or a fight rather than in a comfortable dialogue. Instead of listening, they appeared to be defending against what others had to say. Whether in response to therapist or mate, the pattern was similar. As a consequence, their blood pressure did not fall as quickly after they stopped talking, and occasionally it would not drop back to its resting baseline as would normotensive individuals' blood pressure. Here was another vicious circle in which hypertensive patients appeared to be trapped. Since elevations in blood pressure when speaking were strongly linked to baseline levels, one tended to get caught in a negative feedback loop the longer one engaged in dialogue. Each time a person stopped speaking but did not allow his or her pressure to fall back to baseline levels, that person's blood pressure was inadvertently set to rise all the higher the next time he or she spoke. The mechanics of both hypertensive speech as well as listening skills needed modification. Hence, there appears to be no rhythm to the hypertensive's vascular seesaw when talking to other human beings.

In this light, it became obvious that those people who communicate most intimately with patients play an important role in their cardiovascular health. If hypertensive patients not only significantly elevate their pressure when speaking, but also have difficulty listening to others or attending to their environment, then it is likely that this problem profoundly affects those who try to communicate with them. Extending the metaphor of the vascular seesaw, we realized that if a hypertensive person is on one end of the seesaw, then someone has to be on the other end. It therefore became obvious to us that patients' companions in dialogue have to be engaged in the therapeutic process. They have to discover the same hidden world of vascular dialogue that the computers were revealing to us. Blood pressure has to be treated in the context of a person's everyday life.

As the complex interrelatedness of human dialogue began to crystallize in our minds, and the mosaic of factors that influence

human communicative blood pressure unfolded, other basic questions demanded answers. Is it talking specifically that affects blood
pressure and heart rate; or is it, as the data was beginning to imply,
something far more basic, a process involved with human communication itself?

SILENT COMMUNICATION:
THE WORLD OF THE DEAF

In an effort to delineate the difference between talking and communicating in general, in terms of the blood-pressure and heart-
rate changes we had been observing, a group of deaf individuals
were examined when they communicated by sign language.[34] In
order to carry out this study, we recruited volunteers who were
attending the 1983 annual convention of the Maryland Association
of the Deaf. Thirty-eight white adults (twenty-three men and fifteen
women) volunteered to have their blood pressure monitored by Dr.
Kenneth Malinow, Jay Foreman, and Joseph Lynch when they
were quiet and then when they signed to an interpreter. As in most
other studies, they were instructed to communicate about anything
of interest to them. The volunteers ranged in age from twenty-
three to seventy-four, with an average age of forty-two. All relied
upon signing as their dominant mode of communicating. Each
volunteer was interviewed by hearing interpreters who were highly
skilled in sign language.

As in virtually all previous studies, this deaf population exhibited
significant elevations in blood pressure and heart rate when they
signed. Even more intriguing was the fact that this population also
showed the same trends as speaking populations in terms of the
magnitude of their pressure elevations (see figure 6.10).

When this group was subdivided into those with low resting
blood pressure, those with normal resting blood pressure, and those
judged to be hypertensive,* the trends duplicated those seen in
speaking populations. The higher their resting pressures, the more

---

* Deaf volunteers judged to be hypertensive were defined as either those who were currently
taking antihypertensive medicines, or those who had a diastolic reading greater than 90 during
the pre-signing resting period.

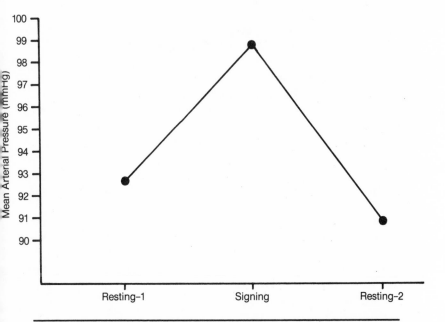

Figure 6.10. Mean arterial pressure changes in a group of thirty-eight adult deaf males and females when they communicated by signing.

they tended to elevate when these deaf people signed. As a group, the hypertensives had a mean pre-signing diastolic pressure of 86, which rose to an average of 103 when they signed. As was true of speaking hypertensives, none of the drugs the deaf hypertensives were taking appeared to be effective in blocking the pressure rises when they signed. For example, one deaf volunteer taking the drug Aldomet (a drug that controls blood pressure by blocking central nervous system activity) had a resting mean arterial pressure of 94, which rose ιo 169 when he signed—an overall increase of 80 percent within sixty seconds of signing.

These findings helped reinforce the idea that face-to-face human communication, irrespective of whether one talks or signs, leads to elevations in blood pressure.*

* These findings also helped us recognize the need to develop a nondrug method to treat hypertension in the deaf. As is true of speaking and hearing populations, it is clear that the deaf also can experience communication struggles that significantly influence their cardiovascular health.

TALKING WITHOUT COMMUNICATING:
SCHIZOPHRENIC DIALOGUE

The blood-pressure increases observed in the deaf led to a re-examination of our original supposition that vocalizing itself can cause the cardiovascular system to respond. We speculated whether reading aloud while one is alone might nevertheless involve human communication. Surely the students in our initial studies (see pages 125–29) could have assumed that we had a purpose in requesting them to read aloud while alone, and thus created their own nonspecific, isolated communication that could not be designed out of the study. Perhaps their reading was akin to talking on the telephone, where another person is not physically present, yet communication is clear and intended. Research data from Dr. Thomas Pickering and Dr. John Laragh at Cornell University Medical School had shown that, in patients whom they had continuously monitored for twenty-four hours, blood pressure often reached its highest levels when a person was talking on the telephone.[35]

All of these questions led us eventually to reconsider situations where communication itself is a real problem. Are there situations where people do indeed talk without communicating? To answer this question, we began to investigate the blood-pressure responses of schizophrenic patients. Schizophrenic patients were of particular interest to us because their disease is characterized by social withdrawal, difficulties in interpersonal communication, and abnormalities in autonomic nervous system responsivity. We wanted to know how the cardiovascular system of schizophrenics would respond when they talked to us. We were not aware of any cardiovascular data recorded on such patients during therapeutic encounters comparable to the data gathered by Wolf with hypertensive patients, and thus we had no idea how they might respond in our research model. In light of the widespread communication difficulties of schizophrenics, it seemed equally possible that their blood pressure might skyrocket when they struggled to talk to us, or that it might not change at all. We had no real way to guess. They might even show marked minute-to-minute fluctuations when they engaged in conversations.

A fourth-year medical student (Dr. John Hsiao) used our model to examine the responses of thirty-seven patients diagnosed as schizophrenic. These patients, none of whom were currently hospitalized, were participating in a research study on the therapy of schizophrenia at the Maryland Psychiatric Research Center.[36] They were monitored by us during one of their routine visits to this highly specialized research facility which, located a few miles southwest of Baltimore, is one of the most advanced centers in the United States solely dedicated to research on the causes and treatment of schizophrenia.*

Patients from this center were chosen to participate in our model for two reasons. First, though all of these patients had been hospitalized for schizophrenic problems in the past, they all were currently functioning in society. Many held jobs, and four had been withdrawn from their medications in an effort to ascertain whether they could function without the need to depend on drugs for the rest of their lives. Second, the nature of their schizophrenic disorder had been carefully documented and classified by a highly sophisticated research team working directly with these patients.†
Unlike so many other schizophrenics, the social, psychiatric, medical, family, and pharmacological histories of these patients were well known.

As in previous studies, the blood pressure and heart rate of these patients was recorded when they were quiet, when they spoke to an experimenter, and when they were quiet once again. Participation in the study was voluntary, and patients were informed in advance about the nature of the study. During the talking phase each patient was asked to describe what he or she had done during the day.

Unlike any other group we had previously studied, the blood pressure of these patients simply did not rise when they talked, and there was virtually no change in their cardiovascular responses. The verbal behavior of these patients was rated on a four-point scale: none, some, normal, and increased rate of speech. Twenty-nine of these outpatients were rated as having normal or increased rates of speech when they talked to Dr. Hsiao, while eight had

* I am grateful to Dr. William Carpenter, director of this facility, for aiding us in these studies.
† Difficulties in diagnosis and lack of standardized criteria used to classify patients' mental status make interpretations of research data in the field of schizophrenia highly problematic.

diminished verbal behavior. The blood pressure of those latter patients actually tended to drop when they spoke. Of the total population of thirty-seven patients, fifteen (41 percent) either did not change or lowered their mean arterial pressure while they talked to Dr. Hsiao—a response pattern markedly different from any we had seen in our previous studies.

While four patients who were off all medication did not increase their blood pressure when they spoke, nevertheless it was possible that the neuroleptic medicines (antipsychotic drugs) taken by these patients might have contributed to the lack of pressure changes observed in the group as a whole. While such a possibility clearly merits additional investigation, no medicines taken by hypertensive patients had produced similar effects. And though these findings must be viewed as preliminary (and are currently being pursued in a series of additional studies), they nevertheless led us to consider an entirely new dimension of the problem of blood-pressure regulation: that is, those life situations that might be characterized by diminished human communication and less social interaction. (For further discussion of this dimension, see chapter 7.)

THE SEARCH FOR MECHANISMS*

We also knew that the psychological, emotional, and social contextual variables described so far in this chapter clearly had to influence blood pressure through bodily mechanisms. Which mechanisms, then, are centrally involved?

As has been pointed out recently by Dr. Peter Sterling and Dr. Joe Eyer at the University of Pennsylvania, basically there are only three physiological ways the body can elevate blood pressure: "The body can (1) increase the amount of salt water in the vascular system (by action of the kidney); (2) decrease the volume of the vascular system (by constricture of vessels); (3) increase the rate at which fluid is pumped through the system (by increasing output of

* Because of the complexity of physiological factors influencing blood pressure, and the technical details of this area, only the most general information will be described in this book.

the heart)."[37] These three mechanisms summarize the following well-known physiological formula:

blood pressure = peripheral resistance × cardiac output.*

While this formula theoretically ought to make it relatively easy to identify and assign weights to the various physiological factors that cause hypertension, the fact is that in only 10 percent of all cases has the physiological cause of the problem been identified. And though the major components of the equation have been isolated, investigators differ sharply about the relative importance of the various neurochemical and physiological factors that influence these mechanisms. Similar sharp controversies swirl around the way variables such as heredity, salt intake, obesity, or renin-angiotensin interact with the cardiovascular system to alter blood pressure. Besides this complex array of factors, another reality must be recognized: that is, the physiological mechanisms that cause short-term, transient elevation in blood pressure need not be the same ones that cause long-term or sustained elevation. These complex factors have recently been summarized in great detail by Dr. Arthur Guyton, a leading authority in the field of hypertension.[38]

Perhaps the complexity of these issues, and the reasons major controversies still abound, can be illustrated by examining just one of the many factors suspected of contributing to hypertension—that is, obesity. Obesity clearly increases the hemodynamic demands placed on the cardiovascular system: that is, the heart has to work harder to force blood through the added mass of body tissue. Yet at the same time obesity can also seriously distort a person's body image as well as one's sense of identity and self-worth. This distortion can, in turn, contribute to marked increases in psychological stress, especially when an obese individual deals with other people. This stress can also lead to increases in blood pressure.

If a complex variable such as obesity is factored into the blood-pressure equation when a person speaks, then the resulting elevations can be traced back to any of several different sources. On the one hand, talking can "load on" to a respiratory and vascular system already overburdened by a person's excess weight. On the other hand, talking can exacerbate the stress an obese person may already feel as a result of a poor self-image. Thus the same act—talking—

* Where cardiac output = stroke volume × heart rate.

can trigger pressure elevations for a variety of reasons, and stimulate a variety of physiological mechanisms that could influence the heart.

Recognition of the many factors that theoretically can contribute to hypertension prompted a leading expert in hypertension, Dr. Irwin Page of the Cleveland Clinic, to propose what he labeled the "mosaic theory" of hypertension. As he pointed out, "Hypertension under this concept [that is, the mosaic theory] can begin in many ways and also develop in many ways. . . . The theory does not rule out the initiation of hypertension by one stimulus. Experience, however, shows that what appears to be one stimulus usually involves multiple mechanisms ranging from genetic to emotional stress."[39]

With this "caveat of complexity" clearly in mind, nevertheless, it is important to understand which bodily mechanisms are involved in pressure elevations when a person speaks.

RESPIRATORY MECHANICS, COMMUNICATION, AND BLOOD PRESSURE

Hypertensive patients in particular appear to speak more rapidly and more intensely when a topic is emotionally provocative. In addition, they frequently appear to stop breathing or to breathe irregularly when they speak. Quite literally, many of these patients talk on and on until they run out of breath. In a grammatical sense, they appear to speak without commas, commas being those places in a sentence where one usually stops to take a breath. There is a certain breathless quality to the hypertensive's speech, so that even when such individuals speak softly and slowly they nevertheless fail to breathe properly. By contrast, the migraine patient speaks far slower and decidedly more softly. Unlike the hypertensive, the migraine patient will, when speaking, sometimes hyperventilate, sighing deeply when a topic seems particularly upsetting.

When we first treated Ed, we frequently interrupted conversations and instructed him to breathe deeply, in order to cut short an emotionally upsetting topic. At first we looked upon deep breathing as an obvious way to relax and a natural way to interrupt talking rather than as some device that would directly lower blood pressure. Yet the more we interacted with hypertensive patients, the more we began to suspect that poor breathing habits, especially during speech, were a significant part of their problem. When instructed to pace their breathing properly, many hypertensive patients are unable to do so. As one perplexed patient remarked, "I don't know how to breathe and talk at the same time."

While a thorough understanding of the physiology of respiration involves lengthy descriptions of a complex set of mechanisms, basically speech itself occurs during the expiratory cycle of respiration. (A quick self-analysis will reveal how difficult it is to talk and inspire air simultaneously.) During the expiratory phase of respiration, several well-known physiological responses occur. Among them, pleural* pressure increases, and pulmonary capillary† volume falls. In response to these changes, the stroke volume‡ of the heart, as well as the cardiac output, increases. The net effect of these changes during normal respiration is that usually pressure in the arteries *increases* during the latter part of inspiration and the early part of the expiration, and then *decreases* during the remainder of the respiratory cycle. During normal speech therefore, stroke volume, cardiac output, and arterial pressure all tend to rise as part of the normal respiratory cycle.

In light of these physiological facts, the question that had to be answered was, what percentage of the elevation in blood pressure during speech can be accounted for by normal changes in the respiratory cycle? To explore this question, fifteen healthy volunteers—two men and thirteen women (most of whom were graduate nursing students)—agreed to participate in a study designed to measure intrapleural§ pressure when they spoke normally and when they spoke rapidly. Since marked fluctuations in intrapleural pressure might have a direct influence on cardiac output, we elected to study phasic changes of intrapleural pressure during speech. Unlike most of our other studies, this experiment required each volunteer to endure certain personal discomfort. In order to measure intrapleural pressure, a long, thin lubricated catheter which had a small deflated rubber balloon sealed on its end, was inserted through the nasal passage and down into each volunteer's esophagus to be

---

* The *pleura* is a delicate serous membrane lining each half of the thorax and folded back over the surface of the lung on the same side.

† *Pulmonary* refers to the lungs; a *capillary* is the vascular bed of the lung across which gas exchange occurs.

‡ *Stroke volume* is the amount or volume of blood ejected from the heart with each heartbeat.

§ *Intrapleural* refers to the space between the pleura on each side of the lungs.

positioned just above the diaphragm. Once the tube was in position, the balloon was inflated with fifteen milliliters of air until it could record the pressure from the lungs as they pushed against the walls of the esophagus. In this way, the intrapleural pressure could be continuously measured both when a person was quiet and when he or she spoke.[40]

After the balloon was inflated, blood pressure and intrapleural pressure were recorded for five minutes by a nurse, Marycarol Rossignol, while the subjects rested quietly. Then for the next ten minutes, these measures were recorded simultaneously when the volunteers read aloud at normal speed and when they read at a faster speed. As in all previous studies, blood pressure and heart rate rose significantly as soon as these students began to read aloud. And as in previous studies, the more rapidly they read, the greater the increases. The same was true of the intrapleural pressure: it rose as a person vocalized and rose proportionately higher with increasing rapidity of speech. Yet though the two were correlated, blood pressure and heart rate increased to a far greater extent than one would have predicted from the increases in intrapleural pressure alone. Thus, changes in total lung capacity only partially explained the magnitude of the blood-pressure changes being observed.

PERIPHERAL RESISTANCE: TALKING WITH ONE'S HANDS

Because peripheral resistance is one of the two major determinants of blood pressure (as described in chapter 2), we next focused our attention on this component of the blood-pressure equation during speech. The "resistance" part of this equation refers principally to the resistance to blood flow offered by the small arterioles. The magnitude of the resistance varies indirectly with their luminal cross-sectional diameter: that is, when the arterioles constrict, pressure in the larger arteries behind them increases; when they dilate, it diminishes. Arteriolar resistance is significantly influenced by the autonomic nervous system, which is profoundly influenced by psychological stress. The question is, Does peripheral resistance change when a person speaks? To answer this question, ten subjects were monitored by a nurse, Gail Holcomb, when they were quiet, when they talked at normal speed, and when they talked rapidly to an experimenter. In addition to the usual recording of heart rate and blood pressure, peripheral blood flow was measured in each person's thumb* by means of a light-emitting diode called a "photoplethysmograph" (derived from the Greek word *pletheim,* "an abundance of blood"). This instrument directs a beam of light through the skin into the vascular bed, and the intensity of the light reflected back denotes the amount of blood flowing through the region.

Again, as in previous studies, the blood pressure of all ten volunteers increased when they spoke; and again, the magnitude of the rise was proportional to the rate of speech. Corresponding to these pressure changes, there were rapid and highly significant changes in blood flow to the thumb as soon as a person began to speak, and the resistance was proportionately greater the more rapid the speech.[41]

This study confirmed our suspicion that peripheral resistance plays an important role in elevating blood pressure during speech.

TISSUE BIOCHEMISTRY AND SPEECH†

One of the primary functions of microcirculation is to deliver oxygen to tissues and, similarly, to transport carbon dioxide away. On the basis of changes in peripheral resistance, we predicted that changes might also occur in the content of tissue oxygen when people speak.

Using a monitoring device called a Transcutaneous‡ PCO_2 monitor, we measured the oxygen content of tissues just beneath the surface of the skin in the forearm of twenty volunteer students. We chose the forearm because several research investigators had demonstrated remarkable vascular reactivity in this region during psychological stress.[42] These investigators had shown that while blood flow decreases in surface regions, such as the fingers, during psychological stress, it simultaneously increases in the forearm region. We measured minute-to-minute changes in tissue oxygen, along with blood pressure and heart rate in the usual research model. As in all other studies, blood pressure and heart rate rose significantly when the students spoke to an experimenter. Oxygen

---

* Resistance in the surface blood vessels in the thumb by no means completely describes changes in arteriole resistance throughout the body; rather, it reflects changes in one localized region.

† I am especially grateful to Dr. Thomas Hobbins, director of the Pulmonary Functions Laboratories of the University of Maryland Hospital, for helping us with these studies.

‡ *Transcutaneous* means "across the skin."

levels on the microscopic tissues of the forearm rose just as quickly and just as dramatically as did blood pressure. The increase in tissue oxygen suggested an increase in blood flow to these tissues.* Though we had predicted this increase, the previous study had shown a decrease in blood flow to the thumb (and thus a predicted decrease in oxygen). The apparent contradiction merely pointed out the differences in vascular reactivity in different vascular beds, or in different parts of the body, when people speak.

All twenty students showed the same response. There was an immediate change in blood gases in the tissues of the forearm when they spoke.[43] The results in terms of increase in tissue oxygen were even more surprising, because of their consistency as well as of the magnitude of the changes. Not a single student talked without his or her tissue oxygen significantly increasing in the forearm region being monitored.

HEARTFELT DIALOGUE: THE CARDIAC
CATHETERIZATION LABORATORY

In a effort to clarify further the mechanisms of the blood pressure–communication response, we extended our studies into the University of Maryland Hospital's Cardiac Catheterization Laboratory.†

In a cardiac catheterization laboratory, techniques permit detailed examination of the heart and the circulatory system. Such techniques are crucial in helping to determine various cardiovascular problems, including coronary heart disease. The technique of cardiac catheterization permits the simultaneous determination of a number of hemodynamic variables and allowed us to study the second major component of the blood pressure equation—cardiac output.

In fourteen patients monitored in this unit by Frances Wimbush, we used the same quiet–talk–quiet model previously described. In the majority of these patients, we demonstrated that when they spoke:

1. Cardiac output increased,

* Although unlikely, a sudden decrease in tissue-oxygen utilization could also account for the change.

† I am deeply grateful to Dr. Robert T. Singleton, director of the Cardiac Catheterization Clinic at the University of Maryland Hospital, for his very generous and kind support of this research project, and to the group of nurses and medical students who helped collect these data. In particular, I am particularly grateful to Patricia Lehr and Nadine Semer for their help.

2. Central aortic pressure rose, and
3. Heart rate increased.

Thus these observations in the cardiac catheterization laboratory suggested that blood-pressure changes during human speech were affected by a combination of factors, including both an increase in cardiac output and peripheral resistance.[44]

In order to verify that these cardiac changes were not peculiar to the stress of the cardiac catheterization procedure itself, each patient was re-examined the following day in his or her hospital room. There were parallel increases with respect to heart rate and blood pressure when these patients spoke, both when they were talking in their hospital rooms and in the catheter laboratory itself. Not surprisingly, however, blood pressure was significantly higher in the catheterization laboratory, a phenomenon due most likely to the stress of such a complex diagnostic procedure.

To be sure, our investigations into the physiological mechanisms underlying blood pressure changes during speech are far from complete. Many additional studies will be required to sort out the mechanism underlying the links between speech and blood pressure. Nevertheless, certain conclusions seem valid.

A remarkable number of physiological changes occur during human speech, including ones in intrapleural pressure, heart rate, peripheral resistance, blood pressure, cardiac output, and tissue-oxygen content. While we initiated these studies to further our understanding of the mechanisms involved in the blood pressure–communication response, we discovered that human dialogue is far more subtle and complex than we had ever dreamed possible, and we gained not only knowledge but a new image of the human body. The entire body, even down to the microscopic levels of circulation and the exchange of blood gases in individual tissues, is involved in human dialogue. Since the cardiovascular system nourishes every cell in the human body, every one of those cells is at least potentially influenced by human dialogue. Thus, however little perceptible by naked eye or listening ear, the entire human body is activated when one speaks—just as when we flick a switch in a dark house at night, every window lights up.

CHAPTER 7

The Social Membrane

> They [Pasteur's critics] said he [Pasteur] was too one-sidedly preoccupied with the apparent cause of the disease: the microbe itself. There were, in fact, many debates about this between Pasteur and his great contemporary, Claude Bernard; the former insisted on the importance of the disease producer, the latter on that of the body's even equilibrium. Yet Pasteur's work on immunity induced with serums and vaccines shows that he recognized the importance of the soil. In any event, it is rather significant that Pasteur attached so much importance to this point that on his deathbed he said to Professor A. Renon who looked after him, "Bernard avait raison. Le germe n'est rien, c'est le terrain qui est tout." (Bernard was right. The microbe is nothing, the soil is everything.) —Hans Selye, *The Stress of Life*

A SERVICEABLE HABIT

Philip was not sick, at least not in the conventional way we tend to think about sickness, when we first met, nor was he my patient. He was instead typical of the three hundred to four hundred people whose blood pressure I monitored during various public lectures I had given over the past six years. In order to demonstrate the link between speaking and blood pressure to audiences who might otherwise dismiss it or fail to appreciate our findings in the clinic, I had grown accustomed to asking for volunteers to have their blood pressure taken during my lectures.

The setting for this lecture was the University of Melbourne, at a general meeting attended by perhaps 250 students and interested lay public. Toward the end of a ten-day lecture tour in Australia in 1979, I found myself speaking in one of those modern chemistry lecture halls where the podium was sunk at the base of the room, while the rows of seats were arranged ever higher toward the back of the hall. As was my usual custom, I asked if someone would be kind enough to volunteer to have his or her blood pressure and heart rate monitored.

From the rear of the hall, a young man raised his hand. He then jauntily bounced his way down the stairs to the front of the hall, looking for all the world like a holdover from the 1960s hippie generation. Dressed in a light red pullover sweatshirt, blue jeans, and tennis shoes, with a somewhat unkempt beard hiding his face, he was far less formally attired than the majority of the audience.

When he arrived at the speaking podium, I belatedly noticed that there was no chair for him to sit on, and so I asked him if he would sit on top of the chemistry table that stretched across the length of the front of the hall. Happy to oblige, he quickly found himself a comfortable spot between a series of gas jets and bunsen burners.

I proceeded to measure his blood pressure and heart rate on the computer for five minutes while he remained quiet. After each measurement I wrote his blood pressure and heart rate on a large blackboard in order to give the audience a sense of the variability in his vasculature, as well as to allow them to see the changes when he spoke.

As I continued to lecture, Philip remained silent. After three recordings, in which his blood pressure registered an absolutely normal level of 120/60, with a heart rate of 60 beats per minute, I noticed several middle-aged women in the middle of the hall laughing heartily to themselves. Assuming them to be laughing either at my accent or at something I had said, I asked them what was so funny.

"Oh, nothing" chortled one of the women, while her two friends began to laugh aloud, no longer able to restrain themselves.

"Come on now, don't be so shy," I goaded. "What's so funny? Is it my accent?"

"Nothing really——ah, we don't want to say."

They half-heartedly pleaded for understanding, while they began to laugh even louder.

"Well if you don't tell me, then you'll have to come down here next and have your blood pressure taken."

The threat seemed to work, for one of the women exclaimed, "Well, then, don't blame me for mentioning it, but does that young man know he's wearing two different-colored socks?"

I scanned the young man's feet—and, indeed, she was right! He was wearing one black and one red-and-yellow sock. Before I could rescue the situation, the entire audience erupted in laughter. Though I felt the need to support him, he seemed to enjoy the situation as much as anyone else, in spite of the fact that over 250 people were laughing at him! Seeing no way to help him directly, I resumed my lecture, hoping the audience would shift their attention back to me. The young man continued to smile silently while the laughter gradually subsided. The computer, neutral about the entire scene, continued to record his pressure every minute. Much to my surprise, Philip's pressure and heart rate registered no reaction to the laughter. One minute after everyone had laughed at him, his pressure still registered 118/60; and two minutes later, it was still only 120/61. The experience of having all those people laugh at him had had virtually no effect on his blood pressure.

Because of this unexpected result, I continued to record his blood pressure for several additional minutes before I asked him to speak to the audience. His pressure remained absolutely normal. Then I asked, "Would you tell us who you are, and then chat about anything you wish to discuss for a couple of minutes." It was a standard request that I had made hundreds of times before in similar situations.

In a soft, yet strong English accent, the young man began to speak to the audience: "Hello——ah——my name is Philip Atten-borough." Losing himself momentarily in thought, he continued, "The reason I volunteered for this experiment is that I thought it would be a marvelous opportunity to chat with a group of Austra-lians. It's been rather much of a cultural shock to find myself here in Melbourne, emigrating as I did just four weeks ago from the midlands of England. I thought it would be a rough transition, leaving home and all, but, God, I don't mind telling you it's been bloody awful. Not that your country isn't beautiful, mind you, or

that the job opportunities are not better here than in Manchester—
but I don't know a bloody soul in this country, and I dare say I
think I'm dying of loneliness."

For another minute or so, Philip continued to tell the audience
that he was a university-trained chemical engineer, twenty-eight
years old, and that he hoped to settle comfortably in Australia. He
also mentioned that he had volunteered for the experiment because
it was the first time he had had the chance to talk about his feelings
since arriving in his adopted country.

The entire time he was speaking, he smiled warmly and appeared
at ease. His blood pressure, however, which had stayed so calm
while the entire audience had laughed at his mismatched socks,
told another story. It surged up to 205/115, while his heart pounded
at 130 beats per minute.

Both the message he gave to the audience, as well as the
cardiovascular changes underneath his calm exterior, led to a
counter explosion of warmth and empathy I have seldom seen
before or since. Warmth literally radiated from everyone in the
room. The Australians erupted with a flood of suggestions that they
felt might help Philip adjust to his new life in their country; and
as they talked, his blood pressure quickly fell back to 115/55, and
his heart rate lowered to 60 beats per minute.

As they continued to give suggestions to Philip, my mind briefly
wandered to Charles Darwin, perhaps because this vast and mag-
nificent country had been important in the formulation of his
thinking. I wondered about Darwin's theory of emotions and his
notion of their expression as a serviceable habit.* I wondered what
was truly "serviceable" in the way Philip had expressed his feelings.
Was his smile simply a way of covering deep feelings hidden in his
vasculature? Was his body preparing itself either to fight or to flee,
with his smile a way of fending off the formidable threat posed by
the audience? And why did his vasculature respond only when he
spoke? Why had his blood pressure not prepared him to fight or to
flee even before he began to speak? Were his words really so potent
a trigger? And if some primitive part of his being wanted to run
away or to fight, why then did another part of him openly admit
to his loneliness? Why did he try to embrace symbolically with

---

* In chapter 9, I shall discuss in detail the importance of Darwin's contributions to the general
framework that guides the way emotions are studied by modern scientists.

words the very people who also led his blood pressure to explode when he spoke to them?

As I thought about these questions, the crucial importance of the social context of the blood-pressure demonstrations suddenly struck me. The relationship between Philip's verbal communications and the changes in his blood pressure and heart rate made it unmistakably clear that there was something truly unique and powerful about talking and the cardiovascular system. While I had witnessed hundreds of comparable cardiovascular changes when people spoke to audiences in the past few years, the more general social context of the phenomenon had escaped my attention. Granted I had not seen an entire audience laugh at a person, nevertheless the unique relationship of talking to the cardiovascular system had occurred in so many settings as to be used by me in lectures to demonstrate the consistency and predictability of the links between talking and the cardiovascular system.

Now I found myself wondering why the stress of sitting in front of a large audience would not by itself cause blood pressure to rise. Philip's blood pressure was absolutely normal while he was quiet; and even though 250 people were looking at him, it remained normal—even when they laughed at him. Similarly hundreds of other volunteers had maintained a relatively low blood pressure and heart rate when they were quiet. Though their blood-pressure and heart-rate increases while speaking were striking, the relative calm of the volunteers' cardiovascular systems while quiet in front of large groups had never previously appeared to be remarkable. Obviously, talking itself altered a person's relationship to the social environment in a way quite different from when one was silent in that same environment.

Winging my way back home several days later, I thought more about Philip, his loneliness, and the interaction between him and that marvelously compassionate Australian audience. Again, the questions repeated themselves; and again, the social context of human communication and the cardiovascular system intruded itself into my consciousness. Were his body and his hidden suffering all that separate from the bodies and feelings of that audience? The question at first struck me as insane. Of course, bodies are separate. We have separate hearts, separate circulations, separate brains, and separate limbs; so clearly, we are separate from each other. Our umbilical cords, the original tie of union with another, is cut at birth, leaving each of us separate and distinct until dealth ultimately sweeps us into the great unknown.

And is there not an elaborate physiological theory, vastly expanded in the late twentieth century, that helps to explain the separateness? Did not Cannon's notion of homeostasis and Claude Bernard's milieu interieur explain how our bodies are separate? No theory makes the separateness of our bodies more complete than Cannon's notion of homeostasis. It is a theory that describes the built-in way each body has to keep itself separated from others, the way each body regulates itself against each and every change in the world beyond the confines of the skin. If it is too warm, then the body can homeostatically sweat; and if it is too cold, the body can homeostatically shiver. Bodies are unique, individuated, and forever separated at birth. That seemed obvious.

My legs were beginning to ache from the long, confining air journey, and I mused about that reality. Clearly my own pain was unique! Clearly my body was separate! There was no doubt about it. My pain was distinct from Philip's loneliness. Bodies are separate. Any thought to the contrary had to be part of the confusion of changing day back into night, and spring back into autumn, as the plane roared northward over the Equator.

Yet the question nagged at me obsessively. What if we are far less distinct and separate than we have been led to believe? What if all our bodies are part of a much larger body—the communal body of mankind? Is human dialogue really a replacement for the umbilical cord we lose at birth, a tethered lifeline that continues to unite us all after birth? All of us drawing sustenance from one unseen common womb that we cannot feel because it engulfs us? Yet all the scientific evidence suggests that our bodies are individual, separate, homeostatically regulated organs that are cast adrift at birth into a vast universe. Somewhere north northwest of Christmas Island at thirty-seven thousand feet, in the crystalline darkness of the equatorial tropics, while my legs still ached, and my mind still wandered, my body slowly drifted asleep.

THE SPEAKER IN THE WORLD

The image of Philip and questions about the nature of human interrelatedness in terms of our individual physical bodies reappeared several years later in an unexpected image. This was a new kind of umbilical cord, one that involved the tethered lifeline of polyethylene oxygen tubes undulating effortlessly in the weightless environment of outer space, attached to a new uterine environment, one that was encased in heat-shielded metal.

Those images from outer space gave me a new way to think about the forces that influence human blood pressure. It was not so much that human blood pressure does not conform to the many physical forces we already know weigh down our vasculature here on spaceship Earth. Rather what became clear, as our clinical and research studies continued, was that a crucial aspect of the space we live in had been left out of the equations. The missing dimension—human interrelatedness—profoundly obscured the real "gravitational forces" determining human cardiovascular health.

There was something about the image of a few men huddled together in the tiny confines of a metal capsule floating weightless in the forbidding panorama of space that heightened my awareness of the interrelatedness of human existence in a new way. Without human speaking to human, bonded in human dialogue, that endless universe, though mind-boggling in its beauty, would be an astonishingly empty and lonely place. Without human eyes and ears, and without a mouth to describe the beauty and the terror of a universe that stretched on forever, there would be nothing out there but silent emptiness.

The pictures from outer space made it apparent that the earth-bound physics of human blood pressure that had evolved into the medical equations for cardiovascular regulation somehow had missed the interpersonal universe of human existence. Medical scientists had looked instead upon the universe of each individual human being, apart from each other and from the rest of nature. As the data confirming the links between blood-pressure elevations and talking, and blood-pressure reductions while listening, attending, or orienting, grew ever clearer, so too did the importance of the interpersonal universe to cardiovascular health. Ever so gradually a new equation about the regulation of the human cardiovascular system began to come clear to me—an equation that factored the importance of dialogue as central to the regulation of the human body.

We speak literally millions upon millions of words in the course of our lives; we listen to millions, perhaps billions of communications from others; we spend every living hour attending to or defending against the living world outside of our skin. Surely the cumulative effects of these human experiences have to affect human cardiovascular health and most likely determine it. Indeed, the more I thought about it, the higher the price appeared to be in terms of blood pressure when, instead of living comfortably in one's interpersonal universe, one needlessly defended oneself against that natural world or withdrew from it. In this light the interrelatedness of Philip's body with other human beings became easier to understand. He shared with them what I began to recognize as a common social membrane which centrally affected his body. Just as the uterine environment surrounds the individual fetus, and as the heat-shielded metal surrounded the astronaut's capsule, so too it occurred to me that a social membrane surrounds each human being, simultaneously separating one from and connecting one to the rest of one's living world. While admittedly odd in terms of the usual concept of a membrane, nevertheless the notion of a social membrane did help my colleagues and me to conceive of how a person's external world meshes with the internal world of physiology to influence human blood pressure, as well as to understand why the cardiovascular system is so responsive to human speech. It seemed to me that the social membrane exists at the outer boundaries of a person's identity, a hypothetical area that demarcates that person from the rest of his or her natural environment. As a membrane, however, its distinguishing characteristic is that it belongs neither to the individual alone nor to the surrounding environment. Rather the membrane is two-sided, a filter that inextricably unites each person to the rest of the living world, while simultaneously keeping one separate. It was this image that allowed us to think about the human cardiovascular system as being profoundly influenced by forces inside as well as outside the individual.

In chapter 6, I described transient increases in blood pressure when people speak and transient decreases in blood pressure when they listen or attend to their environment. These data were cited to support the general thesis that human blood pressure is significantly influenced by two fundamental aspects of dialogue. In addition, I suggested that overall reductions in resting blood-pressure levels of hypertensive patients could be effected by altering their way of communicating with their social and natural world.

In chapter 6 I also suggested that hypertensive and schizophrenic patients represent two extremes on a blood pressure–communication continuum. While hypertensive patients exhibited particularly exaggerated increases in blood pressure when they talked, schizophrenics by contrast showed virtually no change. The striking differences between these groups was the contrasting data that led us to speculate about the importance of the human social membrane. Hypertensive individuals seemed too aware of their social surroundings, too focused on other people, too concerned about the potential threat other people pose to their own fragile sense of personal identity and of self-worth. It was an external focus dominated by a defensive orienting toward a person's fellow humans, not a relaxed focus on the external world but one of hypervigilance. It was a perception of the external world as a constant source of threat. Thus the blood-pressure responses of hypertensive dialogue reflected a chronic hypervigilance and a constant readiness to fight or to flee from a world that seemed essentially adversarial and alien. In a sense, talking forced the hypertensive to deal with an adversarial world at the boundaries of his or her social membrane.

The blood pressure seen during schizophrenic dialogue was quite the reverse. The schizophrenics' focus appeared to be inward, away from those to whom they spoke, as if they no longer had a clear vision of others and thus could no longer see others as a threat. With a sense of identity that had already been badly fragmented, the schizophrenics' sense of others appeared to suffer equally. Instead of hypervigilance, the schizophrenics appeared to have lapsed into a chronic state of withdrawal and hypovigilance. Their dialogue with others had all the earmarks of pseudo talk, lacking in heartfelt dialogue, and was far removed from the social membrane and any sense of a world beyond that membrane. They had drawn away from the boundaries of their own social membrane, into a world where hypervigilance and fight or flight were no longer required.

Assuming the existence of a social membrane, we began to question whether resting blood pressure itself was also determined by a person's overall harmonic dialogue with the environment. If we allow for the various structural or corporeal elements that contribute to blood pressure, does resting blood pressure itself reflect the harmony between one's self and the world beyond the social membrane? Is there a continuum from acute self-awareness and tension at the boundaries of one's social membrane to natural, harmonious coexistence with one's surroundings, all the way to total fragmentation of personal identity—a collapse, if you will, of one's ego—and withdrawal from the boundaries of a personal social membrane? Does resting blood pressure change as the continuum shifts?

Having posed the question in this way, we could examine a new dimension of the communication–blood pressure response: that is, we focused not so much on transient blood-pressure changes when a person speaks, but rather on those more enduring styles of communication that characterize a person's life. In this framework, we sought to evaluate the interpersonal factors in overall resting blood pressure in the context of a person's relationship to his or her own social membrane.

WITHDRAWAL FROM THE SOCIAL MEMBRANE

If hypertension is indeed a reflection of human interaction involving too much tension along the social membrane, does long-term social withdrawal lead to lower blood pressure? What happens to blood pressure if someone withdraws from all human contact? What if a person becomes so emotionally fragmented as to stop talking altogether? If dysfunctional communication elevates blood pressure, will the total cessation of human communication lower blood pressure? What happens if a person withdraws into a world of severe schizophrenia, where one is far removed from the boundaries of the social membrane and loses all sense of personal identity—

where there is no "I" or ego and, therefore, no sense of others?

Once we understood that resting blood pressure and changes in communicative blood pressure can be thought of in terms of a person's relationship to the social membrane, it quickly became apparent that the fact that blood pressure does not rise when schizophrenics talk might reflect a far more fundamental phenomenon, one that influenced their overall resting blood pressure as well. While there had been many studies of resting blood pressure in schizophrenics, no one had previously examined the data in terms of their relative withdrawal from the boundaries of their social existence. Few topics had, over the years, proven to be more complex or more controversial or presented a more confusing picture than the studies of schizophrenic blood pressure.

No sooner had Korotkov devised a method to measure blood pressure in human beings than paradoxical and contradictory reports began to suggest that schizophrenic blood-pressure levels are both lower and higher than those found in normal populations. Investigators argued about the criteria used to diagnose patients as well as about the lack of other normative data that might explain the peculiar cardiovascular findings.

Among the factors confusing the picture were the very terms used to classify schizophrenia. During the decades of the twentieth century, the terms used to identify various forms of this disease changed. Links between schizophrenia and blood pressure were further confused by the appearance and widespread use of antipsychotic medications beginning in the mid-1950s. These drugs tended to dampen or moderate many of the more bizarre or extreme forms of schizophrenic behavior that were once commonplace in mental hospitals. Yet even while the sudden availability of antipsychotic medications confused the picture, it also provided a clear demarcation point. Before the introduction of these medicines, the blood pressure of schizophrenics was not confounded by the uncertain actions of drugs.

Over and above the drug issue, the picture was further confused by the fact that the same schizophrenic can be classified differently at various periods during hospitalization. For example, at one period of hospitalization, a schizophrenic can act very paranoid, perhaps manic, and then later be withdrawn and listless. These changes in behavior can alter one's clinical classification and muddy interpretation of blood pressure. Drugs further compound this problem in that they directly influence blood pressure by altering various aspects of the central nervous system.

In spite of these complexities, the hypothetical link between talking and blood pressure provided a new framework for re-examining the data from previous studies. All of the previous studies could be re-examined in terms both of the relative severity of the disease and of whether patients were in better or poorer social and verbal contact with their social surroundings. This framework thus helped us recognize the significant fact that in virtually every study before the introduction of antipsychotic medicines, schizophrenic patients who were the most socially withdrawn tended to have the lowest blood-pressure levels. With surprising frequency and consistency, investigators reported that the blood pressure of severely withdrawn schizophrenics (usually labeled "catatonic" or "hebephrenic") were the lowest observed in their hospital populations and significantly lower than those in normal populations. Catatonic and hebephrenic patients are characterized by acute social withdrawal and lack of talking and are generally regarded as the most severely disturbed schizophrenics.

The first hint that there might be a connection between low blood pressure and schizophrenia was noted by Stephen Longworth in a paper published in the *British Medical Journal* in 1911.[1] While the diagnostic criteria used in his paper are difficult to evaluate, he did report a surprising number of patients in Suffolk District Asylum who had low blood pressure, and an equally surprising lack of patients with high blood pressure.

At virtually the same time, in 1911, in London, Dr. Ray Gibson described a relationship that was subsequently to appear as a pattern in virtually every study that classified blood pressure of schizophrenics in relationship to their relative social withdrawal. He found that there is a "low blood pressure as a general rule; lowest in cases of catatonia, slightly higher in hebeprenia, and highest in dementia paranoids/paranoid schizophrenics." The systolic blood pressures he recorded were:

Catatonics: men, 112; women, 100
Hebephrenics: men, 118; women, 113
Paranoids: men, 120; women, 128[2]

What differentiated these groups was their relative social contact with their environmental surroundings, as well as their verbal behavior. Paranoid schizophrenics usually were in better verbal contact with others in their environment; while catatonics, as a rule, had completely withdrawn from all reality and contact with others.

In 1923, Dr. Theophele Raphael and his colleagues at Ann Arbor, Michigan, described the case of a fourteen-year-old boy who had been admitted to the state psychopathic hospital.[3] They described the boy, upon admission, as suffering from a classic case of catatonic stupor; he was mute, totally withdrawn, and uncooperative. Nine months later, however, he was markedly improved and in good contact with his environment. When he was admitted, the physicians noticed that he had a very low pulse rate (46 beats per minute) and a blood pressure that averaged 90–100/65–85. Nine months later, when he was talkative, his blood pressure averaged 120/70, and his pulse rate had risen to a normal rate. These investigators suggested that there was a connection between this boy's extreme schizophrenic withdrawal and his low blood pressure.

In 1923, Dr. W. S. Dawson at the Maudsley Psychiatric Hospital in London studied the blood pressure of fifty schizophrenics. Of these cases, twenty-seven were classified as catatonic (including nine they described as "stuporous"), fourteen were labeled simple dementia praecox (early onset schizophrenia), seven were paranoid, and two were hebephrenics. Dawson pointed out that the stuporous schizophrenics formed a particularly interesting group, and noted, "In all except one case the blood pressure was below normal."[4] Again, his general findings of low systolic blood pressure were similar to Gibson's earlier ones:

	Average Systolic Blood Pressure
Catatonics	116
Hebephrenics	117
Simple dementia praecox	117
Paranoid schizophrenics	120

In a follow-up study in the Cheshire County Mental Hospital in England, Dr. G. G. Parkin made 1,338 observations on the blood pressure of various patients. Again, as in previous studies, he found that patients classified as catatonic had significantly lower blood pressures than paranoid schizophrenics.[5]

In the first truly exhaustive study of blood pressure in schizophrenia, Dr. H. Freeman, Dr. R. G. Hoskins, and Dr. F. H. Sleeper examined the blood pressure of 180 patients at the Worcester State Hospital in Massachusetts in 1931.[6] They repeated their measurements both on certain patients as well as with three different investigators taking the same patient's pressure. For comparison's sake, these investigators contrasted their findings against blood pressure readings taken on 323 first-year medical students at Boston University School of Medicine. Though the students were younger in age (and thus one would expect their pressure to be lower), their average systolic blood pressure of 116 was eleven millimeters higher than the schizophrenics' average systolic pressure of 105. There was an even greater difference in diastolic pressures. The students' average diastolic pressure was 71, while the schizophrenic patients' was 55. Diastolic pressure levels thus averaged sixteen millimeters lower in the schizophrenic population. Freeman, Hoskins, and Sleeper added an even more intriguing observation, which was subsequently to be confirmed by other investigators: that is, that schizophrenics' blood pressure did not rise with age the way it did in normal populations. Indeed, though their patients ranged in age between sixteen and sixty, not a single diastolic pressure above 85 millimeters of mercury was observed. Again, as in other studies, patients classified as catatonic had the lowest blood pressure levels, while those classified as paranoid had the highest. None of these differences could be explained by the population's height, weight, or age; and Dr. Freeman suggested that the sedentary life of the patients may have contributed to their generally lower pressure levels.

In 1939, Dr. Milton Miller examined the blood pressure of 193 psychotic individuals.[7] Most of his patients were described as paranoid (60) or depressed (33), only 23 were schizophrenic; and none were described as catatonic or hebephrenic. Again, as in previous studies, those patients classified as withdrawn or schizophrenic had by far the lowest blood pressures in the population (110/78).

In that same year, Dr. Joseph Rheingold examined 129 patients admitted over a five-year period to the Psychiatric Institute of the

University of Illinois College of Medicine.[8] Again the same findings. In general, schizophrenic patients had a mean average blood pressure far below that found in the general population. And again, as shown in the following table, patients who were the most socially withdrawn had the lowest blood pressures:

		Blood Pressure
Catatonic (N = 17)		107/72
Hebephrenic (N = 52)		106/71
Simple (N = 18)		114/78
Paranoid (N = 30)		114/73
Other types (N = 22)		109/74
All schizophrenics	66 males	115/76
	73 females	105/72

A Norwegian study published by Ottar Lingjaerde and his colleagues in 1950 reported findings on 3,000 measurements of blood pressure taken on 423 schizophrenic patients ranging in age from twenty to eighty-five years. These investigators noted that "among schizophrenics below 60 years there are far more hypotensives (low blood pressure) than in normals. Among 122 schizophrenic women below age 40, a systolic blood pressure less than 100 mm Hg. was found in 68 percent."[9]

In one of the more revealing and exhaustive studies ever conducted on the blood pressure of schizophrenics, Dr. F. Mackenzie Shattock and his colleagues exhaustively studied 550 female patients and also a subgroup of patients when they were withdrawn and refractory (catatonic and hebephrenic) as well as when they were in good social contact with their environment. A number of the socially withdrawn patients had extraordinary low systolic blood pressures. For example, 28 withdrawn female schizophrenics had an average systolic pressure of 93. Even more significant, however, were the elevations in blood pressures when these same patients came in "social contact" with their environment. As Shattock noted:

Twelve female schizophrenics who had a low initial brachial blood pressure showed a rise of blood pressure at the beginning of remission, either spontaneous or following E.C.T. (electro-convulsive therapy).

In 6 cases the average blood pressure before spontaneous remission was systolic 89 and diastolic 73; after the spontaneous remission the blood pressure of these patients was systolic 120 and diastolic 85 mm Hg. . . . In another 6 cases the average blood pressure before remission was, systolic

99.5 mm Hg and diastolic 85.1.... after remission following electro-convulsive shock therapy the blood pressure of these patients was systolic 111.8 and diastolic 75.8.[10]

Shattock concluded that "the lowest blood pressure readings in a survey of 550 female patients were almost invariably those of resistive, difficult schizophrenics." Yet at the same time he also pointed out, "There was no obvious reason why refractory schizo-phrenics should have a lower blood pressure, as their physical condition did not compare unfavorably with that of the patients in the socialized group."[11]

Subsequent studies on the blood pressure of schizophrenics reached similar conclusions: the more socially withdrawn, mute, and isolated the patients tended to be, the lower their resting blood pressures.[12]

In a study remarkably similar to Shattock's, Dr. Russell R. Monroe and his colleagues at Tulane Medical School intensively studied 24 schizophrenics, 12 of whom were hypertensive and 12 of whom were hypotensive.[13] These patients were selected from a larger group of 766 institutionalized patients studied by these investigators in 1961. They found that in the population as a whole the incidence of hypotensive blood pressure readings was *three times greater* than that observed in comparative normal populations, while the incidence of hypertension was approximately equal that of normal populations. These investigators also pointed out that these extraordinary low blood pressures appeared with equal fre-quency in both schizophrenic and nonschizophrenic patients—a fact, Monroe and his colleagues suggested, that would imply that the low pressure readings had something to do with some unknown aspect of institutionalization rather than with schizophrenia itself. Five years later, in 1965, these general findings were replicated by Dr. Kurt Witton and Dr. Arnold R. Goldman in a study of 578 patients in a neuropsychiatric hospital.[14] In their population they again found that 109 patients (or 19 percent of the total group) were hypotensive. Again, this rate was three times that found in normal populations. Witton and Goldman also reported that they found only 49 patients who were hypertensive, and that of these, 50 percent were older than sixty-seven. This rate of hypertension was far below that seen in nonpsychiatric populations.

In addition to these overall trends, the twenty-four schizophrenics studied more intensively by Dr. Monroe and his colleagues all appeared to follow a fascinating and consistent pattern. The twelve *hypertensive schizophrenics* were described as follows:

It was our impression after the survey that the hypertensive schizophrenics showed an acute awareness of the nuances in their surroundings. They appeared to be oriented, in contact with the hospital activities, sensitive to changes in the examiner's behavior and emotionally responsive. . . . Their *speech was frequently rapid,* the patient often answering a question before it was completed.* . . .

In contrast to the findings in hypertensive patients, our study of hypotensive patients showed them to be lethargic, clouded, emotionally flat, uninterested in their surroundings, poorly oriented and sparse in their productions. . . . empathy with the examiner was minimal.[15]

The relationship of these patients to their social membrane and its effects in terms of their blood pressure appeared clear. Patients in "too much" contact were hypertensive, while those who were withdrawn and in poor contact with their social membrane were all hypotensive. Even more revealing was their confirmation of the peculiar shifts in blood pressure when a patient's relationship to his or her social membrane shifted. As had been reported earlier by Shattock, Monroe and his colleagues also described the peculiar switching between hypertension and hypotension as the same patients came in contact and then withdrew from their social surroundings:

For 4 of these 12 hypertensive patients we had sufficient data to show significant blood-pressure variations correlated with these behavioral changes. When the individual was belligerent and hostile, neat and clean, and in "good contact" with his environment, the blood pressure would be significantly elevated. When the patient was mute or catatonic or out of contact with his environment, his blood pressure was generally normal or hypotensive.[16]

More recent data has revealed another intriguing dimension to the overall pattern of low blood pressure in withdrawn patients. Working in the Gartnard Hospital in Glasgow, Dr. G. Masterton, Dr. C. J. Main, and their colleagues recently described (1981) in the *British Heart Journal* the results of their retrospective analyses of blood-pressure trends of 116 female psychiatric inpatients, 69 of whom were classified as schizophrenic. The remainder suffered

---

* This verbal behavior is highly reminiscent of the Type A behavior subsequently discovered by Friedman and Rosenman.

from a variety of other psychiatric disorders. All of these patients had been in the hospital for at least one year, and the group as a whole averaged nineteen years of continuous confinement in the hospital. Of the entire group, the schizophrenics tended to have entered the hospital at a younger age and to have stayed far longer than the average. An average of seven measurements of blood pressure were recorded on each patient over the years. Masterton and Main observed that when these women were first admitted to the hospital, their blood pressure was close to that found in normal populations for women their age. What was remarkable, however, was that their blood pressure failed to rise over the next two decades as normal individuals' would. Thus nineteen years later, the patients' systolic blood pressure averaged twenty-eight millimeters lower than normal populations, and their diastolic pressure was almost thirteen millimeters lower. The trends were similar for both schizophrenic and nonschizophrenic women and could not be explained by weight loss, diet, or drugs.[17] The finding that the longer the patients stayed in the hospital, the lower their arterial blood pressure fell compared with normal individuals, confirmed the observations reported by Freeman, Hoskins, and Sleeper several decades earlier.[18]

While not certain about the cause of this surprising effect, Masterton and Main suggested that the social isolation of the patients may have been most important. The authors noted that since diet could not account for the overall finding, "isolation itself could be important" in lowering blood pressure.

Pursuing this finding further, Main and Masterton then examined the blood pressure of 110 female psychiatric inpatients in terms of the type of ward they occupied. Four different wards were studied that varied in relative restrictiveness on freedom allowed the patients. In general, the less restrictive the ward, the greater the social contact among the patients, while the most restrictive had little social contact between patients. As shown in the following table there was a striking relationship between the relative restrictiveness of the ward and the average blood pressure recorded from the patients. Ward A, which was the most restricted (the most disturbed patients), had the lowest blood pressures, while Ward D (the least restrictive) had the highest blood pressures.[19]

	Number of Patients	Blood Pressure	
		Systolic	Diastolic
Ward A	26	117	76
Ward B	21	123	75
Ward C	46	138	85
Ward D	23	143	87

While all of these data point toward social isolation (and a lack of talking) as the crucial factor influencing overall resting blood pressure, two other variables—namely, schizophrenia itself as well as chronic institutionalization—may also have contributed to these findings. A hint that perhaps the low blood pressure of schizophrenics may be a function not solely of institutionalization but rather of a lack of communication was provided in 1979 by B. W. Richards and Fatima Enver, who examined the blood pressure of 486 individuals suffering from Down's syndrome.[20] These investigators had expected blood pressure in these patients to be considerably higher than that found in normal populations. They examined records from ten different institutions and contrasted their findings with 807 subjects who had been living in institutions for comparable periods of time with other types of intellectual deficit. While both those 807 subnormal controls and the Down's syndrome patients had systolic and diastolic levels significantly lower than normal populations, the Down's patients had extraordinarily low blood pressures. The blood pressure of the Down's patients even at age seventy averaged 123/75. The authors concluded that some unknown factor other than institutionalization had contributed to this remarkable finding.

THE PRISONER'S WORLD

In a similar way, in 1930, Dr. Walter Alvarez and Dr. L. L. Stanley examined blood-pressure data in six thousand prisoners and four hundred prison guards and found that the guards had significantly higher readings than the prisoners.[21] Even more impressive was the fact that, unlike normal populations, the prisoners' blood pressure did not tend to rise with age. Blood pressure varied little from the young to the old. Unlike other areas, where dietary factors such as lack of sodium could be cited as potential explanations for the phenomenon, no such factor could be found among the prisoners. The investigators suggested that this surprising finding might be due to the fact that prisoners "had been freed from the hurry and strain and fatigue of earning a living."[22] No mention was made of the solitary life and relative lack of communication enforced by the very structure of prisons. A subsequent study published in 1975 by Dr. D. A. D'Atri and Dr. A. M. Ostfeld revealed that crowding in prisons led to significantly higher blood pressure than that found among people in less crowded settings.[23] Prisoners held in private cells consistently had lower blood pressure than those housed with cellmates.

THE MONK'S WORLD

The data culled from seven decades of research on schizophrenics' blood pressure, as well as on institutionalized prisoners and Down's syndrome patients, all appeared to point in the same direction. When coupled with our findings of the link between talking and blood pressure, the data strongly implied that social isolation and lack of communication contributed to lower-than-normal blood pressures. On the other hand, we could not rule out the possibility that this lowering of blood pressure was caused by a slowdown in muscle activity and the general lethargy of the patients.

There was, however, a way to answer this question. In 1960, Dr. J. Gordon Barrow and his colleagues in Atlanta, Georgia, published the results of a study in which they had carefully assessed various blood serum indices of the cardiovascular health of 150 monks from two Catholic religious orders—Benedictine and Trappist.[24] These investigators had originally initiated these studies to track down various dietary factors that were widely suspected of contributing to the development of atherosclerosis. Barrow and his medical colleagues had deduced that two religious orders, Trappist and Benedictine monks, offered the unique opportunity to study the effects of various dietary factors that were suspected of causing elevations in serum cholesterol and, by inference therefore, of contributing to the development of coronary atherosclerosis. These investigators were interested primarily in these orders because of the differing consumption of fat in the diet of each: Trappist monks neither drank alcohol nor ate meat, while the Benedictines' diet closely resembled that of the typical American. On the average, in this study, the Trappists derived 26 percent of their calories from fat, while the Benedictines received 45 percent of their calories from fat. At issue, according to the Atlanta research team, was the importance of fat in the typical American diet and whether fat contributed to the development of atherosclerosis.

This study was particularly intriguing from our perspective, however, because the Trappists were one of the few religious orders to take a lifelong vow of silence. They spent their lives as silent contemplatives, combining meditative prayer with manual work. Once a man entered the monastery as a monk (usually around age twenty-one), he never spoke again. Even more relevant, they dedicated their life to physical labor, usually working on the farm surrounding the monastery. Thus, these monks might possibly provide answers to questions regarding physical exercise which had been raised by data from institutionalized patients. Unlike the patients, active, vigorous work was an integral part of the Trappist monk's daily life. By contrast, the Benedictine monks, though they also led a life of contemplative prayer, dedicated their religious life to preaching and teaching others. They also communicated regularly with each other in the monastery.

In an exhaustive series of biochemical studies, the medical team measured crucial serum blood factors suspected of contributing to atherosclerosis. Four times a year, they drew blood from seventy Benedictine and eighty Trappist monks, all of whom lived in a communal setting. Among the serum factors examined were the following:

> Total serum cholesterol
> Free cholesterol
> Esterified fatty acids
> Phospholipids
> Total lipids
> Alpha and beta cholesterol

For each of these factors, at every age between twenty and sixty, the Trappist monks had serum levels significantly lower than those found among the Benedictines; and indeed, the Trappists' levels were far lower than comparable levels found in the general population of the United States. Not a single serum measure was higher at any age in the Trappist monks compared with the Benedictines.

Yet the investigators discovered another puzzling fact. Dietary differences could not explain their findings. As they noted in their report:

While the data indicate that the Trappists as a group consume a smaller percentage of fat and have a lower average serum cholesterol than do the Benedictines, an analysis of individual data on each participant shows that individual blood cholesterol when corrected for age cannot be correlated with individual fat intake alone, indicating that *there must be factors other than dietary fat and age which determine serum cholesterol levels.*[25] [Italics added]

Blood-pressure readings unfortunately were not published in this report. Twenty-four years later, I telephoned one of the investigators to inquire whether they had recorded blood pressure in these monks. "Indeed, we did," was the prompt answer.

"Were there differences between the groups in overall resting blood pressure levels?" I asked eagerly, assuming that at long last an answer to the vexing problem of interpreting the low blood-pressure levels of withdrawn schizophrenics would be found.

"I don't recall off hand," the investigator answered apologetically. Then he added with a note of decided pride, "But the data is still stored on computer tapes and I would be happy to look it up for you."

Several days later I telephoned again. This time the investigator was clearly less jubilant—perhaps disgruntled would be a more accurate description—and apologetically he explained that the blood-pressure data had unfortunately been erased from the tapes two months before my call.*

These data are all the more important because of the radical changes that have swept through Catholic religious orders during the past two decades. This study can never be repeated, as no longer do monastic orders take a lifelong vow of silence. Yet these data are significant. All the serum blood factors were lower in the Trappists. Presumably their development of atherosclerosis would also be less common; and, as near as one of the investigators could recall, their blood pressure was also lower.

* Phone conversations with the two other investigators in this project yielded equally disappointing results. One of the investigators did recall that "four or five of the Benedictine monks had symptoms of high blood pressure that were severe enough for me to hospitalize them," but could recall no similar episodes among the Trappist monks. To his best recollection, the blood pressure of the Trappist monks appeared to show the same differences as the blood-serum factors—but he was not absolutely certain. He also added that the data was still stored in boxes and that he hoped to re-examine it sometime in the future.

There was still one other way to look at the effects of social isolation and lack of verbal contact on overall resting blood pressure in individuals who regularly exercise.

HUMAN ISOLATION: LOW BLOOD PRESSURE

A brisk summer breeze from the ocean swirled through the open door of John Kelly's darkened three-room cottage and momentarily stirred the hot ashes lying at the base of the turf-fed hearth before blowing down the leeward side of the green-carpeted mountainside. The wind rustled and shook the purple heather and danced through the fuchsia-laden hedges arching over the ageless stone walls lining the dirt road that wound down the mountainside to the rocky cliffs of Culdaff harbor.

John's whitewashed cottage was enveloped in the monastic, sad quiet that characterizes the Inishowen peninsula of northern Donegal in Ireland. Scattered throughout the valley beneath his farmhouse were a dozen similar small white stone cottages, each with a thin white stream of turf-fed smoke whirling out the chimney in the cool ocean wind and then quickly disappearing. Perhaps the most beautiful, isolated, and unspoiled region in Ireland, this remote peninsula receives few tourists except the émigrés returning home for their summer holidays. John's cottage had stood on the same spot for hundreds of years, and little had changed there for centuries.

It had been a particularly bad day for John. One of his prize cattle had suddenly taken ill, and the local veterinarian was uncertain about its chances of surviving. Years of hard work had so far reaped the rewards of many veterinary bills, and little else. Yet John did not complain. An aging, wiry elf, he was not about to share his bad fortune with me, but asked whether I would play a few Irish songs on his accordion. The reward, he promised with a smile, would be a strong hot toddy* served by his sister.

The ocean winds lifted the heaving waves and sent them crashing in a roar against the cliffs below John's farm. In a knoll beneath

---

* Irish whiskey mixed with boiling hot water and sugar.

his house, a flock of sheep bleated in idyllic pastoral reverie, their sounds only emphasizing the absence of human voices in the region. I could not guess what John thought about or felt as he quietly sipped his hot toddy, though I imagined the loss of his cattle had to be devastating. John spent his days toiling alone in his fields. And in the long summer evenings he walked the four miles down the mountain road into the town of Culdaff, there to spend a few leisurely hours listening to Irish music in his favorite pub. Even there John spent far more time listening than he did speaking.

One fact was clear. On an typical day in the Inishowen country-side, the average person spends far less time talking and far more time listening than people do in Baltimore. But John and his neighbors did not seem lonely. Quite the contrary. They seemed at peace with their environment. They watched the changing weather and the conditions in their fields with a sense of fated resignation that I found hard to grasp. They had long ago learned not to struggle with an Irish weather that could at one moment embrace them in its splendor, only to change without warning to lash them with its brute power. If it rained for a week, then it rained for a week. And when the sun broke through the rain and mist, then they hoped the hay would have time to dry before it rained again. If not, then so be it. Their quiet resignation seemed to have emerged from centuries of wisdom that taught them how to live in harmony with their environment. They simply did not struggle the way I had been raised to struggle.

While little was known about the incidence of hypertension on the Inishowen Peninsula, I guessed that it was not much of a problem for the likes of John. It was a hunch supported by data gleaned from dozens of isolated regions scattered throughout the world. In the industrialized world, blood pressure normally rises markedly during the first two to six weeks of life. After that initial period, blood pressure remains relatively stable, rising ever so slowly during the next few years. Systolic blood pressure is roughly equivalent in ten-year-old boys and girls but, thereafter, rises more rapidly in boys. Between the ages of twenty to forty, systolic blood pressure is typically higher in men than women. By age fifty-five, however, this pattern is reversed, and women typically begin to have higher pressure readings than men. Around age seventy, while systolic pressure continues to rise in both sexes, diastolic pressure actually begins to fall.[26] Thus, in virtually every industrialized country in the world, blood pressure rises slowly but surely throughout a person's life. The pattern has been observed in hundreds of thousands of cases and confirmed in almost every industrialized nation.

The blood pressure of certain groups, however, deviates markedly from these norms and does not rise with age. These exceptions, which are scattered throughout the world, have one factor in common: they are primitive and socially isolated. There are, for example, the Yanomamo Indians, living in northern Brazil. Investigators have discovered that these Indians have an average blood pressure of 106/66 between the ages of ten and nineteen. Yet after age nineteen, these blood-pressure readings do not change but remain at those levels throughout their lives.[27] Investigators have speculated that these remarkably low levels are due to the lack of sodium in the Indian diets. Similar interpretations have been given to comparable findings observed elsewhere. Blood pressure does not rise with age among the aboriginal tribes in Szechwan province in West China,[28] among the Melanesians living in the highlands of New Guinea,[29] among the Samburu[30] and the Zulu warriors[31] in rural Africa, among the natives living in the Solomon Islands,[32] or among the Polynesian natives living in the South Pacific.[33] In every case where investigators have discovered these unusually low blood-pressure readings, the conclusion has always been the same: these findings must be due to the lack of salt in the diets. Virtually no mention or attention has been given to the social isolation of these peoples or to the way they relate to one another.

Evidence also indicates that, as these primitive societies modernize, the blood pressure of their members tends to rise. For example, in 1979, Dr. Stephen T. McGarvey and Dr. Paul T. Baker classified communities in American Samoa as "traditional, intermediate and modern." The designation of these groups within their community was highly predictive of mean group tendencies in terms of resting blood pressure. Those groups classified as "modern" tended to have by far the highest resting levels of blood pressure.[34]

In light of the relatively high level of hypertension of black Americans, a great deal of attention has been paid to comparable rates of hypertension among black Africans. When G. C. Shattuck first attempted to study this problem in Africa in the late 1920s, however, he encountered a peculiar problem. In a monograph published by the Harvard University Press in 1930, he noted that hypertension simply did not then exist in any significant levels in countries such as Liberia.[35] Hypertension did not appear to be the problem among blacks in the remote countries of Africa that it appeared to be in the rural South of the United States. Yet, in 1973, as Dr. Joseph Pobee, chief natural investigator for the World Health Organization Cardiovascular Studies in West Africa, recently pointed out, times have changed. In describing the incidence of hypertension in West Africa, Pobee observed a consistent trend that has been found in a number of African nations. In rural, traditionally isolated tribal areas of West Africa, blood pressure is invariably lower than it is in urban settings, such as Ghana. Yet the very same tribal people have significantly higher rates of hypertension as soon as they move into urban settings.[36]

In the United States, as well, similar examples of low blood pressure can be found. In 1937, Dr. C. G. Salsbury reported the rather remarkable finding he made on the Navajo Indians.[37] During the five years between 1931 and 1936, he observed that, of 4,826 Navajos admitted to the Arizona Mission Hospital, only 4 were found to have hypertension—rates astoundingly lower than those found among black and white Americans (you will recall that anywhere from 25,000,000 to 40,000,000 adult Americans are currently judged to be hypertensive). Similar extraordinary low rates of hypertension among the Navajo Indians living in Arizona and New Mexico were subsequently confirmed by other investigators. For example in 1979, Dr. Frank DeStefano, Dr. John Coulehan, and Dr. Kenneth Wiant recorded blood-pressure readings among 640 Navajo Indians living on the vast Navajo Indian Reservation in northeastern Arizona, northwestern New Mexico, and southern Utah. These Indians lived in widely scattered isolated camp areas in the region. As was true of isolated "primitive" people in other regions of the world, the most fascinating fact was that their blood pressure was low and did not rise with age.[38] These investigators cited the work of Dr. M. Braxton[39] and Dr. M. Sievers[40] who also found low blood pressure in American Indians living on reservations. As happened with the native Africans, however, the rates of hypertension rose significantly when these same Indians moved off their reservations into urban settings.[41]

Unfortunately, while the phenomenon of low blood pressure in isolated peoples has been noted with remarkable consistency, investigators have almost always leaped to dietary or other physical factors to explain their findings. Scant attention has been paid to factors such as the quiet life and the relative social isolation of these peoples.

IMPLICATIONS

All of the data reviewed in this chapter suggest a consistent, and previously unrecognized, factor common to a wide variety of blood-pressure studies. That factor has to do with the amount of time a person remains quiet and socially isolated. While it is obvious that a great deal of additional research would be needed to buttress the formulation of a link between low resting blood pressure and social isolation, nevertheless all available data point toward one. When coupled with the evidence linking talking to blood-pressure increases, the quantity and the quality of verbal contact with others does appear to have a significant influence in determining overall resting baseline blood pressure.

The construct of a social membrane was put forward to help provide a framework for understanding why the cardiovascular system is peculiarly sensitive to human dialogue. I have suggested that the very act of communicating heightens awareness of one's social surroundings and can, in certain instances, heighten tensions along the boundaries of one's social membrane. The very act of speaking can trigger cardiovascular responses more closely approximating a major fight/flight response than any effort to reach out to another human being. Thus, transient elevations in blood pressure and heart rate while speaking can be linked to the very same phenomenon that helps determine overall resting baseline blood pressure—the social membrane.*

What, then, is the hypertensive individual living in a modern industrialized society to do? Obviously, becoming a contemplative monk or a schizophrenic or going to jail cannot be seriously recommended as a cure for cardiovascular disease. Nor can the vast majority of hypertensive individuals retreat to isolated or primitive regions where they would be cut off from their fellow humans. Yet while these are not widely available options, the data do underscore the importance of spending some time each day in quiet reflection, or meditation, turned inward away from the *hyper*tension of one's own social membrane.

A variety of techniques have recently been developed to help hypertensive individuals relax and at least transiently lower their blood pressure. Two investigators in particular, Dr. Herbert Benson at Harvard Medical School and Dr. Charles Stroebel at the Institute of Living in Hartford, Connecticut, have written extensively and persuasively about the health implications of taking time out every day to practice quiet relaxation and meditation. Their studies have shown that such efforts can result in a significant lowering of blood pressure.[42] The construct of the social membrane helps clarify why such a turning inward would help a person lower his or her blood pressure. Though such turning inward would not resolve the tensions emanating from one's social membrane, it would provide an important quieting period of transient relief for a body that would otherwise be taxed by chronic, unremitting tension.

As we shall see in the next two chapters, moments of quiet reflection and meditation also help one come to grips with the central problems inherent in dealing with the social membrane. For, ultimately, the two phenomena are closely linked. Harmony along the walls of one's social membrane is dependent on one's internal harmony, and vice versa.

---

* While it would require a significant amount of additional research, the construct of a social membrane implies that during the course of therapy schizophrenics might confront major increases in blood pressure when they attempt to communicate with others. That is, while the data in this chapter involve schizophrenics who showed no increase, or even a decrease, in blood pressure while talking, I assume that this phenomenon occurred because of a fragmented ego with a resulting lack of sense of others. However, it seems possible that attempts to help schizophrenics reintegrate and restructure their social membrane would also reintroduce the notion of a social world as potentially threatening and hostile. Efforts to negotiate or communicate with such a world could elicit major flight/fight autonomic reactions. In a sense, the schizophrenic might face the dilemma of becoming ever more hypertensive as schizophrenia abated.

CHAPTER 8

The Hidden Dialogue

> Man is the only animal that blushes. Or needs to.
> —Mark Twain

Having thus far considered blood pressure and heart rate as they are linked to human communication, let me now turn to another aspect of the cardiovascular system—blood flow and its connection with the obvious human response of blushing and with its less obvious internal analogues. These responses bring us to a third dimension of the cardiovascular system and its link to human dialogue—a dimension in which heart and circulation can be viewed as more than an object of study and an organ of communication but also as a subject of human experience, of human feelings and of our language for those feelings. These three different dimensions of the human cardiovascular system are most clearly and aptly exemplified by the very human phenomenon of blushing.

My purpose in this chapter is to demonstrate certain fundamental communalities between blushing, migraine headaches, hypertension, and coronary heart disease which link them all to human dialogue. Yet at the same time I must emphasize fundamental differences between these problems—differences that reside in the perceived nature of the vascular message and the ensuing disease. The person who blushes while speaking usually feels the vascular message, and it is seen and responded to by other people as well. By contrast, when a hypertensive elevates blood pressure while speaking— though the response can be thought of as a form of hidden internal blushing—it is neither felt nor seen and is therefore not responded to either by the person whose body is reacting or by other people. The vasomotor reactions in a person prone to migraine headaches fall between these two extremes. As we shall see, aspects of the vascular changes in a person prone to migraine headaches, while speaking, are apparent and can be felt and responded to, or ignored.

In order to introduce the idea of the human heart and circulation both as organ of communication and as subject of human experience, I shall describe my own struggles with blushing while also outlining how these struggles meshed with similar struggles patients were having with their cardiovascular systems.

ASPECTS OF BLUSHING

BLUSHING ON THE OUTSIDE

I suspect I first began learning about the complexity, the subtlety, and, even in some ways, the brutality of stress-induced cardiovascular reactions at a tender age. Even as a young boy, I blushed almost as easily as the wind blows across the open sea. Not the everyday, home-grown garden variety of blushing, mind you; not the subtle shift in color that you often see in people, a slight reddening around the cheeks and eyes, a charming glow. Nothing so merciful was in the cards when Nature wired my body. Whether it was the Celtic genes of my parents, the light coloring of my skin, a certain shyness, a deep-rooted sense of shame, hyperactive blood vessels in my face, an unconscious need to gain attention, an attempt to assault other people with my fiery face—or God knows how many other theories there are to explain it—the simple fact remains that back then as a boy and adolescent, and even today as a middle-aged professor in a medical school, when embarrassed I light up with all the splendor of a harvest moon rising to defeat the blackness of a frosty autumn evening. No pumpkin in all its resplendent autumnal glory could even begin to match the glow of my face when it decides to give me away.

Early in life I was forced to give up trying to be Gary Cooper walking fearlessly down some dusty street at high noon, determined to see justice triumph at any cost, showing not a flicker of emotion. Nor could I pretend that I was John Wayne surrounded by threatening enemies, tight-lipped while fearlessly commanding mere mortals not to be afraid. John Wayne or Gary Cooper, hell! I couldn't even walk across the floor in the eighth grade and talk to a thirteen-year-old girl during an Eddie Fisher recording of "Oh My Papa" without my face lighting up like red fireworks exploding and sparkling in the darkness of a hot Fourth of July evening.

My firefly face was a dead giveaway. It was a fink, a bodily appendage that simply refused to hide my inner secrets. If I was embarrassed—bingo, on came the red. If I was angry, my chameleon surface quickly revealed me to the enemy. No one ever had to ask me what mark I got on a test: an A was gray-white; an F, bright red; and C—well, that was the usual color. If I was frightened, then I had to head for the dark.

If only someone had invented an anti-blushing pill the way they had already invented anti-acids, anti-migraine, anti-hypertensive, anti-colitis, anti-spasm, anti-arrhythmic, anti-pregnancy, and anti-depressant medicines! They seemed to have developed an "anti" for everything except blushing. This peculiar scientific neglect of my problem left me with no option: I simply had to learn to live with my tattletale face. I secretly longed for the day when athero-sclerosis would deaden my vasculature, when nature would give me its own rheostat to help modulate the glow of my face. But fantasies about the glories of old age could not sustain me, nor would my adolescent reality go away. Gradually it wore me down. I had to surrender and learn how to be comfortable being uncom-fortable.

Only years later, as I watched hypertensive and migraine patients' blood pressure, heart rate, blood flow, hand temperature, and even tissue oxygen content rise while they remained unaware—only then did I begin to realize what a wonderful friend I had all along in the hyperreactive vasculature of my face. I saw then that all the embarrassment I had suffered in childhood, adolescence, and manhood had had a purpose. My face had been a merciless but powerfully effective teacher and had forced me to understand intuitively and to accept certain facts about the human body and human feelings that the hypertensive and migraine patients in our clinic did not seem to understand, or that, if understood, were certainly difficult to accept. These patients seemed to think about their bodies and talk about their cardiovascular problems in ways diametrically opposite to the way I had been forced to conceptualize my own body and my cardiovascular reactions. Each patient seemed to see himself or herself as something or someone different from the body in which he or she lived, and to think of the body as a collection of mechanical parts that had nothing to do with the patient's personally. (This problem will be discussed further on pages 223–40.)

NO ONE BLUSHES ALONE

Yet there was one aspect of blushing that forced me to think in an entirely new way about the blood pressure–talking responses described in this book. It took literally thousands of observations before I finally stopped being completely surprised, sometimes even profoundly shocked, at the magnitude of the surges in blood pressure when people talked. The shock was due not so much to the vascular responses as to the striking contrast between these hidden reactions and a patient's surface appearance of absolute calm and lack of awareness. How could such important bodily communications remain absolutely hidden, not just from my view but from the person whose own body was responding? Indeed, when the computer monitor displayed a sudden rise in a patient's blood pressure, he or she was likely to be far more surprised than I.

As study after study reconfirmed the ubiquity of the blood pressure–talking response, we began to think about these hidden vascular responses as a form of blushing. The notion of the human body as a communicative organ, one that can speak with an eloquence surpassing that of spoken words, gradually fused with the realization that it takes two or more human beings to carry on a conversation. When two human beings speak to each other with words, their bodies are also simultaneously engaged in an astonishingly complex dialogue.

These heretofore hidden aspects of bodily communication gradually led me to recognize something else about blushing that I had always intuitively understood but had never fully appreciated: that is, an essential part of the experience of blushing is its public visibility. I cannot recall ever blushing in the dark by myself, no matter what devilish fantasy was coursing through my brain. As near as I can recall, my blushing occurred only when other people were present. How often I wished it was the other way around.*

The reality of blushing as an interpersonal experience had, in common with blood pressure, another aspect which grew ever clearer as we monitored the vasculature of hypertensive patients. Both blushing and blood-pressure elevations when people speak are communications. The importance of blushing had far more to do with the communicative aspects of blushing, its reactive nature, and its consequences than with whether my face lit up a delightful shade of rouge when I was all alone in the dark. By contrast the problem with the blood pressure and heart rate changes when people spoke is primarily due to the fact that these responses are hidden.

I had grown up with an uncomfortable awareness that the presence of other human beings, in combination with whatever struggles were going on inside me, inevitably led my face to light up. Through years of unremitting embarrassment, I came to recognize and understand first-hand the remarkable power we human beings have over each other's bodies. I came to experience, that is, the difference between *physiology* (the machinery of the body), *psychophysiology* (the way the mind influences the body), and, most important, the way other people, or *transactional psychophysiological* forces, influence the body. And it was the transactional experience—blushing—that forced me to be aware of the links between my body and my feelings. For it was other people who not only saw my face turn red but also told me what my blushing face meant: "Are you embarrassed?" The question could be asked in a hundred different ways, but the answer was always the same: "Yes, I have feelings that I would like to deny but cannot hide."

After watching the blood pressure–talking responses in thousands

* Let me emphasize that I am describing transient episodes of human blushing—the physical response best described as "reactive blushing." There are other problems that cause chronic, continuous, and prolonged blushing or flushing, which can occur when a person is alone, and can lead to a serious and embarrassing skin disorder called "rosaceae," characterized by red blotches, pustules, and swelling of connective tissues. Rosaceae has also recently been linked to excessive alcohol intake and a genetic predisposition to alcoholism, as well as to a serious, but undetected vulnerability to diabetes. It may even contribute to various forms of cancer. In a sense, the "delightful red tinge" a person experiences when alone can be symptomatic of serious problems. It has also been suggested that this chronic blushing may be linked to an earlier predisposition to transient blushing when one is emotionally aroused. In this sense, reactive blushing may be an analogue of other types of psychosomatic problems—a bodily state that begins as a reactive response when one is emotionally aroused but that can lead to serious physical disorders.[1]

of cases, I understood that all psychosomatic or psychophysiological reactions involve similar transactional messages—and that one reason these internal responses develop into psychosomatic problems is that they are hidden. Unlike blushing, no one can see these responses, not even the individual whose pressure is rising. And since the response cannot be seen or felt, no one else can tell the individual what these reactions mean emotionally. Thus, such patients hide their feelings, with literally no psychological effort, not only from others but from themselves as well.

Other than straightforward, mechanical, physiological malfunctions, I began to suspect that few people develop hypertension alone, that few "get" ulcers in a social vacuum, and that most migraine headaches are triggered by interpersonal difficulties. Yet for reasons not difficult to comprehend, the vast majority of patients suffering the symptomatic pain and bodily damage of these diseases hold fast to a contrary point of view. Even patients who, as I said in chapter 1, are otherwise quite enlightened about psychosomatic disease have great difficulty coming to grips with the transactional nature of their problems. Cardiovascular regulation, for example, appears to be so solitary, so bound up in one's own individual body, one's own emotional struggles, one's unique developmental history, that it is virtually impossible for a patient to conceive of the problem as involving other people, as being a hidden, bodily way of communicating—a form of blushing, if you will, that leaves both others and oneself unaware of one's discomfort.

The more I listened to patients, the more clearly I saw that, even though they dissociated their vasculature from their sense of personal identity, they nevertheless insisted on maintaining sole ownership of their vascular disease. Each patient was thoroughly convinced that he or she had the "problem," whether it was the migraine inside his or her head, or the hypertension in his or her blood vessels; and so each patient believed it was he or she alone who had to get rid of the problem. It was difficult for patients to grasp the idea that these problems were linked to struggles they were experiencing when they communicated with others; and that, like my blushing, solitary solutions were not likely to solve their problems.

Furthermore, I became increasingly aware of patients' apparently reflex tendency to smile when their cardiovascular systems were changing most dramatically—a tendency that seriously compounded their emotional isolation. For their smiles belied the internal message of their bodies (as I shall discuss later in this chapter) as the blusher's face can never do.

These aspects of the emotional isolation of the patients in our clinic led me finally to recognize the essential importance of blushing and its deep implications as a shared human experience. The sharing involves a sequence of steps that include the following interactions:

1. Blushing is a vascular signal that begins when a person's face first turns red.
2. One may or may not perceive that one is blushing; but since the blush occurs in an interpersonal context, others will recognize the vascular signal.
3. The person who witnesses the blushing will quickly interpret the meaning of the blush and usually conclude that it signals some emotional discomfort, most likely embarrassment.
4. While others are decoding the meaning of the blushing, typically the person who is blushing also will begin to feel his or her discomfort as well.
5. As soon as others begin to recognize that the blusher is uncomfortable, they will begin to search for the source of the discomfort and will usually assume that they may have caused the person embarrassment, or that in some way their ongoing dialogue provoked anxiety.
6. While searching for the source of the discomfort, the blusher will become increasingly conscious of anxiety, recognizing that the embarrassment or shame or anxiety is now manifest to everyone. Once having recognized the discomfort, the blusher will try to get away from the uncomfortable situation.
7. After concluding that they may have caused the blushing, the persons who are perceiving the problem usually automatically take on the role of therapist, in that they try to get the other person to stop blushing and thus curtail the embarrassment and the emotional suffering. This therapeutic role is usually assumed for two reasons: first, most human beings are not sadistic and do not like to see others suffering and, in particular, do not like to confront the fact that they might be the cause of another person's suffering; second, a person's discomfort or embarrassment will quickly become theirs as well.
8. If therapeutic maneuvers designed to stop the blushing fail, and the person continues to be manifestly uncomfortable, eventually everyone involved will break off the encounter and part company.

While there are many variants of this process, generally blushing is an interpersonal vascular signal that usually interrupts all ongoing dialogue and demands a response as an important bodily message. Even more important, it is quickly recognized by all concerned as essentially interpersonal, as a reaction that involves all concerned.

By contrast, the hypertensive or the migraine patient who smiles while simultaneously elevating blood pressure or blocking peripheral blood flow, encourages others to continue with the dialogue—while one's blood pressure rises higher and one's heart beats still faster. The smile encourages the very process that ought to be interrupted because of its potential destructiveness.

Since blushing involves the social membrane, it connects other people to our distress. It leads us to see ourselves, to see and feel our embarrassment, through another person's eyes. It forces us to think about and to feel what others are thinking and feeling about us, and thus establishes our sense of self in reference to others. Other cardiovascular reactions, however, are not so explicit. For example, constriction in blood flow—the very opposite of blushing— is a response that does not usually permit a person insight comparable to that gained from blushing. This loss of interpersonal insight leads to a reciprocal breakdown in communication and to such disorders as migraine headaches.

THE LANGUAGE OF MIGRAINES

NO LANGUAGE BUT A SMILE

Migraine is a common disease characterized by intense, throbbing headaches. According to current concepts, the most immediate cause of the pain is the stretching of nerve fibers secondary to the dilatation of arteries within the cranium. Patients who suffer from migraine headaches, as we shall see, exhibit several peculiarities in common with hypertensive patients, including unusually reactive circulatory systems as well as a lack of awareness of the dramatic shifts in blood pressure and heart rate that are fundamental to the disorder. In contrast to hypertensive patients, however, migraine patients are frequently presented with a physiological signal that is perceptible, if one attends to one's body.

As I have already noted, the abnormalities of the circulatory system in the hypertensive patient and the disordered vascular responsiveness of the typical migraine patient can both be viewed as hidden or internal blushing. That is, just as the ordinary blush denotes an alteration in blood flow—triggered by human interaction—to a particular vascular bed, so too the circulatory changes observed in migraine and hypertensive patients also are triggered by human dialogue.

Patty was, in this regard, a perfect example of a typical migraine patient. On the surface the concerns and diseases that led her and Ed to the University of Maryland clinic appeared to be as different as night and day. Though Ed did realize that elevations in his blood pressure threatened his life, he had originally come seeking help for a problem that he could not feel. By contrast Patty came because painful migraine headaches were crippling her, making it virtually impossible for her to function effectively as a nurse. Sometimes visual blurring accompanied her headaches and had made it difficult for her to see the intravenous drips of the critically ill patients under her care.

Attractive and petite, Patty at thirty-three-years old was the type of women who on first impression seemed to have hardly a care in the world. Bright, effervescent, witty, and pleasant, she would have been a perfect hostess for a daytime television talk show. It was hard to imagine anyone with her outgoing personality being wracked with periods of severe head pain. Nor did she look as though she had endured a succession of emotional traumas in her life. Yet, in addition to stormy relationships with men, including marriage and divorce, Patty's childhood had been dominated by her demanding, overbearing, punitive mother and her father who, as she phrased it, "was browbeaten to death by my mother."

Though her clinical problems and life history differed significantly from Ed's, they had a great deal in common. Both were highly articulate and sensitive. Both also had cardiovascular systems that could change in remarkable ways without the slightest awareness on their part. And both appeared to be totally disconnected from their own bodies. No one would imagine from looking at them that their heart rate, blood pressure, and blood flow could storm out of control while they were engaged in what appeared to be relatively peaceful dialogue.

As with many migraine patients, it was difficult to interact with

Patty and to appreciate fully the depths of her suffering. Perhaps the bleakness of the cold, gray, rainy November afternoon when we met for the fourth time heightened my awareness of the contrast between Patty's pleasant demeanor and her internal suffering. Just before the session I had been staring out of my twelfth-floor window at the rain-shrouded quilt of industrial sprawl and red-brick row houses that characterize southwest Baltimore.

"Thought I'd wear this outfit to combat the weather," Patty commented as she entered my office. "No sense letting nature get the best of you on a day like this." She smiled broadly in response to my comment that her red plaid skirt and matching sweater more than offset the gloomy weather outside. As I attached a thermistor to her finger to measure her skin temperature and wrapped the blood-pressure cuff around her arm, she added, "If I had an office like this, I'd close the curtains on rainy days, and then open them on sunny days. It's bad enough trudging through this mess to get here, but no sense looking at it too. If you don't look, then you wouldn't have to know it's rainy and gooky outside."

While I chuckled in agreement, I wondered whether Patty had touched on a psychological strategy that applied to her migraines. Had she opted to avoid looking at all the emotional pain in her life, hoping against hope that it would all go away? I resisted asking the question, however, believing that such an interpretation would be premature.

For the first fifteen minutes of the session, Patty light-heartedly described various problems she had experienced with patients and doctors during the past week. While she appeared to be in a jovial mood, her cardiovascular system fluctuated markedly. Oblivious to the fact that her heart was racing along at a rate between 110 and 130 beats per minute, she even joked as she referred to her head pain: "The migraines haven't been quite as bad this week, so things must be improving. Maybe your clinic will turn into an uptown satellite of St. Jude's Shrine. I could even see the I.V. drips all week long. The only real bad headache hit me on Saturday, but that was my day off." She smiled as she described her headaches, almost as if she were talking about someone else's pain.

"How are you feeling now?" I asked, trying to call Patty's attention to the fact that her heart rate was averaging around 110 beats per minute, while her blood pressure had dropped to a low of 95/60.

"I think I'm fine," she answered softly. "I think everything's bound to turn out okay in the end. Just find me a man. That's really what we need now."

Patty was alluding to the fact that her husband had left a year earlier. He had remarried, this time a divorced woman with three children, and consequently failed to pay Patty's alimony or to provide any emotional support for their six-year-old son. She had been left, as she had said in a previous session, to "sort things out on my own." In addition to her economic worries, Patty was deeply concerned that her son was growing up without a male figure with whom to identify.

Typical of migraine patients, however, she failed to answer my question about her feelings, so I repeated it for emphasis. "But how are you feeling right now? I mean, what do you think it means when your heart is racing along between 110 and 130 beats a minute. That's faster than it would beat if you were out jogging." Then, as an afterthought, I noted, "I find it difficult to keep up a conversation while jogging. And right now your heart is beating so fast you might as well be jogging. If you want to talk to me, then either I have to run along with you or you have to slow down."

Glancing at the computer for a moment, then looking at me with a quizzical smile, she countered, "Well, like I said, just find us a man. That's bound to get that heart rate lower, and then maybe you can keep up with me. Have you tried the dating game lately? Do you know what it's like to go out and meet a guy at a bar and be looked over like it's meat market time, gang? Believe me, there just aren't that many worthwhile guys out there."

Again, she had not directly answered the question about her feelings. It was clear that part of Patty's struggle resided in the fact that she could not detect or discriminate her own feelings. She simply had no idea when her heart was racing and when it was beating normally. She had no idea when her blood pressure was rising or falling nor could she sense when her hands were freezing cold and when they were warm. Disconnected from some of the major bodily correlates of emotional arousal, Patty was unable to detect the shifts in feeling that accompanied these physiological changes.

The initial part of therapy therefore demanded that she pay attention to the marked changes in her body. Only then could she take the next step, in which she would be taught the emotional meaning of various bodily changes. Her inability to detect the changes was a reflection of the truly profound way Patty had dissociated herself from her own body. Typical of patients with such physical disorders, Patty referred to *her* headaches as "the" headaches and to "that" heart rate rather than "my" heart rate. She did not use possessive pronouns when describing her symptoms or those parts of her body linked to migraines, almost as if these problems belonged to someone else. As had been the case with Ed, our most difficult task was to get her to pay attention to her body and acknowledge it as her own.

Patty proceeded to talk about various concerns in her life. She talked about her worries about her son and the difficulty of balancing her multiple roles as mother, nurse, housekeeper, and sole breadwinner. She also noted that she had no time for her own social life and several times jokingly alluded to the fact that she found dating quite difficult: "This old body ain't getting no younger."

For the first four sessions, her hand temperature never rose above the room temperature of 72 degrees Fahrenheit, more than twenty degrees below normal. Nor could a photoplethysmograph detect any blood flowing in the surface areas of her fingers. Over and above her inability to discuss her feelings or sense her own body, was the remarkable contrast between her pleasant demeanor and her bodily turbulence underneath.

In an effort to force Patty to pay closer attention to her body and the conflicting bodily messages she was giving, I decided to share an image about her paradoxical smile that had occurred to me several weeks earlier: "You know Patty, I've been thinking for the past few weeks about an idea. When I look at you today, I wonder, do you think the Mona Lisa had migraines?"

She laughed aloud at the question as I continued, "Do you think da Vinci was really that clever? I mean when you think about that picture, there's the Mona Lisa smiling her marvelous smile and everyone is captivated by it. Everyone stares at the Mona Lisa's smile, hypnotized by her mystic gaze, just as I'm certain everyone looks at your smile and thinks you're on top of the world."

"Do you think I'd make a good model?" Patty responded,

appearing thoroughly to enjoy the comparison. "I mean, that would be a nice way to supplement my income. Though I'm not as chunky or as well endowed, and I don't have those big dark Italian eyes, well, who knows?"

"But it's not the Mona Lisa's dark eyes or her smile that really interests me," I countered as Patty settled back in her chair. "It's her hands! Why else would da Vinci paint the Mona Lisa's hands? When you look at that painting, there she is smiling her great big smile, while she quietly folds her hands unobtrusively on her lap. Only nobody notices them. Nobody looks at the Mona Lisa's hands. Everybody's preoccupied with her smile. I'm sure it was all a clever ruse. I'm certain the Mona Lisa had migraines. I'll bet you her hands were freezing cold, just like yours, the entire time da Vinci was painting her portrait."

Patty chuckled again while I pressed the issue one step farther. For several weeks I had been trying to get her to pay closer attention to her hands. Specifically I wanted her to notice when they were warm and when cold, so that she would learn to correlate changes in her hand temperature with various events in her daily life. I hoped that she might thus begin to get some sense of when she was anxious or angry and when she was relaxed and at ease. Several years earlier, a group of investigators at the Menninger Clinic in Topeka, Kansas, had shown that if migraine patients were taught to warm their hands through biofeedback and relaxation, they could prevent the occurrence of migraines.[2] Cold hands appeared to be one of the bodily characteristics that typify individuals prone to migraines. The problem appears to be due to reduction of blood flow to the surface areas of the hands, as well as to a generalized hypersensitivity of these vascular regions to emotional stress.

Continuing with my comparison, I asked, "Do you think the Mona Lisa's heart was racing along at a 110 beats per minute while her blood pressure oozed along at 100 systolic millimeters of mercury when da Vinci painted her smile?

"Several of my friends visited the Louvre a few weeks ago, and I called them up after they returned home to ask them about the color of the Mona Lisa's hands. I thought maybe they were bluish white, like your hands. They laughed, of course, and politely told me the painting was rather faded, and that there were about fifty people standing in front of them at the Louvre. Then they asked, in a way that confirmed my suspicions, who looks at the Mona Lisa's hands anyhow? I suggested that they may have missed the whole point of the painting. I told them that I suspected that da Vinci must be chuckling in his grave. He knew all about Mona Lisa, and I'll bet you ten to one his painting was a ruse. I'll bet you that up there in the rafters of the Louvre somewhere above her portrait you can still hear his ghost whispering, 'Look at her hands! Look at her hands!' "

Patty lifted up her hands, looked at them for a moment, pressed them against her face, and then, like a bouncy cheerleader, mockingly sat on them to warm them.

After bantering back and forth for a few more minutes, I called Patty's attention to the fact that her heart rate had fallen to 92 beats per minute, while her blood pressure had risen up to a normal level of 115/75. For the first time since she had come to our clinic, her heart rate had fallen below 100 beats per minute.

She seemed genuinely puzzled, and quipped, "Maybe the Mona Lisa's heart didn't race all the time either?"

"Maybe your heart doesn't race all the time either?" I countered, sensing that she might be ready to begin paying attention to her body. "We could, of course, find out for certain if you took your pulse five or six times each day, along with your blood pressure, and then wrote the numbers down so that we both could have a record."

Patty agreed and added that she knew she ought to pay closer attention to what was going on inside her body.

I then asked her how she expected me to decode her communications, especially when they appeared so contradictory. "Who should I listen to when you speak, Patty? The woman with the lovely smile, and happy-sounding voice, or the woman whose heart sometimes races over 125 beats a minute and whose hands are freezing cold? How in the world could people like your ex-husband carry on a sensible conversation if your body was storming so wildly inside, while you appeared so happy and peaceful on the surface?"

"That's a good question," she answered quickly, while she again stared blankly at the computer tracings of her heart rate and hand temperature. I then asked her how she thought I should interpret the peculiar contradiction between the warmth of her smile and the coolness of her hands, and she answered, "Cold hands, warm heart."

Patty then stopped smiling and fell silent. For a while she quietly watched the physiological monitors as they flashed the unambiguous reality of her internal bodily chaos. Finally she remarked with a pained, semi-forced smile, "I guess I let the insides do the crying for me." Then, sighing deeply, she added softly, "But just remember, when you're smiling, the whole world smiles with you."

I nodded in understanding and scheduled her for another appointment the following week.

After the session I fell once again to staring at the gray mist and rain, and only gradually became aware that I was humming a tune, an echo of the popular song Patty had been referring to in her final remark to me. It suddenly struck me that Patty's attitude toward hiding her pain was entrenched in the music and poetry that permeates our land. She seemed to echo some universal need, something deeply human, something we constantly need to tell each other that is noble. It appeared to be a modern way of convincing ourselves that there is no jungle out there, no inescapable pain, no unavoidable suffering, no life-threatening monsters, no all-consuming darkness. "Cry on the inside, smile on the outside," smile even though our hearts are breaking*—these are the codes we are taught to live by, and they were the codes that dominated Patty's behavior. Such codes, of course, are not all bad. It would be a grim existence if all of us looked despairing every time something went wrong in our lives. There is clearly virtue in focusing on the positive aspects of life and acting as a force that brings joy to other human beings. There is social virtue in being courageous, helping to prop up one another, especially when we are threatened with being overwhelmed by sorrow and grief or consumed by anxiety. And smiling is one way to respond to anxiety. It is a natural way to ease tension and does not by itself lead to migraines, hypertension, or any other psychosomatic problem. This aspect of smiling is common both in healthy individuals and in psychosomatic patients.

* For those readers who are fans of Nat King Cole, I would be remiss if I did not point out that he recorded a beautiful melody entitled "Mona Lisa," in which he asks directly whether the Mona Lisa's mystic smile is in reality only a cover for a broken heart. Certain aspects of the thesis of this book, it seems, have been in the wind for a long, long time.

What becomes a problem for psychosomatic patients, however, and contributes to their bodily problems, may at first glance seem absurd, impossible to believe, and, for those not afflicted by such problems, totally alien to the very way one usually thinks about emotional stress and stress-related physical disorders. The psychosomatic patient does indeed smile even though his or her heart is breaking, only without realizing or feeling it break—the patient feels only the smile. Such patients think—truly believe—they are happy and cannot feel their hearts racing out of control or their hands some twenty degrees colder than normal or their blood pressure boiling up into hypertensive levels. They do not know how they feel, because no one else sees their body responding. No one teaches them about their internal blushing, and they cannot detect that blushing by themselves. Thus no one can educate them about their feelings because their bodily communications are hidden behind a smile.

In order to discuss this anomaly and the multitude of problems that develop from it, I shall first describe the mechanical aspects of the migraine headache, which is but one of a dozen clinical problems in which the interplay between bodily changes and emotional arousal goes undetected. By no means do I intend to provide an exhaustive physiological description of migraines or a definitive text on head pain, but wish rather to help explain why psychosomatic patients in general, and migraine and hypertensive patients in particular, cannot properly identify and label their own feelings and thus are left with no language but a smile.

THE MECHANICS OF MIGRAINES

Migraine is one of several major classes of head pain or headaches. Other types of headache occur with greater frequency, including neuromuscular head pain and temperomandibular joint pain. Unlike other headaches, however, migraines involve the cardiovascular system. The term *migraine*—derived from a Greek term to describe one-sided headaches (*hemi-kranion* ["half-skull"])—is a bit misleading, since this headache occurs on only one side of the head (unilateral head pain) about 50 percent of the time. The head pain often spreads over the entire cranial area and can be mixed with or accompanied by a neuromuscular headache. The migraine is a vascular headache which varies in intensity and duration and may be accompanied by nausea and vomiting, as well as by blurring of vision. The head pain also brings with it, not surprisingly, marked shifts in mood. Before and during an attack, one finds oneself highly sensitive to light (photophobia) and comforted by dark places. Often for hours or even days before the migraine itself, one can sense an impending headache, and it is likely that this dread contributes to the problem. Many individuals so fear the pain of a migraine that they tense their bodies in anticipation before the actual onset of the headache in much the same way a patient tightens up in a dental chair.

The two most common types of migraine are called "classical" and "common." According to a medical committee that defined these types of head pain, classical migraine is a "vascular headache with sharply defined, transient visual, and sensory or motor pro- dromes* or both."[3] It occurs in two phases: a pre-headache phase with an aura or a sense of impending problems; and the headache phase itself. In the classical migraine, the aura phase is brief, usually lasting about thirty minutes. It is accompanied by changes in mood and energy, including euphoria, depression, inertia, irritability, aggressiveness. The aura itself can be, but is not always, followed by the headache itself. Approximately 10 percent to 20 percent of migraine patients suffer from this type of headache.

Common migraine, as the term suggests, is far more prevalent. It is characterized by a less clearcut and more prolonged aura phase, which sometimes lasts for hours and is often not even recognized by the patients themselves. The headache phase is similar to classic migraine, except that the pain generally lasts longer and is likely to recur more often.

The migraine itself is characterized by throbbing, pulsating pain, visual disturbances, nausea, vomiting, and diarrhea. The throbbing pain is caused by the swelling and distension of the blood vessels (vasodilatation) both inside and outside the surface areas of the brain. The swelling, or dilatation, is thought to be triggered by neurochemical agents in the blood stream, and the medicines typically prescribed to alleviate the pain reduce the swelling in these vessels—a class of drugs known as "vasoconstrictors." (Er-

---

* *Prodrome* refers to symptoms or warning signs that give a migraine patient cues that a headache may ensue.

gotamine Tartrate is perhaps the most widely used of this class of medicines.)

It was once thought that approximately 5 percent to 10 percent of the population suffered from migraine, but recent medical surveys have suggested that the incidence may be higher. Recent studies have shown that up to 20 percent to 25 percent of women experience migraine at some point in their lives, and that between 5 percent and 10 percent of men occasionally suffer from it.[4] While authors still differ on the relative incidence in the general population, there is widespread agreement that migraines affect women over men at least on a 2:1 ratio. In a recent survey, women were found to make up 78 percent of 750 migraine patients, a ratio that seems to be in line with the sex incidence of this problem in our clinic.[5] Nor, as we shall see later, is this sex differential merely a statistical quirk; it is, rather, a reflection of underlying psychophysiological and psychodynamic causes of the problem.

In women the history of migraine has certain common features. Usually, though by no means always, the difficulty begins at puberty and disappears at menopause. Since in some women the onset of the headaches is strongly linked to their menstrual cycle, some investigators suspect a link between female hormone levels in the blood and vulnerability.*

While criteria for a diagnosis of migraine have confused the picture somewhat, available data support the fact that women with migraines have a strong family history for the problem. Predisposition for the problem is typically passed from mother to daughter, although sometimes from father to daughter as well. In various studies, positive family histories have ranged anywhere from 10 percent to over 25 percent of all cases studied.

Three possible mechanisms are suggested. The first is a genetically transmitted physiological predisposition. Notable among the phys-

* Estrogen and progesterone affect the blood vessels in the lining of the womb. During the premenstrual phase, the uterine blood vessels become elongated and thick-walled. If progesterone levels drop suddenly, bleeding occurs from the womb, and the pattern can apparently trigger a migraine in susceptible women. In addition, changes in premenstrual blood volume from retention of sodium and water may contribute to the overall vasodilation of the arteries. However, even here the reader must be cautioned about the link between physical-biochemical changes and psychodynamic factors. The onset of one's menstrual period triggers many potential psychological problems that center on issues of femininity, lack of pregnancy, and so on. These, too, can contribute to the psychophysiological stress one can experience during the premenstrual phase. For example, for a woman reared in a family that wanted a boy instead of a girl, menstrual bleeding becomes an "awful" reminder that she is the "wrong" sex and can trigger unconscious resentment, anger, and depression.

iological predisposing factors are the marked lability or changeability of the vasculature in individuals susceptible to migraines. Some scientists have speculated that such individuals suffer from unstable regulation of the autonomic nervous system. Like Patty, these individuals show remarkable shifts in the amount of blood that flows through the surface skin areas of their hands and feet. Sometimes surface blood flow is completely blocked in these regions, followed by periods of greater than normal amounts of blood flowing through the same region. Since surface skin temperature is a reflection of this phenomenon, the hands of migraine patients can exhibit marked swings in temperature—from ice-cold hands at one point to palms soaking wet with sweat minutes later. In addition, data from our clinic suggest that many migraine patients have lower blood pressure and unusually rapid heart rates, especially when they are emotionally upset.[6] Before the development of computer monitoring systems, clinicians were unable to record the continuous blood pressure of migraine patients, and there was little reason to suspect that low blood pressure was a contributing factor to the disease. Indeed, it was widely believed that low blood pressure was not a condition one had to worry about. Yet, as I shall describe in the next chapter, migraine patients occasionally exhibit precipitous drops in blood pressure when they talk about emotionally upsetting topics.

An alternative possibility that could account for the family history link is that the psychological and psychophysiological defenses used by a mother are the very same ones that she then teaches her offspring: that is, mother and daughter communicate to each other through hidden bodily reactions of which neither is aware. In essence, literally by blocking blood flow in her hands instead of by feeling upset, mother teaches daughter how to "handle" emotional stress. Given a biological predisposition to respond to stress by blocking blood flow in the hands, this response pattern would naturally become a way of coping with emotional problems. When confronted with stressful life situations, a woman would be likely to use the same defense her parents used—one involving hidden vascular responsiveness.

There is a third possibility, one that is most likely to prove to have the greatest heuristic value. This explanation holds true for a broad range of psychosomatic disorders, whether hypertension, migraines, colitis, and so on: that is, certain organ systems have a genetically transmitted vulnerability to react to emotional stress. Indeed, vulnerability to many diseases appears to have a strong family history. Thus, if a mother or a father has migraines, there is a strong likelihood their offspring will have migraines. The same is true for hypertension. But what is inherited? As we shall see later in this chapter, a person who, especially when stressed, cannot feel major changes inside his or her body cannot sense his or her own feelings. Thus, if mothers or fathers cannot sense their own feelings, how can they teach their offspring about feelings or sense the feelings of these children? Since the children will inherit the same type of reactive vasculature, the parents will be unable not only to sense their own feelings but to see any signs of emotional stress in their sons or daughters as well. Like their parents, the children will react inside their bodies without exhibiting any external signs of stress. Thus, four things could be transmitted in a complex psycho-genetic package:

1. The genetic predisposition to respond to stress in specific bodily systems;
2. An inability to feel these bodily systems responding to emotional stress;
3. A consequent inability to link these changes to various emotional states;
4. And, most importantly, the fact that these responses cannot be seen or felt by those significant individuals who interact with one, thus creating the possibility for serious emotional miscommunications.

This theory, which is part of the central thesis of this book, assumes that a genetically inherited trait has direct psychological and interpersonal consequences in terms of the communication of human feelings.

When it comes to assessing the psychological status and personalities of migraine patients, there is remarkable agreement in the literature. Beginning with the classic reports of Dr. Harold Wolff (himself a life-long sufferer from migraines),[7] several studies have convincingly shown that migraine headaches are precipitated by emotional stress.* The most commonly cited emotion linked to migraines has been repressed anger or repressed rage. Terms

---

* One of the more complete and comprehensive medical textbooks on headaches is *Wolff's Headache and Other Head Pain,* edited by Donald J. Dalessio, and I highly recommend it for those interested in learning more about migraine headaches.[8]

frequently used to characterize the personality of migraine-prone individuals include the following: meticulous, perfectionistic, conscientious, intelligent, neat, inflexible, rigid, resentful, guilt-ridden, and compulsive.

Perhaps the most peculiar aspect of migraines, from both a physiological and a psychological perspective, is the phenomenon of "let-down headaches:" that is, one may experience a migraine headache not during periods of acute stress or intense work, but rather when one relaxes, when one finally "lets down." Weekends, vacations, or even the first waking moments in the morning frequently mark the onset of migraine. Many patients cite such occurrences as evidence that psychological or psychophysiological explanations cannot be used to account for their vulnerability. They speak of waking up first thing in the morning with a severe head pain. Patty posed this problem the first time she visited our clinic: "If psychological factors are contributing to the problem, then please explain what in the world is stressful about a good night's sleep."

This paradox has an interesting explanation which we have been exploring for several years. During periods of acute or prolonged stress, migraine patients severely constrict blood flow in their peripheral circulation but do not, at these times, experience any headaches. Instead, the only detectable symptom is that their hands and feet, especially their hands, are quite cold relative to the temperature in other parts of their body. This vasoconstriction in hands and feet can last for hours—or even days—depending on the severity and intensity of the stress. Finally, however, when they do relax (for example, when they go to sleep, or take it easy on weekends, or go on a vacation), the vasoconstriction in their hands and feet reverses itself, and blood begins to return to these regions all the more strongly for having been constricted for so long. Marked vasoconstriction becomes excessive vasodilatation—a response that, in turn, appears to be linked to sudden excessive swelling of the cranial arteries and the appearance of headaches. Many migraine patients are confused about these links because, during the migraine itself, their hands will be warm (vasodilated). They erroneously conclude that cold hands are not connected to their headaches because their hands are not cold when their head hurts. In addition, they respond to the sudden appearance of head pain by intensively scrutinizing their environment in an effort to understand what in it could be causing their head pain. In terms of this pain, migraine patients are "wired backward," because they erroneously conclude that periods of rest and relaxation must be stressful and ought to be avoided. They totally overlook the actual periods of stress and even prefer and seek them out because they do not suffer from head pain when they are stressed.

As I have said, the common drug treatment for migraines is a vasoconstrictor, (ergotamines) which reduces the swelling in the cranial arteries. Unfortunately vasoconstrictors also constrict the peripheral circulation, which can lead to a vicious circle with rebound headaches. Thus, the very medicines (vasoconstrictors) that a patient is taking to alleviate head pain will cause the vasoconstriction in hands and feet that precipitated the problem in the first place. In a sense, the situation is similar to the dilemma faced by the individual who drinks alcohol to get "high" in an effort to escape depression, only to be confronted by the "low" caused by alcohol hangover the next morning. This, too, quickly becomes a vicious circle.

To summarize, it appears that migraine headaches are the result of severe and prolonged vasoconstriction in peripheral circulation, which subsequently causes rebound vasodilatation and marked swelling of the blood vessels both inside and outside the cranial regions of the brain.* The rebound spasms can occur when the individual finally begins to relax, after prolonged stress.

DISCREPANT COMMUNICATION: BODY, FEELINGS, LANGUAGE

THE DISCONNECTED BODY

Earlier in this chapter, I suggested that both hypertensive and migraine headaches can be thought of as a form of internal blushing; and also that since others cannot see these vascular

---

* Numerous other theories suggest how various neurochemical agents cause the blood vessels to go into spasm, and involve complex mechanisms beyond the scope of this book. Basically, the vascular smooth muscles are under the dual control of autonomically regulated nerves and agents that circulate in the blood stream, especially catecholamines. It should be enough for the reader to know that the cardiovascular system is itself reactive to emotional stress and that its reactivity is modulated and regulated by the central nervous system and the neurochemical gating mechanism. In addition, migraines have been linked to a wide variety of foods and beverages (especially alcohol), but such data are beyond the scope of this chapter.

changes, they cannot help a person identify the *emotional meaning* of his or her bodily reactions. In addition, since neither the person whose blood pressure increases, nor the person to whom he or she is speaking, perceives these changes, both are necessarily disconnected from important aspects of their emotional dialogue, as well as from their bodily dialogue.

While not everyone who blocks blood flow in the hands, when stressed, or increases heart rate, while elevating or dropping blood pressure, inevitably hurtles toward the serious problems associated with migraines, the fact is that the development of migraine headaches is linked to these response patterns. As I have suggested, it is likely that the physiological potential for the problem is inherited, while the emotional correlates are taught, reinforced, and amplified in early childhood and adolescence. The issue is not qualitatively different from questions about whether one is born with a predisposition to blush or whether one learns to respond that way early in life. In the end, it really makes no difference. For as the blushing individual must confront the vascular reactivity of his or her face and be educated about the corresponding feelings, the migraine-prone or the hypertensive person must develop the same kind of self knowledge.

Just as the blusher quickly dilates facial blood vessels when embarrassed, so too, when emotionally aroused or upset, the migraine-prone individual will quickly block blood flow in his or her hands and feet. Yet this response by itself does not lead to a migraine headache. Responding to stress by clamping down on the blood flow in one's hands ever so often is not the central problem. That reaction, if transient, would be no more of a problem than blushing when uncomfortable. Clinical problems occur only if the response is prolonged for hours or even days. More important, serious problems occur only if one is unaware of the transient responsivity of one's body and of the emotional distress that has produced the changes. The crucial difference between blushing and these hidden bodily responses stems precisely from the fact that, as I have said, blushing is highly visible and is almost always attended to by others. In hypertension or migraines, comparable and even far more excessive vascular reactions are neither seen nor felt and are, therefore, not responded to. People continue discussing whatever they are concerned with, quite unaware of the other person's discomfort.*

In a sense, vasoconstriction and vasodilatation are mirror-image reactions. Since vasodilatation in the face leads to blushing, we can think about vasoconstriction in the hands as blushing in reverse: the migraine patient's hands will turn white, sometimes even slightly blue depending on the environmental temperature. Like the blood vessels in the face of the blusher, so too the surface blood vessels of a migraine-prone individual's hands can function normally one moment and then suddenly constrict, turning from their normal hue to pale white within a few seconds. In a matter of a few minutes the surface temperature of the fingers can drop twenty degrees or more.

It is not at all uncommon to find yourself engaged in a conversation with a migraine patient with a hand temperature of 93 or 94 degrees. Suddenly you touch a topic that leads to vasoconstriction in the hands, and skin temperature will plummet to 72 degrees (the temperature in the room) in less than two to four minutes. Conversely, it is not at all uncommon to chat with such patients for hours, over repeated sessions, and their hands will be ice cold.† Suddenly you touch on a topic that leads to abrupt vasodilatation. In a matter of minutes, their hand temperature will increase by twenty to twenty-five degrees. Sometimes so much blood rushes back into their hands that their palms begin to sweat, and the hands even begin to swell.

The vascular responses in the hands and feet of migraine patients are far more impressive than the marked changes you observe in the vasculature of a blusher's face. Yet there is a feature of the response that is astonishing, counterintuitive, and at first difficult to believe, and that occurs with such regularity that it must be seen as an intricate part of the disease process itself. Since vasoconstriction of the hands, and their consequent coldness, is one of the most common correlates of migraine headaches, one would think that

* As we shall see in subsequent chapters, this problem becomes especially acute in psychotherapy when hypertensive patients are asked to talk at length about their problems even though blood pressure rises higher and higher the longer they continue to talk. In a profound sense, one's attempt to talk about one's emotional problems is part of the very mechanism causing the problem.

† Curiously, even while their hands may be cold, the backs or the underarms of many of these patients will be simultaneously sweating—a fact that suggests that the blood is pooling in markedly different ways in different parts of their bodies.

people afflicted with the problem would be cognizant of this fact. Yet the opposite is generally true. "Are your hands usually cold?" "No, not usually." Such a response from patients when first interviewed in our clinic used to make me wonder whether their headaches had been misdiagnosed. Perhaps they did not have vascular headaches at all. Perhaps they had tension headaches, temperomandibular joint problems, or some other problem causing the head pain.

Trying to make certain by feeling their hands, I was surprised at the coldness of their hands. Frequently a patient would respond to my surprise with an understanding smile, while commenting, "Your hands are so warm! I had no idea my hands were so much colder than yours." An even more common response to the question "Are your hands cold?" is when one touches one's hand to one's cheek in order to find out.

People not afflicted with this type of disorder find it startling that a person cannot automatically sense when his or her hands are cold and when warm. But the reality for many migraine sufferers is just the opposite. Certain appendages and organ systems seem to be totally disconnected from their awareness. They do not feel their hearts racing or their ice-cold hands. Apparently they have endured such bodily conditions for so many years that they no longer even take notice of the changes.

DISCONNECTED LANGUAGE

There was another dimension to this problem that was even more startling, albeit more subtle: that is, the way our patients had disconnected themselves from their bodies literally spilled over into the language they used to describe their own bodies. No matter whether it was a migraine headache, a spastic colon, or hypertension, patients in our clinic uniformly seemed to think and talk about their bodies as a collection of parts that were dissociated from their personal selves. They described their disease in the passive voice and usually in the past tense:

> "I got a bad migraine yesterday. It was really bad."
> "The head is killing me. The hands are cold."
> "The blood pressure went up really high last week. It's so high, I hope I don't get a stroke or a heart attack."

It! It! It! Irrespective of what disease they were suffering from, patients not only uniformly described their problems in the passive voice but also spoke of each bodily problem as an object, as an *it*—as a mechanical part of some machine that had gone wacky. *It*—their headache, colitis, hypertension, ulcers: *it was bad.*

It was striking how differently patients thought about their hypertension, migraines, and spastic colons from the way since adolescence I had been forced to think about my blushing face. Far from being able to point to my face and say, "It was blushing badly yesterday," or "It embarrassed me!,"* I knew my face belonged to me and could only confess to the obvious: "*I* blushed yesterday and *I* was embarrassed!" It was only after watching the perplexity of patients when I tried gently to correct their language, suggesting, for example, "You mean, you gave yourself a headache yesterday?" or, "You mean you drove your own blood pressure up?"—or, after watching many patients' puzzled looks turn to smiles, and hearing the mocking retort, "Are you crazy? Do you think I like migraines? Are you some kind of nut?"—only then was I able to understand how trapped people are in their own language.

Nor is this linguistic problem restricted to the legions of distraught souls suffering the pains of modern stress-induced disease. The mass media and the medical profession itself unwittingly enhance the problem. Every day we are exposed to television commercials that solemnly warn: "If you have hypertension, see your doctor." The advertisement says not, "If you are hypertensive," but rather, "If you *have* it"—as if hypertension were caused by some mysterious infectious bug invading from without. Hypertension is cast as nöun, as object, rather than as adjective or adverb. The word *hypertension* is not used to describe a person but is rather designated as *some thing* a person has. Can one similarly tell the suffering blushers of the world, "If you have a blushing attack, see your doctor"?

---

* Vague linguistic reference to medical problems not only influences how we think these problems develop, but also determines how we try to alleviate them. By labeling symptoms "it," our citizens—and, indeed, a significant proportion of the medical community—have been able to free themselves from any notion of personal involvement in the production of their own problems. "It" is quite different from "I," so it makes perfect sense to seek out *something*—a pill, one hopes—to help treat it, even if "it" is killing them. One—and one's doctors—quickly become caught up in a desperate poker game, constantly upping the ante on one's own body with anti-medicines, hoping that Nature will not call the bluff. And if the anti-medicines don't work, if the game appears in doubt, then one plays one's last trump card and calls in the surgeon to cut "it" out.

Any of a dozen clinical textbooks dealing with hypertension or migraine headaches could be cited to demonstrate the universality of this way of describing one's own body. Typical of the phenomenon is a passage excerpted from an English textbook entitled *Migraines: The Facts,* in which Dr. F. Clifford Rose and Dr. M. Gawel from the Charing Cross Hospital use patients' descriptions to help illustrate the clinical nature of migraine headaches.[9] In these verbatim descriptions one can readily see the pervasiveness of the past tense and the passive voice and the strange way these patients detach certain parts of their body from themselves. The authors do not comment on the patients' language, except to note that they believe this to be a "classical description" of migraine headaches. Their book was on the physiology of migraines, and they did not link this problem to the language used by the patients. I have taken the liberty of italicizing the language to emphasize the linguistic problems I have been describing:

I wake up in the morning feeling happy. The sky seems more blue—in fact, all colours appear more intense. I know this means that later that day, or perhaps the next, *I will get* a *migraine attack. The pain gradually comes on* over one temple, usually the right, and *spreads* over the whole of *that* side *of the head.* At the same time, but sometimes *before the headache begins,* part of my vision blurs, bright stars may appear and move over the field of vision. *The headache becomes worse* and throbbing, I start feeling sick. If I vomit *this seems* to *make the headache* better. With *the headache,* light hurts my eyes so I have to go to bed after drawing the curtains. *The whole attack* lasts about eight hours and leaves me tired and shaken.[10]

Note the language. The patient consistently speaks of her headache as "the headache," while referring paradoxically to her eyes as "my eyes" and "my vision." She has literally fractionated her body and acknowledged certain parts as hers and others as objects. Virtually every patient seen in our clinic uses similar language to describe his or her psychosomatic problems.

For example, after a particularly stressful week, Patty was nearing the end of her eight-month therapeutic venture. She had been free of migraine headaches for the past eight weeks, in part because she had begun to detect her feelings and to deal with them in a fashion that no longer doomed her to throbbing head pain. Our therapy had by no means magically transformed her life into some fairy tale where she married the prince and lived happily ever after. Far from it. Eight months after we first met, she was still struggling to support her son and still coping on her own with a variety of very real life stresses. She had dated men but had been unable to develop an ongoing relationship. While she expressed the strong desire to remarry, she was determined to avoid the mistakes that had led her into a painful divorce.

In this particular session, as we talked about terminating therapy, her heart rate averaged about 75, and her blood pressure fluctuated around 120/70. Her hand temperatures remained at 92 degrees Fahrenheit for the entire hour.

"Haven't been handling anything well," Patty humorously noted, as she summarized a week that had seen her basement flooded in a violent storm and her child sick with the flu. Extending her hands out in front of her, she repeated the phrase for emphasis: "No sirree! They haven't handled anything well lately."

Her statement was a succinct summary of eight months of therapy. One of Patty's favorite terms was how she "handled" various situations: "I can *handle* it," or, "I *handled* that person well." Over the eight months it was remarkable how often she referred to "handling things" when, in fact, one of the major diagnostic signs of her migraines was the way she blocked blood flow in her hands. Having been convinced of one of the triggering mechanisms behind her migraines and of the necessity of attending to temperature changes in her hands, Patty was pleased to tell me she was "no longer handling things," that she no longer allowed her hands to remain ice cold when she was upset. Instead, she used her hands to help her become conscious of her own feelings.

Patty's use of the verb "to handle" was by no means unique to her. Virtually all migraine patients seen in our clinic use the same metaphor to describe how they cope with their problems. Indeed, many patients unwittingly use phrases that provide diagnostic insights into their stress-linked disorders, as though they intuitively sense the mechanisms behind their disease. A couple once came to me to see whether their problem of infertility was psychosomatic. In the hour-long interview the women kept repeating one phrase: "Things are going down the tubes"; "My life is going down the tubes"; "My husband's job is going down the tubes." Everything seemed to be going down the tubes but the baby they wanted.

In a similar way, virtually all hypertensive patients talk about "pressure": the "pressure of the job," the "pressure of the deadlines," the "pressure of golf," the "pressure" they feel from their mates. Everything is talked about in terms of pressure, except for the real problem—their blood pressure. When the migraine patient marries the hypertensive patient, their language grows even more sophisticated. The wife may begin talking about "handling pressure from my husband"!

In addition to using dissociated language and metaphorical allusions to describe their problems, these patients also have significant problems describing their feelings. Typically when queried about feelings, they respond in a rational way, describing what they think rather than what they feel. I believe that this peculiar use of a language devoid of affective terminology originates in the hidden nature of their bodily reactions while communicating with others. These patients literally live in bodies that prevent them from being educated about their own feelings.

NO LANGUAGE FOR FEELINGS: ALEXITHYMIA

While aspects of this problem have been recognized for almost forty years, it has only gained prominent attention in the last decade and is now labeled "alexithymia." The term literally means "without words [a lex] for feelings [thymia]" and has been used to describe a whole class of psychosomatically prone individuals who find it impossible to label their own feelings. Like Patty and Ed, these patients frequently smile and tell you that they are fine, while their blood pressure, heart rate, and blood flow are simultaneously surging out of control. And indeed they do think they are fine.

In 1972 a Harvard psychiatrist, Dr. Peter Sifneos, introduced the concept of alexithymia to describe a problem shared by a large number of patients suffering from various stress-linked medical disorders. He observed that many of these patients had great difficulty describing how they felt. At the time Dr. Sifneos was attempting to understand why so many psychosomatic patients were unable to profit from insight-oriented psychotherapeutic approaches that had been successfully employed to treat other emotional problems. Like other investigators, Dr. Sifneos deduced that psychosomatic disorders are caused by unresolved emotional conflicts outside of a patient's awareness.[11] Therefore it seemed only reasonable to assume that psychotherapy would provide a viable way to help patients become aware of these unconscious conflicts. Yet the reality was quite the opposite. Attempts to use psychotherapy to give these patients insight not only was not helpful but it sometimes was counterproductive. Instead of helping the patients improve their health, attempts to give them insight aroused such emotions that a patient's health would deteriorate.

As described earlier, decades before Dr. Sifneos introduced the concept of alexithymia, psychoanalytic theorists like Franz Alexander had postulated that unconscious psychological conflicts are the cause of a variety of bodily ailments. This orientation, which was validated by numerous clinical observations, led some psychiatrists and internists to assume that psychosomatic problems ought to be amenable to treatment by insight-oriented psychotherapy.

While the general theoretical framework of psychotherapy is well known, it might bear repeating that Sigmund Freud had originally developed a system of therapy whereby patients could talk out their problems and gradually gain insights about the links between their adult difficulties and earlier developmental emotional problems. Free association, a way of describing whatever comes into one's mind, was one way Freud thought patients could gain insights into the nature of their unconscious conflicts.

Yet for reasons that were unclear at the time, Alexander's efforts to use analytically based psychotherapy to treat diseases such as hypertension met with limited success. In a similar fashion, studies that used comparable analytic modes of treatment for other diseases such as ulcerative colitis[12] and peptic ulcers[13] confronted the very same problem. Psychotherapy simply did not seem to be of value to patients suffering psychosomatic problems. Paradoxically, therapies that relied more on supportive approaches and less on insight-oriented therapy appeared to be more helpful.

As early as 1948, Dr. J. Ruesch began to question why psychosomatic patients could not benefit from insight-oriented psychotherapy. Ruesch concluded that many of these patients had "infantile personalities" which, he proposed, contributed to the blockage of normal maturation and the normal way people use verbal means to deal with their emotions.[14] He concluded that any therapy that relies on verbal communications to achieve insight goes beyond the emotional capacity of these patients. Since psychosomatic patients lack the normal capacity to discharge emotional tension through words, gestures, or symbols (including dreams), Ruesch concluded that they are "stuck with their tensions" and that the only mode left for the expression of emotions is their bodies.

In 1952, Dr. Friedman and Dr. Sweet similarly confirmed the peculiar difficulties psychosomatic patients have describing their feelings.[15] These doctors coined the term "emotional illiterates" to underscore the acute struggles psychosomatic patients face whenever they attempt to put their feelings into words, and noted that their patients were genuinely bewildered when it was suggested to them that emotional problems might be the source of their bodily ailments. Like Ruesch's conclusions, Friedman and Sweet theorized that psychosomatic patients have so completely and successfully buried their emotional problems in their bodies that they no longer have any capacity for insight. Echoing these sentiments, Dr. Harley Shands asserted that psychosomatic patients are "unsuitable for psychotherapy." Shands noted that such patients did not seem to profit from insight and, indeed, did not appear to appreciate the reality of their own emotional experiences.[16]

In 1963, two French psychiatrists, Dr. P. Marty and Dr. M. de M'Uzan, published a paper entitled *"La pensée opératoire,"* in which they used the term *"pensée opératoire"* to describe two peculiar characteristics of psychosomatically prone patients. Like other investigators, these French psychiatrists noted the striking paucity of "feeling terms" and lack of fantasy about feelings in such patients. Marty and M'Uzan used the term "operational thinking," or *"pensée opératoire,"* to characterize the way psychosomatic patients responded to questions about their feelings. These authors noted that, rather than anchoring their feelings to changes inside their bodies, psychosomatic patients focused on the most trivial details of external events—that is, on operations in the world. Marty and M'Uzan observed that these patients, when questioned about their feelings, described not what they felt internally but, in painstaking detail, "things they or others did," including the most trivial details of their clinical problems. Unlike the average person who readily describes bodily correlates of feelings such as anger or sadness, these psychosomatic patients answered the same question quite differently, Normally an individual can answer questions such as "How do you know you were angry?" by stating

"Because I felt my stomach churning, or my blood pressure boiling, or my muscles tensing." When psychosomatic patients were asked similar questions, however, they described "events" out there in the world rather than what was going on internally. Marty and M'Uzan also found that their patients demonstrated a conspicuous absence of fantasy and dreams. Their mental activity was dominated by concrete, present-oriented detail and utterly devoid of unconscious fantasies.[17]

Building on the work of these earlier investigators, Dr. Peter Sifneos coined the term *alexithymia* to describe the fact that psychosomatic patients have no words or language to describe their feelings. Working with his colleagues Dr. John Nemiah and Dr. Hellmuth Freyberger at the Massachusetts General Hospital, Sifneos analyzed the verbatim transcripts of a number of psychosomatic patients. Like the French psychoanalysts, Sifneos and his colleagues found that these patients had marked difficulty in verbally expressing or describing their feelings and an absence or striking diminution of fantasy.[18] They were either totally unaware of their feelings or could only describe them in the most elementary fashion.

Typical of the problems alexithymic patients have when they are asked to articulate their feelings is the following case published by Dr. Nemiah and his colleagues:

Related to the difficulties in describing feelings or localizing emotions is the fact that many patients *cannot distinguish among the different kinds of common affects.* [One patient], for example, when asked what it felt like to be frightened, replied: "What does it feel like to be frightened? (Pause). I can't think of the term."
DOCTOR: "Do you feel it in your body?"
PATIENT: "I think it's mostly in your mind."
DOCTOR: "Your mind?"
PATIENT: "It's mostly in your head. Things go through your head."
DOCTOR: "It doesn't affect your body?"
PATIENT: "I don't . . . I can't say for sure. It might. It might. In the stomach maybe."
DOCTOR: "The stomach? And what would you feel there?"
PATIENT: "Knotted up in the stomach."
DOCTOR: "How does that differ from being mad?"
PATIENT: "How does it differ from being mad? Again, I . . . to me, to me all these things are in the same pot. You know, all in one pot."
DOCTOR: "They feel alike?"
PATIENT: "Yeah. The being scared, the being tense, the being aggravated.

To me it's from the head to the stomach ... (long pause) I can't really
... I'd like to say what you want to hear."
DOCTOR: "I want to hear what you feel, that's all."
PATIENT: "Yeah, well ... I can't really say."[19]*

Sifneos concluded that alexithymic individuals are very different
from typical neurotic patients, and thus their treatment has to be
different. He noted that psychotherapeutic approaches that provoke
anxiety in these patients (where their feelings would be stirred up
when their psychological defenses are systematically probed) would
prove counterproductive. Approaches requiring an awareness of
feelings would lead to an increase in frustration and would heighten
rather than lessen physiological distress. To lessen the dangers
inherent in such treatment approaches, Sifneos recommended
supportive and educational treatments, rather than insight-oriented
psychotherapy.[20]

Another problem confronting alexithymic individuals is their
misleading use of language, which causes communication difficulties
because most people use language in a way that is at least partially
inferential. In communication with the alexithymic person, however,
there is pseudo, rather than true, understanding; and the emotionally
"color-blind" do not understand their blindness, nor can others
detect the problem.

Those individuals who have normal color vision, for example,
take their perception of colors for granted, while those who are
color-blind have no idea what they have missed. Color blindness
frequently goes undetected because one cannot miss a phenomenon
one has never experienced. Confusion about the problem is compounded by the fact that the color-blind individual knows there
are words such as *red, yellow,* and *green* and is perfectly capable of
using these color words in sentences without ever having seen or
experienced the colors. So, too, everyone knows such words as *love,
hate, jealousy, ecstasy,* and *envy,* and everyone can use these words
when talking to others. There is, however, a marked difference
between *rationally using feeling terms* that one has never experienced, and using these same terms when one has experienced—
that is, felt—the emotions these terms designate. Psychosomatic
patients can wax eloquent with operational fact-filled descriptions

---

* Note again the dissociated language: the patient tells about *the* stomach and *the* head, rather
than about *my* stomach and *my* head.

of various human emotions even though they have no idea of how these emotions feel. Like a person who has no idea he or she is color-blind, alexithymic individuals do not realize that they cannot detect or properly identify their own feelings, and thus simply do not understand the emotional terminology used by other people.

The problem becomes increasingly exacerbated the more intense one's feelings become. Strong emotional arousal creates especially serious problems for alexithymic individuals. Unable to describe their own feelings, they also lose the capacity to discriminate between and among the bodily correlates of various feelings. An intense surge of blood pressure could just as easily be a storm of hatred or a tidal wave of love. Alexithymic patients have no real way of telling the difference. They cannot tell you what it feels like to be sad, angry, or in love—except in rational terms.*

Another important facet of alexithymia has been described by a Michigan State professor of psychiatry, Dr. Henry Krystal. In a paper on alexithymia and psychotherapy, Krystal noted:

Beside the patients' incapacity to verbalize their emotions and to describe their sensations in respect to affective responses, there is a broader problem as well. These patients, who are often functioning very successfully in their work seem to be "super adjusted to reality." Getting past the superficial impression of superb functioning, one discovers a sterility and monotony of ideas and severe impoverishment of their imagination. The patients' thoughts turn out to be composed of trivial details of their everyday life, and they seem to be devoid of the capacity to get beyond their mundane preoccupations. . . . These patients show a marked impairment in their capacity for creativity, especially in regard to drive gratification fantasy. . . . Such patients' attentiveness to themselves, including their body and health is equally poor. They often show gross neglect of their welfare and impairment in their capacity for self care. McDougall comments on the quality of stony deadness which characterizes these patients' attitude to themselves as well as the world at large and that it is a form of numbness designed to block pain by becoming a "lonely island." One way out is to turn oneself into a rock. Thus many psychosomatic patients continue on their unwavering tightrope, ignoring the body's signs and the mind's distress signals.[21]

* Alexithymia contributes to a variety of other problems, one of which is a predisposition to drug addiction. As adolescents, alexithymics cannot feel their emotional stress and thus are particularly vulnerable to the narcotic-like calming actions of various chemical agents. Unable to sense their emotional problems, alexithymics cannot even recognize their own suffering. Treatment modalities that rely on traditional insight-oriented psychotherapy will meet with failure simply because these patients are trapped inside their own bodies, which can storm out of control without either they or their therapist being aware of it.

Krystal suggested that psychosomatic patients can profit from insight-oriented psychotherapy if certain changes are made in the way the therapist initiates treatment. In 1979, Krystal outlined several steps he believed had to be taken before psychotherapy could be initiated. He suggested that insight and emotional provocations should be avoided until the patient learns certain fundamental lessons about his or her body. Though Krystal lacked the computer technology that allowed us in the clinic to see the dramatic changes in patients' cardiovascular systems when they spoke, and though we were unaware of his recommendations, the initial steps of his treatment overlapped our own to a considerable extent. Krystal emphasized, as we did with Ed and Patty, that the first step in the therapy of alexithymic patients was to teach them about the links between feelings and various bodily states. The therapist's first task, he asserted, was to help these patients become observers of their inner states. He suggested that psychosomatic patients have to recognize their emotional states as signals, and that then, and only then, can they be taught to verbalize these feelings to the therapist.

While precise statistics would be difficult to gather, Krystal's observation that alexithymic patients are often "super-adjusted to reality" also deserves amplification. As already hinted in the case studies cited in this book, many psychosomatically prone patients attain notable professional success, especially in professions whose criteria for success are strictly "objective." Professions that require only that a person do well on objective tests, without any understanding of his or her own feelings, provide fertile conditions for alexithymic individuals to succeed. When confronted by myriad external rules and regulations that require operational thinking, the alexithymic performs exceedingly well. Thus, a significant number of people who suffer from varying degrees of alexithymia function in professions as distinct as medicine, nursing, engineering, science, psychology, education, and law—in none of which is a comprehension of human feelings prerequisite or required for success.* The nationally standardized, objective admissions criteria, which are

---

* Indeed, I suspect that alexithymia would enhance a person's capacity to withstand and endure years of academic stress: finding it difficult to feel or gauge the emotional cost of one's academic "success," one would thus be able to endure stress that would cause the non-alexithymic to withdraw.

used to determine who shall succeed in schools, and who gain entrance into professional schools, have reinforced the belief that feeling one's own human feelings is not relevant to these professions. Individuals who cannot feel their feelings, and who depend on operational modes of thinking, can nevertheless perform exceedingly well in understanding and memorizing reams of objective facts. Thus, their natural predisposition to function exclusively in an operational mode of thought is reinforced by objective examinations which depend almost exclusively on operational constructs.

While many professionals are highly sensitive to subtle emotional interchanges, it also appears that many suffer from alexithymia. Since many professions ultimately require individuals to engage other human beings in emotional interaction, alexithymic individuals like Ed and Patty can find themselves trapped in situations that compound their bodily stress. As we shall see in the final chapter, even professions like psychiatry and psychology—though ostensibly dedicated to the understanding of human feelings—require not that their members feel their feelings, but that they rationally understand human feelings. The end result of this orientation can be truly disconcerting. As shall be described in chapter 10, it is likely that the founder of psychoanalysis, Sigmund Freud, was a prime example of a person suffering from acute alexithymia. Brilliantly rational about human feelings, Freud himself may have had great difficulty feeling his own feelings or, for that matter, feeling those of this patients.

Whether engaged in one of these professions or in a more mundane occupation, however, the more acute their alexithymia, the more these patients will find themselves terribly isolated not only from other people but from their own bodies as well.*

"How are you feeling today?" I usually ask the question in every session as a patient is being attached to machines that monitor blood pressure, blood flow, heart rate, and finger temperature. Early in therapy, the response is predictable. The patient quickly shifts the topic, moving out of the feeling domain, back toward the security of the cognitive realm, the safe realm of thought and reason, by answering, "I think I'm okay." At the same moment, the patient's blood pressure or heart rate frequently increases 25 percent to 50 percent. Such patients answer questions about their

---

* Alexithymic patients tend to marry each other, and it is not uncommon for both husband and wife to have significant psychophysiological problems.

feelings in a rational way that exacts a physical cost. When Patty once so blandly answered questions about her feelings, I exclaimed in some exasperation, "I know *how* you *think,* and *what* you *think,* and *why* you *think,* and *when* you *think,* and *where* you *think,* but I asked you *how do you feel?—not how you think.*"

She smiled at the outburst and again replied, "What do you mean how do I feel today? I just told you that I'm okay."

"I mean are you angry, or sad, or joyful, or enraged, or loving?"

Again she smiled and sighed, "I think I am okay."

Until sensitized and attuned to the alexithymic difficulties of psychosomatic patients, one would hardly notice their peculiar use of emotionless language and their penchant for discussing matters in a cognitive, logical, and rational manner. Their dictionary of facts and rational thoughts is filled with hundreds of thousands of terms, while their dictionary of emotional terms is filled with nothing but blank pages. The meaning of human feelings must be taught to them the same way I was taught about the meaning of my blushing face. It is an education that takes time. It is an education also, as we shall see in the next chapter, that requires the experiential sharing of feelings with other people.

One final aspect of alexithymia needs to be mentioned. Computer monitoring of blood pressure and heart rate, blood flow and skin temperature led us to recognize that not only does the human body vary from moment to moment in the magnitude of changes it exhibits, but the same individual can vary from time to time in his or her capacity to detect these bodily changes. On the assumption that alexithymia is linked to one's inability to detect physiological changes inside one's body, it appears likely that this is not an all-or-none qualitative phenomenon which, like measles, one either has or does not have. Rather it is a quantitative condition, which can exist to a marked or a minor degree. The problem is compounded even further because individuals vary in their capacity to sense and articulate their feelings. Some people are highly sensitive to changes in their body and equally adept at articulating feelings that might accompany these changes. At the other extreme, it is equally likely that other people are completely insensitive to their bodies and poor at articulating any feelings whatsoever. Still other people may be exquisitely sensitive to bodily changes and thus to feeling their feelings, and yet be unsophisticated about communicating these feelings verbally.

THE ROOTS OF ALEXITHYMIA: ORGAN LANGUAGE

Recognition both of the existence of alexithymia and of the problems faced by psychosomatic patients has led investigators to postulate a variety of theoretical possibilities to help explain the disorder. These explanations have ranged from the existence of ill-defined neurological deficits,[22] to problems in early childhood,[23] to cognitive problems.[24] Most of these possibilities have been raised to explain not alexithymia as such, but rather the root cause of psychosomatic disorders. A widely shared underlying assumption is that these various psychosomatic diseases and alexithymia have a similar cause.

One of the more frequently cited neurophysiological explanations was first put forward by Dr. Paul MacLean in 1949. Building on earlier discoveries about brain mechanisms involved in emotions, as well as on psychiatric formulations about the origin of human feelings, MacLean observed that patients with psychosomatic illnesses were often infantile in their behavior.[25] While conducting a series of research studies at the National Institutes of Health, he noted that psychosomatic patients usually responded to emotional stress with physical upheaval much as a frantic infant works itself into a physical frenzy if no one responds to its cries. Similar to other investigators, he too observed the peculiar emotionless language used by these patients. MacLean theorized that these patients suffered from faulty connections between the more primitive emotional centers deep in their brain and the higher brain centers involved in the use of language. Because of this hypothetical neurological deficit, he speculated that these patients were unable to develop a language for feelings and, instead of expressing their feelings through words, were forced to express their feelings through their bodies. It was, as MacLean suggested, a way of expressing emotions through an "organ language." Dr. John Nemiah at Harvard Medical School elaborated on MacLean's theories by suggesting that patients with these problems suffer from a neurological discontinuity between the emotional centers in the brain (the limbic system) and the thinking (cortical) brain centers.

When first using computers to track hypertensive patients' blood pressure and heart rate, we began to sense that the disconnectedness between language and emotions is not neurological in origin—as MacLean had hypothesized—but rather stems from a lack of crucial neonatal experiences. Far from a lack of connection between the brain's emotional and language centers, the problem appeared to be one of *hyper*-connectedness. MacLean's notions of "organ language" began to take on quite a different meaning as we monitored hypertensive and migraine patients. These patients used words in a way that clearly triggered serious bodily disturbances. The problem was that the contrasting "organ language" and spoken language made it difficult for others to decode the alexithymic's emotional communications. Like Patty, these patients used language to mask their feelings as Patty's smile masked her internal crying.

The capacity to monitor patients' bodies continuously during therapeutic dialogue led us to recognize limitations in the original description of alexithymia by Sifneos and other investigators: it is not simply that these patients have "no words for feelings," but rather that they have no words to describe what they cannot feel in their own bodies: they are fundamentally deaf to the language of their own hearts. Patients can gain insight into their problems if they are first taught to listen to their own bodies by therapists who can hear and decode the messages spoken by those bodies. As we shall see, computer monitoring not only helped illuminate the struggles patients have in this regard, but heightened our awareness of the problems of therapists as well.

In the context of issues about sensing human feelings and delineating the difference between human emotions and human feelings, I believe Mark Twain was far more accurate than he intended in his comment that opens this chapter. Indeed, human beings are the only animals that blush—or that need to. We must, in fact, recognize our internal as well as our external blushing in order to avoid unnecessary suffering or even premature death. We must blush to understand that peculiarly human phenomenon— our feelings. For blushing helps us understand what it is about our bodies that make them human: that is, through our emotional relationships to one another, and our use of words to communicate our feelings to each other, we can recognize the fundamental interrelatedness of our bodies and emotions and the communication of these experiences as shared human feelings. We must blush and recognize that blushing in order to learn about human feeling.

CHAPTER 9

Decoding the Heart's Language

> I call myself the last philosopher because I am the last man. Nobody talks to me but myself, and my voice comes to me like that of a dying person! . . . Through you I conceal my loneliness from myself and make my way into the multitude and into love by lies, for my heart . . . cannot bear the terror of the loneliest loneliness and compels me to talk as if I were two. —Friedrich Nietzsche, *Thus Spake Zarathustra*, 1883–91

> I do not ask how the wounded one feels, I, myself, *become* the wounded one.
> —Walt Whitman, *Leaves of Grass*, 1855

In the last two chapters I have extended the relationship of the cardiovascular system and communication to include two new dimensions. Based on the concept of a social membrane these dimensions were cited to help clarify the idea that the heart, and circulation, can be viewed both as an organ of communication as well as a source of human experience and the source of human feelings. The notion of the social membrane was introduced to help delineate these two dimensions and give them meaning in the context of the boundaries as well as of the unique relationships between human beings. Like a biological membrane which allows in and out of the cell those constituents necessary for its survival, so too the social membrane is a selective way of communicating between the individual and constituents in the person's surroundings. It was seen to be a semi-permeable boundary that both separates and unites a person to the rest of his social and natural world.

Among the many issues raised by the clinical vignettes described in this book, two points were emphasized in particular in the last chapter. One is that neither the patients themselves nor anyone else interacting with them seem to be able to recognize the physiological changes that occur when they are engaged in dialogue. They appear to be profoundly cut off from their own bodies. Secondly, the physiological changes that occur resemble the types of bodily shifts that usually are associated with emotional arousal and the perception of feelings. The patients appeared to be peculiar in so far as they manifested the physiological changes usually associated with emotional arousal but did not sense these changes or discriminate them as specific feelings. Thus there seemed to be a fundamental breakdown between the appearance of bodily emotions and the detection and discernment of feelings.

The fact that many people do not feel their emotions raises one of the central questions of this book, and one that will be the focus of this chapter. Namely, how do human beings come to know, to recognize, and to understand bodily emotions as feelings? Is this process intrinsic? Is it a matter of intuition, or are we taught it by others? And if the process requires teaching, how does it occur?

THE LONELIEST LONELINESS

To live one's life in a body that one cannot feel, is, I believe, the loneliest loneliness. The way each of us ordinarily transcends loneliness is by communicating feelings to others—a process that requires us to recognize that we share feelings in common. The word *communicate* literally means to share, and it is the lack of sharing that literally plagues the lives of the patients seen in our clinic. Unaware of their own bodies, they cannot share their emotional life with others.

The use of language to communicate is one of the distinguishing features of human beings. Philosophers have long argued about the nature of this remarkable human trait. Some, like the seventeenth-century British philosopher John Locke have looked upon speech as little more than the movement of air through space, the air coming to impinge on someone else's auditory receptors and triggering consciousness of the event. Others as different in orientation as the philosopher Ludwig Wittgenstein and the zoologist Adolf Portmann have sensed something truly profound in human speech.

When one opens one's mouth to speak, one is, in a sense, attempting to bring the hearer inside one's own world. Ordinarily we tend to think of speech as words projected out, directed at, or aimed toward someone else. Yet a moment of reflection would reveal that quite the opposite is true of *real speech*. For when a person speaks, he or she is inviting others to come inside his or her world, into his or her reality—that is, into his or her body and ultimately into his or her mind's heart. Opening one's mouth to speak signals an attempt to share something inside oneself with someone else. *Real speaking* is communication in the most profound sense: it is an act of communion. In that sense, speaking is an immensely intimate act—a most intimate form of sharing.

To really speak is to invite another into a world that is lived in and through one's body—and herein lies, I believe, the importance of language for the cardiovascular system. Real talk poses difficult problems for the person who is living in a body suffering from the type of disease described in this book. Because of certain life experiences and an inability to live comfortably in one's own body, a person tends to believe that his or her adult world—that is, body—is not worth inviting others into. One's speech confronts them with the dilemma that they are inviting others to a place— one's own body—where one lives only with great pain and discomfort, a pain and discomfort they will have to share. Hence, the invitation is not truly inviting—and, indeed, may invite rejection. The greater the emotional pain, the more one becomes isolated from one's own body; and the more intense one's sense of loneliness and disconnection, the more difficult it is to engage in real talk— that is, to be inviting.

In an effort to protect themselves from this dilemma, these patients seal off their social membrane. Instead of being semipermeable and shared, it becomes an impenetrable barrier, and their speech becomes an act of battering or hiding, rather than an invitation. In order to penetrate the social membrane and commune with such individuals, it is necessary to share in their suffering.

This process becomes especially painful and disruptive when such individuals try to teach their offspring to speak, or when they try to communicate to others in a truly meaningful way. In such instances, talking involves inviting others into one's world of suffering from which one desperately seeks to protect them. For a mother to invite her son, for example, into her world, she would be forced to share her suffering with him. Yet to keep the child out is to prevent him from learning how to communicate emotionally with others and hence to isolate him from his own body, just as the mother is isolated from hers.

This dilemma between parent and child reveals itself in a particularly poignant way during therapy, and again recalls the struggles these patients have with language. In a series of classic studies conducted long before the appearance of the sophisticated monitoring equipment we used in our therapeutic encounters, Dr. Margaret Thaler-Singer and her colleagues developed the concept of engagement-involvement to describe the peculiar tendency of hypertensive patients to maintain emotional distance when interacting with others.[1] These researchers observed that a hypertensive individual who engaged others in dialogue could, by remaining relatively emotionally uninvolved, maintain blood pressure within reasonable limits. If however, the person got too involved or close to others, than he or she became acutely hypertensive.[2]

Computer-tracking devices enabled us to see that this process of engagement and involvement was closely linked to the way our patients used language to communicate. When patients who are prone to psychophysical distress use speech as an act of distancing, battering, or hiding, their bodies are able to tolerate human dialogue, and their blood pressure, blood flow, and heart rate will remain within tolerable levels. However, when these patients try to "really" talk to another, to invite another in, their cardiovascular systems appear to respond as if the patient were terrorized. An adult's efforts to "really" talk in a body that storms out of control without being understood or recognized by others creates, what I call—to use Nietzsche's term—the "loneliest loneliness"; for one is left talking to oneself, as if one truly were two. To help illustrate this point, I will again turn to clinical evidence and describe several patients whose cardiovascular systems surged out of control specifically when they attempted to really talk.

THE MUSEUM OF THE HUMAN BODY

It was late in September 1982 in Rotterdam. The last vestiges of a gentle Dutch summer were reluctantly yielding to cool, moist autumn winds blowing in off the North Sea—not at all like the brilliant autumn I had left in the northeastern United States. I was in Rotterdam for two weeks to share with the staff of the pathology department of Erasmus University Medical School the latest findings on our clinical approach to hypertension. Toward the end of my visit, Dr. J. Rijke-deVries, one of the younger physicians on the staff, asked if I would sit in with her while she spent an hour attempting to apply our techniques with a hypertensive patient she had been treating during the past year.

"The only problem," she noted with a wry smile, "is that the patient does not speak or understand English, so I will act as your interpreter."

Her forty-seven-year-old patient, Jan, was tall, rather thin, and soft-spoken and earned his living as a longshoreman on the Rotterdam waterfront. Dr. Rijke-deVries first explained to him in Dutch who I was and that she was going to record his blood pressure in an entirely new way. She said that the computer would automatically inflate the cuff on his arm, and that, on the front panel, he would see red numbers automatically flashing his heart rate and his systolic, diastolic, and mean arterial pressures each minute.

Then the two began to chat about Jan's hypertension and soon seemed less aware that I was in the room with them. Occasionally, though, Dr. Rijke-deVries would stop and translate certain medical points, such as the fact that Jan was on a "beta blocker" (a class of step-2 drugs used to control hypertension) and that, in general, they were discussing the struggles he was having on his job and his family difficulties. Since her translations tended to interrupt the natural flow of their own communication, I suggested that she simply chat with Jan without being concerned about my under-standing.

Jan spoke with a certain caution and tension. Although, like other hypertensives, he was soft-spoken, his speech seemed controlled in a way that disrupted the natural rhythm of comfortable dialogue. In spite of his gentle demeanor, there was a certain distant or lonely

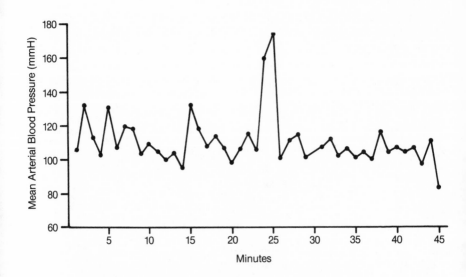

Figure 9.1.   Sudden mean arterial blood-pressure increase in a hypertensive
patient when beginning to speak (minute 23) about certain painful childhood
memories. Note equally rapid fall in pressure when patient was instructed
to breathe deeply.

quality about him, a lack of trust that was underscored by his
controlled speech. It was easier for me to focus on these aspects of
his speech because I did not know what he was talking about.

As shown on the graph in figure 9.1, for over twenty minutes,
Jan's blood pressure and heart rate remained quite normal, fluctuating as hypertensive patients on beta blockers usually respond
when they engage in dialogue. When he spoke, his blood pressure
usually rose 10 percent to 25 percent, into hypertensive ranges;
and when he listened to Dr. Rijke-deVries, his pressure quickly fell
back to normal levels. Yet even while he spoke in his soft, guttural
voice, he seemed to be preoccupied, somewhat removed from the
entire conversation, his attention focused elsewhere, far away.

Jan seemed to be a person who wanted to be heard and
understood, yet was unable to articulate his feelings. I thought his

speech might mask the cries of an infant who cannot explain himself to others. As I explained in chapter 5, our research studies on the blood pressure of newborn babies had led me to think about adult hypertension in this metaphorical way (see pages 115–17). Now in Dr. Rijke-deVries's office, I began to wonder whether deep down, buried from his own awareness, Jan really might feel like an infant crying in the night, a child frantic, unheard by his mother. We had shown that when a newborn baby cries, frequently its blood pressure will increase 100 percent or more.[3] Using the same type of computer now recording Jan's pressure, these studies were the first ever to measure diastolic blood pressure in newborns while simultaneously recording neonatal behavior, such as crying. We had also been able to see the dramatic shifts in the newborns' blood pressure during other activities, such as breast feeding, sleeping, and sucking during maternal interactions.[4]

Acting on my thought, I interrupted the conversation between Jan and Dr. Rijke-deVries, in order to describe to her our studies on newborns. After briefly summarizing our findings, I suggested, "Maybe there's an infant inside Jan crying to be heard. Ask Jan about his childhood! Tell him that I believe that events in childhood can sometimes be linked to an adult's struggles with high blood pressure."

After Dr. Rijke-deVries had translated my request, Jan abruptly turned in his chair and stared at me. He began to speak slightly louder, more rapidly, and with far greater emphasis. And for the first time he spoke directly to me, in spite of the fact that I could not understand what he was saying. Yet though he seemed agitated, he was smiling the entire time he was speaking to me. Within one minute, his pressure rose from 143/83 to 183/136; and within two minutes, it was as high as 210/145.

Alarmed by this sudden rise in pressure, and yet having no idea what in the world he had said, I asked Dr. Rijke-deVries to tell him to be quiet and breathe deeply for several minutes. As reflected in the mean arterial pressure shown in figure 9.1, his blood pressure immediately fell back to 145/83 and then down to 140/81: that is, within two minutes, his systolic pressure was lower than his diastolic pressure had been while he was speaking to me.

While Jan continued to breathe deeply, Dr. Rijke-deVries, also startled by the rapid shifts in his pressure, pointed out to him the dramatic rise and fall in his blood pressure. Then she translated what he had said, "Jan said that when he was a young boy of six, he lived on the waterfront of Rotterdam. Everything in his neighborhood was destroyed when the Nazis firebombed the city. Jan remembers houses in flames and buildings crashing down all around him. He said he was completely terrified, so thoroughly frightened that he could no longer cry."

"But that was not his worst memory," she continued. "He says that when the Allies finally began to drive the Nazis out of Holland, his parents had no food. He says that he got so weak and so thin that he could not get out of bed, and that his father had to go away on long trips in search of food. He said he did not mind starvation as much as what it did to his body. Mainly he felt ashamed of his body—he felt he was nothing—there was nothing to his body but skin and bones—and he felt deeply shamed."

I suggested that Dr. Rijke-deVries explain to Jan that, indeed, there did seem to be a link between his childhood memories and big increases in his blood pressure, and that he had a great deal to discuss with her. I also pointed out to him that, though his blood pressure had surged very high when he spoke about those painful memories, he had done something that quickly lowered his pressure. Jan nodded and smiled, and then continued his discussion with Dr. Rijke-deVries. For the remainder of the session, they spoke quietly together, and his blood pressure gradually fell as low as 129/76.

The dramatic surge in Jan's blood pressure, in spite of his antihypertensive medicines, is far from unusual. Over four years we have seen many similar episodes in other hypertensive patients.* Nor do memories alone of unusual childhood catastrophes produce such marked changes: hypertensive patients appear particularly vulnerable when they touch on topics that elicit complex emotional feelings, as in the following case.

A "LITTLE SECRET"

On the surface Karl was as different from Jan as a Dutch autumn is from a Southern California desert spring. *Gentle* or *soft-spoken* would hardly describe him. A vice president of a medium-sized

---

* Such marked surges in blood pressure have led me to wonder whether they may initiate or exacerbate coronary atherosclerosis. On the assumption that a sudden wave of increased pressure surges down the coronary arteries, it is possible that the inner lining of the artery could be bruised, thus increasing the likelihood of the development of this disease.

construction firm, Karl was built like a middleweight prizefighter; and, indeed, he had tested his mettle earlier in his life in wild barroom brawls. He cursed like an undisciplined seaman, though he frequently apologized to his therapist, Dr. Thomas—"being that she was such a fine lady"—for his coarse language during their therapeutic sessions together. If ever a patient fitted the descriptions of the Type A personality, Karl did. Hardworking, fast-talking, restlessly impulsive, he had come to our clinic, as he phrased it, as "a last-ditch effort to head off a massive heart attack." Indeed, he knew "all about the Type A character" and its links to coronary heart disease and readily acknowledged that "the descriptions I've read in the newspapers fit me to a T."

At fifty-four years of age, Karl had been struggling with hypertension for over twenty years. He had taken a variety of antihypertensive medications for almost a decade. In the spring of 1981, he began to complain of increasing impotency, coupled with serious marital problems, and so his cardiologist began to wean him off his drugs. In midsummer of that same year, after the cessation of his medicines, Karl experienced an acute hypertensive episode and collapsed. He recalled being terrified that he was having a stroke. He was taken by ambulance to a hospital emergency room; his blood pressure was 210/140 upon arrival. In addition to chronic marital stress (his wife had left him to live with another man), Karl was having trouble with his business and with the Internal Revenue Service and was struggling with a son in college. After Karl's hypertensive crisis, his cardiologist placed him back on medicines; and again, he began to feel depressed and impotent. Finally in March 1982, his physician sent him to our university clinic in order to see whether our approach could help.

During his initial session with Dr. Thomas, Karl's blood pressure averaged around 155/95, and his heart rate and blood pressure fluctuated significantly when he spoke. For six sessions Dr. Thomas gently probed various interpersonal issues that appeared to be connected to his hypertension. As therapy progressed, his blood pressure began to drop, and his attitude and general demeanor to change. Initially he resisted watching the computer tracings of his blood pressure. He also rejected the idea that his style of relating to others or of communicating had any direct effect on his body. While he readily acknowledged that his Type A personality and his emotions were linked to his problems with blood pressure, he stated that he believed such factors took their toll gradually, the way a mountain stream slowly cuts deeper into the mountainside." It was difficult for Karl to believe that his way of talking could immediately influence his heart rate and blood pressure.

By the sixth session, however, his attitude changed. Constantly reminded to look at his own blood pressure, he had shifted from the idea of being a patient who presented his "slowly eroding" body to his doctor, to someone who had become actively involved in his own therapy. Hundreds of repeated measurements had led him to understand that his blood pressure was not a static bodily process that changed only gradually over time, but was, instead, a dynamic phenomenon in constant flux. He grew ever more intrigued by changes in his blood pressure that occurred outside of his own awareness. "Damn! that thing sure jumps around," he exclaimed several times during a session, echoing the phraseology used by other patients, like Michael (see chapter 1), to describe his own blood pressure. Like virtually all patients, Karl still talked about his blood pressure as if it were a "thing" traced out on a computer screen, rather than a dynamic component of his essential being.

In order to help him grasp the connection between "him" and "that thing jumping around on the computer," Dr. Thomas suggested that their sixth session together be televised. She felt a video taping of the session would give Karl the opportunity to watch and reflect on the way his blood pressure changed. Toward the end of this session, his blood pressure was averaging around 145/90. He appeared far more relaxed than he had in previous sessions, and openly expressed his appreciation for the supportive care and concern Dr. Thomas had extended to him. He seemed intrigued with the various techniques, including relaxation and proper breathing, that had such an obvious and immediate impact on his blood pressure. It gave him increasing confidence that he could take steps to control his own problems.

Just as their session was almost finished, however, Karl—in an abrupt manner typical of the Type A personality—abruptly changed the topic of conversation. He interrupted Dr. Thomas and, leaning forward in his seat, began to speak rapidly, with an air of hushed excitement. "Called my cardiologist last week, and I told him how things were going here, how my blood pressure was coming down and all—and I asked him if I could cut my diuretic in half. Damn!

I was sick and tired of getting up half a dozen times every night to pee—a man can't hardly sleep with those damn diuretics causing you to get up to run to the bathroom all night long. But he wouldn't budge."

Chuckling a bit to himself, Karl continued, "He's such a careful doctor, you know. He said—so sure of himself, you know the way doctors talk—'Absolutely no way! No way!' Those were his exact words, there's just no way I could cut back on the diuretics just yet!"

Then laughing aloud while gesturing emphatically, Karl repeated the phrase, "No way! No way!" Leaning back in his chair, looking smug and pleased with himself, he continued, "Only problem is I cut those damn pills out a week before I called him! My pressure had come down so nicely in here that I began to wonder whether I could get along without them. Now I'm a very careful observer—and I watched carefully, and there was absolutely no change in my blood pressure. If anything, my damn pressure seemed to be lower."

Pausing again for a moment, he added, "So it's only a little secret! He's such a nice guy, I don't like keeping things from him. But he said so positively, 'No way!'—when it was clear there was a way! I don't like telling him he was wrong, or having to lie to him, but I sure do sleep better at night now. Which do you think is better for blood pressure? Sleeping soundly all night, or getting up half a dozen times to pee! I don't want to embarrass him. Do you think I have to tell him?"

In his excitement, Karl had not noticed that his blood pressure had abruptly surged from an average of 145/90 up to 195/140. While the computer video monitor traced out this major surge, Dr. Thomas calmly noted, "Look at your little secret." And to make sure that Karl would not remain oblivious to the marked change in his blood pressure she repeated, "Look at what your little secret did to your blood pressure! Do you think your little secret is worth such a big price?"

Shocked by the sudden surge in his pressure, clearly reflected on the computer screen, Karl lifted his hands up to his head and muttered, "Oh my God! Oh my God!" Then appearing to recall the lessons he had been taught in earlier session, he stopping talking and began to take deep breaths.

After a minute of silence, and certain that Karl was learning several important lessons, Dr. Thomas added, "So you want your cardiologist to treat you without knowing what drugs you're taking? How is he supposed to know what's going on medically if you start keeping little secrets?

With the air of a man suddenly converted through sheer anxiety to a new way of thinking, Karl rather sheepishly remarked, "I think I'll tell him the next time I see him."

Still appearing alarmed, in spite of the fact that his blood pressure had now fallen below the levels it had been before he began to reveal his "little secret," he said, "Christ, I've never seen my pressure change like that. And you know I didn't feel anything. I didn't feel a damn thing! I didn't feel that damn pressure go up, and I didn't feel it go back down. Nor do I now feel anything other than a bit light headed."

"What do you think that means?" Dr. Thomas asked. "Does it tell you anything about your feelings?"

"Christ!" Karl exclaimed, shaking his head. "I must be totally disconnected from my body and my feelings." Then to himself, he repeated, "I didn't feel a damn thing!"

Within five minutes Karl's pressure had fallen to 142/78, its lowest point since he had first come to the clinic.

Karl revealed other "little secrets" over the next six months and other hidden feelings he discovered by observing the surges in his blood pressure registered by the computer: secrets about the constant pressure his parents put on him to excel, secrets about the fact that this pressure made him afraid of failure, and secrets about his need to dominate and control others. In the process he began to feel the changes in his blood pressure that had previously gone unrecognized. He began to understand that he was using and abusing his body in a way that was threatening his very existence.

By seeing his pressure changes and the way they correlated with certain topics of conversation, Karl began to *feel* his feelings for the first time in his life. "Perhaps," he speculated months later, "I really wanted to die, and my own body was simply obliging me." Gradually he came to grips with the frightening reality that he had been destroying himself, using his cardiovascular system in a way that would inevitably have terminated his life prematurely.

TURNING UP THE THERMOSTAT

By no means do major changes in the cardiovascular system during human dialogue appear only as rapid surges in blood pressure and heart rate. Quite the opposite response can occur in patients whose blood pressure suddenly drops when, in communicating, they allow another person to enter their real world.

An internist had sent Frances to our clinic for migraine headaches and spastic colitis. She had suffered from migraine headaches coincident with her menstrual period since the onset of menarche and they had become more frequent and intense since her marriage nine years before. In her professional life, Frances was by all objective criteria a smashing success, as at thirty-seven years of age she was a senior executive of a large financial institution. She reported that her marriage was generally happy and that her husband successfully ran his own corporation. Their only "real problem," she noted, was her inability to have children. The appearance of fibroid tumors in her uterus with intermittent bleeding when she was twenty-five forced her to have a hysterectomy, precluding the possibility of pregnancy. She did admit that this had "contributed to an unhappy sex life with her husband" and was a "chronic problem in their marriage which they had learned to live with."

Frances's professional accomplishments were all the more remarkable because they stood in sharp contrast to an emotionally turbulent and painful childhood and adolescence. Her early life was littered with the emotional wreckage of severe violations of trust, utter absence of emotional security, and constant withdrawal of parental love. Among the many traumas Frances had endured, she reported that she had been sexually molested by her father's business partner when she was eight years old. When she told her father, he warned her not to mention the incident to anyone lest it hurt him financially, and also suggested at the time that "the incident was at least half [her] fault."

At age sixteen she had been raped by a high school classmate and became pregnant. Her family refused to believe her story about the rape and initially refused to discuss the possibility that she might be pregnant. When it became clear that indeed she was, her parents ordered her to remain in her room each evening while the rest of her family had dinner together. Finally they arranged for her to leave the country, have her baby in a home for unwed mothers, and then give the baby up for adoption. It was after the adoption that her problems with spastic colitis appeared. When Frances was eighteen and in college, her mother had a nervous breakdown. Her parents divorced at that time, and both of them blamed all their marital problems on Frances's pregnancy.

While few readers would be startled by the suggestion that Frances's childhood and adolescent emotional pain were connected to her physical problems, nevertheless it was impressive to see how greatly her body responded when she "really" talked about certain of these traumatic experiences. The fourteenth therapy session illustrates one such episode.

In this session Frances was more optimistic than usual. She was quite encouraged with her therapeutic progress and expressed delight in her freedom from migraine headaches for the past four weeks. She noted that she could not recall so long a period since her adolescence when she had been free from head pain. For the first time she also agreed to have her husband join her in subsequent therapy sessions.

As shown in figure 9.2, during this hour-long session her mean arterial pressure averaged around 85—approximately 10 percent to 15 percent below the levels typical of women her age. Curiously, while Frances's blood pressure was lower than normal, it was typical of the pressure readings of many patients who had come to our clinic for migraine headaches. While a few migraine patients do have high blood pressure and rapid heart rates, low blood pressure (sometimes accompanied by rapid heart rate, sometimes with normal rates) occurs far more frequently in this patient population.

In the course of therapy, Frances had learned to pay closer attention to her hand temperature and, through relaxation, was beginning to be able to regulate her temperature at 90 degrees Fahrenheit. The graph in figure 9.2 of her mean arterial pressure during this fourteenth session shows the usual fluctuations seen in migraine patients during therapy. As can be seen, however, while she was speaking at point L, her blood pressure suddenly plummeted to a low of 67 (a pressure equal to 90/50), thirty millimeters lower than it had been ten minutes earlier. (By way of contrast, Jan's

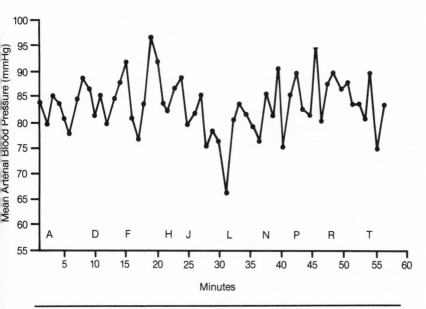

Figure 9.2.   Sudden mean arterial blood-pressure decrease (at point L) in a migraine patient when alluding to her concern for her daughter whom she had given up for adoption at birth.

mean arterial pressure was 148 when he was speaking about his childhood, and Karl's pressure had surged to 151 while he was telling his "little secret"—almost two and a half times greater than Frances's pressure.) Just before her pressure plummeted, Frances had been describing a "wonderful dream" she had had the previous night. She remarked that ordinarily she never dreamed or, if she did, she could not recall the dream. In this dream she is traveling to Paris where she accidentally finds her long-lost daughter. Her daughter is about sixteen years old in the dream. They have a marvelous reunion, touring a number of cities together, and she entertains her daughter the way Frances wished her mother had treated her. She is thrilled that her daughter so readily understands why she, Frances, had to give her up for adoption.

Between points K and L on the graph, after she finished describing this dream, she smiled and quietly added, "I often wonder what she's really like today. It's hard to think about it, but somewhere out there I have a daughter who is a grown-up woman of twenty-one. God, I hope she's happy."

When asked how she felt about having been forced to give up her own child, she responded that she "had worked it all out long ago." While continuing to smile serenely, she softly added that she was "fine." She rejected the suggestion that this issue might still trouble her, then sighed deeply and asked in a voice that seemed filled with peaceful resignation, "How many times can your heart break?"

When the computer registered the sudden drop in her pressure after this remark, she trembled, stared at the screen in silence for about thirty seconds, and added, "God! it's cold in here." While staring at the video screen, she then quietly reflected, "Maybe your heart never stops breaking." Then, like a cheerleader trying to rouse a disheartened crowd to root more enthusiastically for the home team, Frances abruptly changed moods and said in a lively manner, "Let's talk about my husband. That's guaranteed to bring that pressure back up to normal and warm the body. No sense crying over spilt milk!"

THE COSMOPOLITAN LADY

Michelle was every bit as professionally successful as Frances. A lawyer in a firm in Washington, D.C., Michelle's academic accomplishments were truly outstanding. At age thirty-nine not only had she published a number of highly regarded legal briefs, but she was equally respected in her law office. Single, articulate, keenly intelligent, physically very beautiful, always seeming happy, she appeared to be the type of woman who would be the envy of readers of *Cosmopolitan* magazine.

Behind the veneer of success, however, there was another woman who had been wracked with migraines since childhood, as well as a person who had suffered from intermittent colitis and gastrointestinal problems for the past decade. In addition to her migraines, she also suffered from chronic tension headaches. She joked about the fact that the list of medicines she had taken for her headaches had made her a pharmaceutical expert on the treatment of head pain, and noted that she "had tried virtually every combination of medicines that had ever been concocted for head pain." Yet nothing worked. She also tried an extended period of psychotherapy as well as a course of biofeedback. She reported that psychotherapy had been of some personal benefit, though it did little to alleviate her physical symptoms. By contrast, she reported that biofeedback had been of no help whatsoever.

Beyond the list of physical symptoms, Michelle had experienced what seemed to be an unending series of stormy and unhappy relationships with men. When she first met her current male friend, she reported that at long last she believed "that things would work out reasonably well." There was only one real problem with their relationship, and that was his stated intention never to get married again, as he had apparently gone through a very stormy marriage and painful divorce.

In spite of certain reservations, Michelle decided to live with this man and, much to her surprise, became pregnant "quite by accident." She reported that "he was terribly distressed at the pregnancy and, though he did not blame me, he was in no position to marry me." Though raised as a devout Catholic, Michelle saw no alternative but to abort the pregnancy. After this experience, which she described as "the worst experience in my life and one that was utterly devastating," she reported that, as a result, she "totally lost interest in sex."

During the sixth therapy session, Michelle had been calmly talking about a variety of problems in her life. She was particularly disturbed by the fact that her law firm had postponed a decision about making her a partner. While the reason given was economic, Michelle felt the decision was based primarily on sex and stated that "only men seem to make it in [my] firm. They would turn down superwoman herself." In spite of her professional struggles, however, her relationship with her "significant other" was far more pressing. She perceived that it was in danger of breaking up because of her lack of interest in sex. "I can't stand him touching me and I'm hard to get along with. Why should he stay?"

Ever since she had first come to our clinic, Michelle's cardiovascular system had exhibited marked shifts from week to week. Some weeks her heart rate averaged around 100 beats per minute, and other weeks it averaged around 70 beats per minute. Similarly, at times her blood pressure was normal, around 130/65, and at other times, it fell as low as 90/50. Her hands were always ice cold, in spite of the fact that room temperature was kept slightly warmer than normal (76°F).

During this particular session she had been talking about her irritation with her job, and how she had "screwed up her life," and her relationship with men in general. Just before her blood pressure plummeted, I asked her whether she felt alone and abandoned. I compared her existence to that of a person all alone in a small boat on a sea with thirty-foot waves threatening to capsize her at any moment, and then asked, "How can you talk so rationally about your problems? How can you talk so calmly about your job and your love life when you're out on a small dingy that's threatening to capsize in a stormy ocean?"

"Of course I feel abandoned!" Michelle fired back to me, at first seeming to have fixated on my earlier point about her loneliness and abandonment. It was the first time I had ever heard her use the word *feel*. She momentarily slumped back in her chair, and then quickly regained her composure. Her eyes then filled with tears and she added, "How can you talk so readily about love? Don't you see I can't even say the word? Not once in my life did I ever hear my parents use that word. No one ever said I love you to me, and not once in my life have I ever said I love you to anyone." Then, pausing for a moment and shuddering ever so slightly, she added, "I can never forgive myself for that abortion. It was the most devastating experience of my life. God! it was awful! I'd just as soon die."

"Maybe that's what your body's trying to do," I said, as the computer traced the sudden drop in her pressure from 123/71 to 91/50.

"Funny," she answered suddenly attending to her body, "My hands and feet are freezing, and my back and underarms are soaking with sweat. What a crazy body!"

"Maybe that's where all the blood that's suppose to flow to your hands and feet has gone," I added, smiling at my own metaphor. "Maybe all your blood has pooled in the central core of your body and you just don't have enough energy to keep it flowing out to your extremities."

The room grew quiet for a few minutes before I asked, "Did you feel your blood pressure dropping?"

"Are you kidding?" Michelle responded as her blood pressure began to rise to more normal levels. "I don't even know what a feeling is!"

"That's the problem" I countered, hoping to share one additional insight. "Maybe you have to *feel* your feelings before you *know* your feelings! Maybe your feelings are reflected in that dramatic fall in blood pressure."

Michelle smiled, seemed to want to cry, but instead returned to describe her struggles with her boyfriend.

A SUMMING UP

These clinical vignettes describe extraordinary changes that can occur in patients' bodies during what externally appear to be relatively peaceful conversations. In no case were the changes detected by the patient; and, without continuous monitoring, they certainly could not have been detected by anyone else either. Granted that a sophisticated clinician might guess that a patient was a bit more anxious or upset, the fact remains that there was no way to predict or guess the magnitude of these sudden changes in blood pressure and heart rate. While in certain cases the topic being discussed appeared emotionally provocative, in other cases, such as Karl's, the topic appeared far less so than in earlier conversations.

And always, each patient smiled, sometimes even appearing emotionally peaceful, as his or her vasculature abruptly changed. Aside from speaking a bit more rapidly and intensely or breathing irregularly, in general there were no external changes at all commensurate with the autonomic storm raging inside their bodies. It appeared that the effort to "really" talk had physical consequences that were potentially dangerous.

Whatever the physiological mechanisms contributing to these changes, the fact is that these sudden surges can be seen at one time or another in most patients prone to hypertension or migraine headaches, although by no means do they occur in every session. And the direction of the changes—sudden increases in blood pressure in hypertensive patients, and precipitous drops in blood pressure in migraine patients—have appeared with sufficient regularity to make us suspect some causative connection between the direction of the changes and the nature of the disease.

Dysautonomia is the term that seems best to describe the phenomenon: that is, the patient's autonomic nervous system seems hypersensitive to sudden shifts in emotional arousal and is thus vulnerable to sudden major dysfunctional reactions.* It is possible that under stress these patients excrete into the blood stream large amounts of catecholamines which then impinge on structures that are already vulnerable and primed to react.

At present we have no way of knowing whether comparable increases and decreases in blood pressure occur in healthy individuals or in people not prone to these specific psychosomatic disorders. An analysis of this question would require prolonged and repeated conversations in an emotional milieu similar to our therapeutic setting. While such a situation would be difficult to duplicate experimentally, my hunch is that one must already be vulnerable in order to experience changes of this magnitude.

And these changes are not detected by the person in whose body they occur. Indeed, while I am going beyond what we have yet been able to verify empirically, it appears as if the greater the changes—that is, the more massive the emotional upheaval—the less likely is the person prone to these conditions to sense them. Granted that if the changes are pushed to the extreme, as when Karl was rushed to an emergency room in an acute hypertensive crisis, then a person either feels something or collapses (faints or has a stroke, a major "anxiety" attack, or a blinding migraine).

This inability to feel internal changes is a glaring example of what seems to be a major contributing cause of alexithymia. Indeed, as noted in chapter 8, the very term *alexithymia* may be a misnomer. It is not so much that these patients "have no words for feelings" as that they cannot feel the bodily correlates of their own feelings. Virtually every patient who has witnessed these autonomic storms of his or her body has expressed genuine astonishment: as Karl said, "I didn't feel a damn thing!"

* In addition to dysautonomia, other terms have been used to describe analogous phenomena. Several decades earlier, clinicians used *neurocirculatory asthenia* to describe abnormally low blood pressure in certain patients, usually women; a number of clinicians described these patients as thin and frail. The chief sign of asthenia was a sudden decrease in pressure when a patient was stressed.[5] Again, this phenomenon, observed in an era before computer-based monitoring systems, was generally thought of as a sign of depression and frailty but was not linked to human dialogue.

UNFELT EMOTIONS

HUMAN EMOTIONS AS NERVE IMPULSES

When Walter Cannon wrote his book on the physiology of emotions in 1929, he posed a perplexing problem that we at first naïvely believed our computer tracings had at long last solved. Cannon confronted a strange paradox about emotions. He sensed that no matter how clear and how overwhelming the physiological evidence about the influence of emotions on the body might be, there would be deep resistance toward incorporating this knowledge into medical practice:

Although physicians have not infrequent occasions to observe instances of functional disturbance due to emotional causes, there is an inclination to minimize or to slight that influence, or even to deny that it is part of a physician's service to his patient to concern himself with such troubles. Let the patient go to the clergyman for comfort and consolation and for the resolution of his deep anxieties. A too common unwillingness among physicians to regard seriously the emotional elements in disease is due perhaps to the subtle influence of two extreme attitudes and disciplines. On the one hand is the powerful impress of morphological pathology, the study of diseased organs as seen after death. So triumphantly and so generally have the structural alterations which accompany altered functions been demonstrated under the microscope, that any state which has no distinct "pathology" appears to be unreal or of minor significance. Fears, worries and states of rage and resentment leave no clear traces in the brain. What, then, have physicians to do with them? On the other hand, these mysterious and dominant feelings which surge up within us from unknown sources—are they not pure perturbations of the "psyche"? In that case, what, again, have physicians to do with them? If physicians show this indifference, however, is it surprising that men and women, beset by emotional stresses, turn from them and go for help to faith healers and to others who recognize the reality of these disturbing states?[6]

More than fifty years after Cannon made these observations, little had changed. Though virtually every physician readily acknowledges that stress and emotional distress contribute significantly to a wide variety of medical disorders, there is little systematic use of such knowledge in medical practice. We in the clinic suspected Cannon was correct, that perhaps the problem existed because emotions leave no clear traces in the brain. We thought that the computers would help us trace out the physiological correlates of emotions on a video terminal, and that then clinicians would take them seriously. No one, we naïvely believed, would be able to ignore a 50 percent rise in blood pressure when a patient talked about his feelings. And we could store the traces in the computer's memory and play them back over and over again so that no one would doubt their reality.

Our optimism was further fueled by a logical flaw we detected in Cannon's original efforts to solve the paradox he clearly described. For how did he propose to get physicians and patients alike to take emotions seriously as they affect the body? How did he propose to make physicians take seriously fear, rage, grief, loneliness, or love if, indeed, these emotions leave no clear traces in the brain? Cannon's solution, while pragmatic on the surface, proved prophetic in terms of subsequent twentieth-century trends. He opted to approach the topic from the viewpoint of what can be measured. As he described it: "Using the physiological point of view, therefore, I have considered emotions in terms of nerve impulses."[7] Thus he suggested that scientists could study the neurophysiological correlates of "emotions" and eventually find the traces of emotions in the brain. Once the *traces* had been found, then and only then would physicians incorporate this knowledge into medical practice.

No doubt Cannon could not anticipate that a subsequent generation of physiologists would blindly follow his suggestions and develop an elaborate neurophysiology of emotions. In exquisite detail, scientists began to trace various brain centers and nerve tracts that influence organs such as the heart. Unfortunately, while bending their energies in this direction, most physiologists dropped all discussion of "emotions" from their studies and focused instead exclusively on nerve tracts. Gradually the *raison d'être* of Cannon's original work was obscured. By the latter part of the twentieth century, major medical textbooks would appear on such topics as hypertension, and emotions would not even be mentioned, even though elaborate brain mechanisms and complex nervous networks that influence the vasculature were mapped out in exquisite detail. An elaborate neurophysiology was developed that did little to refine understanding of human feelings. As I have pointed out elsewhere, in the years 1970 to 1973, five hundred thousand research articles were cited in the *Index Medicus,* a journal that prints the titles and summaries of most medical and biological studies published everywhere in the world; yet, in this massive outpouring of medical research, there was not a single article connecting the phenomena of love or lack of love to the heart.[8]

In the strangest of ironies, then, the very force that Cannon set out to get physicians to attend to—that is, emotions—was inadvertently excluded from medical studies by the very solution he proposed to remedy the situation.

EMOTIONS IN ANIMALS: FEELINGS IN HUMANS

There were two deep problems contributing to Cannon's dilemma that escaped our attention for almost two decades: one involved the distinction between emotions and feelings; and the other concerned the links between speech and the communication of human feelings. What we failed to appreciate was the significance of the fact that Cannon had based his conceptual thinking about human emotions on a theoretical model he inherited from Charles Darwin. Because of this model, Cannon fell into the same conceptual trap that initially made it difficult for us to appreciate the fundamental importance of the links between human speech and the cardiovascular system. Like Cannon, we too had uncritically accepted the idea that animal physiology was similar to human physiology, and that therefore animals could be used to understand human emotions and stress-linked physiological disorders. Cannon's exquisite demonstrations of the involvement of the autonomic nervous system's influence on the cardiovascular system, for example, had been worked out almost entirely with such animals as cats, rabbits, and dogs. And, indeed, the mechanisms of emotional arousal closely parallel those in human beings. The neurophysiology of emotional arousal is clearly similar in humans and animals. In that conceptual context, it was difficult to conceive of human language as being central to understanding emotions. For the physiology of emotions had been mapped out in animals by Cannon and many other scientists, and animals do not speak.

Yet, as I have emphasized throughout this book, ever so gradually the importance of the links between speech, human physiology, and human emotions began to dawn on us. Only human beings use language that includes words such as *love, hate, anger, jealousy,* and *loneliness.* Only human beings use words to identify feelings, and only human beings use words to communicate their feelings.

In the end we came to realize that only humans discriminate feelings, because only humans share a social membrane and the capacity to speak. To talk about or describe various feelings in animals is nothing but an elaborate exercise in anthropomorphism; it is to attribute to animals a phenomenon that is uniquely human. While a human can attribute emotional meaning to an animal with which one shares a common social membrane, the process can never be reciprocated: animals cannot speak, and no animal can teach a human the "mother tongue." Animals cannot invite humans in to experience their emotional world. No dog can ever teach an infant the meaning of love—or use the word *love*—no matter how loving the dog may appear to be, for no dog can affirm as real an infant's emotional experience. Only human beings consciously experience feelings in a way that is shared through language.

This position is radically different from the central thrust of twentieth-century scientific efforts on this subject. While the scientific literature is both vast and complex, and any attempt to reduce it to a few general statements runs the risk of oversimplification, nevertheless certain fundamental premises can be identified. First, virtually all scientific investigators have localized emotions as phenomena occurring inside the body. Second, emotions have been thought about as phenomena that are essentially the same in humans and in higher animals. Third, the "experience" of emotions in human beings has been viewed as originating in some hyperexcited bodily system which is then decoded by the brain or mind—a notion, as we shall see in chapter 10, that owes its origins to the theoretical writings of René Descartes. The distinction between human feelings and human emotions and their origin in shared experience has been ignored—an oversight that has seriously blurred the links between human relations, human feelings, and bodily functions. Even more to the point, little attention has been paid to the importance of language and of human communication as essential to emotional experience and as a crucial link to psychosomatic disease.

The outlook has not always been so. Long before the nineteenth century, when Darwin advanced his theories, it had been widely accepted that various bodily changes routinely accompany various emotional states. Crying, heart palpitations, sweating, muscle twitching, trembling, breathlessness, diarrhea, and so on, were long regarded as signs of emotional arousal. Shakespeare and other playwrights routinely used such allusions to convey various emotional struggles to audiences who understood their meaning without difficulty.

The idea that emotions could be the object of scientific scrutiny was first raised by Charles Darwin in 1872 in his classic text *The Expression of Emotions in Man and Animals.*[9] This book, published in the wake of his major thesis on the origin of the species, proved to be a fundamental extension of his controversial proposition that humans have evolved from lower animals. Darwin asserted that there is nothing qualitatively unique about human beings. Rather, the difference between humans and the higher animals was seen by him to be merely quantitative, as having evolved. It was a theory that trivialized the unique nature of human speech by asserting it to be "only" the result of neural development a bit more sophisticated than that of animals. Darwin's theory of emotional expression was crucially important because it implied that *not only did humans evolve from animals, but that humans' expression of emotion was similar as well.* He believed emotional expressions to be serviceable habits and, as such, subject to scientific scrutiny. Key to Darwin's entire approach was his penetrating emphasis on the word *expression*—as something that could be measured.

Though seldom recognized as such, Darwin's book on emotions was in many respects far more revolutionary and provocative than his earlier writings on evolution. His book marked the beginning of a new approach, which led other scientists to accept the idea that emotions can be studied objectively. Since his theory of evolution was rooted in genetics and physiology, it was inevitable that the scientific study of emotional expression would similarly be pursued inside an evolving body. Hence, Cannon's work was inevitable. It was, as I have said, the combination of evolutionary theory, coupled with Darwin's conceptual framework about emotions, that made it virtually impossible to conceive any longer of human speech as uniquely linked to human feelings.

Darwin's book stirred a whirlwind of scientific interest in emotions. Within a decade, investigators like William James had blurred the fundamental distinction between emotional expression and emotional experience. In 1890, he posed the question "What is emotion?" and proceeded to outline an entirely new answer to it. He extended Darwin's revolutionary ideas one step farther by proposing that the experience of emotions follows or is secondary to the perception of bodily symptoms. In a view at least partially corroborated by the description of patients in this text, James proposed that one experiences an emotion only if one feels one's heart rate or one's blood pressure rising or some other bodily symptom. A year after William James proposed this idea, a second investigator, the Danish physician and psychologist Carl Georg Lange (1834–1900), put forward a similar thesis but restricted the locus of emotional experience to cues provided by the cardiovascular system alone.[10] The combined views of these two men later came to be known as the "James–Lange theory of emotions."

The outlines of this theory were stated by James as follows:

Common sense says, we lose our fortune, are sorry and weep; we meet a bear, are frightened and run; we are insulted by a rival, are angry and strike. The hypothesis here to be defended says that this order of sequence is incorrect, that the one mental state is not immediately induced by the other, that the *bodily manifestations must first be interposed between,* and that the more natural statement is that we feel sorry because we cry, angry because we strike, afraid because we tremble. . . . that the bodily changes follow directly the perception of the exciting fact and that *our feeling of the same changes as they occur is the emotions.* Every one of the bodily changes, whatsoever it be, is felt acutely or obscurely the moment it occurs.[11] [Italics added]

When this theory was first published just prior to the twentieth century, it troubled psychologists and physiologists alike. It purported to provide a way for scientists to study what historically had been considered the subjective aspect of emotions—their experience. By asserting that the experience of an emotion was coextensive with bodily changes, James implied that that experience was identical with bodily changes. This blurring of the difference between the distinctly human phenomenon of emotional experience and the objective bodily correlates of an emotion paved the way for other scientists to reduce emotions to neural circuitry, which is essentially the same in humans and animals.

It did not take long for physiologists to attack certain aspects of the James–Lange theory, while simultaneously accepting the central core of the thesis. They argued about the locus of emotional experience in the body, while accepting James's fundamental idea

of the body *as the source of and as coexistensive with the emotion.*
What these scientists challenged was the idea that emotions are
caused by changes in the visceral system. While James had proposed
that a rapid heart rate leads to a certain emotional experience, they
insisted that emotional arousal in the brain causes the heart to race
in the first place; hence, emotional experience is in the brain.

In 1927, Walter Cannon raised objections to James's theory and
asserted that emotions are caused by changes in the brain.[12] The
classic research of the eminent neurophysiologist Sir Charles Sherrington had set the stage for Cannon's attack. In 1900, Sherrington
cut the spinal cord and vagus nerves in a dog, thus severing any
connection between brain and visceral nervous system (that is,
lungs, spleen, stomach, and so on); but the dog continued to exhibit
marked evidence of emotional behavior.[13] Cannon used evidence
of this sort to dispute James's idea that emotions are "felt" because
of prior changes in the visceral system, and proposed instead a
"central theory" of emotions (as opposed to James's peripheral
theory).

Dr. Philip Bard, then a professor of neurophysiology at Johns
Hopkins, extended Cannon's theory one step farther by suggesting
that another central brain region, the thalamus, was also necessary
for the expression of emotional behavior.[14] He supported his
position by showing that "shame rage," induced by stripping a cat
of its cortex, could be abolished by then extirpating the thalamus.
Thus the theory of emotions as caused by the central nervous
system came to be called the "Cannon–Bard theory of emotions."
Other investigators questioned these brain regions, believing another
region in the brain—the limbic system—to be the source of
emotional expression.

While both the James–Lange and the Cannon–Bard theories
gathered proponents and have been refined in the intervening years,
they remain the dominant perspectives guiding research in the
field.* Elements of both these theories have appeared in the clinical
vignettes described in this text. I have repeatedly emphasized, for
example, that Cannon's idea about fight or flight played a major
conceptual role in our own understanding of the social membrane

---

* As I shall describe in chapter 10, both the James–Lange and the Cannon–Bard theories of
emotions are merely highly sophisticated elaborations of a philosophical position first enunciated
by René Descartes three centuries earlier.

and of the cardiovascular reactivity of hypertensive patients when they speak to others. Likewise, elements of the James–Lange theory of emotions have significantly affected the alexithymic problems of many of the patients described in this book. Computer feedback of patients' cardiovascular responses when speaking was routinely used to help bring them in touch with feelings that they had not previously detected. And I have emphasized that patients need to be aware of their blood-pressure and heart-rate increases in order to detect shifts in their emotions when they talk with other people.

Thus, the utility of these ideas in terms of bodily processes likely to be involved in emotional arousal is not at issue here. Rather, what is at issue is the limitations of these physiological theories in accounting for the subjective human experience of emotions, as well as for the role that human communication plays in the overall identification and regulation of such experiences as distinct feelings that can be identified and shared through language. Certain cardio-vascular changes, for example, have been shown to be specifically linked to human speech. This dimension of emotional "arousal" is uniquely human and fundamentally different from any of the elaborate and ingenious animal experiments designed to map the central and peripheral correlates of arousal in animals.

It was part of Darwin's legacy that scientists have used animal models in the search for the mechanisms of stress-linked disease. They hope to learn how to create psychosomatic disease in animals so as to develop an efficient means of curing these diseases in human beings. It is a view of human-as-machine that keeps us from noticing the obvious: human beings, and human beings alone, seem especially vulnerable to psychosomatic disease.

It is not that I believe animals cannot be made vulnerable to stress-induced physical disorders, or that they do not suffer from an occasional psychosomatic disorder. I believe, however, that such disorders are relatively rare and are most often created deliberately by humans in laboratories. The animal experiments certainly show us that manipulating the autonomic nervous system can cause disease in animals. It is equally clear that human emotions are inextricably linked to autonomic nervous system activity. Yet the uniqueness of human language and its powerful links to the autonomic nervous system cannot be reproduced in the animal model.

Cannon's plea that physicians take seriously the role of human emotions in physical disease eventually forced us to recognize at least conceptually why his advice was impossible to follow. Part of the problem is that human feelings leave no clear traces in the brain. At first we thought that a useful approach would be to take Cannon literally and develop a computer system that would indeed *trace the vascular correlates of emotions on a video screen.* We were convinced that if blood pressure was seen rising during human conversations, then at long last physicians would be forced to take seriously not only emotions but also human speech. Instead, the computer screens revealed a fundamental conceptual flaw in the entire scientific approach to the study of human emotions and forced us to recognize that they are essentially interactive. Not only do they occur between one's mind and one's body, triggered by speech, but more important, they occur *between two or more people.* This dimension of human feelings *can only be experienced;* it cannot ever be recorded by the most sophisticated computer system conceivable. Indeed, neither machine nor computer can capture or convey the shared *experience* of human feelings that we, and we alone, describe with words.

THE SOCIAL MEMBRANE, EMOTIONS, AND HUMAN FEELINGS

As we saw in the last chapter, the essential experience of blushing is that it occurs during human interactions. And as I have emphasized, it is far more important for the person who is the occasion of the blushing response in another to see it, acknowledge it, and respond to it, than it is for the blusher to be able to control his or her facial blood vessels. It is other people, that is, who inform the individual what it "means" to blush: "Oh, you're blushing. You must be embarrrrassed." "Me embarrassed! You must be kidding." "Well, maybe you're not embarrassed, but you sure do look uncomfortable."

The reflex is peculiarly human. Only human beings deny their feelings, especially those feelings viewed as negative. And the response is just that—a reflex. Few people voluntarily choose to share their emotional vulnerability. We instinctively try to hide our "weakness," our discomforts, our anxieties, and those aspects of our personality that make us aware of our vulnerability. We hide such feelings not only from others but from ourselves as well. It is

not I—the conscious me—who first acknowledges that I am embarrassed. It is my face that gives me away, and another human
being who tells me what it means. There is no way, if my body
allowed me the choice, that I would let myself to be so exposed.

This human problem leads to the central point of this chapter
and to one of the central points of this book. The fact is that other
human beings are absolutely necessary to teach us two crucial
lessons. First, other people are necessary to remind us *that* we feel.
Second, other human beings are necessary to teach us *how* we feel
and *what* we feel. Human beings need as much continuous and
advanced education about their feelings as about any other topic.
Issues of human feelings raise fundamental questions about the
very nature of the human body. The fact is that the process of
learning about human feelings is essentially—that is, biologically—
interpersonal. One cannot have feelings or learn about feelings in
a social vacuum. Nor can one feel one's feelings without one's
living flesh being involved. The human cardiovascular changes
described in this book and their links to human feelings lead to the
inevitable conclusion that the sharing of human feelings involves
the human body in a process that goes far beyond anything that
can be understood by the Cartesian paradigm of a well-oiled
machine.

Yet, at first glance, the involvement of other people in one's own
bodily feelings may not appear radical. The fact is that most people
take their feelings for granted. Most people believe that human
emotions well up internally, and that one has automatic access to
this volcanic part of one's nature. In contrast to their attitudes
toward the mind, many people believe that one needs little or no
training about one's feelings but instead is automatically aware and
innately sophisticated about the most subtle human feelings. Some
people have an even more basic belief that feelings are an amorphous
and primitive animal goo that we share with our quadraped cousins:
one or two or three types of sensation that are really more of a
problem than a help; a system that has the potential of fouling up
human thinking. Still other people believe that reason and feelings
are antithetical, two aspects of human nature eternally at war. The
animal man versus the human man. Finally, some people hold to
the conviction that feelings are attributes of brute animals, machinelike sensations that must be conquered and controlled.

Though we need as much education about human feelings as about the most complex rational thoughts, there are precious few opportunities for such education in modern society. School systems, as I have said, gear virtually all their efforts toward teaching students objective facts and rational thinking. For twelve, sixteen, or twenty years, students learn objective facts, while virtually no formal efforts are expended to teach them about human feelings.* Calculus and physics are seen as highly complex disciplines that require a great deal of training and rigid disciplining of a student's mental faculties. Human feelings such as love, on the other hand, are taken for granted. No training, no exercising, no sensitizing—except, that is, for a rational discussion of these human feelings.

The world of feelings and the language of the heart that computer technology has revealed lead inexorably toward the realization that the problem of human feelings does not exist solely between a person's mind and his or her body. Rather, the problem also exists *between* human beings. Human feelings occur *between* human beings as well as within individual bodies.

Hence it is that, at our laboratory–clinic, my colleagues and I work on the assumption that the emotional meaning of various bodily changes has first to be taught to an individual by other people. This assumption is, indeed, the basis of our unique approach whereby we teach patients to feel and interpret various cardiovascular changes they had not previously detected. In this chapter, I shall extend this assumption to its logical endpoint by putting forward a new thesis, which is rooted in the belief that there is a fundamental distinction between emotions and feelings that is central to understanding the unique nature of the human body. Involved in this thesis is the additional proposition that, while emotions are common to both human beings and animals, only the former have the

---

* For many students, school systems can become a training ground where they are taught not to understand but rather to control their feelings. For those individuals who are already predisposed to be particularly insensitive to their feelings, and who will subject themselves later in life to serious psychosomatic disorders, the entire experience in schools serves to reinforce their problems. Feelings are seen as an irrational force, a dark side of human nature that must be controlled. The academic lesson is that if you cannot control your feelings, then at least you ought to hide them. Since those attitudes and beliefs coincide with and amplify similar parental dispositions, psychosomatically prone individuals often do well in school. Not sensing feelings and compulsively following structure and rules is precisely the type of behavior that prepares one to do well on objective tests. It allows one to spend endless hours learning minute details from texts while simultaneously denying one's anxiety and anger at having to spend so much time competing with fellow students.

potential to share feelings. (Although the terms *emotion* and *feeling* are often used synonymously today, emotions and feelings were for centuries distinguished; but in the seventeenth century, the distinction between them was significantly blurred. In chapter 10, I shall examine how this blurring came about and explain its profound influence on modern perceptions of the human body and on our understanding of the emotional life of human beings.)

LEARNING TO SPEAK THE MOTHER TONGUE

Furthermore, it is not just that feelings must be taught to the individual by other human beings, but that such learning is crucially influenced by those who first teach the child to speak or—perhaps more accurately—by those who first teach the child to speak the "mother tongue." As we shall see, recognition of bodily changes, both as emotions and as feelings, is intimately connected with learning to speak. Central to this teaching is the social membrane, where the meaning of human feelings is first taught through the unique sharing of bodily sensations between "teacher" and "pupil"— that is, between parent and child. At this same nexus also, problems arise that deeply influence a person's subsequent capacity to know and share feelings with others. A parent suffering from the types of problems described in this book faces several difficulties. First, if the parent cannot feel his or her own body, then he or she cannot share that emotional experience with the child. Unable to detect bodily changes in himself or herself, a parent is unable to detect comparable changes in his or her offspring. The parent is unable to confirm or affirm as "real" the emotional experiences of his or her own offspring and is equally unable to link these changes with specific emotional terms. Thus, the defective social membrane of the parent is transmitted to the child, who passes it on to the next generation.

Like all other words taught to a child, those signifying human emotions and *their felt meaning* such as *love, hate, jealousy, envy, rage, resentment, contentment,* and *affection*—must also be taught. The child does not invent these words. Yet unlike words such as *cup* or *ball* or *tree,* which refer to objects out in the world, terms for human feelings refer to experiences that are anchored first and last inside a person's body. For a word such as *cup,* mother and child can each point to an object that is external to them, and agree on its common meaning. Although external objects may trigger the bodily feeling, no external referent *is* that feeling. Such words as *love* or *hate* describe *bodily feelings.* Thus, an accurate understanding of the meaning of these terms depends on a consensual validation that is very different from the process required for learning the meaning of objects out-in-the-world. Mother and child share both the meaning of feeling terms and common bodily experiences along their common social membrane. This reality creates the potential, as well, for serious problems in communication. Though a person is taught words such as *love* and *hate,* for example, these words need not be anchored in bodily feelings; and thus, when one uses such terms to communicate with others, their "meaning" may be very different from the way such terms are understood by others. The problem is similar to the way a totally color-blind person uses words such as *red, green, yellow,* or *blue.* Though one knows there are such words, one has never experienced the colors that other people "mean" when they use the same terms.

When a child comes crying to a mother with a bruised and cut knee, for example, not only does the mother ordinarily comfort her child, perhaps kissing the knee to "make it better"; but, more important, she confirms as real the child's experience of pain and discomfort. She validates the child's statement "I hurt" only because, she, too, knows and feels what it is like to be hurt. While this point may at first sound obvious, most people today tend to think of feelings not as phenomena that emanate from bodily sensations but rather as emanating from the mind and thus as manifestations of psychological rather than physical realities.

As we shall see, this distinction involves more than abstract philosophical hairsplitting. For many bodily experiences less obvious than a bruised knee that "hurts" may not be similarly confirmed by a child's parents and may thus appear less real. Human experiences such as anxiety, fear, anger, love, or lack of love are also brought by a child to mother or father, and the emotional reality of these feelings—that is, their bodily correlates—may or may not be similarly recognized by the parents and thus may or may not be confirmed as real. Such confirmation must occur in dialogue; if it does not, the child will become hopeless about communicating and grow up disconnected from his or her own body. Many such children have arrived decades later as grown-ups in our clinic occupying bodies they no longer "live in" or feel because no one has ever confirmed their emotional life as real.*

This assertion about the bodily origin of human feelings forms the essential core of our therapeutic approach. Just as a mother justifies the very existence of an emotion in an infant's mind by recognizing and acknowledging that infant's bodily realities, so too in our therapy we act to inform the patient of bodily realities the latter has long ignored, and thereby acknowledge the reality of those interpersonal emotional experiences. Though at first glance, such emotional education may appear elementary and straightforward, it leads one to recognize certain unique attributes of human dialogue, human bodies, and human feelings that have long been obscured. It also leads one to see the profound consequences of teaching a child to communicate, to speak the "mother tongue." When first taught, human communication involves a parent's reassurance that the child's emotional experience is real. Beyond confirming these emotional experiences as real, the parent begins to teach the child words to distinguish various bodily feelings— *hurt, lonely, loving, sad, happy.* Each word given to the child, and anchored in a particular bodily feeling, thus forms the foundation upon which a child builds the capacity to communicate his or her feelings to others. Without the mother's reassurance and teaching, the existence of certain feelings becomes illegitimate to the child and alien to the world in which that child must live and grow.

THE SOCIAL WOMB

Several decades before our observations on the links between human communication and the circulatory system and our speculations about the existence of the social membrane, a Swiss zoologist,

---

* As we shall see in the last chapter, the capacity to detect one's own feelings is an issue that goes far beyond the relationship between parent and child and helps identify a central problem that frequently appears in psychotherapy. Like alexithymic parents, psychotherapists can also be seriously limited in their capacity to detect their own bodily emotions, and may thus be unable to share a patient's feelings. Therapists can talk rationally about emotional problems and yet be unable to communicate—that is, share in an experiential manner—what is being felt. Therapy itself can be mired in rational discussion of emotions that is devoid of feelings on the part of both therapist and patient.

Adolf Portmann, described the existence of a phenomenon he called the social womb.[15] Portmann emphasized his belief that at birth the human being is still in an embryonic or incomplete stage of development which requires that he or she be enveloped in a social womb. Portmann saw this developmental or transitional stage as having profound biological significance. He believed that at birth the human being is still *biologically, definitely incomplete;* and that, during the first ten months after birth, the social womb encourages the development of two species-specific characteristics that permit the infant eventually to become human—namely, the capacities to talk and to walk.

It was Portmann's contention that another human being is absolutely necessary in order for the infant to learn how to talk, and that this function is part of essential biological development which prepares the way for the individual to become a *definite* human being with specific characteristics (for example, Japanese, German, English, Buddhist, Catholic, or Jew). Basing his opinion on many ethological observations, he believed that this unique human attribute has to be taught to the infant by other human beings, usually the infant's parents. Such teaching involves a subtle interplay between physiological development and those individuals who envelop the infant in their social womb. Particularly radical is Portmann's belief that the physiological development and the psycho-intellectual (including spiritual) development of the individual are interdependent, and that both require other human beings in order to come to fruition. Each development is defined in terms of the other, and each depends on the other.

Portmann concluded that the social womb is part of a biological condition that makes possible the development of speech and thus facilitates the very process that distinguishes human beings from all other animals. His theory led us to think similarly about the social membrane as far more than a passive communicative conduit between human beings. We began to see that not only is human speech linked to the cardiovascular system and to the social membrane, but that the entire process is uniquely and fundamentally human. We began to recognize that the social membrane has a function in adult life parallel to the function of the social womb for the infant: both foster a biology and an emotional life that is uniquely human. Not only did Portmann recognize that the social womb is necessary for a human being to learn to speak, but he also demonstrated that another human being is required to teach the infant how to speak. In like manner, we began to recognize that the social membrane is absolutely essential for an infant to learn the experiential meaning of various bodily emotions, as well as the meaning of various terms used to describe such emotions.

In the last chapter, I cited the phenomenon of human blushing as an example of an essentially interactive bodily response and emphasized that the emotional meaning of blushing initially has to be taught to the individual by other human beings and that such "education" frequently involves shared emotional—that is, bodily—reactions in the person observing the blushing. In that sense, the entire process is interactive: a bodily reaction that is given meaning by another human being and to which the second human being, in turn, responds. Thus, bodily reactions acquire unique emotional meaning because they occur in the presence of other human beings. To be human means to live through a body that is both biologically incomplete without other human beings and utterly dependent on others for its emotional—that is, human—development and meaning.

When the computer screen first revealed marked blood-pressure rises when a person talked, I thought about the response in terms of human blushing. Yet as patient after patient taught me, computer displays of blood pressure cannot convey all that blushing implies. For blood-pressure numbers and heart-rate data are not exactly like words, nor are they exactly like blushing. They represent communications that fall somewhere between; they constitute a bridge, if you will, between the world of the rational—the world of thoughts and abstract concepts—and the world of human feelings—that is, those human phenomena that are experienced rather than thought about. The essential human aspect of blushing is that it is experienced or felt, not that it is rationally analyzed.

By contrast, the cardiovascular numbers that flash on computer screens each minute as a person talks can be responded to as just that—mere numbers. The problem is that we reflexively respond to numbers—even to numbers telling us something about the human body—rationally rather than by experiencing them. The result is that both patients and therapists can respond to blood-pressure, heart-rate, and skin-temperature numbers in a way that obliterates, rather than enhances, all of the feelings these numbers symbolize. One could no doubt quantify a human blush in a similar way by digitizing the millimeters of increase in blood flow to a person's face as he or she grows more embarrassed—but what those millimeters mean to a blusher or a therapist are likely to be quite different from the experience of a person's face turning bright red during a conversation.

Computer displays of blood pressure and heart rate can be responded to rationally to compound the very disease that afflicts our patients. "Does everybody react this way?" This rational question is asked by virtually every patient—upon first seeing his or her body's reactions displayed on a computer screen—in an attempt to escape the reality of his or her own feelings. No blusher can ask a similar question. For statistical surveys about the incidence of blushing in the population at large are irrelevant to the experience of getting caught with your pants down! There is a world of difference between reading a book about embarrassment, or even admitting you are embarrassed, and feeling your face light up in a bright orange-red glow when you are embarrassed. Rationally understanding or analyzing human emotions and emotionally experiencing feelings clearly involve two different types of human understanding.

Thus, either patient or therapist, or both, can respond to these bodily changes in a strictly rational manner and, in the process, be deluded into believing that they totally "understand" the message. (Readers of this book are subject to this same tendency, because the only way to communicate the central message and the data in this book is in a rational manner.) This rational response leads to unique problems in the therapeutic approach my colleagues and I have developed. What are a therapist's feelings—or, what should they be—as he or she watches the reality of a patient's suffering as revealed on a computer screen? What are those feelings when the therapist is interacting with a human being who appears calm, peaceful, and rational while the computer indicates that the latter's body is pushing ever closer to stroke or heart attack? This is a deeply troubling question, and part of the answer depends on the therapist's capacity to feel his or her own feelings. Earlier in this book, I spoke of physicians, nurses, and even psychiatrists who— however brilliant, rational, and capable—were unable to feel their own feelings. Yet to decode a patient's body—that is to teach a patient the emotional meaning of various bodily changes—the therapist must learn to decode and feel his or her own body as well. One simply cannot teach another person about embarrassment if one has never felt embarrassed oneself.

Thus, the information recorded by the computers raises many problems for therapists. Why does a patient insist on speaking to a therapist even though the computers reveal the former's blood pressure to be very high, and rising higher as the dialogue continues? If the therapeutic dialogue and the concomitant changes threaten to precipitate a stroke or a heart attack, isn't one asking one's therapist to participate in, perhaps even to facilitate, one's own death?

The problems stirred up by recognition of the language of the heart make it easier to appreciate why people readily seek out pills to treat human diseases: the fact is that most people would rather not recognize this language. Take hypertension, for example. If a doctor follows all the normal pharmacological precautions and treats a hypertensive patient with the best available medicines, and the patient dies unexpectedly, then the physician can at least be comforted in the knowledge of having done all in his or her power to do. The patient's body, not the physician's treatment, is seen as the problem. On the other hand, if the pills are replaced with a therapy that relies on human dialogue and on a treatment protocol that is fundamentally interactive, and then the patient dies, whose fault is it? Virtually everyone who is part of a dialogue that leads another person to blush, reflexively blames himself or herself for causing that other person discomfort.

For the decoding of the language of the heart brings one face to face with a reality about human feelings that is at times exhilarating and at other times truly disconcerting. That is, human feelings are not phenomena that simply involve an isolated struggle between an individual's body and mind—a struggle that Nietzsche saw as the "loneliest loneliness." Rather, these phenomena involve shared human experiences of joy and pain. Yet these experiences, as Walt Whitman suggests, exact a price: "I do not ask how the wounded one feels, I myself, become the wounded one."

CHAPTER 10

The Human Dialogue

> Probably all the passions of the soul [that is, feelings] are associated with the body—anger, gentleness, fear, pity, courage and joy, as well as loving and hating; for when they appear the body is also affected. There is good evidence for this. Sometimes no irritation or fear is expressed, though the provocations are strong and obvious; and conversely, small and obscure causes produce movement when the body is disposed to anger, and when it is in an angry mood.
> —Aristotle, *De Anima*

> Dear reader, or better still dear lady reader, recall the bright joyful eyes with which your child beams upon you when you bring him a new toy, and then let the physicist tell you that in reality nothing emerges from these eyes; in reality their only objectively detectable function is continually to be hit by and receive light quanta. In reality! A strange reality! Something seems to be missing in it.   —Erwin Schrödinger, *Mind and Matter**

THE BIRTH OF A NEW CLINIC

In a book entitled *The Birth of the Clinic* (1973), the French philosopher Michel Foucault suggests that the development of modern medical clinics emerged out of a profound revolution in world view that occurred between the seventeenth and the eighteenth

* Erwin Schrödinger is an eminent twentieth-century physicist and the discoverer of wave mechanics.

centuries.[1] Fueled by a growing interest in science which was sparked by the Renaissance and by a general refocusing of attention on the external world, Foucault argues that average citizens began to alter profoundly the way they had traditionally looked at themselves and the world they lived in. Between 1700 and 1800, there was a shift toward a materialistic perspective that led people to believe that what they could see and measure was far more meaningful, important, and rewarding than their earlier faith in the nontangible world of religion.

One result of this shift was a change in the historical relationship between doctor and patient and an ever-increasing emphasis on physical causes of disease. A new belief crept into medicine, one that led physicians to assume that a person could literally be extracted from his or her natural social surroundings and brought to a clinic where the patient's body could be examined in the same way scientists looked at other physical bodies. It was a view that ultimately rendered the rest of one's natural social surroundings utterly irrelevant to one's medical problems.

Foucault notes that this problem deeply concerned the leaders of the French Revolution and was the focus of heated debate. The Revolutionists wanted to place physicians in their communities rather than in centralized hospitals far removed from everyday life. Yet because of a new philosophical orientation they were forced to back off from this commitment and ultimately had to settle for the model of *la clinique,* a place where citizens could literally take their bodily problems. This "birth of the clinic," Foucault believes, led to a diminution of interest in the way social, economic, and political factors influence health. Patients no longer had a social existence that could be seen as relevant to their bodily problems. Instead, a person became an isolated object, a naked group of bodily mechanisms. Nothing was assumed to stand any longer between patient and doctor.

The data described in the preceding chapters suggest to me that we are about to see the birth of a new type of clinic. Though this new clinic will most likely still be removed from the immediate social surroundings of patients, nevertheless one will be able to bring certain dimensions of one's social and economic world along on a visit to one's healers. To see facets of that world, and assess its effects on health, clinicians will request that a patient talk about his or her world while various dynamic physiological factors are measured. For in the new clinic it will be possible, for the first time, to see the outlines of a patient's world in the computer graphics of bodily dialogue.

To properly interpret the graphics, however, clinicians will be required to make a fundamental change in the way they think about the human body. It will no longer be sufficient, for example, to interpret rationally the meaning of various cardiovascular shifts that occur when a patient talks about emotional struggles. Rather, it will also be necessary for clinicians to interpret emotionally and feel the struggles that such bodily codes signify. The social distance built into current ways of looking at the human body—the view of an objective scientist looking at another bodily object that is clearly separate and distinct—will be expanded to include a new type of social connectedness, where two human beings will be able to share commonly felt emotional experiences at their social membrane. In the new clinic, immunization from the emotional experiences of one's fellow man will no longer be seen as either a vital necessity or a particularly virtuous aspect of scientific objectivity. Such detachment will instead be seen as part of a stance that embraces a limited view of the human body in dialogue with others, as well as a restricted view of factors beyond bodily mechanics that influence health.

But in order to appreciate fully what the new clinic could mean in terms of the way we think about health and illness, and what it could mean to society as a whole, we must re-examine the central issue of this book—dialogue and its links to the human body and the emotional life of human beings.

This book began with the observation that the human heart and circulation can be profoundly altered by human speech. After reviewing the philosophical and scientific perspective that initially made it difficult for us to appreciate the full implications of our discovery, I described a variety of environmental, physiological, psychological, and social variables that influenced the magnitude of the phenomenon. Our studies on the links between communication and the cardiovascular system led us to recognize a previously neglected though centrally important cause of a number of diseases, including migraine headaches and hypertension, which helped us develop an effective new therapeutic approach to these problems.

In the course of treating patients, we noticed another previously unrecognized dimension of speaking and the cardiovascular system: the idea that human emotions involve the social membrane, and that the meaning of feeling terms has to be taught through shared bodily experience. Recognition of these factors led us to see something even more profound and unique about the human use of language for communication: namely that human dialogue is inextricably tied to the emotional life of the body.

In this book I have emphasized a particular aspect of human dialogue—an aspect that links words to feelings through shared bodily experiences. The very fact that human beings are capable of sharing feelings through dialogue forces us to marvel, as did the ancient Greek philosophers, about the nature of this remarkable power.

THE FOUNDATIONS OF HUMAN DIALOGUE

It was Greek philosophers and, in particular, three intellectual giants of Western civilization—Socrates, Plato, and Aristotle—who first recognized the central importance of emotional dialogue in human life. These men first understood the importance of what they called the *logos,* which when shared between two human beings came to be known as the *dialogos,* or dialogue. One cannot overemphasize the fundamental importance of the concept of logos in all of Greek philosophy. Bertrand Russell put the central importance of this idea in perspective when he wrote:

The leading notion that runs through Greek philosophy is the logos. It is a term that connotes, amongst other things, "word" and "measure." Thus, philosophic discourse and scientific inquiry are closely linked. . . . *Wisdom,* then, *consists in grasping the underlying formula* which is *common to all things.* . . . But though the universal formula—or Logos—is found everywhere, the many are blind to this and behave as though each had a private wisdom of his own. . . . It is in the last analysis the greatness of Greek philosophy to have recognized the central role of the logos.[2] [Italics added]

While used in a variety of ways by Greek philosophers, basically the term *logos* referred to an attribute of the human soul that *gave form to what would otherwise be without form,* or made definite what was previously undefined, *perhaps even infinite.* Thus logos was what provided meaning or definition to life. In that sense the term literally means either "word" or "formula." As a formula, one other attribute of logos was clearly understood by the Greeks: that is, the individual logos or formula was ultimately connected to a univeral Logos which gave meaning to all dimensions of Greek life. Some thinkers like Plato (and subsequently Descartes) preferred to think of this logos strictly as a formula, arguing that the best way to describe it would be through mathematics—and, in particular, geometry. Others like Aristotle (and subsequently Pascal) thought that the best meaning of *logos* was "word" and thus emphasized language rooted in the body as the best way to get at the essential meaning of the term.

In any event, virtually all Greek philosophers recognized that *words* themselves are abstractions used to describe the essence of phenomena, and as such words truly are formula, or *logoi.* To the Greeks, then, human language was no trivial matter. The process of learning the mother tongue involved the *dialogos,* or the exchange of formulae between mother and child.

It is in the context of the individual logos and the universal Logos and their links to the dialogos that Aristotle once remarked that a "man wholly solitary would either be a God or a brute."[3] This observation succinctly summaries one whole side of his philosophy and helps crystallize much of the collective wisdom of the architects of Western civilization. The Greeks were rooted in sense of place, which helped them focus on the human being's place in the universe. For them a sense of place, a sense of one's body, and a sense of one's identity were related—all linked to a larger logos—the universal Logos. Aristotle believed that the very vitality of the living individual—what we call one's biology—was rooted in man's relationship to his fellow man, and it was precisely that relatedness which led man to develop a larger political life. Thus, for the Greeks, the human body was the basis for the notion of the political body or what came to be known as the "body-politic."

Aristotle, in particular, saw human beings as not just social animals, like other animals in nature, but also as uniquely political. Man, and man alone, was essentially part of a polis—one among many men, connected each to one another through *dialogoi*—and as such possessed the unique capacity to seek out and determine his place in the natural world. Aristotle believed that a human life not lived in the company of others was essentially—that is, "biologically"—incomplete. Thus, the fundamental fabric of his political man was a human being who lived among others, in a way that involved what Aristotle called the passions of man's soul—a deeply emotional human being.

Two thousand years before we were able to watch blood pressure and heart rate change during human dialogue, Aristotle had already defined human emotions as "πάθη λογοι ἔνυλοι εισιη: that is, "the passions of the soul [or what we now call "feelings"] are logoi expressed in matter."[4] The "matter" Aristotle was referring to, as he makes crystal clear in *De Anima,* was human flesh and blood, and the *logoi* were human words. Thus, to Aristotle, human feelings literally were defined as words expressed in human flesh.*

The clarity of Aristotle's thinking about the bodily locus of human feelings recalls again Bertrand Russell's admonition:

Wherever speculative reasoning has flourished in the West, the shadows of Plato and Aristotle were hovering in the background. . . . There is hardly a philosophic problem on which they did not say something of value, and anyone who nowadays sets out to be original while ignoring Athenian philosophy, does so at his own peril.[6]

I mention this admonition to emphasize that Aristotle not only described feelings as words expressed in human flesh, but also made one other crucial distinction that has occupied my last two chapters. In a statement that goes right to the heart of this book, Aristotle observed:

The natural philosopher and logician will in every case offer different definitions in answer to the question what is anger. The latter will call it a craving for retaliation or something of the sort while the former will

---

* While space precludes an extension of these ideas to include various religious issues, I should at least acknowledge the remarkable similarities between Aristotle's views and the opening lines of the Gospel of Saint John. Unlike the other three Gospels, the last was originally written in Greek. And there for the first time a new word was used to describe God—*logos;* and an equally remarkable notion follows close behind: that is, the Logos (the word) becomes flesh and dwells among us. "In the beginning was the Word [*Logos*], and the Word [*Logos*] was with God, and the Word [*Logos*] was God . . . And the Word [*Logos*] was made flesh and dwelt among us."[5]

It is within the context of the Logos becoming flesh that we can sense deep problems in Cartesian philosophy. For if, as Descartes proposed, the human body is solely a machine, then the Incarnation makes no sense whatsoever, and it would make just as much sense for the Divine Logos to occupy a Buick or a water pump as it would for it to become flesh.

describe it as a *surging of blood and heat round the heart.* The one is describing the matter, the other the forms and formula [of anger—that is, the logos of anger].[7]

This distinction precisely echoes the one I have made between emotions and feelings. Certainly Aristotle would have had no quarrel with Darwin's logical efforts to study the *expression* of emotions in humans and animals, as long as it was crystal clear that, in doing so, he was studying the *matter* of emotions but not their form or logos—that is, what these emotions mean essentially.

The one idea I have added to Aristotle's description of feelings is that they are first shared as commonly felt bodily sensations through dialogue at the social membrane. In my definition, the logos of emotions involves a unique sharing in a way that two human beings become one through shared experience. It is, as Aristotle might agree, a sharing of human souls in a way that differed from his original definition of human dialogue.

The definition of feelings as *logoi* or words expressed in flesh contains the seeds of yet another idea that is central to this book. If the logos can be thought of as that which gives form or makes definite that which is potentially indefinite, or infinite, then it seems clear that emotional dialogue encompasses an interaction that is astonishingly rich in possibilities. For implied in the logos of a feeling such as love would be the idea of something potentially indefinite, unformed, perhaps even infinite. In such a light, any notion of real emotional dialogue that leaves the human body unmoved trivializes the infinite potential of the dialogue emerging from the encounter. Nowhere is it easier to comprehend the Greek notion of the possibility of a universal Logos than in emotional dialogue. For if a feeling like love is given its form or logos through human dialogue, then the form at best overflows the usual boundaries and defies mathematical formulations. Could it be that the origin of human feelings as shared experience is the very phenomenon that leads us to ponder the possibility of a universal Logos? And if there is a universal Logos, then is there a formula for love greater than that which resides in the individual human heart?*

---

* While we like to think about the infinite possibilities of human emotions in terms of such a feeling as love, it is easier to see the unlimited potential of darker, destructive emotions—the unbridled human hatred in the twentieth century alone, for example. Certainly love was not the feeling that created the threat of nuclear annihilation that now hangs over all our heads like some unfettered sword of Damocles—nor did love let loose the unlimited, or unbounded, hatred that created Auschwitz, Dachau, and Verdun.

It was precisely this question that came to divide Blaise Pascal and René Descartes in the seventeenth century. For both these men ultimately argued about the nature of human dialogue and how it was linked to the "universal Logos." Descartes argued that the logos in its purest sense was a formula; and that, as I have said, it could best be encompassed in mathematics and analytic geometry. Pascal, on the other hand, opted for an emotional logos rooted in the human body, a logos that went beyond mathematics. When he stated that "the heart has its reason that reason knows not of. ... Do you love by reason?"[8] he was proclaiming a belief that the human heart and feelings of love are inextricably bound in a way both unique and essential to all human dialogue. In defending a position he had inherited from Aristotle, he recognized that the new philosophy espoused by Descartes abandoned the crucial Greek notion of emotional logoi as part of human dialogue, and had replaced it with a strictly rational (in other words, mathematical) dialogue: that is, a dialogue between human beings that had no place for human feelings. In the new Cartesian order, as Pascal detected, one would indeed "love by reason," for human dialogue no longer was linked to its emotional *logoi*. This dramatic move away from the center of Greek philosophy was eventually to touch every aspect of modern life. Human dialogue was extracted from the body by Descartes and placed in the mind; yet he accomplished this transposition so persuasively that by the mid-twentieth century few people thought of themselves as speaking in and through their own bodies.

In 1596, a half-century after Copernicus had published his treatise *On the Revolution of Heavenly Bodies,* René Descartes was born. As noted in chapter 2, he was a contemporary of William Harvey and Galileo, and the larger scientific context of seventeenth-century life profoundly influenced his thinking. For the discoveries of these men and their contemporaries shook the old order based on Aristotelian philosophy that had been Christianized by the scholastic traditions of the Middle Ages. A Christianized version of Aristotelian philosophy was the foundation upon which the Catholic Church built medieval European society. It came as a profound shock therefore when scientists began to demonstrate that many of

Aristotle's key scientific ideas were not correct.* These cracks or flaws in Greek thinking exacerbated a long-simmering uneasiness with the dominance of scholastic traditions in the scientific life of the Renaissance and ultimately allowed Descartes to undermine its very foundations, the Greek vision of what was involved in human dialogue.

Yet in first outlining his new philosophy, Descartes obscured the deeper implications of his thinking. His initial idea appeared simple and innocuous, couched as it was in a scientific description of bodies, and in an analysis of the motion of such bodies, very much along the lines taken by his scientific contemporaries. In the same way as Copernicus had studied the motion of heavenly bodies, and as chemists were studying organic bodies, so too Descartes intended to study the living bodies of humans and animals. And as I noted in chapter 2, this central ideal seemed to be similar to a view expressed by others, like Harvey: namely, that living bodies obey certain well-defined mechanical principles and they ought to be studied according to the law of physics.

Thus Descartes postulated that the organs of living bodies function just like the water-driven, mechanical statues in seventeenth-century French water gardens. On the principle of *reflection*—or the way water spilling into a cylinder can cause it to move, thus reflecting its motion—so, too, can *reflexes* operate in the body. Descartes believed that just as scientific principles could be applied to the regulation of the movement of statues in those gardens, so too could the scientific method be applied to the study of all living bodies. His sense of the correspondence between the movements of statues in French water gardens and the movement of living bodies was prompted in part by his observations that fluids are common to both. Indeed, his interest in this communality first led him to focus on the heart and circulation. He thought of the heart as a kind of steam kettle that heats the blood before it travels to the various organs of the body. He was struck by the fact that each body appears to be made up of separate smaller bodies, and wondered what force or factor unifies these multiple or compound

---

* Also, as I said in chapter 2, Galileo's demonstration of the existence of vacuums in nature was precisely one of the major challenges to Aristotle's belief that nature abhors a vacuum.

bodies and leads them to operate as an entity. He reasoned that blood, being common to every separate organ in the body, had to be a unifying force. Hence, his interest in this remarkable fluid and his subsequent analogy between the operations of a French water garden (that is, hydraulics) and cardiovascular physiology and, by extension, the entire body.*

Yet the overall goal of Descartes's simple notion of rigorously applying the scientific method to the study of physiology was monumental. He intended to create an entirely new medicine. As Descartes himself phrased it, "The conservation of health has always been the principal goal of my studies."[9] It was his intention to overturn what he believed was a medical system in need of a major philosophical overhaul. In spite of technical misconceptions about certain details, such as how the heart works, his overall efforts ultimately were extraordinarily successful: not only did he create an entirely new medicine, but he also ushered in an entirely new social order.†

Descartes began his philosophical writings as part of a search. He wanted to find a way to fuse the power of a resurgent science with what he perceived to be the real theological interest of the seventeenth-century Catholic Church. In essence, he wanted to find a way of integrating the *world of matter*—that is, the world of physical bodies—with the nonmaterial, or spiritual, dimensions of human existence in a way that would circumvent the confusion of scholastic philosophy. He hoped to discover certain incontrovertible truths that would allow him to integrate these two ostensibly different aspects of human existence. After a great deal of personal angst, he settled on two ideas: first, it seemed clear to him that he could not doubt his own existence; and second, he knew the fact of his existence to be true because he could think about it and reflect upon it. Thus, he arrived at his famous dictum: "I think, therefore I am" (*Cogito, ergo Sum*).[11]

* As I noted in chapter 2, precisely this fact led to Pascal's concern about his discoveries of the physics of hydraulics: he realized that the nature of "pressure" would fit perfectly into the hydraulic structures that Descartes had created for human bodies.

† Richard Carter notes: "Descartes' philosophic words, no less than his mathematics and physics, are in fact precisely what he said they were to be: they are vastly elaborated foundations for his medicine. The unique goal of Descartes' thought was an improved medical therapy, and even his philosophy is a medical philosophy. Therefore, to the degree it is correct to say that modern philosophy takes its questions from the philosophy of Descartes, it is also correct to say that modern thought starts from questions posed by Descartes' medical research and theory into questions concerned with such matters as the definitions of life, the neuro-anatomical basis of perception and thinking, and the relation between mind and body."[10]

Once having arrived at this philosophical starting place, he sought out the source of this marvelous power to think and arrived at the conclusion that thought can occur only because human beings have souls. So far his course was conventional: that is, Descartes, like the Greek philosophers before him, saw "thinking" as a process that does not involve matter. By definition, thought was predicated on the existence of a nonmaterial power that had been labeled "soul" by the pre-eminent thinkers of Western civilization including Aristotle and Plato.

It was at this junction, however, that Descartes made a radical departure from traditional philosophy by categorically asserting that only human beings have souls, and therefore only humans can think. He placed human beings in a unique position different from all other creatures on earth. Unlike earlier Greek thinkers and scholastic philosophers, such as Augustine and Thomas Aquinas, who tended to place man within nature in harmony with the rest of creation—and with its Creator—Descartes stated that man is different in a novel way. Man alone is conscious. Animals cannot think because they have no consciousness, precisely because they do not have souls. He asserted, instead, that animals are nothing more, and nothing less, than "automata"—autonomous, self-regulated, preprogrammed, soulless robots.

While this distinction between humans and animals may not seem earth shattering, it contained the seeds of his true revolution—the separation of the body from all meaningful human dialogue. For it followed inevitably that if animals were soulless robots, animal physiology could only be part of the workings of a complex machine. Stated another way, physiological systems would no longer require a soul to perform their vital functions. In this view, animal physiology—and, indeed, by extension human physiology—was seen as functioning the same way that statues functioned in French water gardens. Thus, the body played no essential role in human dialogue since it no longer needed a soul to perform its vital functions. In that way, Descartes removed the Greek idea of logos from living bodies and limited it to a soul that was restricted to the human mind.

By separating soul from body, Descartes, in essence, created two realities for humans: one, a machine body; and the other, a mind or soul which interacts both with the machine body as well as with other human beings. Thus human beings relate to each other in dialogue only through their minds.

And yet as profound as this conceptual revolution was, Descartes went farther and enunciated a dogma that, though seldom recognized or acknowledged even today, blurred a historic distinction the Greeks had made between thoughts, emotions, and feelings. In essence, Descartes redefined human feelings as being merely confused thoughts. He proposed that there really is no distinction between thoughts and feelings—*except in their origins.* Thoughts and feelings arise from the soul, said Descartes, or from outside the machine body, while emotions stem from disturbances inside the body. The seeds for this remarkable position had been planted the moment he postulated that the physiological organ systems of animals are nothing more than mechanical components of a complex machine. Descartes saw that animals move in space—that dogs bark, birds sing, and cats meow. What was radical was his idea that this motion, this *e*-motion—literally, "out of motion"—is only the action and reaction of a complex machine to this or that stimulus.

He postulated that emotions arise from certain secretions of the internal organs of the body, and that these organs secrete high-energy substances into the blood stream which then make their way to the brain. So far the transport process was strictly mechanical and was identical in both humans and animals. Mechanical transport was seen as a result of the hydraulic force that moves a machine to action. It is at the moment these high-energy substances reach the brain that Descartes located the great difference between humans and animals. For the soul allows humans alone to be aware of the excessively rapid motion of the particles of these biochemical secretions as "feelings," or what Descartes called "passions." Animals, on the other hand, having no soul and thus no awareness, do not "feel" the perturbations caused by these high-energy substances in the brain. Thus we arrive at his central thesis: *the underlying mechanics of stimulus-response is the same in humans and animals, but only humans can detect these perturbations in the brain and be aware of them as feelings.*

First, then, Descartes traced the source of emotions back to the machinery of the body, and then he said that the crucial difference between the mere occurrence of biochemical changes in the body and the perceptions of emotions as feelings is the existence of consciousness. He maintained that animal-robots do have more or less the same biochemical and physiological mechanics underlying human emotions and that these were the major force driving animals to move. What animals lack is any awareness of these mechanics: they lack a soul. It follows from this proposition that *emotions can be outwardly expressed without being felt in animals.*

THE DISAPPEARANCE OF THE BODY IN HUMAN DIALOGUE: FREUD AND PAVLOV

In a bold stroke, Descartes rendered human physiology and human emotions completely independent of human dialogue. He had redefined the world of the irrational—the world of feelings—as rational, as essentially a world of thought. Descartes's fundamental dictum "I think, therefore I am" was chosen with great care. He did not say, nor could he have ever said, "I feel, therefore I am," without at the same time acknowledging that he was transposing feelings into thoughts.

Descartes's philosophical position marked the beginning of modern loneliness. His dictum "I think, therefore I am" is, I believe, one of the loneliest cries ever uttered by Western man: I alone exist: I alone think. That loneliness was further heightened when Descartes classified animals as robots and yet gave these robots the physiological correlates of what would be called "emotions" in human beings. Emotions, in turn, would subsequently be seen as strictly a scientific problem. By definition, a robot does not, nor does it need to, relate to another robot in any way different from the way statues related to water in French water gardens. There is no dialogue between robots. Animals were, as he called them, "automatons." Furthermore, by placing the hydraulic correlates of emotions in the physiology of robots, Descartes stripped human beings of the emotional—that is, physiological—basis of human relatedness. Thoughts came to be the only way that human beings could relate. Human relationships were to become strictly rational. In this new view, the feeling of love is merely an imprecise thought; loneliness has nothing to do with physical health. Even more to the point, Descartes made the human body utterly irrelevant to human dialogue.

This shift away from the Greek ideas about human dialogue was a far cry from Aristotle's definition of feelings as words expressed in flesh. While the roots of these ideas spread into many facets of modern life, perhaps nowhere was their impact greater than on a relationship that is peculiar to twentieth-century life: that of patient and psychotherapist.

It is only in this century that, I believe, the full manifestations of the notion of *la clinique* matured to encompass and complete the essential system of mind and body initiated by Descartes. This "clinic" went far beyond the notion of considering a person's body as a naked group of mechanisms outside of his or her natural social environment. Instead, it embraced the idea that one could bring one's mind to a clinic to be examined and treated irrespective of the body. A new form of therapeutic dialogue was conceived, in which one was extracted both from one's natural social surroundings as well as from one's body to engage another human being in a rational dialogue about one's mental suffering in order to alleviate it.

THE LONELY COUCH: SIGMUND FREUD

It was a remarkable approach when Sigmund Freud first conceived of it in the 1890s, and it still is today. The patient lies down on a couch and talks—not face to face with the analyst, mind you, because the analyst is seated behind the patient out of the latter's field.* The analyst instructs the patient to free-associate, to talk about everything, including the most trivial details of everyday life. Rarely does the analyst speak. The patient talks, while the analyst listens. The patient can stare at the cracks in the ceiling while talking, but talk he or she must. One can free-associate for fifty minutes about anything one wishes, four to five times a week for six or seven years, as one voyages on a long journey backward. Back through long-forgotten childhood experiences, back through repressed memories and unconscious struggles, back through a maze of bizarre dreams and strange slips of the tongue, back until

---

* Freud assumed that face-to-face dialogue would impede one's efforts to understand one's own unconscious struggles. He also recognized that such factors as his own facial expressions could communicate emotional messages to a patient and potentially confuse or blur the latter's unconscious struggles with his or her conflicts.

the adult edifice of one's personality has been stripped of all pretense and civility, until the "primal" struggles of childhood are laid bare. And by the end of that journey the patient will know every crack and subtle nuance in the ceiling of the analyst's office.

From that couch in Vienna poured forth some of the most commonplace and influential words and concepts of twentieth-century life. *Id, ego,* and *superego; conscious, unconscious,* and *preconscious;* the interpretation of dreams and the dynamic meaning of symbols; concepts of neurosis and psychosis, Oedipal struggles and infantile sexuality; repression and denial; and an encyclopedic list of unconscious defense mechanisms. In a dazzling display of genius, Sigmund Freud laid the foundations for what he called his "science" of psychoanalysis, upon which most forms of psychotherapy are now based.

Throughout this text I have made little effort to trace the psychophysiological distresses of individual patients back to struggles in childhood, but instead, for lack of space, have chosen to assert, quite simply, that such struggles are part of the overall therapeutic picture. To certain of these struggles, however—such as parental alcoholism, the loss of parents, parental alexithymia, early abuse or neglect—I have alluded in passing, not because they do not play an important role in a person's adult struggles with human dialogue or with hypertension and migraine headaches, but rather because they have been admirably described in the past by other psychoanalytic theorists such as Franz Alexander. Indeed, one of the core tenets of this book underscores my essential agreement with Freudian psychodynamic theory in respect to the conflicted nature of a patient's dialogue, which is made evident by cardiovascular changes during speech. Although our therapy of transactional psychophysiology is essentially interactive, it relies heavily on many of the psychodynamic formulations first enunciated by Freud.*

The problem with Freud's psychodynamic formulations resides not so much in his theoretical formulations and clinical astuteness, as in the utility of his methods as a means of treating psychosomatic patients, and in deeper issues about the nature of emotional

---

* The same is also true with insights first promulgated by Ivan Pavlov. As outlined in chapter 3, much of my own conceptual thinking is rooted in the Pavlovian paradigm as taught to me by one of Pavlov's students, W. Horsley Gantt. Nor is there any doubt that many of the cardiovascular changes seen in patients when they talk are, in essence, conditional autonomic reponses triggered by issues rooted in a patient's past life.

understanding as a shared human experience. Freud, of course, lacked our technical capacity to monitor the human body and thus could not appreciate the dynamic connection between the human cardiovascular system and talking.

When I first demonstrated to a psychiatric colleague how blood pressure rises when a person speaks, he remarked, "Well, it's clear Sigmund Freud knew what he was doing when he got the patient to talk! By remaining quiet, at least he spared his own cardiovascular system. Maybe he unconsciously felt the vascular stress of face-to-face dialogue and thus opted for the only personally healthy method available to him."

This humorous conjecture that Freud may have tried to escape from the cardiovascular stress of human dialogue helped me to understand a deep problem inherent in Freud's entire conceptual framework of human emotions. The central core of his theory is that human emotions can be looked at objectively by both therapist and patient, and that a patient can rationally understand his or her emotions without ever having to sense, describe, or understand the meaning of various bodily changes. Even if we assume that Freud was profoundly influenced by Descartes's thinking in this regard, nevertheless we must wonder why or how Freud could make such a crucial mistake. It was that question which led me to suspect that his peculiar blindness had to have been caused by his own bodily struggles, including a serious misunderstanding of the interplay between emotional experiences, the nature of human feelings, and dynamic shifts in his own cardiovascular system.

Freud himself suffered lifelong episodes of cardiovascular distress that were triggered by a variety of unpleasant interactions with other people. His own cardiovascular lability may have kept him from detecting or understanding his feelings in any other than a rational or objective way. Among other cardiovascular problems, Freud suffered throughout his life from severe bouts of migraine headaches. While, at first glance, this problem may appear to have little to do with his overall conceptions of the nature of human emotional conflicts, it is my belief that it made it difficult for Freud accurately to detect his own feelings—especially negative ones—while engaged in dialogue with another person. It appears likely that he had the very same alexithymic problems—that is, the inability to feel his own feelings—that plagued virtually every patient described in this book. Like them, in all likelihood Freud had a hyperreactive cardiovascular system that he could not feel, and thus he would have been unable to gain insight about episodes or interactions that triggered major stress reactions inside his body. And, like the hypertensive psychiatrist described in chapter 1, Sigmund Freud could have been brilliantly rational and superbly insightful about the psychodynamic causes of emotional conflicts, yet at the same time been unable to feel his own or his patients' feelings.

One other thought needs to be added, especially in light of recent assaults on certain aspects of Freud's character. In all likelihood, Freud himself must have been—like the patients I have described— fundamentally altruistic, trying to care for others without first caring effectively for himself.

Besides migraines, he suffered most of his life from neurocirculatory asthenia, which is characterized by palpitations of the heart and a highly reactive cardiovascular system. Neurocirculatory asthenia is now widely recognized to be associated with prolonged or extreme anxiety states and is usually accompanied by episodes of extreme fatigue. Freud frequently complained of periods of utter and absolute exhaustion.

In his detailed biography, Ernest Jones (a student of Freud's) described Freud's migraines as follows:

> All his life Freud was subject to incapacitating spells of migraine, quite refractory to any treatment. It is still not known whether this complaint is of organic or functional origin. The following remark of his would suggest the former: *"It was as if all the pain was external; I was not identified with the disease, and stood above it."* That was written when he was too weak to stand but yet felt perfectly clear mentally. It reminded me of a similar remark many years later when I condoled with him over a heavy cold: "It is purely external; the inner man is intact."[12] [Italics added]

Freud's description of his migraines and his head pain are couched in the same dissociated language used by patients in our clinic. The pain is not "my" pain but is viewed instead as a phenomenon outside or external to his personal sense of identity.

Freud was also predisposed to periodic fainting spells, which were probably caused by the same labile cardiovascular symptoms that contributed to his migraines. Perhaps the most famous episode of fainting occurred in Munich in 1912 during a particularly unpleasant encounter (which Freud tried to control) with his most famous associate, Carl Jung, who, like many others of Freud's associates, first deeply admired and then subsequently fought with him. Freud described his fainting in Munich as follows:

I am resigned to being declared a candidate for eternity on the basis of my attack in Munich. Recently Stekel* wrote that *my behavior* was already showing the "hypocritical feature." All of them can hardly wait for it, but I can answer them as Mark Twain did under similar circumstances: "Reports of my death are grossly exaggerated."[13]

Later Freud wrote, with what appears to be far clearer insight, to another of his colleagues, Ludwig Binswanger, about this same episode:

My fainting attack in Munich was surely provoked by psychogenic elements, which received strong somatic reinforcements (a week of troubles, a sleepless night, the equivalent of a migraine, the day's task). I had had several such attacks; in each case there were similar contributory causes, after a bit of alcohol for which I have no tolerance. Among the psychic elements there is the fact that I had a quite similar seizure in the same place in Munich, on two previous occasions, four and six years ago. In light of a most careful diagnosis, it seems scarcely possible to attribute my attacks to a more serious cause, for instance, a weak heart. *Repressed feelings, this time directed against Jung,* as previously against a predecessor of his, naturally play the main part.

The agreement reached in Munich will hardly hold for long. His attitude precludes this. I would gladly renounce any kind of personal relations with him, and merely preserve the official connection. By the way, it seems that the reason my visit to Kreuzlingen† so greatly disturbed him [Jung] was, as he said, that he had assumed I was conspiring against him with his enemies, you and Haberlin! I beg you to slow down the process by remaining utterly discreet about everything concerning him and me.[14] [Italics added]

All the elements are here: interpersonal struggles; repressed anger; bodily predisposition. Yet at the same time we can almost hear Freud desperately searching for the triggering mechanism. For the issue confronting him was not one simply of understanding the psychodynamic and interpersonal conflicts underlying his problems, but one of fainting in front of his "enemies"—that is, playing his hand badly in public, so to speak—as well as of avoiding mercilessly excoriating himself with pain. His retrospective analysis of his own

---

* Wilhelm Stekel was one of Freud's earliest followers.
† A Swiss mental hospital.

problems did not stop him from fainting nor did it ever block his migraines.

Dr. Richard Restak, a neurologist in Washington, D.C., recently pointed out that Freud's initial interest in cocaine was most likely based in part on his "desperate efforts to obtain relief from migraine headaches."[15] Apparently Freud missed one other fact about his migraines: their coincident appearance with his adolescence, their acute intensification when he married, and their disappearance in his old age.* Thus, his attacks seem to have been rooted in the same problems that plagued many of his patients and probably were the source of his brilliant insights—struggles regarding his own psychosexual development.

Freud's insights about migraines were perhaps most clearly revealed in his psychological biography of President Woodrow Wilson that was not published until 1967, almost thirty years after his death.[16] What apparently fascinated Freud about Woodrow Wilson were his terrible struggles with migraine headaches. Fourteen different times in his life, Wilson's health broke down totally, and he suffered from chronic headaches, nervousness, fatigue, and indigestion—the very problems that troubled Freud. Sifting through the psychodynamic details of Wilson's early life, Freud concluded that "the conflict between his femininity and his exalted Super-Ego which demanded that he should be all masculinity" was the root psychodynamic cause of his problems.[17] If one carefully scrutinizes Freud's life, his analysis of Wilson appears to be an act of self-revelation.†

* Of equal interest is the fact that one of Freud's closest friends, and his personal physician for a decade, Wilhelm Fliess, also suffered from the same problem. They corresponded regularly with each other about their headaches. Fliess treated Freud's migraines, with no success.

† In light of their common medical problems, it is fascinating to add that Freud harbored a passionate dislike of Woodrow Wilson. So vehement was his negative attitude that, to his credit, Freud felt compelled to warn his readers of it at the beginning of his analysis of Wilson. He wrote in part: "When an author publishes his opinion of a historical personage, he seldom neglects to assure his readers at the outset that he has endeavored to keep himself free from bias and prejudice, that he has worked 'sine ira et studio,' as the beautiful classic phrase expresses it. I must, however, commence my contribution to this psychological study of Thomas Woodrow Wilson with the confession that the figure of the American President, as it rose above the horizons of Europeans, was from the beginning unsympathetic to me, and that this aversion increased in the course of years the more I learned about him and the more recently we suffered from the consequences of his intrusion into our destiny. . . . To be sure, when I was led through the influence of [William] Bullitt [diplomat and Freud's co-author] to a more thorough study of the life of the President, this emotion did not remain unchanged. A measure of sympathy developed, but sympathy of a special sort mixed with pity, such as one feels when reading Cervantes for his hero, the naive cavalier of La Mancha."[18] Since their struggles with migraines were similar, I believe these remarks reflect similar unconscious attitudes Freud harbored toward himself.

Yet my point is not to center on the frailties of Sigmund Freud or to expose his migraines as being caused by emotional struggles. Were this the extent of my interest, I might as well have added the weighty observation that Freud was also a human being. In suffering from severe migraines, he had something in common with Carolus Linnaeus, Thomas Jefferson, Ulysses S. Grant, Alfred Nobel, Alexander Graham Bell, George Bernard Shaw, Upton Sinclair, and Princess Margaret—each of whom may also have suffered from comparable psychodynamic conflicts and had cardiovascular systems similar to those I have described.

In speaking of Freud, however, I take issue with his views of a phenomenon he labeled "countertransference" and his struggles with it in therapy. In 1913, responding to a question about countertransference, Freud wrote:

It is one of the most difficult ones [questions] technically in psychoanalysis. I regard it as more easily solvable on the theoretical level. *What is given to the patient should indeed never be a spontaneous affect, but always consciously allotted,* and then more or less of it as the need may arise. Occasionally a great deal, but never from one's own unconscious. This I should regard as the formula. In other words, one must always recognize one's countertransference and rise above it, only then is one free oneself. To give someone too little because one loves him too much is being unjust to the patient and a technical error. All this is not easy, and perhaps possible only if one is older.[19] [Italics added]

Thus Freud saw the couch as the best way of protecting the patient against the unconscious feelings of the therapist in countertransference. Yet the best evidence available suggests that Freud himself was not particularly adept at feeling his own feelings but rather hid them from himself in his hyperreactive vasculature. It is not hard to imagine the therapeutic conflict that ensued, one between a patient's expression of his or her own private feelings and Freud's hidden emotional cardiovascular response and his inability to sense his own feelings or those of his patients.

I believe it was this problem that persuaded Freud that, in the social isolation of the analyst's couch, a patient can best learn about his or her feelings by rationally understanding the psychodynamic issues and psychological struggles involved. Thus, on Freud's couch feelings were not experienced but were rationally analyzed as the residue of imprecise conflicting thoughts previously buried deep in the unconscious. The essential interpersonal nature of human feelings was lost. Instead, human feelings were frozen by a Cartesian vision that reduced them to a solipsistic encounter between head and heart.

Rooted as it was in a far deeper philosophical tradition which went largely unrecognized, Freud's *scientific analysis* of the human psyche was tied to the very same principles of physiological reflexes and of the conservation of energy that guided another central figure of twentieth century life: Ivan Pavlov. Freud's therapy was deemed "scientific" precisely because he made the human subject into an object. Both the free-associating patient on Freud's couch and the salivating dog in Pavlov's isolation chamber were removed from their natural world and examined. Their visions and the social consequences of their views both stemmed from the same source—René Descartes.

THE ISOLATION CHAMBER: IVAN PAVLOV

"We have changed nothing since he died in 1936. You see that his office has been kept exactly as it was when he last worked there. His Nobel Prize is still on his desk as well. You will see that his laboratory is the same also. For over forty years nothing has changed."

As we clambered up the concrete spiral staircase that led to Ivan P. Pavlov's famous tower laboratories in Leningrad, the strong basso voice of my Russian host echoed off the cold stone walls with pride and enthusiasm. He continued, "There are many other scientific institutes in Russia, but to care for Pavlov's Institute—that is the very first honor in all of Russian medicine." When we reached the top of the tower, he swung open the creaking cast-iron door that Pavlov had used to seal off the animal chamber from all external sounds, and said "See for yourself, see how remarkable was his vision. Already at the beginning of the twentieth century Pavlov could see the whole future clearly."

Then laughing heartily, as if he felt I shared his joy, he buoyantly asked, "So what do you think now?" His bright, dark eyes scanned my face, while he continued without waiting for an answer: "You must fly with us to Soviet Georgia to see our beautiful country. My family would be honored to take you there. I am so happy to meet one of Professor Gantt's students. No doubt you have learned everything about Pavlov from your dear teacher! But think of it! Think of it! Pavlov built this long before others understood this new science. And we have changed nothing!"

A brooding, cold, leaden sky had blanketed Leningrad the entire time I was there, and the interior of Pavlov's experimental animal chamber was chill and dank, not unlike a morgue. In the waning days of October, the bone-chilling subarctic air contrasted sharply with the warmth of my Russian host.

As the tour of Pavlov's laboratory continued, my mind began to wander to the larger context of this city and nation that were its home. In the swampy reaches of the Gulf of Finland, legions of serfs had carved endless canals out of the icy Russian peat and muck, draining vast areas of swamps to create their Venice of the North. In that forbidding wellspring of half a dozen fabled Russian rivers, they built a regal city and made it the winter home for their czars. It was destined to become the birthplace of the Bolshevik revolution, nurtured by the blood of nameless serfs who had marched to pay their czar homage at the dawn of the twentieth century, only to be greeted by steel and bullets. Eventually Petersburg became Leningrad; and in the Second World War, it endured nine hundred days of siege, engulfed in indescribable pain and suffering, in which an estimated one and one quarter million of its citizens perished. Thinking of the violent cataclysms and radical changes this city had endured, I could not help but marvel that, in a nation and a city that did not lack for heroes, Ivan Pavlov, a mere physiologist, was nonetheless a genuine Russian hero.

The son of a Russian priest, the first of his countrymen to win the Nobel Prize, he became world-famous for his discovery of the conditional reflex. While machinegun fire and cannons were rattling through the streets of Leningrad, marking the beginning of the revolution, Ivan Pavlov was carrying out his own revolution, within the monasterylike silence of his laboratory. He dreamed of building a moat around his tower building so that the rumbling of the cannon fire would be absorbed by the water and thus reduce the vibrations and muffle the sounds of battle. No efforts were spared to help guarantee the scientific precision of his experiments. The drops of saliva streaming from a dog's parotid gland in response to a conditional signal were far too precious to be disturbed by the military struggle convulsing the streets.* Any extraneous environmental disturbance could alter the conditional salivary response and thus had to be controlled. While the revolution toppled the old order, Pavlov's dogs remained in their tower chambers, isolated from all external stimuli except those that could be precisely measured, providing the scientific and philosophical ammunition that was to become part and parcel of the new socialist order.

For Lenin sought in Pavlov's work support for his definition of the new Soviet man, one who would be born again in dialectic materialism, part of a new socialist order that would free the working class from centuries of bondage and the philosophical trappings of the ruling élite.† No more bourgeois philosophy or enslaving principles! No more religions to be an "opiate for the masses"!

What did Lenin see in Pavlov's research, which Bernard Shaw had laughingly dismissed as much ado about nothing, a mere rediscovery of tricks that animal trainers had used for centuries? Why did Pavlov's socially isolated dogs appeal to the leaders of the new socialist revolution?

* One of Pavlov's research assistants testified to the remarkable tenacity of his teacher: "During the revolution it was very difficult to get to the laboratory at all, because besides other things there was often shooting and fighting on the streets. However, Pavlov was generally present even though nobody else was. One of those days when I was about ten minutes late for an experiment, I found Pavlov already there punctually, though no one else had come. Seeing that I was not on time, he immediately lit into me with his customary vivaciousness 'Why are you late Sir?' I asked him if he did not know there was a revolution going on outside. 'What difference does a revolution make when you have work in the laboratory to do!' "[20]

I must emphasize that Pavlov himself was an enigma. Neither communist or socialist, he was dismayed by the upheaval in his native land and by the excesses of the revolution. When a portrait of the Prince of Oldenburg was removed from Pavlov's institute and thrown in a dump, he rescued the portrait and hung it in his own office. He had the remarkable courage to defend the virtue and courage of his disgraced benefactor at a time when such defiance could lead to a person's execution. Later, however, Pavlov came to believe that the Bolshevik revolution had improved the lot of the average Russian peasant, and in that sense he supported its ideals.

† In gratitude, in 1921, Lenin signed a decree instructing government agencies to "create as soon as possible the most favorable conditions for safeguarding the scientific work of Academician Pavlov and his collaborators." That same decree instructed a government agency to suppy Pavlov and his wife double food rations—this in a period when many people were in want of food.

In 1935, the fifteenth international congress of physiology was held in Leningrad. Following the convention a reception was given for the delegates by the Soviet government in the Kremlin. In a speech to the delegates, Pavlov said, "How exceptionally favorable is the position of science in my fatherland! I want to give only one example to illustrate the relation which arose in our country between the government and science. We, the leaders of scientific institutions, are really alarmed and uneasy over the question whether or not we are in a position to justify all those means which the government places at our disposal. As you know, I am an experimenter from head to foot.

"My whole life has consisted of experiments. Our government is also an experimenter, only on an incomparably higher plane. I passionately desire to live in order to see the victorious completion of this *historical social experiment*" (italics added).[21]

Lenin and his predecessors, Marx and Engel, fully realized that only a certain kind of animal lives in society—an animal that is "social." They also believed that the behavior and the beliefs of human beings depend absolutely and completely on the environmental (including economic) conditions in which they live. Marx therefore had asserted that the state, as a representative of the social collective, had to seize control of these conditions for the economic benefit of all. Marx had seen how the nineteenth-century working class in Europe and the peasant class in Russia had been duped into accepting their miserable lot in life, their exploitation rigidly enforced by the propaganda—that is, the philosophical beliefs, the religious structures, and the economic controls—of the ruling élite. And, at the same time, he believed revolutionary change to be not only possible but inevitable, the end result of social evolutionary forces that would ultimately lead to a new social synthesis. Marx's ideas were rooted in nineteenth-century science and were especially congenial to the revolutionary ideas of Charles Darwin.* In his graveside eulogy to Karl Marx, Engel stated:

Just as Darwin discovered the law of development of organic nature, so Marx discovered the law of development of human history: the simple fact, hitherto concealed by an overgrowth of ideology, that mankind must first of all eat, drink, have shelter and clothing, before it can pursue politics, science, art, religion, etc.; that therefore the production of the immediate material means of subsistence and consequently the degree of economic development attained by a given people or during a given epoch form the foundation upon which the state institutions, the legal conceptions, the ideas on art, and even on religion, of the people concerned have been evolved, and in the light of which they must, therefore, be explained, instead of *vice versa,* as had hitherto been the case. . . . Such was the man of science. But this was not even half the man. Science was for Marx a historically dynamic, revolutionary force.[22]

What kind of revolutionary science would soon lead half the people on earth to live under the absolute control of state-run bureaucracies? What kind of science convinced Marx that he was merely a spokesman for an evolutionary force that would lead inevitably to a new social order? As Engel made clear in his graveside remarks, the wellspring of Marxian dialectic materialism, the fountainhead of the new social order, was rooted in science

---

* Even today a statue of Darwin stands outside the walkway that leads to Pavlov's Institute.

and closely akin to the Darwinian notions of evolution.* Karl Marx had deduced something about science and the scientific method that went far beyond observations made in the laboratory: that is, *the scientific method was the organizing principle of the new social order.* While he failed to appreciate that Descartes's *Discourse on Method* had made precisely this same point, nevertheless Marx did comprehend the consequences of this philosophical viewpoint. It was precisely Descartes's idea about the human body that led Marx to create a theoretical system that holds as part of its central dogma a belief in mind as a by-product of bodily organization and in the state or bureaucracy as a sort of living organism modeled on Descartes's living soulless animal organism. In Marx's view, neither state nor individual bodies any longer need souls. Thus was born the soulless modern "body-politic." Darwinian evolution, for example, was seen by Marx as a way not only to understand man's materialistic origins but, even more importantly, to conceive of how societies would inevitably evolve. The workers had the power to unite as one collective social evolutionary force that would inevitably overthrow the ruling élite.

Pavlov's scientific research (initially supported by the Russian nobility in the days of the czar) was precisely the type of data the new social order needed, for his conditional reflex experiments provided a radically new context for interpreting the social environment. Pavlov viewed "social stimuli" as merely a complex set of environmental stimuli that elicit conditional responses from the organism. The nature of the conditional responses to "social stimuli" was dependent on prior experiences (that is, earlier conditioning). It was precisely the same view that Marx had enunciated in the realm of politics. Since the working class had been conditioned, by a variety of bourgeois structures (that is, religion, education, law), to accept economic misery, Marx proposed that the way to change such conditioning was to overthrow the economic system that fueled and controlled the environmental conditions creating their misery. A revolution would have to occur that would change the social consciousness of the working class. Pavlov's

* While the Marxist philosophical heritage can be traced back to the teachings of Hegel and his exposition of the dialectic (which was itself grounded in the philosophical writings of Rousseau), Marx replaced the dialectic idealism of his teacher with the dialectic materialism of science.

isolated dogs provided the scientific evidence that explained how the environment determines not only what a dog would salivate to but also, by inference, what the working class would, as it were, "salivate" to as well.

Another implication of Pavlov's experiments initially escaped general attention. In a truly profound sense, they implied that living organisms only have "insides" that are genetically programmed to respond stereotypically to external stimuli: that is, there is no *real or essential world* but only a world to which living organisms are conditioned to respond. As Engel had said in his eulogy, that was precisely Marx's true insight and, by extension, the real implication of Pavlov's discovery. The evolution of politics, art, economic structures, and religion were all dependent on environmental conditioning. There were no *a priori* truths, preordained commandments, pre-existing order, or grand theocratic mandates, as the ruling élite had claimed and justified with entrenched philosophical and religious structures. To the contrary, these structures were themselves seen as nothing but elaborate conditional signals designed to influence the way people behave.

Yet, paradoxically, Pavlov's conditioning experiments, linked to Marxist philosophy also simultaneously helped to obliterate the notion of the individual, since the human being was defined in the new socialist order as someone who responds only to environmental signals. Gone, then, was the notion of real or essential human relationships bounded by emotional dialogue—that is, the logos and Logos of the ancient Greeks. Gone, too, were the means for humans to relate naturally to one another and to their external world. In the most remarkable of ironies, the socialist revolution and new social order found the explanation for the nature of *social* relationships in the isolation of a Pavlovian chamber. Individual human beings were seen as "higher" animals wired to respond reflexively to a wide variety of complex environmental signals (including other human beings), and thus human relationships themselves could be determined by the state which controlled the environment for the collective economic good.*

* While Westerners tend to believe that it is only citizens of totalitarian regimes who are victims of government propaganda, and environmental manipulation, similar social conditioning has had an equally profound influence on human relationships in noncommunist countries. Such influence helps explain the disintegration of family life and the rise of loneliness and estrangement in the Western world, as human beings everywhere struggle to rearrange their relationships according to the new "social" philosophy and twentieth-century scientific technology.

If his extension of the idea of reflexes to include social relationships appeared radical, it was only because the underlying physiological theories about the human body were themselves radical. As Pavlov himself duly noted, the idea of the reflex was first enunciated by René Descartes in the seventeenth century. Unlike many other scientists who fail to appreciate the philosophical origins or implications of their work, Pavlov was at least clear in this regard. At the very beginning of his book *Conditioned Reflexes,* he wrote:

The physiologist must take his own path, where a trail has already been blazed for him. Three hundred years ago Descartes evolved the idea of the reflex. Starting from the assumption that animals behaved simply as machines, he regarded every activity of the organism as a *necessary* reaction to some external stimulus, the connection between the stimulus and the response being made through a definite nervous path: and this connection, he stated, was the fundamental purpose of the nervous structures in the animal body. This was the basis on which the study of the nervous system was firmly established. . . . Descartes' conception of the reflex was constantly and fruitfully applied in these studies.[23]

The fact that Descartes's ideas permeate virtually all modern theories of the body helps explain why Pavlov's views were quickly accepted in countries that adhered to radically different political and economic systems.

THE BODY-POLITIC

Two thousand years ago, when Aristotle first enunciated the notion of the body-politic, he provided a vision of a Greek society in which people had the potential to live together in unity and harmony because they shared one principle in common—the logos. Today, although the outlines of that ancient Greek vision have been largely forgotten, a strange universal agreement about part of it remains. For in spite of sharply diverging economic and political systems, there is virtually no difference in the way communist, socialist, and capitalist systems view the human body. Scientific medicine today is essentially no different in Washington or Moscow, Beijing or Paris, London or Leningrad, Berlin or Bucharest, Tokyo or Tangiers. The same generic medicines are prescribed for migraine headaches and hypertension in Warsaw and Rome, in New Delhi and New York. All share the same Cartesian beliefs about the human body. Nor are there substantive differences in the way environmental and social factors are perceived as influencing the human body. There is virtually universal agreement that the body is a self-contained, homeostatically self-regulated, reflexively pre-wired machine designed for self-preservation. There are, furthermore, startingly similar views about the nature of social relationships, at least insofar as the human body is concerned.*

How, then, do nations establish their ideas about the body-politic if their views of the human body are all more or less the same? Are our views about the body-politic indeed so different? Are the differences in the West simply a philosophical residue of an age that predates Descartes?

As I suggested in chapter 2, the twentieth-century development that permitted the measurement of blood pressure in human beings was but a technological ripple in a philosophical tide that Descartes had harnessed three centuries earlier. Far more important than the technology used to measure living blood was the astonishing idea that blood has a pressure that can be completely defined mathematically. Acceptance of this belief, which reflected an acceptance of the general premise that biology can be wholly encompassed by mathematics and physics, proved to be a powerful organizing principle of all modern societies. For if the human body can be completely understood by a scientific method that systematically unravels the mechanisms of various organs, then by extension society itself can likewise be understood as merely the complex

---

* This fact leads to the surprising conclusion that nations no longer believe that political, economic, and philosophical differences have any bearing on the overall health of their citizens. Otherwise, the facts would be allowed to speak for themselves, and longevity and health statistics would be cited in support of a particular nation's political system. Since such statistics are not used to defend political systems, we can conclude that virtually all nations now accept the notion of the human body as a genetic machine. Thus, it is that sharply increased mortality and morbidity rates of impoverished groups, such as black Americans or Third World nations, from diseases such as hypertension, are seen as physical problems. Ghettos are seen as causing social, psychological, spiritual, economic, and interpersonal problems, and even health problems stemming from environmental conditions such as poor sanitation and infectious disease but not from specific social discrepancies in relation to the larger community. A perspective acknowledging the links between social existence, human dialogue, and health would force us to come to grips with the disconcerting idea that if we accept the links between physical health and communal dialogue, then we would have to see ourselves as participating in an attack on our fellow citizens. Little wonder then that we continue to blame black hypertension on the renal system and sodium imbalance. The alternative is to see ourselves as members and participants in a social system that causes certain of its members to lose a decade or more of life.

organization of a collection of bodies. Social, corporate, and governmental bureaucracies were destined to be created to operate according to the same mechanistic principles that guided the operation of individual bodies. Each part of the bureaucracy would have its own function, designed to solve specific problems automatically, and all geared to solve the more general problems of the larger body.

At first this belief fueled great optimism and hope in Western societies. Many people embraced the idea that human beings can be organized in such a way as to be able to solve all problems, including all those to do with health. The overall organization of the bureaucracy was to be determined by enlightened human reason studiously dedicated to solving problems in strict accordance with the principles of the scientific method. The general outlines of this belief were, as I have said, formulated by René Descartes in his attempt to create a new medicine and, by extension, a new political order founded on the principle that living bodies can be understood by dissecting their mechanisms. It was Descartes's contention that all bodies—whether animal, human, social, or political—operate by mechanisms that can be rationally—that is, objectively—understood. In addition, he believed that complex bodies—including the human body—are organized so as to provide internal solutions for their own problems: each part or subcomponent of the body responds to the hydraulic demands of its other parts. Otherwise, Descartes maintained, complex bodies would be unable to maintain their integrity as a unit and would disintegrate. This optimistic belief led to the implicit assumption that all human dilemmas have rational solutions. But, in the twentieth century, it was precisely this assumption that helped to fuel the Holocaust, when a state organization coldly and efficiently exterminated millions of human—that is, machine—bodies as a rational "final *solution*" to its Jewish "problem." After the corporal rubble of Auschwitz and other concentration camps, and the "corporations" that dispassionately used the labor pool of tortured and tormented human beings they supplied, it was all too obvious that there was no longer anything necessarily sacred—or, indeed, even human—about human bodies, human corporate structures, or the human body-politic. Nor was there any longer a distinction between the amoral mechanical workings of a human body and the amoral mechanical functioning of corporate and state bureaucracies.* All were seen as mechanisms designed to solve problems. In one case, the problem was internal regulation; in the other, economic and social regulation. Thus, over the course of three centuries, the definition of what it means to be a human being had slowly but surely changed. In the twentieth century, human beings emerged triumphant over nature, with the remarkable power to control any number of physical bodies—including their own—yet separated and ruptured from their own nature and their own structures in a way that leaves each person utterly alone. In a sense, man has become his own universal Logos; the Incarnation had been reversed, for human beings have come to believe that their minds controlled the machinery of nature.

LIFE AND HUMAN DIALOGUE

At the beginning of this chapter, I suggested that we are about to witness the birth of a new type of clinic, one based on the view—not that the human body is more than a group of sophisticated, isolated biological mechanisms to be treated—but also one that understands that the human body is inextricably bound up in and profoundly influenced by human dialogue. Yet as Foucault suggested, in outlining the confluence of philosophical, social, and scientific issues that fostered the first clinic in the eighteenth century, the birth of a clinic such as I have described in this book is also part of a philosophical shift far deeper than that encompassed by our discoveries of the link between human speech and the heart. For, as suggested by the history of the twentieth century, the vision of the human body as solely a group of sophisticated mechanisms has reaped its own whirlwind—and cries out to be changed.

History now stands in mute and pained testimonial to the fact that mankind will be saved neither by feelings alone nor by reason

* While many people still see the Holocaust as a convulsive, irrational act engineered by a few perverted madmen, the facts reveal another reality. While the implications of the modern acceptance of vast mechanistic bureaucracies that operate oblivious to the moral implications of their actions, have been examined in depth by Hannah Arendt,[24] Raul Hilberg,[25] Richard Rubenstein,[26] and other writers, the deeper philosophical roots of this problem peculiar to our time remain unexamined.

alone. Either feelings or reason pushed to an extreme in human affairs, especially when isolated from each other, leads inevitably to man's inhumanity to man. This was not René Descartes's vision when he struggled to work out his new philosophy. He intended to create a new society and a new medicine designed to end the ignorance, superstition, suffering, and cruelty of the age he lived in. The motives guiding his vision were not dark or evil but rather reflected his hope that human beings would be able to live in a better world, a world of reason, where the logos of all human dialogue could be apprehended in the crystalline purity of mathematical logic. It was, as I have suggested earlier, an idea that at first sparked great hope and optimism in the West. Yet it was also a blind hope which was crushed forever in the madness of the sheer rationality of Auschwitz, where the mathematical idea of a final solution bore witness to a terrible flaw in the philosophical foundations of modern Western civilization. For it was there, in one of the most sophisticated of all Western nations, that men who were clearly rational were also clearly incapable of hearing the cries of human suffering. For, if Germany was the most scientific—that is, rational of all nations—and if it had the most advanced medicine in the Western world, it was also a medicine totally deaf to those cries. To believe, however, that such deafness was peculiarly German, or the result of an aberration in what has otherwise been an inexorable movement toward greater enlightenment, is to feed the very same disease that produced this human catastrophe in the first place.

As with every birth, the shape and form of the new clinic cannot be fully known until it has had time to mature. There, are, however, certain aspirations that will, I hope, guide its development. Three principles seem especially important. First, human life, dialogue, and health need to be seen in the framework of the larger world we all live in. When we speak to each other, I hope it will be with an awareness of the universe we all share. Second, I hope that we can see both reason and feelings as housed inside the same human body, and that they must thus always overlap. For then, and only then, can we human beings fully appreciate the richness and the infinite possibilities in every human dialogue. Third, and perhaps most important, it is my hope that the new clinic will foster a world in which when any of us cries, inarticulately or feebly or in bodily suffering, there will be other people to hear, to understand, to share, and to respond.

Contained in the "In Exitu" of the medieval Gregorian chant is the central drama of every human life. Lonely, haunting, ascetic, stark, this hymn recalls the exile of the Jews wandering in the wilderness of Sinai. It recalls the loneliness of a tribe in exile, the distress of having no place to live, the restless quest for a homeland, a promised land where one could live a life shared with others in Jerusalem. Throughout this book, patient after patient has recounted painful aspects of this human drama as each person, in exile from his or her own body, has sought relentlessly to find some home, some sense of place, some way of relating to others and an end to their engulfing isolation and loneliness. And, as these patients' suffering has made clear, to be unable to live in one's body is to have no place to live." It is a life of exile. To find one's home and to rediscover one's own body is to discover a life with others in the Jerusalem of the human heart.

At times I have found myself trembling when meeting the eyes of a patient—looking at me, searching, hoping earnestly to discover for the first time the emotional meaning of his or her elevated blood pressure, rapid heart rate, or freezing hands. At such moments I have felt Schrodinger's reality—deeply felt it—for surely there is far more to their eyes than optical sensors whose only function is to detect light quanta. And I have trembled then precisely because I have caught a glimpse of the infinite universe behind those eyes and the reality of a universal Logos uniting us in dialogue. And it is at such moments, in the quiet sharing of reason and feelings in dialogue, that I have felt most alive and human.

APPENDIX

Transactional Psychophysiology

TREATING DISEASES OF DYSFUNCTIONAL HUMAN COMMUNICATION

The interactions of patients described in this book involve a new systematic clinical approach to the treatment of a variety of stress-induced disorders. While it was not my intention in this book to focus on specific details of transactional psychophysiology—the therapeutic approach my colleagues and I use at the Psychophysiological Clinic at the University of Maryland—nevertheless certain clinical cases were useful in highlighting issues unique to it.* Although each patient has a particular constellation of life experiences as well as of bodily reactions, general aspects of our approach are common to all patients. While the following principles can be applied to a variety of disorders, for economy of space the therapeutic steps described here apply specifically to hypertension.

STEPS IN TRANSACTIONAL PSYCHOPHYSIOLOGY THERAPY

Transactional psychophysiological therapy (T.P. therapy) basically involves computer-assisted continuous monitoring of various bodily systems (such as blood pressure, heart rate, blood flow, skin

* All of the steps of transactional psychophysiology therapy outlined in this appendix have been developed with Dr. Sue Thomas and have been published in a preliminary version in chapter 1 of *The Healing Heart: Psychological Intervention in Cardiovascular Disease.*[1] These steps and treatment issues will be described in far greater detail in a technical manual by Sue Thomas, James Lynch, Herbert Gross, and Paul Rosch, to be entitled "Transactional Psychophysiology: A New Non-Drug Treatment for Stress-Linked Diseases."[2] This treatment approach, however, requires specific training and supervision if it is to be clinically effective.

temperature, muscle activity), while a person engages a therapist in dialogue. As I noted in chapter 8, many internal vascular reactions can be thought of as analogues of blushing. Just as no one blushes alone, so too the internal vascular system—including blood pressure, heart rate, and blood flow—is highly responsive to human interaction. Monitoring equipment allows these hidden components of the cardiovascular system to be seen and responded to as emotional communications in much the same way as a person responds to blushing.

The overall goal of T.P. therapy centers on diminishing the cardiovascular component of the fight or flight response typically observed in hypertensive dialogue. Though we believe that patients cannot directly control blood-pressure elevation during stressful dialogue, they can be made aware of their cardiovascular changes and taught to attend to them while speaking. A variety of physical maneuvers also can be taught to help modulate the magnitude of changes in blood pressure and heart rate. These maneuvers include slowing the rate of speech, deep breathing, muscle relaxation, nondefensive attending to others, and, when necessary in order to relax, periods of social withdrawal and quiet meditation.

T.P. therapy is based on the assumption that patients with stress-linked physical disorders have in common certain interpersonal struggles that lead them from health to illness; it is these common struggles that the therapy is designed to address systematically. Each step in therapy leads the patient to a progressively deeper understanding of the difference between healthy and unhealthy human dialogue and of how the human body contributes to that dialogue. Movement from one step to the next depends on the understanding and incorporation of certain basic principles.

The major steps in the T.P. therapy of hypertension involve:

1. Psychophysical assessment;
2. Observation of vascular reactions in an interpersonal world;
3. Linking the cardiovascular system to human communication;
4. Linking the cardiovascular system to an awareness of human feelings;
5. Seeing the therapist and "significant" others as essential aspects of transactional psychophysiological dialogue;
6. Learning to feel and modulate cardiovascular reactions when relating to others;

7. Recognizing emotional issues involved in changes in cardiovascular physiology; and
8. Recognizing family systems and environment as homeostatic regulators of the vascular system.

STEP 1. PSYCHOPHYSIOLOGICAL ASSESSMENT

The first step in T.P. therapy involves five components:

1. Complete medical examination as well as detailed medical history;
2. Assessment of current medical status, including details of clinical problems and medications;
3. Detailed social and family history;
4. In-depth psychological assessment; and
5. Psychophysiological assessment of patient in dialogue.

Any patient exhibiting symptoms of hypertension requires careful medical evaluation in order to rule out possible organic contributions to the problem, as well as to assess possible secondary organ damage that might have resulted from prolonged or extremely high blood pressure. Assuming that such an evaluation has already been conducted, the first step of the T.P. assessment involves an intake interview conducted by a clinical nurse specialist with a master's degree. A nurse is particularly well suited to conduct the interview because he or she can encourage the patient to feel that his or her problem (the patient's) is rooted in the body. Thus, a nurse not only assures that adequate medical data will be gathered but also helps support the social defense mechanisms of the patient by emphasizing that the problem is not "merely psychological"—a term that many patients equate with imaginary problems or ones that are not organic. In general, patients whose high blood pressure is psychophysiological are very resistant to a psychological interpretation of their cardiovascular problems (as indeed was Sigmund Freud himself, as we saw in chapter 10). We therefore feel that the more the intake procedure resembles a traditional medical one, the more likely is the patient to accept it—at least during the crucial initial phase of therapy.

During an hour-long interview the nurse obtains the patient's medical history—including onset, duration and aggravating circumstances of the problem—and also reviews all associated symptoms and relevant medical problems. These include any signs of diabetes, heart failure, abnormal kidney function, and visual problems which might suggest serious hypertensive disease or possible end-organ damage. All risk factors for hypertension and cardiovascular disease are also checked. These include a family history of hypertension, overweight, elevation in blood sugar, cholesterol levels, serum lipids, and smoking behavior. A detailed medication history and current drugs are also recorded.

Following this medical review, the nurse conducts a brief social, family, and occupational history. A particular effort is made to assess potential major sources of stress and conflict in the patient's interpersonal life.

The patient is then given a computerized battery of standardized medical and psychological tests by the nurse. These tests are designed to assess a patient's mental status. A patient who has serious thought disturbances, or appears to be experiencing serious emotional disturbance, is not considered ready for T.P. therapy. Significant disturbance in mental status renders difficult the process of insight and control inherent in the interactive dialogue of T.P. therapy. In such cases, therefore, the patient would be recommended to continue with a pharmacological means of controlling blood pressure.*

As part of the intake protocol, the nurse also monitors a variety of bodily systems (including heart rate, blood pressure, and skin temperature) when the patient is quiet and when he or she is discussing some ordinary aspect of life (such as job or home life). These data are gathered not only to evaluate bodily changes when the patient communicates, but also as a baseline reference point for subsequent physiological monitoring.

STEP 2. OBSERVATIONS OF VASCULAR REACTIONS
IN AN INTERPERSONAL WORLD

This step in the therapeutic process involves four components:

1. Seeing blood pressure, blood flow, and heart rate as dynamic rather than static bodily processes;
2. Learning to "own" one's body by acknowledging that the cardiovascular system is part of one's identity;
3. Recognizing one's cardiovascular system as being highly sensitive to interpersonal interaction; and

* Such cases are relatively uncommon in our clinic—perhaps because most of the patients are referred by physicians who already understand the complex nature of our treatment.

4. Understanding the relationship between internal homeostasis and social homeostasis.

Before being helped to lower blood pressure, a patient must first learn to observe changes in blood pressure when engaging another person in dialogue. In order to achieve such awareness, the patient must first be introduced to the notion that blood pressure and heart rate are not static components of a relatively unchanging body. Quite the contrary. The very essence of being alive is to live in a body that is in constant dynamic flux. In a sense, the patient must be reintroduced to his or her body and taught that he or she has much to learn about how his or her cardiovascular system responds, especially when dealing with other people. Gradually the idea of a cardiovascular system in constant flux is extended to include the idea of a system highly responsive to human interaction. As the patient assimilates this idea, it is suggested that factors outside of the body, especially interpersonal relationships, are as important to the cardiovascular system as various adaptive mechanisms inside the body. This initial step in the therapeutic process can take as long as four to six hour-long sessions, depending on how fixed a patient's ideas are about his or her body.

STEP 3. LINKING THE CARDIOVASCULAR SYSTEM TO HUMAN COMMUNICATION

This next step in T.P. therapy involves a series of component issues that are designed to teach the patient basic facts about communication–cardiovascular relationships. Among them, the following dimensions of communication are linked to changes in blood pressure:

1. Fast talking versus slow talking;
2. Listening, talking, and human dialogue;
3. Breathing and relaxing while talking;
4. Emotional content of speech; and
5. Language as a cry and language as a communication.

In this step of T.P. therapy, the patient begins to move beyond an overall appreciation of the dynamic nature of the cardiovascular system to a deeper sense of certain specific factors that cause blood pressure to change significantly. While watching tracings of his or her blood pressure and heart rate, the patient is shown the difference between rapid and slow speech, deep breathing and shallow breathing, and the overall impact of quiet relaxation on blood pressure. Once these mechanical dimensions of speech and their links to cardiovascular regulation are understood, the patient will be prepared to appreciate the difference between passively relaxing and actively attending to his or her environment. Two components of dialogue—speaking and listening—are shown to the patient, on computer tracings, to have significant and reciprocal influences on blood pressure. Having learned these ideas, the individual is introduced to the way emotional arousal both influences the mechanical aspects of speech and alters other physiological mechanisms that affect the cardiovascular system. Gradually the patient is introduced to various emotional issues within the context of the ongoing therapeutic dialogue and systematically probes their links to cardiovascular functions. The individual is taught the difference between communicating in a inarticulate way (much as a baby cries) and effectively communicating in a way that does not lead to exaggerated cardiovascular reactions. In addition, the patient is also instructed to begin recording blood pressure at home both before and after five minutes of relaxed deep breathing. In order to be sensitized to the links between emotional arousal and blood pressure, patients are also instructed to estimate their blood pressure before they actually measure it, as well as to note how they are feeling.

STEP 4. LINKING THE CARDIOVASCULAR SYSTEM TO
AWARENESS OF HUMAN FEELINGS

This step of T.P. therapy addresses discrete aspects of the relationship between human feelings and changes in the cardiovascular system. Among the issues raised are:

1. Emotional implications of being unaware of major bodily changes, especially during dialogue;
2. Feeling bodily changes;
3. Labeling bodily changes as meaningful in an emotional context; and
4. Recognizing bodily changes as signals that ought to be listened to, and accepted, rather than rejected.

During this stage of T.P. therapy, continuous attention is focused on the nature of the cardiovascular changes that occur during the therapeutic dialogue. Patients are reminded to look at the changes in their heart rate and blood pressure, especially when they communicate, and frequently asked to interpret what they believe such changes imply. During this stage of treatment, the therapist also begins to raise issues of emotional significance to the patient. Every effort is made to titrate the level of arousal so that the blood pressure does not rise excessively. The patient is instructed to introspect about his or her feelings in order to correlate them with cardiovascular changes. During this stage, the person is also reminded that it is far more important to feel feelings than to control them. The patient is taught that he or she cannot begin to understand feelings until he or she first learns to recognize them. Emphasis is also placed on examining the premises underpinning certain emotional states, such as chronic states of fight or flight, in order to help the patient alter his or her perceptions of the dangers really posed by other people in the external world. It is also emphasized that a patient does not have "good" and "bad" bodily reactions but rather has human reactions to which he or she must attend.

As I emphasized in chapter 9, this stage of therapy not only hinges on the efforts put forward by the patient but is also crucially determined by the therapist's capacity to feel and to share these feelings. This stage of therapy centers on the importance both of the social membrane as the nexus for teaching the patient about feelings and shared human experience as well as of language which one uses to communicate emotional meaning to other people.

STEP 5. SEEING THE THERAPIST AND "SIGNIFICANT" OTHERS AS AN ESSENTIAL ASPECT OF T.P. DIALOGUE

This step is perhaps the most difficult to grasp in the therapeutic process. It basically involves a conceptual reorientation about the influence of interpersonal factors on the cardiovascular system. While difficult to explain in a brief fashion, the theoretical issues involve at least three components:

1. Bodily responses in countertransference;
2. Life-threatening bodily changes as a countertransference problem; and
3. The fact that no one blushes alone.

Fundamentally this step extends a patient's awareness—as well as the awareness of people who interact with the patient—to include the idea that the human body is highly responsive to social "set and setting" variables. This idea is juxtaposed against the traditional idea that blood pressure is regulated solely by internal bodily mechanisms. In a sense, the "hypertensive problem" is expanded to include not only the person whose blood pressure is elevated, but also all those who come in contact with him or her. The idea is put forward that these "significant" others frequently contribute inadvertently to the general problem. A patient must recognize, for example, that blood pressure not only transiently responds when he or she talks to a mate or a therapist, but that his or her overall resting blood pressure is also influenced by the quality of such interaction. Thus, both pleasant and unpleasant interactions can be compounded so as to "set" the resting blood pressure of a patient. In addition, it is equally important for those individuals who interact with the hypertensive patient—including the therapist and the mate—to come to grips with the very same reality. This issue is explained in light of the idea that no one blushes alone. Just as blushing is a vascular response that has real interpersonal communicative implications, so too have hidden hypertensive reactions.

This is an especially problematic phase of therapy because usually neither the hypertensive individual nor those who interact with him or her sense any real discomfort and are thus unable to appreciate blood-pressure responses as being anything but mechanical. It is especially difficult to see these changes as communications, particularly since they historically have neither been felt by the individual nor seen by others and are frequently masked by a smiling and pleasant demeanor that belies one's internal struggles. On the other hand, when computers reveal these previously hidden struggles, other people may see themselves as the "cause" of the hypertensive person's reactions and thus tend to retreat from dialogue. Much like the analogy to blushing, the essentially transactional nature of bodily communications must be understood. If one accepts the role of "helper" in such interaction—by attempting to calm a person's blood pressure, for example—then one must also come to grips with one's potential helplessness. One could literally "fail" in one's efforts to calm the other person and thus trigger countertransferential feelings of guilt. In addition to this complex problem, the interlocking nature of emotions as shared human experience must be addressed. Basically, the discrepancies between overt and covert bodily communications must be heard and decoded, and then one's reactions to such discrepant signals must be analyzed.

As is true in traditional dynamically oriented psychotherapy, this stage of bodily countertransference is the most difficult of all the stages of T.P. therapy.

STEP 6. LEARNING TO FEEL AND MODULATE CARDIOVASCULAR REACTIONS WHEN ONE RELATES TO OTHERS

In this stage of therapy, emphasis is once again focused on various physiological factors that influence blood pressure. Basically, the influence of these factors is discussed in respect both to when the patient is alone and to when he or she engages others in dialogue. Several crucial issues are addressed:

1.   Short-term effects of deep breathing and muscle relaxation;
2.   Long-term influence of proper breathing, muscle relaxation, and graded exercise; and
3.   Central nervous system mediation of the cardiovascular system.

Basically, the patient is again educated to the way various mechanical factors influence blood pressure, and to how these mechanisms operate when one is emotionally aroused. The patient is led to understand that any permanent alteration in blood pressure involves certain fundamental changes in overall health habits. It is emphasized that one can be emotionally aroused, even emotionally upset, and yet still breathe normally and exercise regularly. In that way, a person comes to learn that it is possible to engage others in dialogue, even stressful dialogue, without becoming acutely hypertensive. An analogy is drawn between playing a vigorous sport when one is in good physical shape versus when one is in poor physical shape: the better one's physical shape, the more able one is to play the game. So, too, in terms of dialogue, the better one's cardiovascular "shape," the better one can engage in stressful dialogue.

Finally, the patient learns about various central nervous system mechanisms that influence blood pressure, and about the various psychological states that have to do with these mechanisms. Again, as in step 3, the individual is reminded about the links between attending to others and to one's natural environment in a relaxed manner and the way this attention is linked to the lowering of blood pressure.

STEP 7. RECOGNIZING EMOTIONAL ISSUES INVOLVED IN CHANGES IN CARDIOVASCULAR PHYSIOLOGY

In this third major and last phase of therapy, the general orientation shifts toward a comprehensive understanding of major life issues that have an overall influence on the cardiovascular system and on a persons' health in general. Among the issues addressed are:

1. Current interpersonal issues that influence cardiovascular physiology;
2. Early life experiences that influence one's communicative style;
3. Difference between recognizing an emotional issue and altering one's physiological response to it; and
4. A genetic predisposition to respond in specific physiological systems and the emotional consequences of that predisposition.

In general, during this final phase of therapy, a patient is informed that early experiences have a significant impact on an adult's communicative patterns. As described in chapter 9, for example, a hypertensive parent, or parents, may have interacted with the patient when he or she was a child in a way that hampered emotional understanding: that is, a mother who suffered from alexithymia, say, would have difficulty feeling her own feelings and thus would imperfectly teach emotional awareness to her offspring. Such links allow a patient to see his or her own experiences in a larger context, which includes the profound impact of early developmental experiences. In addition, the patient learns that blood pressure can be used as a sensitive barometer to monitor and assess shifts in interpersonal struggles in adult life, as well as to pinpoint areas (such as job or home life) that might be contributing to overall feelings of stress.

As I emphasized in earlier phases of treatment, the patient is also taught that there is a significant difference between understanding and recognizing that one's vascular system is responding and controlling that response. As with blushing, it is far more important to recognize that one is reacting than it is to control the response; for the response must be looked at as a communication that ought to be listened to rather than controlled. And again as in the case of blushing, the patient is told that a predisposition to exaggerated blood-pressure responses may be due either to genetic or to early environmental experiences. What is important, however, is that one understands not so much the origins of the problem as the emotional consequences of one's pattern of responding.

Finally, each person is led to understand that he or she must conduct any dialogue with others in full awareness of the limitations of his or her body. The elderly, for example, must recognize that atherosclerosis and the loss of vascular resiliency can create a condition where blood pressure will tend to rise more abruptly when one speaks than it does in a younger person. Therefore, the elderly person may have to modify his or her style of speaking accordingly, perhaps by breathing more regularly when speaking as well as by talking at a slower, less intense pace.

STEP 8. FAMILY SYSTEMS AND ENVIRONMENT AS HOMEOSTATIC REGULATORS OF THE CARDIOVASCULAR SYSTEM

In this final step of therapy, the patient is led to see the way his or her predisposition to hidden cardiovascular reactions can influence an entire family system. Cut off from awareness of his or her own body, the patient is likely to be equally cut off from awareness of other people; and even more to the point, others will be equally unaware of the patient's feelings. Thus, in this final phase of therapy, the external and the internal dialogue are extended to include those other key people in a patient's life. It is emphasized that blood pressure is as important a communication system as are spoken words, and that the language of the heart must be carefully attended to and heeded. Before terminating therapy, patients are informed that they must continue to monitor blood pressure for the remainder of their life, and warned not to ignore the signals of their cardiovascular system.

Finally, we tell patients that they are not conventionally "cured": that is, their blood pressure is not going to remain constant. It is our belief that hypertensive patients have a genetic predisposition to respond to stress with transient elevations in blood pressure, while migraine patients will block peripheral blood flow, just as I will continue to blush whenever I am embarrassed. Thus, our patients are charged with a lifelong responsibility to monitor their cardiovascular system and are instructed to return for a follow-up visit if an elevated pressure does not return to acceptable levels within a few days or if they experience recurrent headaches.

NOTES

Introduction

1. *The New York Times,* 31 October 1984, p. A18.
2. James J. Lynch, *The Broken Heart: The Medical Consequences of Loneliness* (New York: Basic Books, 1977).
3. Ibid., pp. 217, 218.

Chapter 1. Bodies in Revolt

1. S. Cobb and R. Rose, "Hypertension, Peptic Ulcer and Diabetes in Air Traffic Controllers," *Journal of the American Medical Association* 224 (1973):489–92.

Chapter 2. The Vital Sign

1. National Center for Health Statistics, "Office Visits for Diseases of the Circulatory System. The National Ambulatory Medical Care Survey, U.S., 1975, 1976." Publication no. (PHS) 79–1971, Department of Health, Education, and Welfare, Hyattsville, Maryland, 1979.
   J. J. Lynch et al., "Human Speech and Blood Pressure," *Journal of Nervous and Mental Disease* 168(9[1981]).
2. William B. Kannel, "Role of Blood Pressure in Cardiovascular Morbidity and Mortality," *Progress in Cardiovascular Diseases* 17(1[July/August 1974]):5–24.
3. *Cardiovascular Primer for the Workplace.* Health Education Branch, Office of Prevention, Education, and Control. National Heart, Lung, and Blood Institute. U.S. Department of Health and Human Services. Public Health Service. National Institutes of Health. NIH Publication no. 81–2210 (January 1981).
4. Ibid.
5. W. B. Kannel; and P. Sorlie, "Hypertension in Framingham," in O. Paul, ed., *Epidemiology and Control of Hypertension* (Miami: Symposia Specialists, 1975).
   Veterans Administration Cooperative Study Group on Antihypertensive Agents, "Effects of Treatment on Morbidity in Hypertension: I. Results in Patients with Diastolic Blood Pressure Averaging 115–129," *Journal of the American Medical Association* 202(1967):1028–34.
   Veterans Administration Cooperative Study Group on Antihypertensive Agents, "Effects of Treatment on Morbidity in Hypertension: II. Results in Patients with Diastolic Blood Pressure Averaging 90 through 114 mm Hg," *Journal of the American Medical Association* 213(1970):1143–52.

6. M. J. Reichgott and B. G. Simons-Morton, "Strategies to Improve Patient Compliance with Antihypertensive Therapy," *Primary Care* 10(1[March 1983]):21.

7. Harvey quoted in F. A. Willius and T. E. Keys, *Classics of Cardiology* (New York: Dover, 1941), vol. I, p. 15. William Harvey's manuscript notes for "An Anatomical Disquisition on the Motion of the Heart and Blood in Animals" (1628) are now in the British Museum.

8. Ibid.

9. René Descartes, *Philosophic Works of Descartes,* 2 vols., E. S. Haldane and G. R. T. Ross, trans. (New York: Dover, 1955; Oxford University Press, 1967).

10. Hales quoted in Willius and Keys, *Classics of Cardiology* [8], pp. 131–55. The original source of Hales's *Account* is the third edition published in London in 1733.

11. Blaise Pascal, *Traité de la Pesanteur de la Masse de L'air* (Paris: Guillaume Deprez, 1663).

12. For Pascal, see *Dictionary of Scientific Biography* (New York: Charles Scribner's, 1974), vol. X, pp. 330–42; and *Encyclopedia Americana* (New York: American, 1977), vol. XXI, pp. 362–64.

13. Pascal, *Pensées* (Paris, Guillaume Deprez, 1670).

14. Ibid.

15. Pascal, *Traité* [11].

16. Willius and Keys, *Classics of Cardiology* [8], p. 131.

17. James J. Lynch, et al., "Heart Rate Changes in the Horse to Human Contact," *Psychophysiology* 11(4[1974]):472–78.

18. L. A. Geddis, *The Direct and Indirect Measurement of Blood Pressure* (Chicago: Year Book Medical Publishers, 1970), pp. 75–77. Original source: L. Luciane, *Human Physiology,* F. A. Wilby, trans., vol. I (London: Macmillan, 1911), 592. Original article: S. Riva-Rocci, "Un nuovo sfigmomanometro," vol. 47 (Torino: Medical Gazette, 1896), pp. 981–96.

19. M. E. Geddis, H. E. Hoff, and A. S. Badger, "Introduction to the Ausculatory Method of Measuring Blood Pressure—Including a Translation of Korotkoff's Original Paper," *Cardiovascular Research Bulletin* 5(1967):57–74.

20. M. Douglas. *Natural Symbols: Explorations in Cosmology* (London: Barries and Rockliss: Cresset Press, 1970; New York: Random House, 1972).

Chapter 3. The Human Machine

1. D. Roffman and S. A. Thomas, "Treatment of Hypertension," in M. Weiner and G. A. Pepper, eds., *Clinical Pharmacology and Therapeutics in Nursing,* 2nd ed. (New York: McGraw-Hill, 1985).

2. H. Weiner, *Psychobiology of Essential Hypertension* (New York: Elsevier, 1979).

3. M. Friedman and R. Rosenman, *Type A Behavior and Your Heart* (New York: Alfred A. Knopf, 1974).

4. Blood Pressure Study, 1979, Society of Actuaries and Association of Life Insurance Medical Directors of America (November 1980).

5. T. S. Kuhn, *Structure of Scientific Revolutions* (Chicago: University of Chicago Press, 1970).

6. W. H. Gantt, "The Role of Teleology in Behavior," editorial, *Pavlovian Journal of Biological Science* 14(3[1979]):157–59.

W. H. Gantt, "Who Am I? Who Are You?" editorial page, *Baltimore Sun,* 25 April 1979.

W. H. Gantt, "Perspectives Fifty Years after Pavlov," *Journal of Behavioral Therapy and Experimental Psychiatry* 10(2[1979]).

W. H. Gantt, "The Role of Teleology in Behavior," editorial, *Pavlovian Journal of Biological Science* 14(1[1979]).

W. H. Gantt, "The Century's Ebb," editorial, *Pavlovian Journal of Biological Science* 13(3[1978]):133–34.

W. H. Gantt, "Do Consciousness and Free Will Require Physical Energy?," editorial, *Pavlovian Journal of Biological Science* (1977).

A. M. Harvey, "W. Horsley Gantt—A Legend in His Time," *The Johns Hopkins Medical Journal* 139(3[September 1976]):121–26.

W. H. Gantt, "Autokinesis, Schizokinesis, Organ-System Responsibility: Concepts and Definitions," *Pavlovian Journal of Biological Science* 9(4[1974]):187–91.

W. H. Gantt, *"A Scientist's Last Words,"* in J. W. Cullen, ed., *Legacies in the Study of Behavior* (Springfield, Ill.: Charles C Thomas, 1974), pp. 46–61.

W. H. Gantt, "Ivan Petrovich Pavlov," *Encyclopaedia Britannica,* 15th ed. (1974), pp. 1095–97.

James J. Lynch, et al., "Pavlovian Conditioning of Drug Reactions: Some Implications for Problems of Drug Addiction," *Conditional Reflex* 8(4[1973]): 211–23.

W. H. Gantt, "Objectivity and Subjectivity: Pain," *Conditional Reflex* 8(4[1973]):187–92.

W. H. Gantt, "Reminiscences of Pavlov," *Journal of Experimental Analysis Behavior* 20(1973):131–36.

W. H. Gantt, "Analysis of the Effect of Person," *Conditional Reflex* 7(2[1972]):67–73.

W. H. Gantt, "B. F. Skinner and His Contingencies," editorial, *Conditional Reflex* 5(2[1970]):63–74.

W. H. Gantt, "The Distinction Between the Conditional and the Unconditional Reflex," *Conditional Reflex* 3(1[1968]):1–3.

W. H. Gantt, "Pavlov's Higher Nervous Activity," *Conditional Reflex* 3(4[1968]):279–84.

J. J. Lynch and W. H. Gantt, "The Heart Rate Component of the Social Reflex in Dogs: The Conditional Effects of Petting and Person," *Conditional Reflex* 3(2[1968]):69–80.

J. J. Lynch and W. H. Gantt, "Comparison of the Conditional Reflex to the Unconditional Reflex in Classical Heart Rate Conditioning: The Effect of Person and Its Interaction with Shock," *Conditional Reflex* 3(2[abstract, 1968]).

W. H. Gantt, "Pavlovian, Classical Conditional Reflex, A Classical Error?," *Conditional Reflex* 2(4[1967]):255–57.

W. H. Gantt, "On Humility in Science," *Conditional Reflex* 2(3[1967]):179–83.

W. H. Gantt, "Introduction to Dos Passos editorial," *Conditional Reflex* 2(1[1967]).

J. E. O. Newton and W. H. Gantt, "History of a Catatonic Dog," *Conditional Reflex* 3(1[1967]):45–61.

W. H. Gantt, "Neurophysiological Psychiatry: Descartes to Pavlov and After," in I. Galdston, ed., *Historic Derivations of Modern Psychiatry* (New York: McGraw-Hill, 1967), pp. 139–57.

W. H. Gantt, "The Meaning of the Cardiac Conditional Reflex," *Conditional Reflex* 1(3[1966]):139–43.

J. F. Reus, J. J. Lynch, and W. H. Gantt, "Motor Response Device," *Conditional Reflex* 1(2[1966]):135–36.

W. H. Gantt, "Conditional or Conditioned, Reflex or Response?," *Conditional Reflex* 1(2[1966]):69–74.

W. H. Gantt, editorial, *Conditional Reflex* 1(1[1966]):1–2.

W. H. Gantt, et al., "Effect of Person," *Conditional Reflex* 1(1966):18–35.

Sandra Anderson and W. H. Gantt, "The Effect of Person on Cardiac and Motor Responsivity to Shock in Dogs," *Conditional Reflex* 1(3[1966]):181–90.

W. H. Gantt, "Reflexology, Schizokinesis and Autokinesis," *Conditional Reflex* 1(1966):57–68.

W. H. Gantt, "Comments: Impact of Pavlov on Psychiatry," *American Journal of Psychiatry* 121(1965):1213–15.

W. H. Gantt, "Autonomic Conditioning," *Annals New York Academy of Science* 117(1964):132–41.

W. H. Gantt, "The Role of the Heart in Psychosomatic Medicine," editorial, *Medical Tribune,* 30 August 1963.

W. H. Gantt, J. E. O. Newton, and Fred L. Royer, "Effect of Person," *American Academy of Neurology,* exhibit, 26–29 April 1961.

Fred L. Royer and W. H. Gantt, "The Effect of Different Persons on the Heart Rate of Dogs," Eastern Psychological Association, Philadelphia, 7–8 March 1961.

W. H. Gantt, J. E. O. Newton, and J. Stephens, "Effect of Person on Conditional Reflexes," *Psychosomatic Medicine* 22(1960):322–23.

W. H. Gantt, *Experimental Basis for Neurotic Behavior* (New York: Hoeber, 1944).

7. E. Schrödinger, *What Is Life? Mind and Matter* (London: Cambridge University Press, 1967), p. 135.

8. See titles in note 6.

9. J. E. O. Newton and W. W. Ehrlich, "Coronary Blood Flow in Dogs: Effect of Person," *Conditional Reflex* 1(1966):81.

10. J. J. Lynch, et al., "The Effects of Human Contact on Cardiac Arrhythmia in Coronary Care Patients," *Journal of Nervous and Mental Disease* 158(1974):88–99.

J. J. Lynch, et al., "Human Contact and Cardiac Arrhythmia in a Coronary Care Unit," *Psychosomatic Medicine* 39(1977):188–92.

S. A. Thomas, J. J. Lynch, and M. E. Mills, "Psychosocial Influences on Heart Arrhythmia in a Coronary Care Patient," *Heart and Lung* 4(1975):746–50.

J. J. Lynch, et al., "Psychological Aspects of Cardiac Arrhythmia," *American Heart Journal* 93(1977):645–57.

11. J. J. Lynch, et al., "The Effects of Human Contact on the Heart Activity of Curarized Patients in a Shock-Trauma Unit," *American Heart Journal* 88(1974):160–69.

12. Ibid.

13. J. J. Lynch, *The Broken Heart: The Medical Consequences of Loneliness* (New York: Basic Books, 1977).

14. Ibid.

15. P. Sterling and J. Eger, "Biological Basis for Stress Related Mortality," *Social Science and Medicine* 15E(1981):3–42.

16. I. H. Page, "Some Regulatory Mechanisms of Renovascular and Essential Hypertension," in J. Genest, E. Koiw, and O. Kuchel, eds., *Hypertension* (New York: McGraw-Hill, 1977).

17. A. C. Guyton, *Arterial Pressure and Hypertension* (Philadelphia: W. B. Saunders, 1980).

18. Veterans Administration Cooperative Study Group on Antihypertensive Agents, "Effects of Treatment on Morbidity in Hypertension: Results in Patients with

Diastolic Pressure Averaging 115 through 129 mm Hg," *Journal of the American Medical Association* 202(1967):1028–34.

Veterans Administration Cooperative Study Group on Antihypertensive Agents, "Effects of Treatment on Morbidity in Hypertension: Results in Patients with Diastolic Pressure Averaging 90 through 114 mm Hg," *Journal of the American Medical Association* 213(1970):1143–52.

19. Hypertension Detection and Follow-Up Program Cooperative Group, "Five Year Findings of the Hypertension Detection and Follow-up Program. I: Reduction in Mortality of Persons with High Blood Pressure, Including Mild Hypertension," *Journal of the American Medical Association* 242(1979):2572–77.

20. Multiple Risk Factor Intervention Trial Research Group, "Multiple Risk Factor Intervention Trial Risk Factor Changes and Mortality Results," *Journal of the American Medical Association* 248(12[1982]):1465–1501.

21. M. J. Reichgott and B. G. Simons-Morton, "Strategies to Improve Compliance with Antihypertensive Therapy," *Primary Care* 10(1[1983]):21–27.

22. E. Brandt, "Assistant Secretary for Health's Advisory on Treatment of Mild Hypertension," *FDA Drug Bulletin* 13(1983):24–25.

23. James J. Lynch, et al., "Interpersonal Aspects of Blood Pressure Control," *Journal of Nervous and Mental Disease* 170([1982]):143–53.

Chapter 4. Lethal Dialogue

1. S. A. Thomas, et al., "Patients' Cardiac Responses to Nursing Interviews in a CCU," *Dimensions of Critical Care Nursing* 1(4[July–August 1982]):198–205.

S. A. Thomas, et al., "Denial in the Coronary Care Patient—An Objective Reassessment," *Heart and Lung* 12(1[January 1983]):74–80.

2. Ibid.

3. I. P. Stevenson, et al., "Life Situations, Emotions, and Extrasystoles," *Psychosomatic Medicine* 11(1949):257–72.

4. R. Coleman, M. Greenblatt, and H. Solomon, "Physiological Evidence of Rapport during Psychotherapeutic Interviews, *Diseases of the Nervous System* 17(1956):71–78.

H. Mayer, B. Stanek, and P. Hahn, "Biometric Findings on Cardiac Neurosis II EKG and Circulatory Findings of Cardiophobic Patients During Standardized Examination of Circulatory System," in Topics of Psychosomatic Research (Ninth European Conference on Psychosomatic Research, Vienna, 1973), pp. 284–88.

L. H. Sigler, "Emotion and Atherosclerotic Heart Disease I: Electrocardiographic Changes Observed on the Recall of Past Emotional Disturbances," *British Journal of Medical Psychology* 40(1967):55–64.

S. Wolf, "Cardiovascular Reactions to Symbolic Stimuli," *Circulation* 18(1958):287–92.

5. F. Alexander, "Psychoanalytic Study of a Case of Essential Hypertension," *Psychosomatic Medicine* 1(1939):139–56.

F. Alexander, "Emotional Factors in Essential Hypertension," *Psychosomatic Medicine* 1(1939):173.

F. Alexander, *Psychosomatic Medicine: Its Principles and Applications* (New York: W. W. Norton, 1950)

L. Moses, G. E. Daniels, and J. L. Nickerson, "Psychogenic Factors in Essential Hypertension," *Psychosomatic Medicine* 18(1956):471–85.

M. Reiser, et al., "Life Situations, Emotions, and the Course of Patients with Arterial Hypertension," *Psychosomatic Medicine,* May–June 1951.

M. Thaler, H. Weiner, and M. Reiser, "Exploration of the Doctor-Patient Relationship through Projective Techniques," *Psychosomatic Medicine* 19(1957):228–39.

S. Wolf, et al., *Life Stress and Essential Hypertension* (Baltimore: Williams & Wilkins, 1955).

6. J. J. Lynch, *The Broken Heart: The Medical Consequences of Loneliness* (New York: Basic Books, 1977).

7. W. S. Agras, "Relaxation Therapy in Hypertension," *Hospital Practice,* May 1983, pp. 129–37.

W. S. Agras, et al., "Relaxation Training," *Archives of General Psychiatry* 37(1980):859–63.

H. Benson, et al., "Decreased Blood Pressure in Borderline Hypertensives Who Practice Meditation," *Journal of Chronic Disease* 27(1974):163–69.

H. Benson, et al., "Decreased Systolic Blood Pressure through Operant Conditioning Techniques in Patients with Essential Hypertension," *Science* 173(1971):740–42.

H. Benson, et al., "Decreased Blood Pressure in Pharmacologically Treated Hypertensive Patients Who Regularly Elicited the Relaxation Response," *Lancet* 1(1974):289–91.

H. Benson, and R. K. Wallace, "Decreased Blood Pressure in Hypertensive Subjects Who Practice Meditation," *Circulation* 46 (supplement II [1972]):130.

H. Benson, B. R. Marzetta, and B. A. Rosner, "Decreased Blood Pressure Associated with the Regular Elicitation of the Relaxation Response: A Study of Hypertensive Subjects," *Contemporary Problems in Cardiology,* vol I: *Stress and the Heart,* ed. by R. S. Eliot (Mt. Kisco, N.Y.: Futura, 1974).

B. Blackwell, et al., "Transcendental Meditation in Hypertension," *Lancet* 1(1976):223–26.

J. P. Brady, L. Luborsky, and R. E. Kron, "Blood Pressure Reduction in Patients with Essential Hypertension through Metronome-Conditioned Relaxation: A Preliminary Report," *Behavior Therapy* 5(1974):203–9.

H. L. Deabler, C. Fidel, and R. L. Dillenkoffer, "The Use of Relaxation and Hypnosis in Lowering High Blood Pressure," *American Journal of Clinical Hypnosis* 16(1973):75–83.

J. J. Lynch, et al., "Interpersonal Aspects of Blood Pressure Control," *Journal of Nervous and Mental Disease* 170(1982):143–53.

C. Patel and K. K. Datey, "Relaxation and Biofeedback Techniques in the Management of Hypertension," *Angiology* 27(1976):106–13.

C. Patel, M. G. Marmot, and D. J. Terry, "Controlled Trial of Biofeedback—Aided Behavioral Methods in Reducing Mild Hypertension," *British Medical Journal* 282(1981):2005–8.

J. E. Shoemaker and D. L. Tasto, "The Effects of Muscle Relaxation on Blood Pressure of Essential Hypertensives," *Behavioral Research and Therapy* 13(1975):29–43.

M. A. Southam, et al., "Relaxation Training," *Archives of General Psychiatry* 39(1982):715–17.

8. L. Moses, G. Daniels, and J. Nickerson, "Psychogenic Factors in Essential Hypertension," *Psychosomatic Medicine* 18(6[1956]):471–85.

M. Reiser, et al., "Life Situations, Emotions, and the Course of Patients with Arterial Hypertension," *Psychosomatic Medicine* 13(3[1951]):133–39.

9. F. Alexander, "Psychoanalytic Study of a Case of Essential Hypertension," *Psychosomatic Medicine* 1(1939):139–56.

F. Alexander, "Emotional Factors in Essential Hypertension," *Psychosomatic Medicine* 1(1939):173.

10. S. Freud, *Basic Writings of Sigmund Freud* (New York: Random House, 1938).

11. W. B. Cannon, *Bodily Changes in Pain, Hunger, Fear and Rage* (New York: Appleton-Century-Crofts, 1929).

12. Ibid., p. 93.

13. Ibid., pp. 193–94.

14. Alexander, "Psychoanalytic Study" [9].

15. M. F. Reiser, M. Rosenbaum, and E. B. Ferris, "Psychologic Mechanisms in Malignant Hypertension," *Psychosomatic Medicine* 13(1951):157.

16. Ibid.

17. Moses, Daniels, and Nickerson, "Psychogenic Factors" [8].

18. A. P. Shapiro, comments in *Psychosomatic Classics: Selected Papers from Psychosomatic Medicine, 1939–1958* (New York: S. Karger, 1972), p. 56.

19. H. Weiner, *Psychobiology of Essential Hypertension* (New York: Elsevier, 1979).

20. F. Alexander, T. M. French, and G. H. Pollock, *Psychosomatic Specificity* (Chicago: University of Chicago Press, 1968), p. 30.

21. S. Wolf, et al., *Life Stress and Essential Hypertension* (Baltimore: Williams & Wilkins, 1955).

22. Ibid., p. 96.

23. Weiner, *Psychobiology* [19].

24. See titles in note 5 and Weiner, *Psychobiology* [19].

25. Weiner, *Psychobiology* [19], p. 29.

26. W. J. Grace and D. T. Graham, "Relationship of Specific Attitudes and Emotions to Certain Bodily Diseases," *Psychosomatic Medicine* 14(1952):243.

Chapter 5. No Language But a Cry

1. B. Gribbin, A. Steptoe, and P. Sleight, "Pulse Wave Velocity as a Measure of Blood Pressure Changes," *Psychophysiology* 13(1976):86–91.

P. Walsh, A. Dale, and D. E. Anderson, "Comparison of Biofeedback Pulse Wave Velocity and Progressive Relaxation in Essential Hypertensives," *Perceptual and Motor Skills* 44(1977):839–43.

Chapter 6. Examining the Cardiovascular–Communication Links

1. S. M. Kaplan, et al., "Hostility in Verbal Productions and Hypnotic 'Dreams' of Hypertensive Patients (Comparisons Between Hypertensive and Normotensive Groups and Within Hypertensive Individuals)," abstract in *Psychosomatic Medicine* 22(1960):320.

2. G. Innes, W. M. Millar, and M. Valentine, "Emotion and Blood-Pressure," *Journal of Mental Science* 105(1959):840–51.

3. R. Adler, et al., "A Context Study of Psychological Conditions Prior to Shifts in Blood Pressure," *Psychotherapy and Psychosomatics* 27(1976–77):198–204.

4. M. Friedman and R. Rosenman, *Type A Behavior and Your Heart* (New York: Alfred A. Knopf, 1974).

5. T. M. Dembrowski, et al., "Components of Type A Behavior Pattern and Cardiovascular Responses to Psychomotor Performance Challenge," *Journal of Behavioral Medicine* (1978).

T. M. Dembrowski, J. M. MacDougall, and R. Lushene, "Interpersonal Interaction and Cardiovascular Response in Type A Subjects and Coronary Patients," *Journal of Human Stress* 5(1979):28–36.

6. S. A. Thomas, et al., "Denial in the Coronary Care Patient—An Objective Reassessment," *Heart and Lung* 12(1[1983]):74–80.

S. A. Thomas, et al., "Patients' Cardiac Responses to Nursing Interviews in a CCU," *Dimensions of Critical Care Nursing* 1(4[July–August 1982]):198–205.

S. A. Thomas, J. J. Lynch, and M. E. Mills, "Psychosocial Influences on Heart Rhythm in Coronary Care Unit," *Heart and Lung* 4(5[1975]):746–50.

7. J. J. Lynch, et al., "Human Speech and Blood Pressure," *Journal of Nervous and Mental Disease* 168(1980):526–34.

8. Ibid.

9. J. J. Lynch, et al., "The Effects of Talking on the Blood Pressure of Hypertensive and Normotensive Individuals," *Psychosomatic Medicine* 43(1981):25–33.

10. S. Wolf, et al., *Life Stress and Essential Hypertension* (Baltimore: Williams & Wilkins, 1955).

11. K. Malinow, et al., "Automated Blood Pressure Recording: The Phenomenon of Blood Pressure Elevation During Speech," *Angiology* 33(7[1982]):474–79.

12. T. G. Pickering, et al., "Blood Pressure During Normal Daily Activities, Sleep and Exercise: Comparison of Values in Normal and Hypertensive Subjects," *Journal of the American Medical Association* 247(issue 7[1982]):992–96.

T. G. Pickering, et al., "Ambulatory Monitoring in the Elevation of Blood Pressure in Patients with Borderline Hypertension and the Role of the Defense Reflex," *Clinical and Experimental Hypertension* A-4(1982):675–93.

G. A. Harshfield, et al., "Situational Variations of Blood Pressure in Ambulatory Hypertensive Patients," *Psychosomatic Medicine* 44(1982):237–45.

13. E. Friedmann, et al., "The Effects of Normal and Rapid Speech on Blood Pressure," *Psychosomatic Medicine* 170(3[1982]):143–53.

S. Hall, et al., "Measurement of Neonatal Blood Pressure: A New Method," *Psychophysiology* 19(2[1982]):231–36.

J. M. Long, et al., "The Effect of Status on Blood Pressure during Verbal Communication," *Behavioral Medicine* 5(2[1982]):165–72.

K. Malinow, et al., "Automated Blood Pressure Recording: The Phenomenon of Blood Pressure Elevations During Speech," *Angiology* 33(7[1982]):474–79.

J. J. Lynch, et al., "The Effects of Talking on the Blood Pressure of Hypertensive and Normotensive Individuals," *Psychosomatic Medicine* 43(1981):25–33.

J. J. Lynch, et al., "Human Speech and Blood Pressure," *Journal of Nervous and Mental Disease* 168(1980):526–34.

J. J. Lynch, et al., "Interpersonal Aspects of Blood Pressure Control," *Journal of Nervous and Mental Disease* 170(3[1982]):143–53.

S. A. Thomas, et al., "Changes in Nurses' Blood Pressure and Heart Rate While Communicating," *Journal of Research in Nursing and Health* 7(1984):119–26.

S. A. Thomas, et al., "Blood Pressure and Heart Rate Changes in Children When They Read Aloud in School," *Public Health Reports* 99(1[1984]):77–84.

14. J. J. Lynch, et al., "Blood Pressure Changes While Talking," *Israeli Journal of Medical Science* 18(5[1982]):575–79.

15. E. Lynch, et al., "Blood Pressure and Heart Rate Increases in Kindergarten

Children during a Routine School Task," manuscript to be submitted to *Child Development*, 1984.

16. M. Friedman and R. Rosenman, *Type A Behavior and Your Heart* (New York: Alfred A. Knopf, 1974).

17. E. Friedman, et al., "The Effects of Normal and Rapid Speech on Blood Pressure," *Psychosomatic Medicine* 44(6[1982]):545–53.

18. C. E. Thoresen, et al., "Feasibility of Altering Type A Behavior Pattern after Myocardial Infarction. Recurrent Coronary Prevention Project Study: Methods, Baseline Results and Preliminary Findings," *Circulation* 66(1[1982]):83–92.

19. P. J. Rosch, "Stress, Cholesterol and Coronary Heart Disease," *Lancet* 2(1983):851–52.

20. J. Staessen, et al., "The Effects of Aging on Blood Pressure," in Franz Gross and Toma Strasser, eds., *Mild Hypertension: Recent Advances* (New York: Raven Press, 1983), pp. 315–26.

21. T. G. Pickering, et al., "Blood Pressure during Normal Daily Activities, Sleep and Exercise: Comparison of Values in Normal and Hypertensive Subjects," *Journal of the American Medical Association* 247(7[1982]):992–96.

T. G. Pickering, et al., "Ambulatory Monitoring in the Elevation of Blood Pressure in Patients with Borderline Hypertension and the Role of the Defense Reflex," *Clinical and Experimental Hypertension* A-4(1982):675–93.

G. A. Harshfield, et al., "Situational Variations of Blood Pressure in Ambulatory Hypertensive Patients," *Psychosomatic Medicine* 44(1982):237–45.

22. J. M. Long, et al., "The Effect of Status on Blood Pressure during Verbal Communication," *Behavioral Medicine* 5(2[1982]):165–72.

23. S. A. Thomas, et al., "Blood Pressure and Heart Rate Changes in Children When They Read Aloud in School," *Public Health Reports* 99(1[1984]):77–84.

24. I. M. Moriyama, D. E. Kreuger, and J. Stamler, "Cardiovascular Diseases in the United States," Vital and Health Statistics Monograph (Cambridge, Mass.: Harvard University Press, 1971).

25. H. A. Tyroler, "Race Education and 5-Year Mortality in HDFP Stratum I Referred-Care Males," in F. Gross and T. Strasser, eds., *Mild Hypertension: Recent Advances* (New York: Raven Press, 1983), pp. 163–75.

26. E. Friedmann, et al., "Animal Companions and One-Year Survival of Patients after Discharge from a Coronary Care Unit," *Public Health Reports* 95(4[1980]):307–12.

27. E. Friedmann, et al., "Social Interaction and Blood Pressure: Influence of Animal Companions," *The Journal of Nervous and Mental Disease* 171(8[1983]):461–65.

28. A. Beck and A. H. Katcher, *Between Pets and People* (New York: G. P. Putnam, 1983).

29. J. J. Lynch, "The Cardiac Orienting Response and Its Relationship to the Cardiac Conditional Response in Dogs," *Conditional Reflex* 2(2[1967]):138–52.

30. F. K. Graham and R. K. Clifton, "Heart Rate Changes as a Component of the Orienting Response," *Psychological Bulletin* 65(1966):305–20.

E. N. Sokolov, *Perception and the Conditioned Reflex,* translated by Stefan W. Waydenfeld (New York: Macmillan, 1963).

31. Sokolov, *Perception* [30].

32. Lynch, "Cardiac Orienting Response" [29].

33. Graham and Clifton, "Heart Rate Changes" [30].

34. K. Malinow, et al., "Blood Pressure Changes While Signing in a Deaf Population," unpublished manuscript.

35. G. A. Harschfield, et al., "Situational Reactivity of Blood Pressure in Essential

Hypertensive Patients During Normal Activities," *Psychophysiology* 18(1981):163.

36. J. Hsiao, et al., "Blood Pressure Changes in Schizophrenics When They Talk," unpublished manuscript.

37. P. Sterling and J. Eyer, "Biological Basis for Stress Related Mortality," *Social Science and Medicine* 15E(1981):3–42.

38. A. C. Guyton, *Arterial Pressure and Hypertension* (Philadelphia: W. B. Saunders, 1980).

39. I. H. Page, "The Mosaic Theory of Hypertension," in K. D. Bock and P. T. Cottier, eds., *Essential Hypertension* (Berlin: Springer, 1960).

40. S. A. Thomas, et al., "Changes in Blood Pressure, Intra-pleural Pressure and Finger Blood Flow during Normal and Rapid Speech," unpublished manuscript.

41. Ibid.

42. M. D. Abramson and E. B. Ferris, "Responses of Blood Vessels in the Resting Hand and Forearm to Various Stimuli," *American Heart Journal* 19(1940):541–53.

H. Barcroft, et al., "The Mechanism of the Vasodilatation in the Forearm Muscle During Stress (Mental Arithmetic)," *Clinical Science* 19(1960):577–86.

V. Fencl, Z. Hejl, and J. Jirka, "Circulatory Changes Underlying Blood Pressure Elevations during Acute Emotional Stress (Mental Arithmetic) in Normotensive and Hypertensive Subjects," *Clinical Science* 18(1959):269–79.

V. Fencl, et al., "Changes of Blood Flow in Forearm Muscle and Skin during an Acute Emotional Stress (Mental Arithmetic)," *Clinical Science* 18(1959):491–98.

D. Kelly, C. C. Brown, and J. W. Schaffer, "A Comparison of Physiological and Psychological Measurements on Anxious Patients and Normal Controls," *Psychophysiology* 6(1970):429–41.

H. Konzett and K. Strieder, "Differentiation of Stress Stimuli by Measuring Forearm Blood Flow," *Federal Proceedings* 29(741[Abstract 2801, 1970]).

M. Ulrych, "Changes of General Haemodynamics during Stressful Mental Arithmetic and Non-Stressing Quiet Conversation and Modification of the Beta-Adrenergic Blockage," *Clinical Science* 36(1969):453–61.

43. J. J. Lynch, et al., "Oxygen Tension Changes in Forearm Skin Tissue during Talking and Rest," unpublished manuscript.

44. F. Wimbush, et al., "Patient Responses to Two Stressors: Communication and Cardiac Catheterization," unpublished manuscript.

Chapter 7. The Social Membrane

1. S. Longworth, "Blood Pressure in Mental Disorders," *British Medical Journal* (1911):1366–68.

2. Ray Gibson, "The Pathology of Dementia Praecox, Especially in Relation to the Circulatory Change," *Archives of Neurology and Psychiatry* 5(1911):182.

3. T. Raphael, J. Parsons, and M. Woodwell, "Schizophrenic Catatonia with Associated Metabolic and Vegetative Features," *Archives of Neurology and Psychiatry* 9(1923):471–77.

4. W. S. Dawson, "A Study of the Endocrine-Autonomic Disorders of Dementia Praecox," *Journal of Mental Science* 69(1923):182–99.

5. G. Pankin, "Some Observations on the Study of Blood-Pressure in the Insane," *Journal of Mental Science* 73(1927):240–55.

6. H. Freeman, R. G. Hoskins, and F. H. Sleeper, "The Blood Pressure in Schizophrenia," *Archives of Neurology and Psychiatry* 27(1932):333–51.

7. M. Miller, "Blood Pressure Findings in Relation to Inhibited Aggressions in Psychotics," *Psychosomatic Medicine* 1(1[1939]):162–72.

8. Joseph Rheingold, "Autonomic Integration in Schizophrenia," *Psychosomatic Medicine* 1(3[1939]):497–513.

9. O. Lingjaerde, C. L. Laane, and H. Strom, "The Variation of Blood Pressure with the Age in Schizophrenics," *Journal-Nordisk Medicin* 43(1950):167–70.

10. F. Shattock, M. Oxon, and D. London, "The Somatic Manifestations of Schizophrenia: A Clinical Study of Their Significance," *Journal of Mental Science* 96(1950):32–63.

11. Ibid.

12. G. Masterton, et al., "Low Blood Pressure in Psychiatric Inpatients," *British Heart Journal* 45(1981):442–46.

13. R. R. Monroe, et al., "A Comparison of Hypertensive and Hypotensive Schizophrenics," *Psychosomatic Medicine* 23(6[1961]).

14. K. Witton and A. R. Goldman, "Some Considerations on Blood Pressure Patterns in a Mental Hospital Population," *Journal of Nervous and Mental Disease* 140(1[1965]):58–63.

15. Monroe et al., "A Comparison" [13].

16. Ibid.

17. G. Masterton, et al., "Low Blood Pressure in Psychiatric Inpatients," *British Heart Journal* 45(1981):442–46.

18. Freeman, Hoskins, and Sleeper, "Blood Pressure" [6].

19. C. J. Main and G. Masterton, "The Influence of Hospital Environment on Blood Pressure in Psychiatric Inpatients," *Journal of Psychosomatic Research* 25(3[1981]):157–63.

20. B. Richards and F. Enver, "Blood Pressure in Down's Syndrome," *Journal of Mental Deficiency Research* 23(1979):123–35.

21. W. C. Alvarez and L. L. Stanley, "Blood Pressure in Six Thousand Prisoners and Four Hundred Prison Guards," *Archives of Internal Medicine,* 12 November 1929, pp. 17–39.

22. Ibid.

23. D. A. D'Atri and A. M. Ostfeld, "Crowding—Its Effects on Elevation of Blood-Pressure in a Prison Setting," *Preventive Medicine* 4(4[1975]):550–66.

24. J. Gordon Barrow, et al., "Studies in Atherosclerosis III. An Epidemiologic Study of Atherosclerosis in Trappist and Benedictine Monks: A Preliminary Report," *Annals of Internal Medicine* 52(2[1960]):368–77.

25. Ibid.

26. J. Staessen, et al., *"The Effects of Aging on Blood Pressure,"* in F. Gross and T. Strasser, eds., *Mild Hypertension: Recent Advances* (New York: Raven Press, 1983), pp. 315–27.

27. W. J. Oliver, E. L. Cohen, and J. V. Neel, "Blood Pressure, Sodium Intake and Sodium Related Hormones in the Yanomamo Indians, A 'No Salt' Culture," *Circulation* 52(1975):146–51.

28. W. R. Morse and Y. T. Beh, "Blood Pressure amongst Aboriginal Ethnic Groups of Szechwan Province, West China," *Lancet* 1(1937):966–67.

29. I. Maddocks, "Blood Pressure in Melanesians," *Medical Journal of Australia* 1(1967):1123–26.

30. A. W. Williams, "Blood Pressure Differences in Kikuyu and Samburu Communities in Kenya," *East Africa Medical Journal* 46(1969):262–71.

31. B. Gampel, et al., "Urbanization and Hypertension among Adult Zulus," *Journal of Chronic Diseases* 15(1961):57.

32. L. B. Page, A. Damon, and R. C. Moellering, "Antecedents of Cardiovascular

Disease in Six Solomon Island Societies," *Circulation* 49(1974):1132–46.

33. A. M. Prior, et al., "Sodium Intake and Blood Pressure in Two Polynesian Populations," *New England Journal of Medicine* 279(1968):515–20.

34. Stephen T. McGarvey and Paul T. Baker, "The Effects of Modernization and Migration on Samoan Blood Pressures," *Human Biology* 51(1979):461–80.

35. G. C. Shattuck, *The African Republic of Liberia and the Belgian Congo; Report of the Harvard Expedition to Liberia* (Cambridge, Mass.: Harvard University Press, 1930).

36. J. O. M. Pobee, "Epidemiological Report from West Africa," in Franz Gross and Toma Strasser, eds., *Mild Hypertension: Recent Advances* (New York, Raven Press, 1983), pp. 33–54.

O. O. Akinkugbe, and O. A. Ojo, "Arterial Pressures in Rural and Urban Populations in Nigeria," *British Medical Journal* 2(1969):222.

37. C. G. Salsbury, "Disease Incidence among the Navajo," *Southwestern Medicine* 21(1937):230–33.

38. F. DeStefano, J. Coulehan, and K. Wiunt, "Blood Pressure Survey on the Navajo Indian Reservation," *American Journal of Epidemiology* 109(3[1979]):335–45.

39. M. Braxton, "Blood Pressure Changes among Male Navajo Migrants to an Urban Environment," *Canadian Review of Sociology and Anthropology* 7(1970):189–200.

40. M. Sievers, "Historical Overview of Hypertension among American Indians and Alaskan Natives," *Arizona Medicine* 34(1977):607–10.

41. Braxton, "Blood Pressure Changes" [39].

42. H. Benson, B. R. Marzetta, and B. A. Rosner, "Decreased Systolic Blood Pressure in Hypertensive Subjects Who Practiced Meditation," *Journal of Clinical Investigation* 52(1973):8a.

H. Benson, H. P. Klemchuk, and J. R. Graham, "The Usefulness of the Relaxation Response in the Therapy of Headache," *Headache* 14(1974):49–52.

H. Benson, "Your Innate Asset for Combatting Stress," *Harvard Business Review* 52(1974):49–60.

H. Benson, J. F. Beary, and M. P. Carol, "The Relaxation Response," *Psychiatry* 37(1974):37–46.

H. Benson, "Transcendental Meditation—Science or Cult?" *Journal of the American Medical Association* 227(1974):807.

H. Benson, "Yoga for Drug Abuse," *New England Journal of Medicine* 281(1969):1133.

H. Benson and M. Z. Klipper, *The Relaxation Response* (New York: William Morrow, 1975).

Charles F. Stroebel, *The QR or Quieting Reflex* (New York: G. P. Putnam, 1982), p. 221.

Chapter 8. The Hidden Dialogue

1. J. Wilkin, "Flushing Reactions: Consequences and Mechanisms," *Annals of Internal Medicine,* 95(1981):468–76.

2. S. Fahrion, "Autogenic Biofeedback for Migraine," *Psychiatric Annals* (May 1978):219–34.

Joseph D. Sargent, Elmer E. Green, and E. Dale Walters, "Preliminary Report on the Use of Autogenic Feedback Training in the Treatment of Migraine and Tension Headaches," *Psychosomatic Medicine* 35(2[1973]):129–35.

3. Ad Hoc Committee on the Classification of Headache, National Institute of Neurological Diseases and Blindness, "Classification of Headaches," *Neurology* 12(1962):378.

4. C. F. Rose and M. Gawel, *Migraine—The Facts* (New York: Oxford University Press, 1979).

5. H. Adams, M. Feurlstein, and J. Fowler, "Migraine Headache: Review of Parameters, Etiology and Intervention," *Psychological Bulletin* 87(2[March 1980]):217–37.

A. H. Crisp, et al., "Some Clinical, Social, and Psychological Characteristics of Migraine Subjects in the General Population," *Postgraduate Medical Journal* 53(November 1977):691–97.

S. Dimond and J. Gedina, "Review Article: Current Thoughts in Migraine," *Headache* 20(1980):208–12.

6. J. J. Lynch and S. A. Thomas, "Heart Rate and Blood Pressure Changes in Migraine Patients during Therapeutic Dialogue," unpublished manuscript.

7. H. G. Wolff and M. M. Tunis, "Analysis of Cranial Artery Pressure Pulse Waves in Patients With Vascular Headaches of the Migraine Type," *Transactions of Associations of American Physicians* 65(240[1952]).

8. H. G. Wolff, *Wolff's Headache and Other Head Pain,* edited by D. J. Dalessio, 4th ed. (New York: Oxford University Press, 1980).

9. Rose and Gawel, *Migraine: The Facts* [4].

10. Ibid.

11. J. G. Flannery, "Alexithymia," *Psychotherapeutics and Psychosomatics* 30(1978):193–97.

P. C. Kimball, "The Languages of Psychosomatic Medicine," *Psychotherapeutics and Psychosomatics* 28(1977):1–12.

H. Krystal, "Trauma: Consideration of Severity and Chronicity," in H. Krystal and W. Niederland, eds., *Psychic Traumatization* (Boston: Little, Brown, 1971).

J. Nemiah, "Denial Revisited: Reflections on Psychosomatic Theory," *Psychotherapeutics and Psychosomatics* 26(1975):140–47.

J. C. Nemiah, "Alexithymia, Theoretical Considerations," *Psychotherapeutics and Psychosomatics* 28(1977):199–206.

J. C. Nemiah and P. E. Sifneos, "Psychosomatic Illness: A Problem of Communication," *Psychotherapeutics and Psychosomatics* 18(1970):154–58.

R. Pierloot and J. Vinick, "A Pragmatic Approach to the Concept of Alexithymia," *Psychotherapeutics and Psychosomatics* 28(1977):156–66.

P. E. Sifneos, "A Reconsideration of Psychodynamic Mechanisms in Symptom Formation in View of Recent Clinical Observations," *Psychotherapeutics and Psychosomatics* 24(1974):151–55.

P. E. Sifneos, "The Prevalence of Alexithymic Characteristics in Psychosomatic Patients," *Psychotherapeutics and Psychosomatics* 22(1973):255–62.

G. J. Taylor, "Alexithymia and the Counter-Transference," *Psychotherapeutics and Psychosomatics* 28(1977):141–47.

12. F. Alexander, *Psychosomatic Medicine* (New York: W. W. Norton, 1950).

E. Lindemann, "Psychiatric Problems in Conservative Treatment of Ulcerative Colitis," *Archives of Neurology* (Chicago) 53(1945):322–24.

13. A. Garma, "Internalized Mother as Harmful Food in Peptic Ulcer Patients," *International Journal of Psychoanalysis* 34(1953):102.

F. T. Knapp, M. Rosenbaum, and J. Romano, "Psychological Factors in Men with Peptic Ulcer," *American Journal of Psychiatry* 103(1947):700.

J. C. Nemiah, "The Psychological Management and Treatment of Patients with Peptic Ulcer," *Advanced Psychosomatic Medicine* 6(169[1971]).

14. J. Ruesch, "The Infantile Personality: The Core Problem of Psychosomatic Medicine," *Psychosomatic Medicine* 10(1948):134–44.

15. M. B. Freedman and B. S. Sweet, "Some Specific Features of Group Psychotherapy and Their Implications for Selected Patients," *International Journal of Group Psychotherapy* 4(1954):355–68.

16. H. C. Shands, "How Are Psychosomatic Patients Different from Psycho-Neurotic Patients?" *Psychotherapeutics and Psychosomatics* 26(1975):270–85.

17. P. Marty and M. de M'Uzan, "La Pensée Opératoire," *Revue François Psychoanalysis* 27(supplement [1963]):1345.

18. J. C. Nemiah, H. Freyberger, and P. E. Sifneos, "Alexithymia: A View of the Psychosomatic Process," in O. Hill, ed., *Modern Trends in Psychosomatic Medicine, vol. III* (London: Butterworths, 1976), pp. 430–39.

19. Ibid, p. 432.

20. P. E. Sifneos, "Problems of Psychotherapy of Patients with Alexithymic Characteristics and Physical Disease," *Psychotherapeutics and Psychosomatics* 26(1975):68.

21. H. Krystal, "Alexithymia and Psychotherapy," *American Journal of Psychotherapy* 33(1979):17–31.

22. K. D. Hoppe and J. E. Bogen, "Alexithymia in Twelve Commissurotomized Patients," *Psychotherapeutics and Psychosomatics* 28(1977):148–55.

23. J. McDougall, "The Psychosoma and Psychoanalytic Process," *International Journal of Psychoanalysis* 1(1974):461–66.

24. Marty and de M'Uzan, "La Pensée Opératoire" [17].

25. P. D. MacLean, "Psychosomatic Disease and the Visceral Brain," *Psychosomatic Medicine* 11(1949):338.

Chapter 9. Decoding the Heart's Language

1. M. Thaler-Singer, "Psychological Dimensions in Psychosomatic Patients," *Psychotherapeutics and Psychosomatics* 28(1977):13–27.

2. M. Thaler-Singer, M. F. Reiss, and H. Weiner, "An Exploration of the Doctor-Patient Relationship through Projective Techniques: Their Use in Psychosomatic Illness," *Psychosomatic Medicine* 19(1957):228–39.

3. P. S. Hall, S. A. Thomas, E. Friedmann, J. J. Lynch, "Measurement of Neonatal Blood Pressure: A New Method," *Psychophysiology* 19(1982):231–36.

4. P. S. Hall, J. J. Lynch, S. A. Thomas, and E. Friedmann, "The Effects of Breast Feeding and Bottle Feeding on the Blood Pressure and Heart Rate of Newborn Infants," unpublished manuscript.

5. John C. Nemiah, "Neurasthenic Neurosis" in Alfred M. Freedman, H. I. Kaplan, and Benjamin J. Sadock, eds. *Comprehensive Textbook of Psychiatry II,* vol. 1, 2nd ed. (Baltimore: Williams & Wilkins, 1975) p. 1264.

6. W. B. Cannon, *Bodily Changes in Pain, Hunger, Fear and Rage: An Account of Recent Researches into the Function of Emotional Excitement* (New York: Appleton, 1929).

7. Ibid.

8. J. J. Lynch, *The Broken Heart: The Medical Consequences of Loneliness* (New York: Basic Books, 1977).

9. C. Darwin, *The Expression of the Emotions in Man and Animals* (New York: Philosophical Library, 1955).

10. Carl Georg Lange, *Ueber Gemüthsbewegungen,* H. Kurella, trans. (Leipzig: 1887) p. 75.

11. William James, "On Emotion," in *Principles of Psychology,* vol. 2 (New York: Holt and Company, 1890).

W. James, "What is an Emotion," *Mind* 9(1884):188–205.

W. James, *Emotions: Their Parameters and Measurements,* L. Livi, ed. (New York: Raven Press, 1975).

12. W. B. Cannon, *Bodily Changes in Pain, Hunger, Fear and Rage: An Account of Recent Researches into the Function of Emotional Excitement* (New York: Appleton, 1929).

13. C. S. Sherrington, *Integrative Action of the Nervous System* (New York: Scribner, 1906).

14. Philip Bard, "A Diencephalic Mechanism for the Expression of Rage with Special Reference to the Sympathetic Nervous System," *American Journal of Physiology* 84(1928):490–515.

15. Adolf Portmann, "Lebensforschung unserer Tage," *Universitas* 3 (Februar 1955). (*Contemporary Biological Research Part I,* R.B. Carter, trans.)

Adolf Portmann, "Lebensforschung unserer Tage," *Universitas* 3 (März 1955). (*Contemporary Biological Research Part II,* R.B. Carter, trans.).

Adolf Portmann, "Lebensforschung unserer Tage," *Universitas* 3 (April 1955). (*Contemporary Biological Research Part III,* R.B. Carter, trans.)

Adolf Portmann, *Handbuch der allgemeinen Pathologie,* vol. 1, (Berlin, Heidelberg, New York: 1969), pp. 187–204. (*The Problem of Living Things,* R. B. Carter, trans.)

Adolf Portmann, "Der Mensch im Felde der Evolutionstheroie," in *Meyers Enzyklopaedischem Lexikon* (Mannheim, Wein, Zurich: Bibliographisches Institut, 1971). (*Human Beings in the Perspective of the Theory of Evolution,* R. B. Carter, trans.)

Adolf Portmann, "Das Lebendige als vorbereitete Beziehung," *Erranos-Jahrbuch* 24(1955):485–506. Nachdruck (1965): *Aufbuch der Lebensforschung,* pp. 13–32. (*The Living Thing as a Pre-Arranged Relationship,* B. Carter with E. B. Carter, trans.).

Adolf Portmann, "Der Weg Zum Wort: Stufen lebendiger Kommunication," *Erranos-Jahrbuch* 39 (1970), (Leiden: E. J. Brill, 1973):397–424. (*The Path Leading to Words: Levels of Living Communication,* R. B. Carter, trans.)

Chapter 10. The Human Dialogue

1. M. Foucault, *Naissance de la Clinique: Une Archeologie du Regard Medical* (Paris: Presse Université de France, 1972).

2. Bertrand Russell, *Wisdom of the West* (London: Rathbone Books Limited, Crescent Books, 1959).

3. Aristotle, "De Anima," in *On the Soul,* with commentaries and glossary by Hippocrates. G. Apostle, trans. (Grinnell, Iowa: Peripatetic Press, 1981).

4. Ibid.

5. John 1:1 and 14.

6. Russell, *Wisdom of the West.*

7. Aristotle, "De Anima."

8. Blaise Pascal, *Pensées* (New York: Washington Square Press, 1965).

9. René Descartes, "Discourse on Method" in *Oeuvres,* vol. 4, p. 329, 1, 16–19, as quoted in Richard B. Carter, *Descartes' Medical Philosophy—The Organic Solution to the Mind-Body Problem* (Baltimore: Johns Hopkins University Press, 1983) p. 7.

10. Richard B. Carter, *Descartes' Medical Philosophy—The Organic Solution to the Mind-Body Problem* (Baltimore: Johns Hopkins University Press, 1983).

11. René Descartes, *The Philosophical Works of Descartes,* vol. 1, E. S. Haldane and G. R. T. Ross, trans. (New York: Cambridge University Press, 1979, [c. 1911]).

12. Ernest Jones, *The Life and Work of Sigmund Freud: The Formative Years and the Great Discoveries 1856–1900,* vol. 1 (New York: Basic Books, 1953), pp. 169–70.

13. Ludwig Binswanger, *Sigmund Freud: Reminiscences of a Friendship,* Norbert Guterman, trans. (New York: Grune and Stratton, 1957).

14. Ibid.

15. Richard M. Restak, review of *The Freudian Fallacy,* by E.M. Thornton, in "Book World," *Washington Post,* 18 March 1984.

16. S. Freud and W. C. Bullitt, *Thomas Woodrow Wilson, Twenty-Eighth President of the United States: A Psychological Study* (Boston: Houghton Mifflin, 1967 [c. 1966]).

17. Ibid.

18. Ibid., pp. xi–xiii.

19. Binswanger, *Sigmund Freud.*

20. Ivan P. Pavlov, *Lectures on Conditioned Reflexes: Twenty-Five Years of Objective Study of the Higher Activity (Behavior) of Animals,* vols. 1 and 2, W. H. Gantt, ed. and trans. (New York: International Publishers, 1941).

21. Ivan P. Pavlov, *Conditioned Reflexes and Psychiatry,* vol. 2, Appendix 2, W.H. Gantt, ed. and trans. (New York: International Publishers, 1941).

22. Karl Marx, *The Portable Karl Marx,* Eugene Kamenka, ed. (Harmondsworth, Middlesex, England: Penguin Books, 1983).

23. Ivan P. Pavlov, *Conditioned Reflexes* (New York: Dover Books, 1960 reprint of the 1927 Oxford University Press, G.V. Anrep, trans.) p. 4, as quoted in Richard B. Carter, *Descartes' Medical Philosophy—The Organic Solution to the Mind-Body Problem* (Baltimore: Johns Hopkins University Press, 1983) p. 3.

24. Hannah Arendt, *Crises of the Republic* (New York: Harcourt Brace Jovanovich, 1972 [c. 1969]).

Hannah Arendt, *On Violence* (New York: Harcourt Brace and World, 1969).

Hannah Arendt, *The Origins of Totalitarianism,* 2nd ed. (New York: Meridian Books, 1958).

25. Raul Hilberg, *The Destruction of the European Jews* (Chicago: Quadrangle Books, 1967).

26. Richard L. Rubenstein, *The Cunning of History: The Holocaust and the American Future* (New York: Harper and Row, 1978 [c. 1975]).

Appendix

1. S. A. Thomas, "Steps in Transactional Psychophysiology Therapy" in *The Healing Heart: Psychological Intervention in Cardiovascular Disease,* Andrew M. Razin, ed.(California: Jossey-Bass, in press).

2. S. A. Thomas, J. J. Lynch, H. Gross, and P. Rosch, *Transactional Psychophysiology: A New Non-Drug Treatment for Stress-Linked Diseases.* (New York: Basic Books, in press).

INDEX